A CENTURY OF COMMUNICATION STUDIES

This volume chronicles the development of communication studies as a discipline, providing a history of the field and identifying opportunities for future growth. Editors Pat J. Gehrke and William M. Keith have assembled an exceptional list of communication scholars who, in the eleven chapters contained in this book, cover the breadth and depth of the field. Organized around themes and concepts that have enduring historical significance and wide appeal across numerous subfields of communication, *A Century of Communication Studies* bridges research and pedagogy, addressing themes that connect classroom practice and publication.

Published in the one-hundredth anniversary year of the National Communication Association, this collection highlights the evolution of communication studies and will serve future generations of scholars as a window into not only our past but also the field's collective possibilities.

Pat J. Gehrke is Associate Professor of Speech Communication and Rhetoric at the University of South Carolina. His research interests include the history of communication education, rhetorical theory, communication ethics, and public political discourse.

William M. Keith is Professor of Communication at the University of Wisconsin, Milwaukee. His research interests include the history of public participation in the United States, communication pedagogy and disciplinarity, and the rhetoric of science.

A CENTURY OF COMMUNICATION STUDIES

THE UNFINISHED CONVERSATION

Edited by

PAT J. GEHRKE

AND

WILLIAM M. KEITH

Routledge
Taylor & Francis Group

NEW YORK AND LONDON

First published 2015
by Routledge
711 Third Avenue, New York, NY 10017

and by Routledge
2 Park Square, Milton Park, Abingdon, Oxon, OX14 4RN

Routledge is an imprint of the Taylor & Francis Group, an informa business

© 2015 Taylor & Francis

Library of Congress Cataloging in Publication Data
A century of communication studies: the unfinished conversation/edited by
Pat J. Gehrke and William M. Keith.
    pages cm
    Includes bibliographical references and index.
    1. Communication—Study and teaching—United States—History.
    2. Communication—Research—United States—History. 3. National
    Communication Association (U.S.) I. Gehrke, Pat J., 1970– editor.
    II. Keith, William M., 1959– editor.
    P91.5.U5C47 2014
    302.207'073—dc23
    2014022495

ISBN: 978-0-415-82037-0 (hbk)
ISBN: 978-0-415-82036-3 (pbk)
ISBN: 978-0-203-36691-2 (ebk)

Typeset in Minion Pro
by Florence Production Ltd, Stoodleigh, Devon, UK

Printed and bound in the United States of America by Publishers Graphics,
LLC on sustainably sourced paper.

CONTENTS

CONTRIBUTORS

John M. Allison, Jr. is Associate Professor and Chair in the Department of Communication Studies at the University of North Texas. He researches and teaches narrative theory, particularly the narrative structure of everyday life, and southern fiction, which he also adapts for the stage. His publications include "Narrative and Time: A Phenomenological Reconsideration"; his performance work includes adaptations of fiction by Lee Smith, Clyde Edgerton, and Flannery O'Connor.

James A. Anderson is Professor of Communication and Director of the Center for Communication and Community at the University of Utah. He was president of the International Communication Association and is an ICA Fellow. His research interests have spanned research methodologies, communication theory and philosophy, media, and organizations, and are now focused on community engaged scholarship. His most recent books examined organizational ethics, media violence, and media research methods.

Reynaldo Anderson is Assistant Professor in the Department of Humanities at Harris-Stowe State University. He has written extensively about cultural studies, intercultural communication, Africana studies, and social media. His recent publications include *Molefi Kete Asante: The Afrocentric Idea and the Cultural Turn in Intercultural Communication Studies* (2012), (with John Jennings) *Afrofuturism: The Visual Imagery of Kanye West* (2014), and *Black Atlantic Heretics of Empire 1919–1965: The Caribbean Intersectionality of Amy Jacques Garvey, Elma Francois, and Claudia Jones* (2014).

Ronald C. Arnett is Chair and Professor of the Department of Communication & Rhetorical Studies and the Henry Koren, C.S.Sp., Endowed Chair for Scholarly Excellence at Duquesne University. He is the author/co-author of nine books. His recent works include *Communication Ethics in Dark Times: Hannah Arendt's Rhetoric of Warning and Hope* (2013, Southern Illinois University Press), *An Overture to Philosophy of Communication: The Carrier of Meaning* (2013, Peter Lang), and *Conflict between Persons: The Origins of Leadership* (2014, Kendall Hunt).

David Beard is Associate Professor of rhetoric in the Department of Writing Studies at the University of Minnesota, Duluth, where he researches the history and theory of rhetoric and pedagogy. He has published in journals including the *International Journal of Listening*, *Archival Science*, *Philosophy and Rhetoric* (with William Keith), *Southern Journal of Communication*, and *Enculturation* (with Joshua Gunn), among other outlets. With Richard Enos, he edited *Advances in the History of Rhetoric* (Parlor Press).

Graham Bodie is Associate Professor of Communication Studies at Louisiana State University and Agricultural & Mechanical College. He is recognized as an international expert on listening and the social cognitive underpinnings of human communicative behavior, having authored over seventy published papers in outlets such as *Human Communication Research*, *Communication Monographs*, *Communication Research*, *Communication Yearbook*, and the *International Journal of Listening*. Dr. Bodie has received early career awards from the Southern States Communication Association and National Communication Association, and the distinguished Research Award from the International Listening Association.

Frank E.X. Dance is John Evans Distinguished Professor Emeritus of Communication Studies at the University of Denver Department of Communication Studies. Past president and fellow of the International Communication Association and past president of the National Communication Association he has served as editor of the *Journal of Communication* and of *Communication Education*. He has written and published widely about speech communication theory, communication theory, and been a long time champion of "speech" as a disciplinary marker.

Mary Domenico is a PhD student in the Department of Communication Studies at the University of North Carolina, Chapel Hill where she studies contemporary communication ethics through the lenses of rhetoric, psychoanalysis, and feminist theory. Her publications include "Psychoanalytic Analysis" (*Critical Media Studies: An Introduction*, edited by Brian L. Ott and Robert L. Mack, 2014) and (with Sonja K. Foss and Karen A. Foss) *Gender Stories: Negotiating Identity in a Binary World* (2013).

William F. Eadie is Professor of Journalism and Media Studies at San Diego State University and the current editor of the *Western Journal of Communication*. He was formerly an associate director of the National Communication Association. He edited the two-volume *21st Century Communication: A Reference Handbook* for Sage Publications, and he has written several articles on the historical nature of communication study and the role that scholarly societies have played in creating a discipline of communication. He is currently working on a book titled *When Communication Became a Discipline*.

Pat J. Gehrke is Associate Professor in the Speech Communication and Rhetoric Program and the Department of English at the University of South Carolina. He has published original research in communication ethics, public argument, political rhetoric, rhetorical theory, history of communication, and philosophy of communication, including his 2009 book, *The Ethics and Politics of Speech: Communication and Rhetoric in the Twentieth Century* (Southern Illinois University Press).

Marnel Niles Goins is Associate Professor in the Department of Communication at California State University, Fresno. Her areas of interest are small group and organizational communication, with special emphasis on peer groups, decision-making, and gender and race studies. She recently published an edited volume entitled *Still Searching for Our Mothers' Gardens: Experiences of New, Tenure Track Women of Color in "Majority" Institutions.*

Joshua Gunn is Associate Professor of Communication Studies and Affiliated Faculty of Rhetoric and Writing at the University of Texas at Austin. He teaches and researches at the intersection of rhetorical, cultural, and media studies.

Sheena Howard is Assistant Professor at Rider University in Lawrenceville, NJ. She has been twice named as a Frederick Douglass Scholar at Clarion University (2009) and West Chester University (2010), at which she held faculty positions in the Communication Department.

William M. Keith is Professor in the Department of English at the University of Wisconsin, Milwaukee. He has written widely about the history of public participation in the United States, and the history of communication pedagogy and disciplinarity. His publications include *Democracy as Discussion* (2007), "We Are the Speech Teachers" (2011), and (with Christian Lundberg) *Public Speaking: Choices and Responsibility* (2013).

Michael K. Middleton is Assistant Professor of Communication and Director of Forensics at the University of Utah. His areas of research interest include rhetorical theory and criticism, social movements, and cultural studies. His current research focuses on homeless social movements in the context of the 2008 recession, as well as the intersections between ethnography, performance, and rhetoric. He has been published in these areas in the *Western Journal of Communication*, the *Southern Communication Journal*, and *Communication, Culture, and Critique.*

Charles E. Morris III is Professor of Communication & Rhetorical Studies and LGBT Studies at Syracuse University. His books include *Queering Public Address, Remembering the AIDS Quilt*, and with Jason Edward Black, *An Archive of Hope: Harvey Milk's Speeches and Writings.* For his work on queer rhetorical history, he has twice been the recipient of the Golden Monograph Award, as well as the Karl Wallace and Randy Majors Awards, from NCA. He is co-founding Editor-in-Chief of *QED: A Journal in GLBTQ Worldmaking.*

Brian L. Ott is Associate Professor of Rhetorical and Media Studies in the Department of Communication at the University of Colorado, Denver. His chief research interest concerns how media texts equip people to live their everyday lives. He is author of *The Small Screen: How Television Equips Us to Live in the Information Age* (2007) and *Critical*

Media Studies: An Introduction (2010/2014), as well as a co-editor of *It's Not TV: Watching HBO in the Post-Television Era* (2008), *Places of Public Memory: The Rhetoric of Museums and Memorials* (2010), and *The Routledge Reader in Rhetorical Criticism* (2013).

Catherine Helen Palczewski is Professor of Communication Studies and Affiliate Faculty in Women's and Gender Studies at the University of Northern Iowa. Her work focuses on how marginalized groups rhetorically construct their messages to gain access to, and be legible in, the dominant public sphere. She received the Francine Merritt Award for Outstanding Contributions to the Lives of Women in Communication in 2010 from the Women's Caucus of NCA. She directed the AFA/NCA Biennial Conference on Argumentation in 2013 and edited its selected works: *Disturbing Argument* (2014). Her co-authored publications include *Gender in Communication* (2014) and *Rhetoric in Civic Life* (2012).

Ronald J. Pelias taught performance studies from 1981 to 2013 in the Department of Communication Studies at Southern Illinois University, Carbondale. He works on the stage primarily as a director and on the page as a writer committed to non-traditional forms of scholarly representation. His most recent books exploring qualitative methods are *A Methodology of the Heart: Evoking Academic & Daily Life* (2004), *Leaning: A Poetics of Personal Relations* (2011), and *Performance: An Alphabet of Performative Writing* (2014).

Gerry Philipsen was a faculty member in communication at the University of California, Santa Barbara from 1972 to 1978 and at the University of Washington since 1978. He works on the history of the communication discipline in the twentieth century, ethnography of communication, and speech codes theory, of which he is the originator. In 2013 he was named a National Communication Association Distinguished Scholar.

Tracy Stephenson Shaffer is Associate Professor in the Department of Communication Studies at Louisiana State University where she researches and teaches performance studies and film. Her publications include "Performing Backpacking" (2004), *Performance Studies: The Interpretation of Aesthetic Texts* (with Ronald J. Pelias, 2007), "Mapping Mediatization in *The Life and Times of King Kong*" (2009), "Music as Performance Method" (2010), "Playing in the Dark with Sue Monk Kidd" (2013), and "Performance as Practice" (2014). In addition to written publication, she also creates original work in the HopKins Black Box theater on LSU's campus.

J. Michael Sproule is Professor Emeritus of Communication Studies, San Jose State University and is a past president of the National Communication Association (2007). He has twice received the NCA's Golden Anniversary Monograph Award: in 1988, for his article, "Propaganda Studies in American Social Science: The Rise and Fall of the Critical Paradigm," and in 2012, for "Inventing Public Speaking: Rhetoric and the Speech Book, 1730–1930." His nine books or editions thereof include *Propaganda and Democracy* (1997) and *The Rhetoric of Western Thought* (2011).

Timothy D. Stephen is Professor in the Department of Communication at University at Albany (SUNY), New York. His work focuses on communication in intimacy in contemporary and historical perspective, and on patterns of scholarly productivity across the communication field in the United States.

ACKNOWLEDGMENTS

The editors have benefited from the time, talents, and dedication of a number of people who helped see this volume to completion: our NCA advisors, Carole Blair, Dawn Braithwaite, Gerry Philipsen, and Jerry Hauser; the staff at the NCA national office, especially Nancy Kidd and Trevor Parry-Giles; Linda Bathgate and her remarkable staff at Routledge; Anthony Stagliano, our indefatigable editorial assistant; the University of Utah Marriott Library Special Collections (home of the NCA archives) staff; and John Bowers, for helpful advice and perspective. The chapter authors deserve special praise, working under tight deadlines and delivering outstanding and creative work. We would be remiss not to acknowledge the support, on so many levels, of Gina Ercolini and Kari Whittenberger-Keith, who make so much possible.

INTRODUCTION

A Brief History of the National Communication Association

Pat J. Gehrke and William M. Keith

The owl of Minerva begins its flight only with the falling of the twilight.
[Die Eule der Minerva beginnt erst mit der einbrechenden Dämmerung ihren Flug.][1]

G.W.F. Hegel

What is the use of a disciplinary and organizational history? Practically speaking, we should get the events and narratives of one hundred years researched and written; as events recede into the past, they become harder to research and recall. But history can do far more than that: it can illuminate the past as well as the present. As Hegel pointed out long ago, wisdom (the "owl of Minerva") may often be retrospective; at the end of an era, it becomes possible to understand assumptions and patterns invisible to those who made the history. One hundred years is, in a sense, an arbitrary turning point; 2014 doesn't have to be the end of a disciplinary trajectory. Yet 2014 serves as well as any as a point in time at which to reflect on who we have been and what we have done—and thus who we are and what we do.

The central fact of our history is the ambiguity of "we." "We" can mean *e pluribus unum*, a unified entity that emerges from diversity, but it can also refer to a multiplicity of voices, sometimes in harmony, but not necessarily unified. A simple account of "what we study and how we have studied and taught it" would make a nice story, but it would be difficult to reconcile with the textual and archival evidence: Our field and association have never had a stable identity. We don't mean to imply an "identity crisis," which entails this condition is problematic. Rather, we argue and believe the chapters in this volume demonstrate that the unique strengths and weaknesses of the field flow from a dynamic scholarly identity, always in flux, never at rest.

In a sense, we have never really been a discipline (which makes us no different from most), if what is meant by discipline is having a stable, definable identity that includes all relevant scholars and teachers, and excludes all non-relevant ones. Our reality is messier and much more interesting than that. Disciplinarity may actually function as an ideal that must not be fulfilled, since its fulfillment would eliminate most of what is creative and generative in our work. Disciplinarity, in its ideal state, must be respected and devoutly pursued, but endlessly deferred. Our bargain with ourselves is to strive toward a unity, which for principled reasons we could never accept.

As several authors point out, an easy way to track changes in identity would be changing labels—from oratory, to speech, to communication. We want to claim that these labels don't name new, stable essences, but rather the points of tension around which our disciplinary history has evolved. In many ways, our history has been a dialectic between unity and diversity. Unity represents the pull toward commonality of ideas, practices, politics, and institutions, whereas diversity represents the pull toward inclusion of difference of ideas, practices, politics, and institutions. Excessive unity can breed exclusion and control; diversity can beget fragmentation and incoherence. The critical point of tension for the association and the discipline has been between narrow, solid, well-defined, coherent research and efficiency versus a broad membership, intellectual cross-pollination, inclusiveness, and democratization. The only strong claim we make here is that change in the discipline is driven by the pull toward one pole or the other—and sometimes both at once; the history of the association is the history of grappling with this problem. Both sides have costs and benefits, though the costs have not always been as clear as the benefits at a given moment. In particular, the organizational imperatives of running an academic association ("herding cats," in the popular metaphor) have often been in tension with the intellectual and political diversity of the membership.

In this introduction, we would like to fill out this thesis by giving a general history of the association, outlining its chronology as well as some movements and milestones. What does "history" mean in this context? To make our methods clear, we need to distinguish, roughly, between traditions and critical genealogies as complementary approaches to understanding our history. Traditions are those stories that we (where "we" can include many subgroups within the discipline) tell ourselves about where we came from, and how a historical context provides meaning for what we teach and research. Sometimes these stories are invocations of a large intellectual tradition ("It all goes back to Aristotle . . ."), and sometimes they are anchored in a series of citation classics, those books and articles that define an intellectual progression leading to the present state of scholarship. Traditions are generally informal, and often rehearsed at the beginning of a graduate course, or in a proseminar to a PhD program. Traditions are various, protean, and not well documented, since there is little opportunity to publish about them.

Critical genealogies are attempts to trace and document, in a scholarly fashion, the intellectual, organizational, and institutional events and processes that result in the teaching and scholarship we see now. Critical genealogies follow the intellectual conversation, the multi-voiced back and forth that can cross decades, sometimes in formal publications, sometimes in other outlets. But they also attend to the contexts that make these conversations possible, from the larger social and political setting, to the institutional conditions of research and teaching, to the organizational and interpersonal dynamics among teachers and scholars. For example, we will sometimes use the term "National Communication Association" or NCA in referring to events of a century ago. While strictly speaking it should be the National Association of Academic Teachers of Public Speaking (NAATPS) for events until 1920, the NCA is the descendent, organizationally and intellectually, of the NAATPS and so, for all its abundant differences from its predecessor, in a genealogical sense it names the same entity.

We intend this book to be a contribution to a critical genealogy of the field of communication. It also, thereby, celebrates the lively, important, and consequential conversations that span the past hundred years of scholarship and teaching. We could not hope to produce a truly complete picture of the field; that would be a gigantic undertaking (see Wolfgang Donsbach's *Encyclopedia of Communication*), well beyond a single book. Scholars in the field volunteered to write these chapters, and the excellence of their work in no way implies its completeness.

Likewise, this book marks the centennial of the National Communication Association, the largest and most significant association for scholars and teachers of communication studies in the United States. However, this volume is not a simple celebration of the past hundred years, filled with saccharine stories or romantic reminiscences. Instead, it reflects a mature celebration of our discipline, wherein we take the centennial moment as an opportunity for critical self-reflection. Thus, we offer this volume in the ancient tradition of self-writing: a practice of caring for ourselves by writing our stories and taking stock of what we have done, who we are, and who we are becoming.

Founding an Association: 1910–1914

The story of the founding of the National Communication Association (NCA) and, by extension, the modern era of American communication studies, most commonly begins with the 1914 conference of the National Council of Teachers of English. While no doubt this was when the NCA was founded in the form of the National Association of Academic Teachers of Public Speaking (NAATPS), the years immediately prior set the stage for that 1914 meeting. At the beginning of the twentieth century, just as writing instruction was evolving into its own modern form, oral education and the rhetorical tradition consisted of oration (original speeches), declamation (delivering famous speeches), and elocution (the art of expressive delivery).[2] While some of this training occurred in private schools or with personal tutors, it also had become standard in college and university education across the country. Teachers in these traditions had been meeting since the end of the nineteenth century in associations like the National Speech Arts Association (NSAA) and the National Association of Elocutionists (NAE). At the beginning of the twentieth century, however, different practical and civic concerns and rising theories of psychology were taking hold in higher education. These motivations and theories brought a generation of public speaking teachers who sought to build an alternative to the elocutionary tradition.

In 1910, James Winans of Cornell University and Paul Pearson at Swarthmore College organized a group of these teachers into the Public Speaking Conference of the New England and the North Atlantic States (later known as the Eastern Communication Association). The first conference was held at Swarthmore on April 15 and 16, 1910.[3] Herbert Wichelns characterized that early conference and the association it built as a sometimes uncomfortable joint venture of the declining elocutionists (represented most prominently by Thomas Trueblood) and the rising public speaking teachers (such as

John Frizzell and Wilbur Kay).[4] The first program of the 1910 conference included topics such as what courses should be taught in public speaking, the relationship between music and public speaking, how departments of public speaking serve colleges, and pedagogies of the Rush and Delsarte systems of elocution. Thirteen people presented and, by design, the association originally restricted membership to teachers from universities and colleges, including teachers' colleges, not opening itself to secondary school teachers until 1920.[5] The Eastern Association began publishing what was arguably the first academic journal of speech in 1911, *The Public Speaking Review*, which ceased publication three years later. Its self-declared purpose was to be the first such publication "by teachers for teachers."[6] While college and university education in public speaking was the *Review*'s focus, it also published regularly on high school public speaking.

During the same period that the public speaking teachers in the Northeast had been organizing and building their publication, English teachers around the country, and particularly those interested in the teaching of writing, had been working to form an autonomous organization more friendly to their purposes than the Modern Language Association. In 1911, thirty-five teachers of English, who had met at the English roundtable of the National Education Association and almost half of whom were from high schools, founded the National Council of Teachers of English. Disciplinary distinctions were forming quickly, however; James Winans, the head of the Department of Public Speaking at Cornell University, emerged as perhaps the only figure common to the National Speech Arts Association, the Eastern Conference on Public Speaking, and the National Council of Teachers of English. A natural progression might have suggested an alliance between speech and writing teachers, yet a combination of circumstances and interests in both the Eastern Public Speaking Conference and the NCTE led to the founding of the NAATPS.

Since at least 1910, James O'Neill (then at Dartmouth and later at Wisconsin) had been campaigning for an independent speech association and independent speech departments. He met Winans at a Dartmouth debate competition, and they began to explore their common interests and advocacy. At the 1913 meeting of the Eastern Conference, O'Neill, a few months before moving to the University of Wisconsin, made an impassioned plea for the independence of public speaking from English and other disciplines; Winans also advocated for independence at that same meeting. O'Neill and Frederick Robinson of the College of the City of New York even drafted a "declaration of independence" for speech.[7] These conversations led to the deliberately provocative speech O'Neill gave later that year as a keynote at the 1913 National Council of Teachers of English conference. Responding to claims made at the previous year's NCTE conference that the teaching of speech occurred best under the umbrella of English, O'Neill argued for a "dividing line between departments of Speech and English," claiming that no "good work" in speech would be possible until it was free from the English departments. Reception was reportedly quite mixed.[8]

Having built a coalition of invested teachers and laid the rhetorical groundwork for separation at the NCTE and in the Eastern Public Speaking Conference, O'Neill, Winans, and their allies set the goal of founding the new association in 1914. A committee composed of Charles Woolbert of Illinois, C.D. Hardy of Northwestern,[9] and O'Neill set about preparation for the 1914 NCTE meeting. Hardy wrote to teachers of public speaking and polled them on their desire for a new association. Having received replies from 116 teachers at ninety-three institutions, Hardy presented his results at the business meeting of the public speaking committee of the NCTE in 1914, and his data aid in understanding the condition of public speaking at the time. Only thirty-eight institutions placed public speaking in departments of English. Fifty-one of the institutions already had independent departments of public speaking, speech, oratory, or elocution. Four institutions were listed as "other" or offering miscellaneous replies. Nonetheless, out of the 116 respondents all but three were in favor of a new national organization for teachers of public speaking. On the question of whether that association ought to be independent from existing organizations, the replies were less unanimous. In fact, in the original poll only forty-one of the 116 respondents voted for an independent organization, forty-two voted for affiliation with the NCTE, ten with the NSAA, sixteen with the NAE, and five replies were listed as miscellaneous. Because no majority emerged on the question of independence (and likely also because the plurality had not produced the desired result), a second ballot was sent with only two options: affiliation with the NCTE or autonomy. The vote for independence carried without a majority and by a single vote, with fifty-seven voting for autonomy, fifty-six voting for affiliation with the NCTE, and four giving other or miscellaneous replies.[10]

With Hardy's information, the committee set about discussing the motion to form a new national association for public speaking teachers; the few stories we have about that discussion come almost entirely from the creators of what is now the National Communication Association. However, we do know that the question of forming a new association was, in the end, tabled by a vote of eighteen to sixteen. Unsatisfied with this result, O'Neill and sixteen other college and university teachers of public speaking held their own "rump" convention the next morning in a parlor of the Auditorium Hotel (currently part of Roosevelt University).[11] O'Neill later defended the legitimacy of that Saturday morning conference of the select seventeen in this way:

> First, that more than two of the people voting to table this motion were public readers—not teachers—or teachers in other departments than public speaking; secondly, this vote was taken at a time when the attendance was small—a number of strong supporters of the motion being absent at the time, and, thirdly at least two (I think three) of the men who voted to table this motion were present at the conference the next morning and voted for all the motions passed at that meeting.[12]

In the end, seventeen college and university teachers settled on a name, the National Association of Academic Teachers of Public Speaking, decided to found a journal (the *Quarterly Journal of Public Speaking*), and committed to gathering as many members as they could. The founding members of the association were

I.M. Cochran, Carleton College
Loren Gates, Miami University
J.S. Gaylord, Winona Normal
H.B. Gislason, University of Minnesota

H.B. Gough, DePauw University

Binney Gunnison, Lombard College

C.D. Hardy, Northwestern University

J.L. Lardner, Northwestern University

G.N. Merry, University of Iowa

James M. O'Neill, University of Wisconsin (First President)

J.M. Phelps, University of Illinois

F.M. Rarig, University of Minnesota

L. Sarett, Northwestern University

B.C. Van Wye, University of Cincinnati

J.A. Winans, Cornell University

I.L. Winter, Harvard University

C.H. Woolbert, University of Illinois

We cannot reconstruct the full range of motivations of the seventeen, but from their own statements we know they were concerned with issues of tenure, promotion, dignity and influence of work, marginalization within English and the NCTE, and control over their own convention programming. This last matter, agency in programming convention panels, has been emphasized separately by Robert Jeffrey and Giles Gray.[13] The NCTE had centralized control over not only the association but also the annual conference. The area committees of the NCTE did not decide who or what would be presented and so the speech teachers felt unrepresented by the NCTE officers and feared the teachers of writing who dominated the organization were not able judges of the topics or speakers most useful to the public speaking teachers. Likewise, it bears mentioning that the new NAATPS was founded without a single representative of K–12 education, even though the NCTE was highly invested in teaching English in elementary and secondary schools and populated by many teachers from those schools. As with the founding of the Eastern Public Speaking Conference, the emphasis on academic teachers of public speaking appears to have translated into a bias favoring college and university teachers.

Building the Discipline: The First Thirty Years[14]

While Herman Cohen has pointed out that "ambiguity and a measure of parliamentary uncertainty" marked the founding,[15] over the next thirty years the association and the discipline of speech grew dramatically across the United States. For the first few years, the fledgling NAATPS met concurrently with the NCTE, which maintained its own public speaking committee. The first convention in 1915 was at the Congress Hotel in Chicago, near the Auditorium Hotel where the NCTE was meeting. At that first conference in 1915, twelve of the nineteen presenters were from universities, three were from colleges, two from normal schools or teachers' colleges, and two were from high schools; this ratio differed markedly from the distribution of presenters at the simultaneous NCTE conference, where faculty from teachers' colleges and primary/secondary institutions were more prominent. Nonetheless, by the end of 1915 the

NAATPS had grown from seventeen to 160 members.[16] In that first year, the new association had also begun publication of its academic journal, the *Quarterly Journal of Public Speaking*. O'Neill was the journal's first editor and declared it would focus on research; in fact he promised "right of way" and "practically unlimited space" to articles giving the results of research that came through the NAATPS.[17] Filling the journal in the first years was a challenge and O'Neill wrote to many people who presented at the NAATPS and Eastern meetings begging them to write up their talks for publication.[18]

The focus on college and university public speaking, the insistence upon the "academic" moniker, and O'Neill's desire to publish research can give the wrong impression to current readers. All these terms were understood at the time within the context of teaching. *Research* referred to studies and explorations of what was taught, what ought to be taught, and how best to teach it. *Academic* referred to the teaching that occurred in formal educational institutions, predominantly at the college and university level, as opposed to private elocution instruction. As even a cursory review of the first decade of the *Quarterly Journal* will testify, teaching dominated the disciplinary conversation. Teaching was so much the focus that a 1915 call for a symposium on methods in the journal referred exclusively to the pedagogical question: By what methods ought we teach public speaking?[19]

Even while openly hostile to public readers (performers) and non-academic teachers, and generally less than welcoming to elementary and secondary teachers, by 1920 the NAATPS had grown to 700 members, while the NSAA, the NAE, and the public speaking committee of the NCTE had all ceased operating. Dues at this time for the National Association were $2.00 annually, rising to $2.50 in 1921 ($32.67 in 2014 dollars adjusted for inflation).[20]

While this new association found its early decades embroiled with Progressive politics, two world wars, and the Great Depression, we do not have space to rehearse those stories here. We have each written, as have others, on the role of pragmatism and progressivism in the early discipline, and the relationship between speech education and wartime during the era.[21] Instead, we want to emphasize how dramatically the new association, the discipline, and its departments grew in its first thirty years. Certainly the sheer growth in members, rising to over 4,000 by 1938, is impressive. Perhaps even more impressive is that this growth occurred simultaneous with a dramatic expansion in the national and regional organizations that might claim the attention and finances of teachers and scholars of speech across the country, as well as being unabated by the Great Depression. In 1925 the American Academy of Speech Correction was formed for those focused on speech pathology and audiology, today known as the American Speech-Language-Hearing Association (ASHA). Sometimes referred to as "speech sciences" (in addition to "speech correction" and "speech pathology"), the ASHA was meeting independently of the speech teachers by 1937. Additionally, between 1929 and 1931 the Western, Central, and Southern regions of the United States each established their own speech associations to match the Eastern region. In 1936 two new associations were formed for teachers of theater, the American Educational Theater Association (AETA) and the National Association of Dramatic and Speech Arts (NADSA).

Unity in Diversity: The Post-War Era

The years of austerity and redirection of national energies during World War II saw a significant decline in association membership, but by 1949 the association, now the Speech Association of America (SAA), had rebuilt its membership to over 5,000. The growth of the association reflected the rising strength of speech as a discipline and a booming interest in the study and teaching of communication at the mid-century. From the 1940s through the 1950s, "communication" was the buzzword not only for teachers of speech but also for teachers of English and related fields. As chapters by J. Michael Sproule and Gerry Philipsen in this volume document, the rise of communication (both the term and the idea) did not begin exclusively during World War II, nor was it solely a function of the new technologies of the time. Instead, "communication" represented a paradigm shift in our theories of how human interaction, language, speech, writing, and social organization function. During these years English, speech, journalism, and media experienced something of a rapprochement. The National Council of Teachers of English formed the Conference on College Composition and Communication, reaching out to speech teachers in the effort, and for a brief moment it appeared that writing and speaking instruction might be unified, but it was not to be.[22] Teachers and scholars in speech formed the National Society for the Study of Communication, which would become the International Communication Association in 1969; this group shifted its focus to include mediated communication as well as emerging social science methodologies. As C.H. Weaver wrote, these moves reflected rising desires to foster "methodologies, philosophies, courses, and curricula in so-called basic communication, speech, journalism, radio, and other mass media (including English, etc.), which would implement training more directly for the needs of human relations at all levels."[23] These trends were likewise reflected in the growth of omnibus departments of speech where all of these subjects were taught.

Inevitably, with so many different emphases and interests populating departments of speech and the Speech Association of America, conflict arose about the terms used to name and describe the activities of the discipline, as well as issues of representation and control of the national association. In the early 1950s, these issues reached a crisis point and a general outcry arose to do something, with camps generally split between a more unified and narrow focus to the association, versus a less coherent but more broadly democratic and inclusive association. As Paul Bagwell wrote in 1952, "various members of our Association have expressed dissatisfaction concerning what they have termed separatist movements and the growth of specialisms within the Speech Association of America."[24] Likewise, reflecting the same kinds of difficult cooperation and conflicts over recognition and power that brought about the 1914 defection from the NCTE, many members of the discipline and the association saw themselves as sidelined, subordinated, or simply under-represented. Perhaps most significant were the complaints of members from theater and media (radio, television, and film). By the beginning of the 1950s, theater teachers already had significant options in other national associations, and theater faculty such as Jack Morrison, president of the AETA, were particularly vocal in expressing their dissatisfaction with how the national and regional speech associations treated them.

Echoing the complaints speech teachers had made about the NCTE forty years earlier, Morrison argued both in private letters and in publication that the control of theater panels at the conventions by speech people was both inappropriate and ineffective.[25] Faculty working in radio-TV-film units expressed similar complaints at the same time, while faculty in speech and hearing sciences were already departing from the broader speech discipline.

These complaints, combined with the continued growth of the national association, led former president of the SAA, Wilbur Gilman, to propose a reorganization of the association, the most complete version of which he published in an April 1952 *Quarterly Journal of Speech* article, entitled "Unity in Diversity."[26] What came to be called the "Gilman Plan" was to transform the SAA into an umbrella organization that could gather together all the other independent organizations that had anything to do with speech, hearing, debate, media, or theater, with each retaining its relative independence while being organized as sub-units of the broader national association. While this proposal for a federated structure was loudly debated and eventually rejected by nearly all the associations it had hoped to capture,[27] both its theme of "unity in diversity" and the underlying idea of relatively autonomous divisions in a federated structure triumphed just two years later. In 1954, the NCA (then the SAA) revised its constitution to create independent divisions to reflect the varied emphases and interests of its members. The divisions now had their own officers, access to some of the association funds, but most importantly control of their own programming at the national convention.[28] Under this new structure each division had relatively autonomous control over its domain, but also had a significant role in the decisions of the national association. While the new structure did little to address the rise and growth of independent associations in areas like speech pathology, theater, and media, the new federated structure did facilitate the tendency for members of other associations also to maintain a dual membership with the SAA.[29]

These two turns at the beginning of the 1950s, the first toward the term *communication* and the second being the new structure of the association, laid the groundwork for a period of both extraordinary growth in membership and a dramatic expansion of inclusiveness. From the mid-1950s to the early 1970s, the association saw significant growth, including increases in the number of convention panels focused on, and members from, K–12 education. In part this was due to a rising interest in speech at secondary schools and high schools during the 1950s, but without the kinds of structural changes that had taken hold by 1954 these teachers may not have turned to the Speech Association of America, but instead to an alternative organization, such as the NCTE or AETA. In many ways, this period represents the broadest integration of the discipline across fields, methods, and levels of education of any time in the century. Thus, by the mid-1960s the Speech Association of America had twenty different divisions and had become the wellspring for scholarship and pedagogy in all areas of communication. In 1965 those divisions were listed as:

> Administrative policies and practices;
> American forensic association;
> Behavioral sciences;

Business and professional speaking;
Discussion and group methods;
General semantics and related methodologies;
Graduate study and instruction;
High school discussion-debate;
History of speech education;
Interpretation;
Parliamentary procedure;
Radio-television-film;
Rhetoric and public address;
Speech and hearing disorders;
Speech for foreign and bilingual students;
Speech for religious workers;
Speech in the elementary school;
Speech in the secondary school;
Theater and drama;
Undergraduate speech instruction; and
Voice phonetics and linguistics.[30]

The relative autonomy of each division and growth in the number of divisions created a certain detente in which the debates of the previous forty years between science and humanities were largely suspended while each of the discipline's two dominant epistemologies pursued their own paths. Similar to many other disciplines in the 1950s, and resonant with C.P. Snow's 1959 diagnosis of the science/humanities rift in academic culture, speech and communication in the 1950s began to form two cultures—the social sciences and the humanities—and the conversations between them steadily diminished. By 1975 the rift was complete enough for Thomas Sloan of Berkeley to condemn both of the "two houses" in the association, noting that their mutual antipathy variously positioned them as "humanist and behaviorist" or "rhetorician and communicator."[31] As Cohen noted, a debate between the humanistic, psychological, and sociological orientations toward the study of speech invigorated the discipline almost from the moments of its founding.[32] Early speech scholars such as Woolbert had called for a rise of psychological and scientific study of speech in the 1910s, the speech pathologists had been developing an increasingly rigorous science in the study of speech and hearing throughout the period, and scholars such as Elwood Murray at Denver were conducting laboratory studies of speech in a variety of contexts in the 1930s.[33] The tools and sophistication of social scientific work in the 1950s, particularly the capacity to do complex statistical analyses of large data sets, are no doubt primitive by the standards of social scientists in the twenty-first century, but the scholarship done at the mid-century lay the foundation that by the late 1960s grounded a diversity of work that was empirical, social scientific, and predominantly psychological in both its sources and methodologies.

Meanwhile, the humanistic study of speech in the 1950s and 1960s found a new potency in the term *rhetoric*. While scholars in the discipline had commonly referenced rhetoric since the beginning of the century, for the first few decades it was simply one term among a cluster of terms for the humanistic and democratic traditions in speech. *Public speaking, public address, oratory,* and *speech* were, most often, more important to the early authors than *rhetoric,* and *speech* was clearly the master term. The early journals present a smattering of articles on classical rhetoric and rhetoric certainly had its champions (especially Everett Hunt), but the dominant trend, as exemplified by Craig Baird, was toward theorizing and critically analyzing speech, of which rhetoric was merely a subfield.[34] In the early 1950s, this began to change as humanistic scholars of speech discovered the work of Kenneth Burke, particularly as presented and interpreted by Marie Hochmuth Nichols.[35] Working from Burke, emerging philosophies of public discourse from Europe, and a rising American interest in existentialism, rhetoric provided scholars in the 1950s and 1960s an alternative to speech that was not simply classicist but created a living tradition. If the dominant trend in the early century had been to re-articulate the American traditions of democracy to each new generation through understanding how speaking and speech created and sustained a democratic culture, the new rhetoric project of the mid-century was universal, leveling cultural difference into an analysis of *homo symbolens,* humans as symbolizing animals. Breaking to some extent with the progressive and pragmatist tradition of the early discipline, the humanistic tradition in the discipline began to conceive of itself as the study of rhetoric, with the attendant subfields of rhetorical theory, rhetorical criticism, public address, history of rhetoric, and so on. The exuberant fecundity of this approach would lead to perceptions of an excessive expansion of the rhetorical tradition, necessitating conversations like those at the National Development Project on Rhetoric's two conferences in 1970: the Wingspread Conference and the National Conference on Rhetoric.[36]

For most of the 1950s and 1960s, these divergent and diverse orientations grew into a number of vibrant departments and an association that averaged between 6,000 and 7,000 members for most of that period. Not one of the twenty divisions could claim to dominate the national association at the time. In fact, in the mid-1960s the largest divisions could claim no more than 17% of the association's membership. In 1965 theater and drama was the largest with 950 members, while rhetoric and public address was second with 889. On the opposite end the smallest were speech in elementary education with one hundred members and parliamentary procedure with eighty-four. While we do not have precise numbers for every division over the years, we do know that in the mid- to late 1960s, in addition to the divisions mentioned above, the undergraduate speech instruction and radio-TV-film divisions were among the largest.[37]

As the status of that undergraduate speech instruction division testifies, the teaching emphasis that had dominated the first decades of the discipline may have declined by the 1960s, but it was certainly not absent. The abstracts for the 1968 annual convention show that 15% of the panel titles explicitly emphasized some element of teaching, training, or instruction. K–12 education likewise was a minority but still noticeable presence, making explicit appearance in 10% of the panel titles.[38] These numbers may appear relatively small, but they should be understood in light of two facts: first, none of the twenty divisions claimed more than 17% of the total membership during the period and, second, that these are the panel titles and not the titles of individual papers. For a point of comparison, we could locate only four panels in total during the 2013 National

Communication Association convention that explicitly referred to any level of K–12 education, which would be 0.3% of the total 1,192 panels that year.

Of course, managing this kind of diversity and dealing with a membership this size presented organizational and institutional challenges for the association. Amazingly, the dues in 1963 were raised, but only to $5.00 annually; after adjustment for inflation this was even cheaper than the $2.00 membership in 1914. In an effort to connect with private foundations, between 1962 and 1963 the association moved its headquarters to New York City, at great expense, and began the trajectory toward a full-time professional staff.[39] The expenses of professionalizing the association and high costs of the move created the need for a dramatic increase in dues in 1967, when they jumped to $10.00 (equivalent to $70.00 in 2014).[40] Nonetheless, the increase provided sufficient financial support for the association to generate positive net income each year.

Conflict and Consolidation

The late 1960s through the 1970s was in some ways a period of crisis for the association as well as significant change, a crisis in the classical sense of the word: a point in time requiring significant judgment to make critical decisions and choose a path forward. How one judges the decisions made by the members and officers of the association during the 1960s and 1970s likely reflects one's own politics and philosophy of education and scholarship, just as the choices did then. Whether leaders realized it or not, these decisions were again about how to manage unity and diversity.

Beginning in roughly 1965 with the activities of a group of graduate students and young scholars calling themselves the "Young Turks," the association's legislative assembly displayed a growing interest in and engagement with contemporary political events.[41] The legislative assembly's attention to American political events of the 1960s gained momentum over the next few years, reaching an unprecedented level in 1968. When they met in Chicago in late December, the "police riots" of four months earlier, where Chicago police had beaten and tear-gassed masses of protesters and bystanders at the Democratic National Convention, and the early December release of the Walker Report on those riots[42] were still fresh in the minds of the membership. The legislative assembly debated the condemnation of the association for failing to move its convention out of the city and members brought to the floor and debated multiple resolutions ranging from statements of disapproval to embargoing Chicago as a convention city.[43] In the end, some ambiguity remains about the exact results of some of those votes, but the administrative committee, reflecting on the debates and votes of the legislative assembly, decided to move the 1970 convention from Chicago to New Orleans. Less than two years before the convention, the association cancelled its contracts with hotels, apparently without providing the hotels with remuneration, found a new location for the convention, and did not return to Chicago until 1972.[44]

The following year continued the political debates in the legislative assembly, including objections to statements made by Vice President Spiro Agnew, but more importantly 1969 through 1974 saw the independent development of both the Black Caucus and Women's Caucus. The histories of each are detailed by chapters in this volume, but several events merit mention. First, the rise of the Black Caucus and the Women's Caucus did not occur by either caucus asking permission from the legislative assembly or the administrative committee. They were, instead, organized independently of the officers of the association and presented themselves not so much in a request for recognition but each by a statement of its principles and a declaration of its presence. The response of the association at the time was to acknowledge the two caucuses and eventually provide them some meeting space and convention panels, while formally organizing them into a "social relevance committee" and later a commission on "the profession and social problems." Reviewing the reports of these committees and documents from the legislative assembly and administrative council in the early to mid-1970s reveals that this structure was both unproductive and unsustainable. In 1974, the commission stated without equivocation that it had been a fundamental mistake to try to place the Women's Caucus and Black Caucus into one committee. In their information report that year, they wrote, "Grouping the various minority problems under one umbrella commission has made for a less efficient operation of the commission ... There is little equivocation between the Women's Liberation Movement and the struggle for survival among Black Americans."[45] It was clear that a single representative, be it a person, a committee, or commission, could not give voice to or address the challenges of the diversity of people in the association. Very shortly after, the two caucuses were functioning independently and received more formal recognition by the association, such as their own program panels at the convention and inclusion of their annual reports in the minutes of the Legislative Council.[46] A few years later in 1978, as Morris and Palczewski document in their chapter in this volume, the Caucus on Gay and Lesbian Concerns also organized and quickly thereafter began organizing convention panels and publishing its own bulletin.

At the same time as the political debates and the challenges of diversity came to the fore, the association was trying to decide how to manage its own growth. Perhaps most importantly, the twenty divisions that had emerged since 1954 and growing caucuses, committees, and commissions led some to call for consolidation and clarification of the organization's mission and title. 1970 saw perhaps one of the most dramatic changes in the history of the association when it not only changed its name from the Speech Association of America to the Speech Communication Association (SCA), but also implemented a new constitution that whittled down those twenty divisions to nine. To characterize this consolidation of diverse elements as contentious would be a significant understatement. While the membership eventually approved the new constitution by an overwhelming margin, the process of its production began with a committee of only four people who were appointed by the Administrative Council: J. Jeffrey Auer, John E. Dietrich, Douglas Ehninger, and William Work.[47] Those four then appointed a broader body of "consultants."[48] These two groups of members, all of which had been appointed rather than elected, then drafted the new constitution. An elected committee of fifty members then served as the final check on the constitution in a short convention meeting that was not without controversy but eventually sent the document to the full membership for a vote. Of those fifty, none were from K–12 institutions and roughly two-thirds were from schools we would recognize as research universities with graduate education programs.[49] Though the vote of the membership passed the new constitution by a wide margin, only about a third of the members voted and there was a strong sense that some divisions and groups felt poorly represented or marginalized in the process of drafting the new constitution and especially by its final form.[50] Acknowledging members' concerns and problems with the new constitution, an unsigned editorial occupying the center column of the front page of *Spectra* in February of 1970 reported that "the Administrative Council urges ratification of the new Constitution and By-Laws and that the Council, cognizant of the dissatisfaction expressed by some groups regarding certain structural features . . . expresses confidence that the amendment procedures provided are adequate to bring about change."[51] The nine divisions remaining were:

Forensics;
Instructional development;
Interpersonal and small group interaction;
Interpretation;
Mass communication;
Public address;
Rhetorical and communication theory;
Speech sciences; and
Theater.

The same nine divisions, with some minor modifications in name, were the only divisions in the association for many years to come.[52]

A comparison of those nine divisions with the twenty that existed in 1969 reveals a number of areas removed from the association's purview. Yet diversity did not disappear. Over the next few years, some of those previous divisions became independent organizations that would affiliate with the newly renamed Speech Communication Association. The period between 1971 and 1977 saw the founding of the Religious Communication Association, the Association for Communication Administration, the Commission on American Parliamentary Practice, the Society for the Study of Symbolic Interaction, the American Society for the History of Rhetoric, and the International Society for the History of Rhetoric. Some of these new associations would become relatively or even fully autonomous, while others largely functioned as interest groups of the Speech Communication Association while formally being independent. Other associations that were founded prior to the constitution change also saw growth during this period, most notably TESOL, the Teachers of English to Speakers of Other Languages association, which was founded in 1966 and grew substantially through the 1970s. Likewise the American Speech-Language-Hearing Association (ASHA) grew during these years, having become the home for certification standards for audiologists and speech language pathologists during the 1960s. The International Communication Association, having just changed its name from the National Society for the Study of Communication in 1969, also grew dramatically from 348 members in 1969 to 2,173 in 1979.[53] Work and Jeffrey report that at least some of that growth resulted from scholars interested in business and professional communication who left the SCA after the 1970 constitution change.[54] Theater faculty also appear to have left for other organizations, dropping nearly a third of its members between 1971 and 1973 (from 1,440 to 993).[55] Rhetoric also saw much activity and growth in the late 1960s and through the 1970s in a variety of symposia, institutes, and projects; the Rhetoric Society of America (RSA) was formally founded in 1968 and began regular quarterly publication of its academic journal, *Rhetoric Society Quarterly*, in 1976.[56] However, it did not begin to offer regular conferences until the mid-1980s and took many more years before it attracted a significant number of communication scholars and teachers. Having jumped from 528 members in 2006 to 1,164 members in 2010,[57] the RSA now exists as a serious alternative for rhetoric scholars in both Communication and English, though their professional networks still operate predominantly through the NCA and NCTE.

The 1970s were also a period of decline in K–12 members and panels. Under the 1970 constitution, many of the teachers previously affiliated with the elementary or secondary divisions now found themselves in the instructional development division significantly outnumbered by members of the former undergraduate instruction division. Likewise, members of the association whose primary concern was teaching and who participated in the instructional development division as a home for that emphasis increasingly voiced concern that the national association no longer shared their focus. A proposal to change the names of the journals to match the rising focus on communication was hotly debated in the association, but the proposed change of *The Speech Teacher* to *Communication Education* inspired especially heated and protracted debate. In general, the association officers, including the director of the Publications Board at the time, expressed some sympathy but the change went ahead with the promise that the journal would be "a journal for the teacher ... with practical, well-conceived ideas and resources for developing speech competencies in their students."[58] The discussion of that name change originally included a proposal for a new publication focused on the practical matters of teaching speech at the undergraduate and high school level while *Communication Education* might turn more toward the publication of research,[59] but instead *Communication Education* published a mix of research reports (the bulk of its page count each issue) and practical teaching materials (usually five or more short guides for teachers) in each issue until the early 1980s. As practical instructional material declined in the journal, almost completely disappearing by 1983, the need for a new publication focused on teaching brought about *The Speech Communication Teacher* in 1986 (today *Communication Teacher*).

However, for whatever remaining attention was paid to teaching in *Communication Education*, little of it was directed to K–12 education. In general, it appears that in the latter half of the 1970s and throughout the 1980s the association lost much of its connection to K–12 educators. The decline of K–12 participation at the national convention is reflected in minutes of the 1976 April meeting of the Administrative Committee, requesting that year's conference planner to try to give special attention to scheduling panels to attract more K–12 teachers.[60] In that same year, the association attempted to respond to "requests received from numerous individuals and groups within the association" and open a space for K–12 and community college teachers by making new "sections," in particular "working environments" of education that had disappeared when their divisions were eliminated in 1970.[61] Finally, in 1978 the association eliminated one of its Associate Executive Secretary positions, which had focused on bridging the gap between higher education and practices in K–12 programs. At the time, that position was occupied by the former chair of the instructional development division, Barbara Lieb-Brilhart, who wrote to the administrative committee in that same year that her experience in the position and her contacts with the officers and members of the association had disabused her of the notion that the association had any commitment to bridging that gap. She warned at the time that the association risked becoming "solely for purpose of scholarly exchange."[62]

The conflicts and consolidation of the association during the 1970s no doubt diminished its breadth and the association's membership declined as well. The association had grown dramatically at the end of the 1960s; from 1966 through 1973 it oscillated between 6,677 and 7,240 members. In 1974 the membership dropped to 5,799 and did not break 6,000 again until 1987. These numbers alone do not definitively imply a failure or even a misdirection of the association and the significant dues increases of the 1970s almost certainly played a role in declining membership. We would argue, however, that the decline in the pedagogical dimension of the association weakened it during this period; though we also recognize that many would value the increased sense of unity and emphasize the growth of a research focus during this time. As more than one chapter in this volume will remind us, part of the debate in the 1980s was whether we should still care about the education and training of undergraduates, particularly the first-year public speaking course. Likewise, it would be interesting to further explore the question of whether the national association lost a key opportunity to positively affect American public discourse by diminishing its role in K–12 education, but this question would have to be asked with an awareness of the arguments beginning with O'Neill in the 1910s (and others later) about the need for an organization specifically focused on higher education and research.

The latter years of the 1970s saw the association grappling with its choices and trying to chart its future. By 1976, the association had moved its headquarters once again, this time to northern Virginia in an effort to build connections to government agencies, and increased its annual dues to $25.00. Even after adjustment for the high inflation of the period, those dues in 1976 represent more than a 150% increase over the 1963 rate (and notably 63% of the 2014 membership dues). After the dramatic drop in membership in 1974 failed to be reversed in the next two years, the association tasked James Sayer to assess the "needs" of former members who had not renewed their membership. Presenting his report in 1977, he identified the following as the primary concerns expressed by former members: first, a lack of a central focus to the association combined with the tension between "ability to work in all areas of communication" and having "a narrower definition of the organization"; second, waste and inefficiency in the national office and the high cost of the move from New York to Virginia; third, a general lack of utility of the national office and association services for members; and fourth, the relative uselessness of the convention and the journals as "practical help for teachers."[63] It would be easy to argue that the next two decades of the association focused (among other things) on precisely the concerns found in Sayer's report. To what extent these concerns are valid problems for the national association and the discipline, or represent good or bad choices made for the direction of communication studies, or have been ameliorated in more recent years, are open questions of both historical and policy interest.

Into the Present

Many of the chapters in this volume tell much of the history from the late 1970s to present, so we will not repeat those stories here, but significant structural changes in the association do merit mention. Most notably, from 1985 to 2002 changes in the constitution and bylaws reversed the trends toward concentration and strove to diversify and democratize the association. Rising areas and changing interests in communication studies led to the development of two new divisions: Organizational Communication in 1983 and International and Intercultural Communication in 1984. However, the existing constitution required that approval of such changes (and even of name changes for divisions) be treated as constitutional amendments with a mail ballot and requiring a two-thirds affirmative vote.[64] Commissions, meanwhile, provided a mechanism that bypassed this process, as they could come into existence by petitioning the Legislative Council and were considered by the association "in effect mini-divisions" though their constitutional status was vague at best.[65] Caucuses meanwhile had no formal status in the constitution and were growing in number with the addition of the La Raza Caucus and the Asian/Pacific American Caucus organizing between 1989 and 1992.

From 1987 to 1989, the association worked on drafting a new constitution to clarify and codify the purposes of sections, caucuses, divisions, and commissions, as well as provide a mechanism for establishing and dissolving such units without requiring constitutional amendment. The resulting constitution, which the full membership passed in 1991, gave members a clear and relatively easy pathway for establishing new units in the association, with commissions requiring only 100 signatures and divisions needing 300 signatures. It also set as policy that divisions, sections, commissions, and caucuses would receive financial support and guaranteed panel slots based on their membership numbers.[66] Association membership numbers for this period of time are difficult to acquire, but we do know that in 1989 membership was 6,376 and in 1992 it was around 7,000.[67] As a result of these changes, by 1996 the association formally recognized nineteen divisions, fifteen commissions, four sections, and six caucuses, including the Disability Issues Caucus. The largest of these were the Rhetoric/Communication Theory Division with 1,796 members and the Interpersonal/Small Group Interaction Division with 1,570 members.[68]

The second major shift during this period took place in 2002, when the association undertook another revision of the constitution, this time driven by an expressed desire to "make NCA's governance structure as democratic and responsive to member needs as possible."[69] After a lengthy process, including a series of open public forums on the constitution held at the national convention, the changes were passed by the membership in 2002. The new constitution eliminated the distinction between divisions and commissions (the "mini-divisions") and instead renamed all these units as divisions.

It retained the relationship between division size and financial support and convention program panels, but also provided the divisions, sections, and caucuses proportional representation in a larger legislative assembly, which was also empowered to make policy more directly. It also gave divisions, sections, and caucuses greater leeway in determining how they selected their own representatives to the assembly. While less dramatic than the change in 1991, the new constitution was nonetheless important in the development of the association as a broadly inclusive organization and the democratization of its governance. For at least a while, the diversity behind our unity seems to have again taken prominence. As of this year, 2014, the association hosts forty-four divisions, seven sections, and six caucuses, with membership in recent years generally holding between 7,000 and 8,000 persons.[70]

Across this history, from the founding of the National Association of Academic Teachers of Public Speaking in 1914 through the centennial of the National Communication Association in 2014, what we find is that as the association goes, so goes the discipline. It may not be that their fates are intertwined, or that one persistently guides the other, but the study of the NCA is at minimum a useful lens or possibly even a synecdoche for the study of the discipline. If there is a theme that seems to emerge across the century, we might argue that theme was captured in that mid-century phrase, "unity in diversity." The stakes in each period seem not only to be the swing of the pendulum between these two poles but also the principles that define and organize the key terms.

The chapters in this book chart the evolution of the terms, concepts, theories, and methodologies that united and divided us over the last century. J. Michael Sproule begins with the eighteenth-century roots of pedagogy, and traces the steps by which teachers of speech and writing thought they could intervene with students, first improving the quality of their language and language use, and later the quality of students' effectiveness. He shows how the study of communication, writ large, in fact does flow naturally from what originally seemed to be arcane concerns over minutiae of pronunciation and delivery. Gerry Philipsen understands this transition somewhat differently. He is worried, as are Joshua Gunn and Frank Dance, about what we have lost in the transition from "speech" to "communication" as well as what we have gained. From 1914 through the middle century, "speech" was the term that not only named the substance of our study and teaching, but provided the name for our departments, association, and journals. For Philipsen, the term names an important achievement of intellectual and practical synthesis, and was diminished when it became one among many means for the purpose of "communication," which soon supplants it as the master term. Gunn and Dance track the process by which "speech" fell into disrepute; as with any concept which bears the burden of synthesizing the diverse concerns of a discipline, they contend we lose important theoretical and practical resources when we marginalize "speech," regardless of what is gained in "communication."

These critical analyses are followed by two chapters which attempt to stabilize the big picture of change in the field using content analytic techniques. James Anderson and Michael Middleton quantitatively analyze over 9,000 articles from our journals, in three time periods, 1951–1960, 1975–1985, and 2001–2010. They look at the discipline as a knowledge-generating enterprise, and so analyze these articles according to epistemological location, theoretical lineage, and specific theories, and are able to draw interesting conclusions about where theorizing and research have been and might be going. Timothy Stephen's chapter uses an analysis of all the titles in an array of journals to create a complex account that not only shows the growth and shrinkage of standard areas over time, but the emergence of new ones and the interrelationships between areas.

The next two chapters plumb diversity in the history of the association on several levels. Charles Morris and Catherine Palczewski, in both broad strokes and specific detail, trace the intellectual, institutional, and political ways in which the field became aware and engaged scholars, teachers, and members who are women and LGBTQ. They discover that NCA is still a discipline and an association in transition when it comes to equality, acceptance, and inclusion, though the changes over the century have been striking. Reynaldo Anderson, Marnel Niles Goins, and Sheena Howard look at both the theoretical sources and obstacles to incorporating the Afrocentric idea into the study of communication, as well as the development of the Black Caucus and the emergence of intersectional areas of study.

The four chapters that conclude the book focus on the histories of specific sub-fields. Tracy Stephenson Shaffer, John Allison, and Ronald Pelias examine the history of performance studies as well as the role of the body in speech. Performance was once the central feature of the field, and the transition from the aesthetic body of the first half of the century to a focus on the "everyday" body has brought with it an expansion of performance studies in ethnography. David Beard and Graham Bodie probe the history of listening; at one time listening was an extremely popular course and is still regarded as an essential skill. Yet they show that listening research never became central to the field, though it may be returning in new forms. Brian Ott and Mary Domenico outline the approaches communication and rhetoric scholars have taken to meaning; this is a vast topic, and their historical survey illuminates important dimensions of the use of these theories for communication scholars, even when the theories generally have not originated in our field. Ronald C. Arnett creates an account of "communicative meeting," the traditions in communication scholarship that focus on communication as a moment of deep interpersonal sharing and contact. William Eadie concludes the book by identifying major trends from the last century and indicating where things might go in the future.

We offer the following chapters to the discipline with gratitude to the scholars who wrote them, as well as to the scholars, teachers, and professionals who inspired them.

Notes

1 Preface to *Elements of the Philosophy of Right*, translation our own.
2 J. Michael Sproule, "Inventing Public Speaking: Rhetoric and the Speech Book, 1730–1930," *Rhetoric and Public Affairs* 15, no. 4 (2012): 563–608.
3 Magdalene Kramer, "History of the Speech Association of the Eastern States," *Today's Speech* 1, no. 1 (1953): 1.

4 Herbert A. Wichelns, *A History of the Speech Association of the Eastern States* (Speech Association of the Eastern States, 1959): 4–6.

5 Kramer, "History," 2.

6 Wichelns, *History*, 6.

7 Frank M. Rarig and Halbert S. Greaves, "National Speech Organizations and Speech Education," in *History of Speech Education in America: Background Studies,* ed. Karl R. Wallace (New York: Appleton-Century-Crofts, 1954): 498.

8 Reports on the reception are quite lean, but some indications of the tensions are offered by O'Neill, who wrote that he knew he "was getting what is known as a 'mixed reception'" and that he ended the talk with a quotation from Finley Peter Dunne's popular fictional character, Mr. Dooley, "If I've said anything I am sorry for, I'm glad of it." James M. O'Neill, "James M. O'Neill, First President," in *The Past is Prologue: 75th Anniversary Publication of the Speech Communication Association*, ed. William Work and Robert C. Jeffrey (Annandale, VA: Speech Communication Association, 1989). See also Rarig and Greaves, "National Speech Organizations," 498–499.

9 O'Neill, "First President," 4.

10 James M. O'Neill, "The National Association," *Quarterly Journal of Public Speaking* 1, no. 1 (1915): 52–53. See also Rarig and Greaves, "National Speech Organizations," 499.

11 A long-standing belief holds that this meeting occurred at the Palmer House Hotel, however, two sources confirm it was, in fact, the Auditorium Hotel: "The First Meeting of the National Association," *Quarterly Journal of Public Speaking* 1, no. 3 (1915): 308–310; and O'Neill, who writes, "A small group who gathered around a table in one of the parlors in the second floor of Auditorium Hotel in Chicago" in "After Thirteen Years," *Quarterly Journal of Public Speaking* 14, no. 2 (1928): 243.

12 O'Neill, "The National Association," 54.

13 Frank Rarig, WSCA Oral History Project A0327, Western States Communication Association records, MS 620, J. Willard Marriott Library, University of Utah; O'Neill in "After Thirteen Years," 244; Robert C. Jeffrey, "A History of the Speech Association of America, 1914–1964," *Quarterly Journal of Speech* 50, no. 4 (1964): 432; Giles Wilkeson Gray, "The Founding of the Speech Association of America: Happy Birthday," *Quarterly Journal of Speech* 50, no. 3 (1964): 344.

14 For readers particularly interested in this early formative period, we highly recommend Herman Cohen's unparalleled study of the first thirty years of the National Communication Association: *The History of Speech Communication: The Emergence of a Discipline, 1914–1954* (Annandale, VA: National Communication Association, 1994).

15 Cohen, *History*, 30.

16 For most of our membership numbers, we have relied upon Robert C. Jeffrey, "A History of the Speech Association of America, 1914–1964," in *The Past is Prologue: 75th Anniversary Publication of the Speech Communication Association*, ed. William M. Work and Robert C. Jeffrey (Annandale, VA: Speech Communication Association, 1989): 31–32. However, in some cases we have corrected their numbers using the membership records and reports in the National Communication Association records, MS 673, at the J. Willard Marriott Library, University of Utah. All membership numbers reflect total individual and institutional memberships, but do not include library memberships.

17 "The 'Quarterly Journal' and Research," *Quarterly Journal of Public Speaking* 1, no. 1 (1915): 84–85.

18 See Northwestern University Special Collections, The James P. O'Neill Files, Box 2, Folder 1.

19 "A Symposium on Methods," *Quarterly Journal of Public Speaking* 1, no. 1 (1915): 75–76; for more on the dominance of teaching as the purpose of the discipline see William M. Keith, "We are the Speech Teachers," *Review of Communication* 11, no. 1 (2011): 83–92.

20 Adjustments for inflation throughout this chapter were calculated using the United States Department of Labor, Bureau of Labor Statistic, CPI Inflation Calculator: www.bls.gov/data/inflation_calculator.htm.

21 See chapters 1–3 from Pat J. Gehrke, *The Ethics and Politics of Speech: Communication and Rhetoric in the 20th Century* (Carbondale, IL: Southern Illinois University Press, 2009); and chapters 1–4

from William M. Keith, *Democracy as Discussion: Civic Education and the American Forum Movement* (Lanham, MD: Lexington Books, 2007).

22 Sharon Crowley, "Communication Skills and a Brief Rapprochement of Rhetoricians," *Rhetoric Society Quarterly* 34, no. 1 (2004): 89–103.

23 Carl H. Weaver, "A History of the International Communication Association," in *Communication Yearbook*, ed. B.D. Ruben (New Brunswick, NJ: Transaction Books, 1977): 607–618.

24 Paul D. Bagwell, "The Gilman Plan for the Reorganization of the Speech Association of America: A Symposium," *Quarterly Journal of Speech* 38, no. 3 (1952): 331.

25 See letters exchanged between then AETA president Jack Morrison and SAES (ECA) president Calvin Callaghan in Eastern Communication Association Records, ACCN 1474 Box 7 Folder 17, J. Willard Marriott Library, University of Utah, Salt Lake City; Morrison then published this argument, see Jack Morrison, "Speech and Theatre," *Western Speech* 15, no. 1 (1951): 27–30.

26 Wilbur E. Gilman, "Unity in Diversity," *Quarterly Journal of Speech* 38, no. 2 (1952): 123–132.

27 The negative reaction can be seen in the comments of past presidents and various association leaders in Bagwell's 1952 symposium on the Gilman plan as well as Roy C. McCall's "Divide and Be Conquered," *Western Speech* 17, no. 3 (1953): 149–154.

28 Jeffrey, "History," 442–443.

29 While exact data on joint membership is hard to come by, we do have anecdotal claims of this practice throughout the debate over the Gilman plan, as well as data from a 1967 survey of association members, in which of 1,330 responses, 291 were also members of AETA, 173 of the NEA, 145 of the AFA, 122 of the NSSC, and various smaller amounts members of ASHA, NCTE, MLA, and other organizations. "SAA Member Opinionnaire," National Communication Association records, MS 673 Box 113 Folder 5, J. Willard Marriott Library, University of Utah.

30 *Constitution and By-Laws, Officers and Committees, 1965–1966*, National Communication Association records, MS 673 Box 21 Folder 16, J. Willard Marriott Library, University of Utah.

31 Thomas Sloan, "A Plague on Both our Houses?" *Spectra* 11, no. 3 (1975): 1–2.

32 See Cohen's discussion of Everett Hunt, Charles Woolbert, and Mary Yost in chapter 3 of *The History of Speech Communication*.

33 See Judith Brownell, "Elwood Murray's Interdisciplinary Analogue Laboratory," *Communication Education* 28, no. 1 (1979): 9–21; and "Elwood Murray's Laboratory in Interpersonal Communication," *Communication Education* 31, no. 4 (1982): 325–332.

34 For example, see Lester Thonssen and A. Craig Baird, *Speech Criticism: The Development of Standards for Rhetorical Appraisal* (New York: Ronald Press, 1948).

35 Most significantly, Kenneth Burke published a four-part series in *Quarterly Journal of Speech* from 1952–1953 immediately following an essay arguing for the importance of Burke's work to speech scholars by Hochmuth Nichols: Marie Hochmuth, "Kenneth Burke and the 'New Rhetoric,'" *Quarterly Journal of Speech* 38, no. 2 (1952): 133–144; Kenneth Burke, "A Dramatistic View of the Origins of Language," *Quarterly Journal of Speech* 38, no. 3 (1952): 251–264; "A Dramatistic View of the Origins of Language: Part Two," *Quarterly Journal of Speech* 38, no. 4 (1952): 446–460; "A Dramatistic View of the Origins of Language: Part III," *Quarterly Journal of Speech* 39, no. 1 (1953): 79–92; "Postscripts on the Negative," *Quarterly Journal of Speech* 39, no. 2 (1953): 209–216.

36 Lloyd F. Bitzer and Edwin Black, eds., *The Prospect of Rhetoric: Report of the National Development Project* (Englewood Cliffs, NJ: Prentice-Hall, 1971).

37 Leroy T. Laase, "1965 Information Report," National Communication Association records, MS 673 Box 15 Folder 5; W. Knox Hagood, "1967 Information Report," MS 673 Box 15 Folder 13; Charles R. Petrie, "1967 information report," National Communication Association records, MS 673 Box 15 Folder 13; James W Gibson, "1968 Information Report," National Communication Association records, MS 673 Box 15 Folder 17, J. Willard Marriott Library, University of Utah.

38 *1968 Speech Association Annual Convention Abstract Book*, National Communication Association records, MS 673 Box 213 Folder 1, J. Willard Marriott Library, University of Utah.

39 William Work and Robert C. Jeffrey, "Historical Notes: The Speech Communication Association, 1965–1989," in *The Past is Prologue: 75th Anniversary Publication of the Speech Communication*

Association, ed. William Work and Robert C. Jeffrey (Annandale, VA: Speech Communication Association, 1989), 42.

40 Jeffrey, "History," 434–435.

41 The formal statements and association's acknowledgment of the "Young Turks" did not come until 1968–1969, but their activities are visible in the association in earlier years of the 1960s. After gaining the attention of the leadership of the association in 1968, they met together and with association officers at the 1969 convention. In 1970 they wrote in *Spectra*, "We seek a forum for dissent and political representation within the SAA." "A Communication from the 'Young Turks,'" *Spectra* 6, no. 1 (1970): 6. See also "Young Turks," *Spectra* 4, no. 5 (1968): 4.

42 The phrase "police riots" was used by the Walker Report to describe the incident, in part to recognize that the police had initiated the violence and been the root cause of the rioting. That report was released just weeks before the 1968 SAA convention.

43 "1968 Action Reports to the Legislative Assembly," National Communication Association records, MS 673 Box 15 Folder 16 J. Willard Marriott Library, University of Utah.

44 See "Summary Minutes, SAA Administrative Council" and "1969 Action Report to the Legislative Assembly," National Communication Association records, MS 673 Box 15 Folder 203, J. Willard Marriott Library, University of Utah. Additionally, see "Chicago, 1968," *Spectra* 5, no. 1 (1969): 1–2; "1970 Convention Site Selected," *Spectra* 5, no. 4 (1969): 6; and the letters to the editor in *Spectra* 6, no. 1 (1970): 11.

45 "1974 Information Report of the Commission on the Profession and Social Problems," National Communication Association records, MS 673 Box 22 Folder 10, J. Willard Marriott Library, University of Utah.

46 "SCA Legislative Council 1976 Information Report," National Communication Association records, MS 673 Box 22 Folder 17, J. Willard Marriott Library, University of Utah.

47 "Constitutional Conference Authorized," *Spectra* 5, no. 2 (1969): 1.

48 "Structure Committee Consultants Named," *Spectra* 5, no. 5 (1969): 8.

49 "Constitutional Conference Delegates Named," *Spectra* 5, no. 6 (1969): 1–2.

50 Some hints of this dissatisfaction linger between the lines of the unsigned editorial in the February 1970 *Spectra*, "Editorial," *Spectra* 6, no. 1 (1970): 1–10; but additional evidence comes from the discussion of "groups disenfranchised by the constitution" in Work and Jeffrey, "Historical Notes," 39.

51 "Editorial," *Spectra* 6, no. 1 (1970): 1–10.

52 The durability of this division structure can be witnessed in both the next many years' issues of *Spectra* as well as the reports to the Legislative Assembly and Administrative Council found in National Communication Association records, MS 673 Box 22 Folders 6–12 and Box 23 Folder 1, J. Willard Marriott Library, University of Utah.

53 Personal correspondence with Sam Luna, International Communication Association Headquarters, March 18, 2014.

54 Work and Jeffrey, "Historical Notes," 39.

55 "Speech Communication Association Division Membership Records," National Communication Association records, MS 673 Box 113 Folder 7, J. Willard Marriott Library, University of Utah.

56 *Rhetoric Society Quarterly* was preceded by a newsletter of the RSA from 1968 through 1975, which had irregular publication and generally did not carry original scholarly articles. The RSA conferences began in Arlington, TX, in 1984 largely thanks to the energies of Charles Kneupper.

57 Membership numbers provided by RSA President Kendall R. Phillips, personal correspondence, March 28, 2014.

58 "ST-CE," *Spectra* 11, no. 3 (1975): 2; see also the description of the issues and attitude of the Publications Board as perceived by the editor of *The Speech Teacher* in the letter from Mary M. Roberts to R.R. Allen, April 27, 1974, National Communication Association records, MS 673 Box 27 Folder 18, J. Willard Marriott Library, University of Utah.

59 See minutes, agendas, and supplement materials of the Educational Policies Board in the National Communication Association records, MS 673 Box 27 Folders 18–19, J. Willard Marriott Library, University of Utah.

60 "Summary Minutes, SCA Administrative Committee, 1976," National Communication Association records, MS 673 Box 15 Folder 23, J. Willard Marriott Library, University of Utah.

61 "Constitutional Amendments Proposed," *Spectra* 12, no. 1 (1976): 10.

62 Barabara Lieb-Brilhart, "Statement Delivered at the AC Meeting," May 9, 1978, National Communication Association records, MS 673 Box 16 Folder 1, J. Willard Marriott Library, University of Utah.

63 "Summary Minutes: SCA Administrative Committee, Oct 17–19, 1977," National Communication Association records, MS 673 Box 15 Folder 25, J. Willard Marriott Library, University of Utah.

64 See Linda Putnam, "Organizational Communication Amendment," *Spectra* 19, no. 4 (1983): 1–2; and "Constitutional Amendment," *Spectra* 20, no. 2 (1984): 1.

65 "Subgroup Taxonomy," *Spectra* 20, no. 7 (1984): 16.

66 "LC Endorses Changes to SCA Constitution and Bylaws," *Spectra* 26, no. 1 (1990): 1; "SCA Members to Vote on Constitutional Changes," *Spectra* 26, no. 5 (1990): 1–8; "New Unit Affiliation Takes Effect in July," *Spectra* 27, no. 4 (1991): 1.

67 1989 is the last year available in Jeffrey's table. The 1970 estimate comes from James Gaudino, "Strong Member Support Strengthens SCA in 1992," *Spectra* 28, no. 11 (1992): 18. Due to a fire in the national association office and issues with early membership tracking software, it appears no numbers are readily available for 1990 to 2001.

68 James L. Gaudino, "SCA Units and Membership Continue to Grow," *Spectra* 32, no. 3 (1996): 4–5.

69 Bill Ballthrop, "Answers Given to Questions on the Proposed Constitution and Bylaws," *Spectra* 38, no. 6 (2002): 8. See also Bill Balthrop, "Proposed Constitutional Amendments Just Part of a 'Changing' NCA," *Spectra* 38, no. 1 (2002): 2–3.

70 Membership fluctuations in the past two decades appear more strongly related to convention site than in the early years, with 2008 and 2010 being high marks with over 8,000 members in January of those years, each following a November convention in Chicago, and the 2012 Orlando, Florida convention being a low point resulting in 6,428 members in January 2013.

References

"1970 Convention Site Selected." *Spectra* 5, no. 4 (1969): 6.

Bagwell, Paul D. "The Gilman Plan for the Reorganization of the Speech Association of America: A Symposium." *Quarterly Journal of Speech* 38, no. 3 (1952): 331–342.

Ballthrop, Bill. "Answers Given to Questions on the Proposed Constitution and Bylaws." *Spectra* 38, no. 6 (2002): 8.

——. "Proposed Constitutional Amendments Just Part of a 'Changing' NCA." *Spectra* 38, no. 1 (2002): 2–3.

Bitzer, Lloyd F. and Edwin Black, eds. *The Prospect of Rhetoric: Report of the National Development Project.* Englewood Cliffs, NJ: Prentice-Hall, 1971.

Brownell, Judith. "Elwood Murray's Interdisciplinary Analogue Laboratory." *Communication Education* 28, no. 1 (1979): 9–21.

——. "Elwood Murray's Laboratory in Interpersonal Communication." *Communication Education* 31, no. 4 (1982): 325–332.

Burke, Kenneth. "A Dramatistic View of the Origins of Language." *Quarterly Journal of Speech* 38, no. 3 (1952): 251–264.

——. "A Dramatistic View of the Origins of Language: Part Two." *Quarterly Journal of Speech* 38, no. 4 (1952): 446–460.

——. "A Dramatistic View of the Origins of Language: Part III." *Quarterly Journal of Speech* 39, no. 1 (1953): 79–92.

——. "Postscripts on the Negative." *Quarterly Journal of Speech* 39, no. 2 (1953): 209–216.

"Chicago, 1968." *Spectra* 5, no. 1 (1969): 1–2.

Cohen, Herman. *The History of Speech Communication: The Emergence of a Discipline, 1914–1954.* Annandale, VA: National Communication Association, 1994. "Constitutional Amendment." *Spectra* 20, no. 2 (1984): 1.

"Constitutional Amendments Proposed." *Spectra* 12, no. 1 (1976): 10.

"Constitutional Conference Authorized." *Spectra* 5, no. 2 (1969): 1.

"Constitutional Conference Delegates Named." *Spectra* 5, no. 6 (1969): 1–2.

Crowley, Sharon. "Communication Skills and a Brief Rapprochement of Rhetoricians." *Rhetoric Society Quarterly* 34, no. 1 (2004): 89–103.

Eastern Communication Association Records. J. Willard Marriott Library, University of Utah. (Note: These records have been relocated to Ball State University.)

"Editorial." *Spectra* 6, no. 1 (1970): 1–10.

"The First Meeting of the National Association." *Quarterly Journal of Public Speaking* 1, no. 3 (1915): 308–310.

Gaudino, James L. "SCA Units and Membership Continue to Grow." *Spectra* 32, no. 3 (1996): 4–5.

——. "Strong Member Support Strengthens SCA in 1992." *Spectra* 28, no. 11 (1992): 18.

Gehrke, Pat J. *The Ethics and Politics of Speech: Communication and Rhetoric in the 20th Century.* Carbondale, IL: Southern Illinois University Press, 2009.

Gilman, Wilbur E. "Unity in Diversity." *Quarterly Journal of Speech* 38, no. 2 (1952): 123–132.

Gray, Giles Wilkeson. "The Founding of the Speech Association of America: Happy Birthday." *Quarterly Journal of Speech* 50, no. 3 (1964): 344.

Hegel, G.W.F. Preface to *Elements of the Philosophy of Right*, translation our own.

Hochmuth, Marie. "Kenneth Burke and the 'New Rhetoric.'" *Quarterly Journal of Speech* 38, no. 2 (1952): 133–144.

Jeffrey, Robert C. "A History of the Speech Association of America, 1914–1964." In *The Past is Prologue: 75th Anniversary Publication of the Speech Communication Association*, edited by William Work and Robert C. Jeffrey, 31–32. Annandale, VA: Speech Communication Association, 1989.

Keith, William M. *Democracy as Discussion: Civic Education and the American Forum Movement.* Lanham, MD: Lexington Books, 2007.

——. "We are the Speech Teachers." *Review of Communication* 11, no. 1 (2011): 83–92.

Kramer, Magdalene. "History of the Speech Association of the Eastern States." *Today's Speech* 1, no. 1 (1953): 1.

"LC Endorses Changes to SCA Constitution and Bylaws." *Spectra* 26, no. 1 (1990): 1.

Letters to the Editor. *Spectra* 6, no. 1 (1970): 11.

McCall, Roy C. "Divide and Be Conquered." *Western Speech* 17, no. 3 (1953): 149–154.

Morrison, Jack. "Speech and Theatre." *Western Speech* 15, no. 1 (1951): 27–30.

National Communication Association Records. J. Willard Marriott Library, University of Utah.

"New Unit Affiliation Takes Effect in July." *Spectra* 27, no. 4 (1991): 1.

O'Neill, James M. "After Thirteen Years." *Quarterly Journal of Public Speaking* 14, no. 2 (1928): 242–243.

——. Files. Northwestern University Special Collections.

——. "James M. O'Neill, First President." In *The Past is Prologue: 75th Anniversary Publication of the Speech Communication Association*, edited by William Work and Robert C. Jeffrey, 3–4. Annandale, VA: Speech Communication Association, 1989.

——. "The National Association." *Quarterly Journal of Public Speaking* 1, no. 1 (1915): 52–53.

Putnam, Linda."Organizational Communication Amendment." *Spectra* 19, no. 4 (1983): 1–2.

"The 'Quarterly Journal' and Research." *Quarterly Journal of Public Speaking* 1, no. 1 (1915): 84–85.

Rarig, Frank M. and Halbert S. Greaves. "National Speech Organizations and Speech Education." In *History of Speech Education in America: Background Studies*, edited by Karl R. Wallace, 490–517. New York: Appleton-Century-Crofts, 1954.

Roever, James E. "A Communication from the 'Young Turks.'" *Spectra* 6, no. 1 (1970): 6.

"SCA Members to Vote on Constitutional Changes." *Spectra* 26, no. 5 (1990): 1–8.

Sloan, Thomas. "A Plague on Both our Houses?" *Spectra* 11, no. 3 (1975): 1–2.

Sproule, J. Michael. "Inventing Public Speaking: Rhetoric and the Speech Book, 1730–1930." *Rhetoric and Public Affairs* 15, no. 4 (2012): 563–608.

"ST-CE." *Spectra* 11, no. 3 (1975): 2.

"Structure Committee Consultants Named." *Spectra* 5, no. 5 (1969): 8.

"Subgroup Taxonomy." *Spectra* 20, no. 7 (1984): 16.

"A Symposium on Methods." *Quarterly Journal of Public Speaking* 1, no. 1 (1915): 75–76.

Thonssen, Lester and A. Craig Baird. *Speech Criticism: The Development of Standards for Rhetorical Appraisal.* New York: Ronald Press, 1948.

Weaver, Carl H. "A History of the International Communication Association." In *Communication Yearbook,* edited by B.D. Ruben, 607–618. New Brunswick, NJ: Transaction Books, 1977.

Western States Communication Association Records. J. Willard Marriott Library, University of Utah.

Wichelns, Herbert A. *A History of the Speech Association of the Eastern States.* Speech Association of the Eastern States, 1959.

Work, William and Robert C. Jeffrey. "Historical Notes: The Speech Communication Association, 1965–1989." In *The Past is Prologue: 75th Anniversary Publication of the Speech Communication Association,* edited by William Work and Robert C. Jeffrey, 38–58. Annandale, VA: Speech Communication Association, 1989.

"Young Turks." *Spectra* 4, no. 5 (1968): 4.

1.

DISCOVERING COMMUNICATION
Five Turns toward Discipline and Association

J. Michael Sproule

The one-hundredth anniversary of the National Communication Association provides occasion to explore connections between our organization and the emergence of communication as a fully realized academic area focused on human interaction as variously mediated by speech, writing, print, electronic channels, and culture. What we find is a three-century transformation by which the term *communication* transitioned from a designator for the *purpose underlying* various oral-literate media to a high-level *disciplinary moniker unifying* both channels and socio-cultural processes. This more explicit awareness of the holistic connection between audience and source represents the outcome of five successive, although not always harmonious, turning points. The tale first takes us to the early eighteenth century when the term *communication* gained currency as part of the project to elevate vernacular English as a purposive vehicle in both spoken and written formats. Somewhat diminishing this early emphasis on source–audience connectivity was a second turn, after the 1820s, by which theorists and teachers separately elaborated the *expressive instrumentalities* of elocution and composition. A third important transformation point dates to the years after 1915 when proponents of public speaking began to re-emphasize the pivotal role of communicative objectives in expressive speech. Separately, in *fin de siècle* social science, we find the beginnings of a fourth key turn whereby *communication* increasingly functioned as a conceptual lever for understanding the societal implications of symbolic exchange. Parallel projects of 1940s wartime scholarship and teaching further advanced this purposive-societal perspective. Here quantitative social scientists undertook studies of *mass communication* while at the same time teachers of speech and composition joined forces in unified communication courses that integrated speaking, writing, listening, and reading. Finally giving communication study its full disciplinary breadth was a fifth conceptual-disciplinary metamorphosis after the 1960s whereby scholars and teachers expanded the bailiwick of communication study by giving more explicit attention to culture's role in social interaction.

Elevating the Vernacular

The 1700s represents an apt starting point for communication history in view of several transformations of rhetorical theory and pedagogy flowing from the mania for improving the English language as discursive medium. Because English, speech, and journalism all grew from a shared purpose to widen interaction through the common tongue, we may presumptively give an affirmative answer to the yet persisting question, "Is communication a discipline?" Such an interpretation stands in opposition to the discipline's supposed original sin of having been conceived in irredeemable fragmentation as allegedly proved by latter-day fissures among composition, literature, speaking, news, compliance gaining, marketing, electronic media, and so on.

When examined holistically, the works of major eighteenth-century British rhetoricians all point in the direction of a vernacular synthesis variously useful for bringing provincial elites to the King's English, introducing the middle class to literary culture, and enabling the democracy of debating societies.[1] Accordingly, classicists John Lawson (1758) and John Ward (1759) both blended ancient oratorical rhetoric with eighteenth-century considerations of genius, taste, the sublime, prose writers and genres, stylistic purity and perspicuity, and the composition of sentences. Thomas Sheridan (1780 and 1781) and John Walker's (1810, 1834, and 1971) broad intent to reform and regularize both oral and written English becomes evident when we juxtapose their lectures on elocutionary reading (respectively, 1762 and 1781) to their equally important rhetorical grammars (respectively, 1781 and 1785) and pronouncing dictionaries (respectively, 1780 and 1791). Finally, the works that Wilbur Howell designates as constituting a British New Rhetoric emerge as the treatises most influential in edifying the English vernacular in both its oral and written iterations. Best represented by George Campbell (1776), Hugh Blair (1783), and later Richard Whately (1828), the New Rhetoric theorists promoted wide-ranging vernacular interchange not only by treating written grammar, usage, sentence construction, style, and literary taste, but also by elucidating the oral elements of pronunciation, articulation, purposive speaking, expressive literary reading, and (in Blair and Whately) gesture.

The orientation of rhetoricians to an audience-accessible vernacular further becomes clear from their pedagogical writings that followed John Locke (1692) and Benjamin Franklin (1749) in making English pronunciation, writing, and literature central to education. James Burgh (1745) favored schooling grounded in the correct and intelligible speaking and writing of the mother tongue; and Sheridan (1769) circulated a plan to "methodize the whole of the English language" through college-preparatory English grammar, oral reading of English prose and poetry, and reinstating "the lost art of speaking." Similarly, Joseph Priestley (1796) and Noah Webster (1790) lamented how the modern languages, though central to social and intellectual life, currently were insufficiently cultivated. To remedy this deficiency, Samuel Knox (1799), Principal of Baltimore College and author of a synthetic rhetoric textbook, wanted "the study and thorough knowledge of the native language" to become "the leading consideration" of liberal education through a regimen of composition, pronunciation, rhetoric, elocution, oratory, belles lettres, taste, and criticism. With British and American rhetoricians championing a broad-based English education, Douglas Ehninger's tidy apportionment of Enlightenment-era rhetoric into four schools of thought (classical, psychological-epistemological, belle-tristic, elocutionary) obscures the common-language imperative by diverting attention to what were differing starting points in a like-minded theoretical-pedagogical enterprise.[2]

Abridged versions designed for colleges and academies helped diffuse the vernacular-English mission of the New-Rhetoric treatises, most notably the numerous abstracted treatments of Blair's *Lectures*. Even more influential were compilations drawing from multiple works. These schoolbooks, best designated as *advanced rhetorics*, offered college and academy students an integrated introduction to vernacular English by selectively drawing from Blair, Campbell, Whately, and other contemporary handbooks such as those of John Holmes (1755) and John Stirling (1733). Here Knox's rhetoric (1809) and other treatise-synthesizing textbooks continued the pattern of combining writing and speaking, most often by appropriating from Blair's sections on composing and literature, also typically including Campbell's treatments of usage and verbal criticism. Later advanced rhetorics drew from Whately on argument types, refutation, presumption, and burden of proof. Initially somewhat idiosyncratic in their borrowings, advanced rhetorics progressively took on a more conventionalized aspect, transitioning into the English composition book. Yet the earliest composition texts shared the integrative orality-literacy approach of the treatises and advanced rhetorics, most notably by including the oration as one important context for composing.[3]

Treatise books—and related advanced rhetorics and composition manuals—typically garner the greatest attention in rhetorical history for having served as mainstays of academy and college instruction. Yet it is clear that the vernacular imperative encom-passed more than the *horizontal* span of subject-matter orality and literacy found in higher-level works. The project also included a *vertical* component relating to levels of instruction beginning with elementary primers, spellers, grammars, and readers. The pedagogical and cultural influence of these humbler works stemmed less from intellectual weight and more from their reaching a far larger audience in a time when less than 1% of students graduated from high school.[4] Primers and spellers uniformly utilized an ascending oral-recitation method that commenced with sounding out letters, syllables, words, and sentences and that continued with upper-grade pupils delivering longer selections (the religious orientation of which resulted from the prior-day practice of using catechisms, psalters, and Bibles for reading lessons). Some early introductory textbooks brought together spelling, grammar, and reading as in Thomas Dilworth's popular *New Guide* (1740). However, by the later eighteenth century, separate spellers, grammars, and readers collectively provided a broad-based vernacular pedagogy of language recognition, pronunciation, recitation, and appreciative literary expression. Even grammar study, seemingly an apotheosis of print-on-page English, then included as one of its four standard departments something called *prosody*, defined as the correct and appropriate pronunciation and delivery of prose together with the principles of versification.

In a context where reading aloud to the class constituted the basic pedagogy from grade school to college, *rhetorical readers* ultimately became the pivotal schoolbook used in locales spanning grammar school, academy (an institution sometimes equivalent to first-year college), university, and adult learning. Rhetorical readers may be recognized by their two-part organization, first, a brief introductory section covering principles of oral expression followed by a far lengthier classified anthology of essays, speeches, plays, and poems. This speaking/writing amalgamation of purposive and literary texts represented a pedagogical synthesis ideal for many settings. In grammar schools, speaking-oriented readers facilitated declamation in the upper grades; in academies, they provided the fundamentals of elocution (oral reading plus speech delivery); and across the educational spectrum, they constituted the earliest available literary anthologies—accounting for their extensive presence in university libraries. Initially most popular were rhetorical readers imported from England, notably those of Burgh (1761), William Enfield (1774), William Scott (1779), and Lindley Murray (1799). Burgh's evocative instructions for expressing seventy-seven passions made his text a particular favorite until after the Revolution, when British imports increasingly were replaced by American-authored readers, notably those of Webster (1785/1806) and Caleb Bingham (1797). Rhetorical readers were particularly sought out by adult learners such as Lincoln who studied from Scott, and Frederick Douglass who took "every opportunity" to read Bingham.[5] Autodidacts had reference not only to schoolbooks—spellers, grammars, and readers—but also to handbooks specifically designed for private study or workaday reference, manuals adapted principally to business and secondarily to polite society. Practical guidebooks chiefly offered either classified letters (e.g., requesting payment) or business arithmetic (e.g., weights and measures), although many combined model letters and numerics and added exemplary legal documents (e.g., powers of attorney) and/or useful social graces such as forms of address and "familiar letters" (i.e., polite social correspondence). A few, such as George Fisher's *American Instructor* (1748), undertook an additional, explicitly English-vernacular mission variously embracing pronunciation, oral reading, physical delivery, style (tropes and figures), and rhetorical organization.

Not only was the notion of close audience–source connection inherent in all academic and popular works promising competency in the common tongue, but the very term *communication* occurs frequently in the higher-level treatises as well as in the treatise-derived advanced rhetorics and composition textbooks. Here John Locke's *Essay Concerning Human Understanding* (1690) proved pivotal for containing the first significant use of *communication* as an integrative concept denoting minds linked through symbols. Locke's innovation was to give broader meaning to the traditional locution of *communicatio*, a term previously employed in rhetorical theory as a label for that figure of style in which a speaker rhetorically questions listeners or hypothetically consults imagined interlocutors. In an "Epistle to the Reader," Locke described his entire treatise as having originated with regard to resolving doubts through discussion. From this dialogic perspective, Locke appropriated *communication* as an operative principle for such of his postulates as "To make words serviceable to the end of communication, it is necessary . . . that they excite in the hearer exactly the same idea they stand for in the mind of the speaker." Although Locke's treatment of idea-communication was criticized by George Berkeley (1710), and did not figure in later philosophies of mind, the notion abided in the background of rhetorical study as a consequence of Locke's *Human Understanding* having been the most extensively used college textbook of moral philosophy through the 1860s.[6]

Although influenced by communicative idea exchange, *à la* Locke, rhetoricians failed fully to exploit the theoretical-pedagogical implications of this principle; instead, audience-adapted message making remained as a taken-for-granted outcome of expressive techniques well executed. In Thomas Sheridan and Joseph Priestley, we find direct connections drawn between *communication* as explicated in *Human Understanding* and insights about conveying thoughts and feelings through clarity of words and earnestness of address. While like-minded uses of *communication* in Campbell, Blair, and Whately are less explicitly reflective of Locke, nevertheless the "Big-Three" new rhetoricians shared with Sheridan and Priestley a tendency to treat the message-building elements of rhetoric (words, sentences, style, and argument) as actively operating upon audience-related faculties, sympathy, passions, and attitudes toward issues and advocates. Such may be observed even in Campbell's psychologically oriented treatise that begins with his famously subsuming receivers under four objectives sought by speakers, namely, "to enlighten the understanding, to please the imagination, to move the passions, or to influence the will." Campbell subsequently emphasizes how these ends might be attained by applications of evidence, moral reasoning (experience, analogy, testimony, probability), and language characterized by purity, perspicuity, and vivacity. Particularly illustrative is his twofold description of persuasion as (1) "communicating lively and glowing ideas" by connecting actions to motivations (e.g., honor or pity) and (2) offering "forcible arguments" for rational conviction.[7]

Refining Expressive Instruments

Communication (in the Lockean sense) enjoyed a continuing presence in nineteenth-century textbooks, although ideational congruence between source and audience remained subordinate to *things delivered*—as in a speaker's oral articulation, a writer's words, or a literary work's embodying authorial genius. Particularly indicative of the post-1820s emphasis on techniques well executed were textbooks of elocution, composition, and literature that gave pedagogical prominence to *expression* rather than to *communication*.

With regard to refining elocutionary expression, two related kinds of schoolbooks for academy and college—the *elocutionary reader* and the *elocutionary manual*—proved particularly important by replacing the anthological emphasis of the old rhetorical readers with a more concepts-focused pedagogy. Representative of the *elocutionary readers* is Ebenezer Porter's influential *Rhetorical Delivery* (1827) which, although retaining a concluding collection of texts, commenced with two instructional sections. Porter first supplied an array of terms related to voice, face, and gesture by which readers and speakers could expressively convey feeling; then he clarified articulation, inflection, emphasis, and modulation by marking passages according to his system of notations for monotone, rising or falling inflection, circumflex (rising *and* falling), and eight varieties of modulation. Where books such as Porter's retained the traditional collection of extracts, later *elocutionary manuals* fully embraced the instructional format of concepts illustrated by short diacritically marked selections. In the hands of Robert Fulton and Thomas Trueblood (1896), such a prescriptive pedagogy brought forth more than 300 conceptual refinements supported by over 250 figures, diagrams, lists, charts, and tables.

So culturally influential was the highly technical approach to delivery that it entered the grammar-school curriculum. Here the Burgh-style readers yielded to graded-series readers consisting of four to six volumes in which the directions for oral expression advanced in complexity as the selections increased in difficulty. Typically books Four, Five, or Six in a series took the form of an elocutionary reader as exemplified by the introductory "Principles of Elocution" in William McGuffey's *Sixth Reader* (1857). In addition to this principles-plus-examples treatment of articulation, inflection, accent, emphasis, pauses, vocal qualities/tones, and gesture, McGuffey's first five anthologized selections doubled as exercises in articulation. Many of his subsequent readings came with diacritical marks for inflection. The increasingly technical approach to expression visible in textbooks from grammar school to college reflected their authors' assimilation of the detailed elocutionary work not only by Sheridan and Walker but also by Joshua Steele (his 1779 markings for vowel sounds, diphthongs, melodic slides, pauses, emphasis, cadence/meter, and length of syllables), Gilbert Austin (his 1806 diagrammatic science of gesture), and James Rush (his 1827 systematic classification of vocal characteristics).

Notwithstanding the prevalence of techniques-based elocutionary expression across the educational spectrum, this somewhat mechanical pedagogy increasingly faced competition from meaning-centered approaches that typically foregrounded the label of *expression*. S.S. Curry (1910) emerged as leader in a movement to center instruction on how thought processes guided vocal and bodily action. A related pedagogy, best exemplified by William Chamberlain and Solomon Clark (1897), detailed many text-interpretive strategies by which a speaker might expressively convey authorial meaning through pausing, grouping words, and using voice and body to highlight major ideas and emotions as they unfolded in the text. Despite differences of emphasis, however, the technical, thinking-speaking, and interpretative methods all kept focus on a speaker's outward projection of thoughts and feelings, with a corresponding presumption that effectively executed expression brought about communication. The same held true in a category of non-academic guidebooks marketed for civic display and home entertainment, a genre better known as *parlor elocution*. Volumes such as Henry Northrop's (1894) were decoratively bound and typically contained an introductory how-to précis consisting of photographs or drawings of speakers giving dramatic vent to such emotional states as anger or pride.

Trends elevating expressive instrumentalities over communicative objectives were not restricted to elocution but emerged equally in English composition textbooks. One sign of expressionism's dominance in writing pedagogy was that, after the 1850s, textbooks for college and academy increasingly downplayed or omitted oratory as a context for composing such that, by 1896, audience-conditioned oral persuasion virtually disappeared from writing instruction. Even more reflective of the symbols-given-out emphasis was the increasingly standardized template that, as illustrated by A.S. Hill's *Rhetoric* (1895), focused on how to unleash, in ascending order, the expressive powers of words (chosen for propriety), sentences (of perspicuity and balance), paragraphs (exhibiting unity and force), and style (simultaneously chaste and figurative). This dedication to outward projection culminated in a roster of four discourse modes—description, exposition, narration, argumentation—with each of these New-Rhetoric-inflected categories serving as chapter-length repositories for message-making tactics that included how to secure argumentative conviction by testimony, claims of presumption, and avoidance of fallacies. A later genre of more bare-bones writing handbooks pared away composition's few remaining rhetorical vestiges—notably the figures and discourse forms—in favor of a strictly how-to pedagogy. These short manuals in the mode of Edwin Woolley (1907) provided classified and numbered directions for proper spelling, punctuation, penmanship, diction (e.g., avoiding barbarisms or triteness), word choice (e.g., precision and brevity), usage (e.g., "which" versus "that"), the logic of sentence construction, and paragraph division (to assist both eye and thought), all accompanied by exercises for practice.

Expressionist tendencies in elocution and composition were accompanied by kindred developments in literary study after the Civil War when leading universities redeployed into separate departments in which the research mission—embodied in disciplinary journals and professional associations—greatly influenced the curriculum. Initially supplying English with the necessary research-paradigm *bona fides* was evolutionary-scientific philology. However, literature gradually improved its relative departmental clout as a result of the many books and articles produced by specialists whose signature professional method was the historical-appreciative criticism of great works of imaginative literature. This scholarly explication of creative genius enabled literary study to overcome its humbler origins as a popular-amateur activity, encompassing both taste and communicative purpose, undertaken in town and college literary societies and further manifested in somewhat more elevated reviews by well-read ministers and lawyers who assessed such matters as whether a poem exhibited correct and appropriate language or whether a novel accommodated moral probity. From this vantage point of traditional belles-lettres erudition, the Rev. William Ellery Channing (1841) had praised Wordsworth's poetry more for its truth-elucidating power than for its beauty. Such a practice of evaluating literature for socio-moral enlightenment explains why the old rhetorical readers were home to the practical genres of oration, essay, and history. The later turn to textual connoisseurship sundered functional and aesthetic matters, an approach observable in George Cathcart's *Literary Reader* (1874), where artistry of language took center stage in presentations of Wordsworth and others, and where the author's life and times served to explain literary genius. Even more consummately aesthetic *fin de siècle* literary anthologies by George Metcalf (1912) and others largely purged oratory and narrative history from the canon, but retained the somewhat purposive essay owing to its stylistic gentility (i.e., proverbial wisdom, allusions, imaginative description, and spiritual self-revelation).

Nineteenth-century elocution, composition, and literature consistently moved away from the purposive-communicative connection of source and receiver and toward expressionist manifestations of author-text intentionality. With regard to elocution and composition, the impetus to refine particular instrumentalities stemmed from the attractions of rhetorical technologies as variously manifested in diacritical markings, gestural templates, lists of stylistic figures, rosters of discursive form, and numerically organized schemes. In literature, Hayden White describes a somewhat more ethereal process of "mystification" by which literary study recognized only a text's expressive and performative dimensions while ignoring or denigrating its more mundane purposive-communicative elements. White's "ideology of aestheticism" also helps explain the rise of anti-technical oral reading in the mode of Curry, Chamberlain, and Clark. Ultimately most significant is that complementary transformations in elocution, composition, and literature came together in the universal employment of *expression* as denotation for symbols emitted by speakers, authors, and texts—with a concomitant de-emphasis of *communication* in the sense of audience–source immediacy. Accordingly, while elocutionist Porter acknowledged that "delivery in its most general sense" involves "the communication of our thoughts to others," he consistently employed *expression* as the operative principle, not only highlighting the term in his table of contents, but also deploying it in regard both to voice as agency of sentiment and to countenance as window into the soul. The same pattern may be found in Hill's composition manual where *communication* served as underlying metric as in "Rhetoric may be defined as the art of efficient communication by language," but where *expression* functioned actively in the book's many linguistic operations. Accordingly, Hill's index showed two entries for *expression* and none for *communication*. In like manner, literary anthologies over-whelmingly featured the expressive rather than the purposive agency of language as when Metcalf defined literature as any "piece of writing" that gives pleasure "because of its artistic form and expression."[8]

Communicative Objectives

At the same time that expression-focused studies were on the rise in American education, the roots of what became the communication discipline were growing by virtue of popular public speaking outside of academe. A number of nineteenth-century social contexts and institutions supplied a nurturing environment for this more audience-adaptive kind of address, among them the literary and debating societies, the lyceum and lecture system, stump speaking in politics, and a more interpersonally attuned and audience-sensitive preaching. The closely related literary and debating societies touted their atmosphere of instructive and convivial "mutual improvement" in which members might try out and polish their work. As described in diary entries for 1840 by Isaac Mickle, the process was doubly engaging, for not only did this 18-year-old draw sustenance from privately practicing articulation and movement with a friend, but his oratory drew comments from fellow literary-society members. In addition to participatory speaking in the societies, audiences after the 1820s flocked to hear regional and national experts address literary, scientific, and (later) political topics in town and village lyceums—a practice that, beginning in New England, spread westward with the railroad. Lyceum lecturing demanded an energetic and direct kind of public address, not only in view of the need to fill the hall, but also because popular speakers competed against the more recreationally oriented fare provided by jugglers and minstrel groups. The Age of Jackson was also one characterized by the growth of stump speaking, a kind of address less in accord with learned oratorical-elocutionary codes and more attuned to immediate attitudes and sentiment. Mickle sardonically reflected on a stump appearance by John W. Bear, the infamous "Buckeye Blacksmith," whose Whig-party address in favor of "hard cider and hard money" relied less on forging "the chain of an argument" and more on branding opponents as "loafing rascals . . . without either shirts or characters, brains or honesty." Preaching also came under the influence of trends toward more accessible and involving public address as when the renowned Rev. Channing advised young ministers that, under modern-age conditions, "religion must be communicated in a more exciting form." He recommended replacing "dry, pedantic" sermonizing with preaching that spoke directly to the audience's situation—a kind of address that, appealing both to intellect and sentiment, offered not merely external doctrinal or Biblical evidence, but rather tapped into "the inward proofs" of human sensibility and moral feeling.[9]

New kinds of popular guidebooks came into print in support of the direct, plain, specific, and evocative kind of address found in debating and literary societies, lyceum lecturing, on the stump, and in audience-adapted preaching. Available for members of the speaking clubs were James McElligott's (1855) and other reference guides laying out a sample constitution, parliamentary procedure, and tips for responding to common interests with straightforward, audience-aware extemporization. The Rev. Henry Ware's (1824) influential ten-step program for ministers advised uttering ideas "as they rise fresh" such that a preacher would "communicate directly with the hearts of his fellow men, and win them over."[10] Similar extempore preaching books by Abbe Bautain (1859/1916) and William Pittenger (1883) enjoyed further prominence for attracting a general readership. However, most influential among the popular speechmaking works were guidebooks offered by veterans of the lecture circuit such as Thomas Higginson (1887) and George Jacob Holyoake (1849). In *Public Speaking and Debate*, in print between 1849 and 1919 in various versions, Holyoake acknowledged a number of traditional concerns such as proper pronunciation; however, his recipe emphasized earnestness and sincerity in place of affectation, knowing the mind of the audience to permit adaptation, finding and pursuing common ground, getting straight to the point, exciting curiosity, and speaking according to sense with proper vocal modulation inevitably resulting.

The modern academic public speaking book emerged between 1890 and 1930 chiefly as a result of teachers and theorists assimilating lessons from audience-centered debating, lecturing, and preaching as codified in popular speech guidebooks. Where composition, elocution, and oral-English classes still emphasized the correct and proper expression of forms—diction, pronunciation, grammar, sentences, paragraphs, kinds of discourse, gestures—reformed speechmaking defined itself as a medium of accessible, audience-centered communication. No one was more important in this transition than James Winans, whose widely cited *Public Speaking* (1915) not only referenced the plain speaking of Holyoake, Bautain, and related authors, but was the first explicitly to tap modern psychological authorities (chiefly William James (1892) and Walter Scott (1907)) to provide direct entry points to the audience independent of expressionist presumptions. Fundamental to Winans's method was "a sense of communication" whereby speakers made words meaningful by keeping ideas connected to listeners rather than relying upon expressive techniques. His archetypal speaker was dialogic, extemporaneous, earnest, and mindful of listeners' attention, interest, and viewpoints. Although Winans treated matters of voice and gesture, he advised that faults of delivery tended to disappear when speakers thought of themselves as conversationally engaged. Through the 1920s, the genre of textbooks developed by Winans and his cohorts competed with other speech books of more expressive bent that were variously derived from nineteenth-century rhetorical readers, elocutionary manuals, and composition texts. Nevertheless, by the mid-1920s, the public speaking book largely had taken on its present-day form and, in addition, the Winans-influenced communicative approach held sway in books designed for argumentation and debate, extemporaneous speaking, and business speech.[11]

By presenting public speaking as interactive communication rather than instrumental expression, Winans and like-minded others initiated a true paradigm shift by which a long-subordinated discursive principle emerged as the defining ideal—thereby supplying the first requisite for creation of a discipline, namely, a Great Idea. Yet in the history of American intellectual life, recognition of a discipline necessitates that an overarching paradigmatic principle such as *communication* be accompanied by evidence of institutional endorsement, including independent academic departments, a repertoire of courses, a research program showcased in academic journals and professional associations, and a cadre of graduate-student recruits to perpetuate the enterprise.[12] Here the work of Winans and his cohorts proved foundational not only for recasting theory and pedagogy but also for institutionalizing the communicative turn through creation of both the National Association of Academic Teachers of Public Speaking (i.e., NCA) and academic departments of "speech" rather than "elocution" or "expression."

Communication as Research or Teaching Field

Before the disciplinary study of symbolic interaction coalesced under *communication*, conceptualizations of speech and writing emphasized the particular media of presentation including English (as the common tongue), elocution, composition, public speaking, and journalism. Although pre-1860s attention to broad-spectrum *rhetoric* seemingly belies this generalization, the old Graeco-Roman rubric not only had atrophied by 1900 but gradually had become virtually synonymous with English composition until the Cornell revival of rhetorical theory.[13] Yet it was the study of film, radio, and television—media independent of print or face-to-face contexts—that finally created the conditions under which *communication* increasingly emerged as the dominant designator for social influence.

Notwithstanding the later association of *mass media* with electronics, the concept dates to the era of print when theorists and teachers first recognized the implications of large-circulation newspapers, popular magazines, and books that were creating national audiences through technologized production (telegraph, linotype, wood-pulp paper, and steam presses). Academe's first response came in the form of professionalizing trends that, beginning with news-writing courses in English, culminated in journalism departments and schools developed under the influence of state press associations. Mass-circulation publishing soon brought the phenomenon of large-scale persuasion to the attention of theorists in the emerging social sciences. Here the older view of sociopolitical opinion as informed conversations among members of the educated public—as in literary or debating societies—found itself in competition with a newer notion of social influence as the arousing of interest and feelings among members of an urban crowd. The former and more sanguine conception of the people was to be found in the widely used works of James Bryce (1899), a political theorist who believed that, for the most part, public opinion unfolded through rational public discussion. Opposing was the pessimistic crowd psychology of Gustave Le Bon (1895) and others that fixated on an allegedly irrational urban mass consisting of immigrants and minimally educated native speakers. Yet while some theorists of social irrationality, such as Walter Lippmann (1925), gave up on the public, other pioneers in collective behavior, notably sociologists Charles Cooley (1909) and Robert Park (1923), staked out a middle ground by recognizing that, notwithstanding limitations in the public mind, mass communication could further positive developments, both individual and social.

Whatever the implications for democracy of mass publishing, issues of media and society became even greater after film and radio dramatically broadened the potential audience. The Hoover Committee's *Recent Social Trends* report (1933) regarded the resulting "mass impression on so vast a scale" as significant for having "never before been possible." In assessing "The Agencies of Communication," the Committee noted advertisers pressuring newspapers, public-relations professionals disguising their promotions, movies "shaping attitudes and social values," and radio "promot[ing] cultural leveling." The Hoover report reflected the mid-1930s tendency for the social-problems component of media study to overshadow the social-process perspective of Cooley and Park, a mindset resulting from the large bibliography of popular and academic works exposing opinion manipulation not only by the World War I belligerents but also by domestic institutions and interest groups. Accordingly, the term *propaganda* tended to predominate over that of *communication* until post-Pearl Harbor considerations of national survival brought renewed attention to the positive potentials of mass persuasion.[14]

In contrast to the society-level theorization about newspapers, film, and radio sometimes found in sociology, psychology, and political science between the wars, departments of speech and English more typically regarded electronic channels as simply extending the established crafts of speaking and composing, such that, analogous to journalism-writing courses in English, speech faculty simply added radio speaking and production. Yet faculty drawn from all these departments would help to lay the proto-paradigmatic foundations of what became post-World War II communication study as a result of their answering the call to wartime service in two parallel programs, the one oriented to theory and research, and the other consisting of combined courses bringing together composition and public speaking. The theory-research tangent sprang from the Rockefeller Foundation's communication seminars for social-influence researchers. One such participant, political scientist Harold Lasswell (1949), secured a Rockefeller grant to further refine his content-analysis procedures that, under the auspices of the Library of Congress, provided data used by the Justice Department to prosecute domestic propagandists whose messages paralleled Axis outputs. Even more extensive was the work of social scientists in the Army's Research Branch—including Paul Lazarsfeld and Carl Hovland (1949)—who conducted surveys of the soldiers as well as experimental assessments of training and orientation films. One result of this work was that, by 1949, listings in *Psychological Abstracts* under *communication* began to outnumber those for *propaganda*. Sociologist Alfred McClung Lee attributed this terminological shift to the wont of social scientists to avoid "add[ing] something menacing to the notion of communications" inasmuch as "propaganda points to the social purpose of a communication."[15]

Wartime military imperatives had a second impact on communication study in producing combined "Communication" courses that, at the behest of the Army and Navy, brought together public speaking and English composition for reasons of a more efficient delivery of basic education. As refined through the early 1950s, these courses presented a fourfold curriculum of reading, writing, speaking, and listening. Notwithstanding a subsequent reversion to separatism, 1940s basic Communication produced two lasting organizational outcomes, the both of which helped transform *communication* from a *concept* miscellaneously signifying outcomes to an incipient *field* straddling the humanities and social sciences. One of these associations, the National Society for the Study of Communication (NSSC), originated at the 1949 convention of the Speech Association of America (SAA; i.e., NCA) and met jointly with the SAA as late as 1963. The other, the Conference on College Composition and Communication (CCCC), reflected the interests of writing teachers and, accordingly, began in association with the National Council of Teachers of English. Although neither the NSSC nor the CCCC immediately redefined their respective disciplines of speech and English, both helped foreground considerations of interactive process over the long-dominant craft-guild mindset of purposes, techniques, instruments, and professionalism.[16]

Certain self-segregating tendencies in the field approach, however, acted to retard recognition of *communication* as a general discipline-defining principle. By limiting the field's origins to the wartime work of Lasswell, Lazarsfeld, Hovland, and Kurt Lewin, Wilbur Schramm's "Four Fathers" thesis represented the apotheosis of treating communication as merely an interdisciplinary niche where, in Schramm's vision, elite institutes dedicated to quantitative mass-media research would bring together faculty in journalism and social science. In less sanguine private comments, however, Schramm acknowledged that no more than a third of the nation's thirty-nine accredited journalism units either sponsored "mature research activity" or were even open to integrating it into the program. Although Schramm's institutes eventually proved ideal at only a few well-resourced universities, Four-Fathers and research-institute thinking reigned supreme through the 1970s in the International Communication Association (ICA, the former NSSC). Nevertheless, ICA president Everett Rogers later acknowledged the intellectual constraints whereby "this limited [quantitative-data] approach was preferred as safer for younger scholars."[17]

Addressing Culture

The increased post-1960s attention to the role of culture represents a further element of the process by which broader disciplinary understandings of *communication* replaced narrower field conceptions. From the standpoint of the millennial-era focus on race, class, gender, ethnicity, cultural criticism, cultural capital, mediated culture, ideology, and international settings, it seems difficult to imagine a time when scholars treated audiences as either actually or potentially homogeneous with respect to messages. Despite culture's prominence in contemporary NCA divisions and journals, it is appropriate, at the organization's one-hundredth anniversary, to remind ourselves that such was not always the case.

Academicians in English, elocution, public speaking, and journalism evidenced little sensitivity to cultural differences during the *fin de siècle* era when objectively refining techniques for message production far outweighed audience considerations. To the contrary, the long-standing focus on "correctness" and "propriety" in spoken and written English reflected a class-based worldview that associated deficiencies in diction and pronunciation with less favored regions and ethnicities. At the same time, proponents of the literary canon sought the "objectively" best products of genius. Similarly, histories of journalism emphasized mainstream producers, production, professionalism, and efforts to capture the mass audience, although acknowledging certain publications catering to women, religion, and other supposedly unrepresentative spheres. By the 1940s, however, efforts to preserve cultural correctness were on the wane. Influenced by studies of historical grammar and usage, composition teachers gradually became less enamored of prescriptive diction and usage, and modern speechmaking adopted standards of pronunciation and dialect based on what was acceptable to popular audiences. At the same time, journalism historians paid heed to how such bedrock principles as objectivity sprang from nineteenth- and twentieth-century cultural currents.[18]

Perhaps the most enduring obstacle to making culture central in communication study was the widespread assumption that attitude measurement and/or rhetorical-critical analysis sufficiently accounted for audience responses. Through the 1970s, mass-media surveys and experiments were delivering streams of response data to establish law-like generalizations about selective predispositions (to exposure, retention, or recall), ego involvement, fear appeals, and the impact of TV programming. Lazarsfeld's finding that only 4% of respondents reported differences in the voting patterns of family members illustrates this search for homogeneity.[19] Edwin Black (1978) described a like-minded tendency in neo-Aristotelian criticism to presume a fundamental uniformity of populations based on putative enthymematic agreements about values. Here the typical rhetorical analyst not only foregrounded speaker purpose and textual outputs but emphasized how an immediate audience—divorced from the larger historical and ideological context—rationally took account of arguments.

But by the 1960s, many trends pointed up the importance of cultural differences with regard to audiences. Reflecting Cold-War-era considerations, Robert Oliver's *Culture and Communication* (1962) piqued scholarly curiosity about the impact on international understandings and diplomacy of differing cultural preconceptions (e.g., truth or empathy) and varying linguistic expectations (e.g., ambiguity or self-assertion). Other researchers became conversant with communication-relevant anthropological work including Edward Hall's *The Silent Language* (1959) and Erving Goffman's (1959) studies of face-to-face cultural presentation. These and many other such works not only laid the foundation for intercultural communication but also, by showcasing symbolic processes in less public settings, stimulated research in interpersonal interaction. At the same time, the social struggles of the later 1960s alerted rhetoricians to cultural discourses of (in the idiom of the time) Black Power, Chicano rhetoric, and women's consciousness raising. Looking to ground their critical investigations, scholars rediscovered such classic Frankfurt-School contributions as Max Horkheimer's and Theodor Adorno's (1944) treatment of film, radio, and magazines as a uniformity-inducing system of manipulation and, later, referenced Herbert Marcuse's (1964) explorations of contemporary pressures to uncritical affirmation. The burgeoning literature of British cultural studies included John Fiske and John Hartley's (1978) explication of television's many embedded symbolic codes such as its association of officially sanctioned violence with efficiency. As Philip Wander observed (1983), the critical turn was also an ideological turn that combined skepticism about official explanations with a recognition that vested interests shaped public address. As a result, we now find contemporary NCA journals devoting increasing space to critical, cultural, and performance scholarship such that even traditional rhetorical history now takes cognizance of oratorical culture, cultural rhetorics, and rhetorical hybrids.

Cultural considerations enabled *communication* to complete its transition both from *concept* denoting expressive outcomes and from narrow quantitative *field* to recognition as a unique paradigmatic domain, thereby consummating earlier movements toward an accessible vernacular, a lively "sense of communication," and integrative communication research and teaching. Chief among the signs that *communication* at last had won status as a disciplinary Great Idea was the term's utility in broadening the mission of academic associations and departments formerly named to reflect particular media. Previous to 1968, the only national academic organizations foregrounding *communication* were the two post-war societies of specialized focus, i.e., the NSSC/ICA and the CCCC. But in 1970, the SAA greatly advanced its move away from the limited craft-guild treatment of orality by rechristening itself as the Speech Communication Association, and later in 1997, the National Communication Association. In 1976, the Association for Education in Journalism broadened its own long-standing focus on reporting-editing professionalism by appending to its name "and Mass Communication" (AEJMC). Accompanying these organizational changes were early calls by Garth Jowett (1975) and others for holistic histories of communication in preference to chronologies limited to particular media (e.g., speechmaking or newspapers) and/or particular methodologies (e.g., Jesse Delia's 1987 history of quantitative communication research).

Yet a fundamental impediment to an integrated discipline of communication remained through the millennium in the continuing allure of organizing and defining communicative interaction along the lines of what was deemed "the proper study," to borrow from the title of Stuart Chase's 1948 book commissioned by the Social Science Research Council and the Carnegie Corporation to establish quantitative methods as definitive for social inquiry. One still encounters individuals who long for the good old days when *journalism* meant newspapers and when *speech* held pride of place in what is now the NCA. A similar impulse may be observed in Rogers's (1994) commendable, but still limited, effort to stretch the historical-intellectual boundaries of Schramm's "Four Fathers." Here Thomas Kuhn explains how intellectual myopia can produce a "drastic distortion" of a discipline's history when scholars memorialize only those trends "leading in a straight line to the discipline's present vantage," or we may add, to some idealized condition. Narrow perspectives have had consequences as becomes clear in Stuart Hall's dismissal of an allegedly "misguided attempt . . . to constitute communication as a self-sustaining, disciplinary specialty." Hall's stipulation flowed from his taking account of only the post-war competition between "the dominant [quantitative-effects] paradigm in communication theory" and the "critical alternatives."[20]

The long-standing practice of defining communication study variously from the standpoint of a single medium, from guild practices, or from a stipulated methodology all have played a part in impeding recognition of the central disciplinary role of the NCA. Particularizing tendencies of the twentieth century gave great salience to the AEJMC's impressive links with the news industry and the ICA's confident orthodoxy in contrast to the NCA's seemingly humbler endeavor to serve both teaching and research and to accommodate both qualitative and quantitative scholarship. Further directing attention away from the NCA was its willingness not only to host joint meetings with large break-away societies representing theater education and speech and hearing (from the 1930s into the 1960s) but also to incubate what became separate associations, notably the NSSC and the American Society for the History of Rhetoric.[21] Yet while the NCA's openness once obscured its centrality, now the association's integration of humanities, social sciences, performance studies, and professions—together with its support for teaching, research, and service—should win for it recognition as a paradigmatic standard bearer in an ever more interconnected world. The NCA may rightly expect a bright future in an intellectual milieu where *communication* denotes *discipline* more than *subordinate concept* or *limited field*, and where both internationalism and the convergence of digital media validate an association pursuing holistic understandings.

Notes

1 Thomas P. Miller, *The Formation of College English* (Pittsburgh, PA: University of Pittsburgh Press, 1997).

2 John Locke, *Some Thoughts Concerning Education* (1692; Repr., Cambridge: Cambridge University Press, 1895): 74–76, 148, 162–166; Benjamin Franklin, *Franklin's Proposals for the Education of Youth in Pennsylvania* (1749; Repr., Ann Arbor, MI: Clements Library, 1927): 14–21; James Burgh, *Thoughts on Education* (1745; Repr., Boston: Rogers and Fowle, 1749): 11–12; Thomas Sheridan, *A Plan of Education for the Young Nobility and Gentry of Great Britain* (1769; Repr., Ann Arbor, MI: Xerox University Microfilms, 1970): xxii–xxiii; also, Thomas Sheridan, *British Education* (1756; Repr., New York: Garland, 1970): 132–177; Joseph Priestley, *Miscellaneous Observations Relating to Education* (1st U.S. ed. New London: J. Springer, 1796): 21; Noah Webster, "On the Education of Youth in America," in *Essays on Education in the Early Republic*, ed. Frederick Rudolph (Cambridge, MA: Belknap Press of Harvard University Press, 1965): 46–49; Samuel Knox, "An Essay on the Best System of Liberal Education Adapted to the Genius of the Government of the United States," in *Essays on Education in the Early Republic*, ed. Frederick Rudolph (Cambridge, MA: Harvard University Press, 1965): 301. See Douglas Ehninger, "Dominant Trends in English Rhetorical Thought, 1750–1800," *Southern Communication Journal* 18 (1952): 3–12.

3 J. Michael Sproule, "Inventing Public Speaking," *Rhetoric & Public Affairs* 15 (2012): 574–575.

4 Historical Statistics of the United States Millennial Edition Online. Database, San Jose State University, Table Bc 258–264.

5 Frederick Douglass, *Narrative of the Life of Frederick Douglass* (1845; Repr., New York: Signet, 1968): 54.

6   John Locke, *Essay Concerning Human Understanding* (1690; Repr., in *Great Books of the Western World*, ed. Robert M. Hutchins, 52 vols., Chicago: Encyclopaedia Britannica, 1952): 35:286. Locke's conversancy with the figures, *Human Understanding*, 35:299, and *Education*, 163, 165. *Human Understanding* as textbook in Louis F. Snow, *The College Curriculum in the United States* (1907; Repr., New York: AMS Press, 1972). *Cassell's New Latin Dictionary* (New York: Funk and Wagnalls, 1960): 120, shows *communicatio* dating to Cicero; also see *The Compact Edition of the Oxford English Dictionary* (Glasgow: Oxford University Press, 1971): 1:485. Locke would have encountered *communicatio* in Thomas Wilson, *The Art of Rhetoric* (1560; Repr., ed. Peter E. Medine, University Park: Pennsylvania State University Press, 1994): 212; John Smith, *The Mysterie of Rhetoric Unvail'd* (1657; Repr., New York: Georg Olms, 1973): 152; and (Bernard Lamy), *The Art of Speaking* (1676; Repr., ed. John T. Harwood, Carbondale, IL: Southern Illinois University Press, 1986): 237. Page citations are to respective reprints. Locke on communication in Wilbur S. Howell, *Eighteenth-Century British Logic and Rhetoric* (Princeton, NJ: Princeton University Press, 1971): 489–502; and John D. Peters, *Speaking into the Air* (Chicago: University of Chicago Press, 1999): 63, 80–89; George Berkeley, *The Principles of Human Knowledge* (1710; Repr., in *Great Books of the Western World*, ed. Robert M. Hutchins, 52 vols., Chicago: Encyclopaedia Britannica, 1952): 35:407–412.

7   Thomas Sheridan, *A Course of Lectures on Elocution* (1762; Repr., Menston, England: Scolar, 1968): v–xii; Joseph Priestley, *A Course of Lectures on Oratory and Criticism* (1777; Repr., ed. Vincent M. Bevilacqua and Richard Murphy, Carbondale, IL: Southern Illinois University Press, 1965): 56–58, 108–111; George Campbell, *The Philosophy of Rhetoric* (New ed., 1850; Repr., ed. Lloyd F. Blitzer, Carbondale, IL: Southern Illinois University Press, 1963): 1, 78; Hugh Blair, *Lectures on Rhetoric and Belles Lettres* (2 vols., London: W. Strahan and T. Cadell, 1783): 1:97–98; Richard Whately, *Elements of Rhetoric* (7th ed. 1846; Repr., ed. Douglas Ehninger, Carbondale, IL: Southern Illinois University Press, 1963): 20.

8   Hayden White, "The Suppression of Rhetoric in the Nineteenth Century," in *The Rhetoric Canon*, ed. Brenda D. Schildgen (Detroit: Wayne State University Press, 1997): 21–22; Ebenezer Porter, *Analysis of the Principles of Rhetorical Delivery as Applied to Reading and Speaking* (4th ed. Andover: Flagg & Gould, 1831): 13; Adams S. Hill, *The Principles of Rhetoric* (Rev. ed. New York: Harper, 1895): iii; John C. Metcalf, *English Literature* (Richmond: B.F. Johnson, 1912): 9.

9   Charles Morley, *A Guide to Forming and Conducting Lyceums, Debating Societies, &c.* (New York: A.E. Wright, 1841): 7; Thomas W. Higginson, "The American Lecture-System," *Macmillan's Magazine* 18 (May 1868): 48–49, 52; Philip E. Mackey, ed., *A Gentleman of Much Promise: The Diary of Isaac Mickle, 1837–1845* (2 vols., Philadelphia: University of Pennsylvania Press, 1977): 1:60; William E. Channing, "The Demands of the Age on the Ministry," in *The Works of William E. Channing, D.D.* (8th ed. 6 vols., Boston: James Munroe, 1841 [1824]): 3:146, 150.

10 Henry Ware, Jr. *Hints on Extemporaneous Preaching* (Boston: Cummings, Hilliard, 1824): 15, 93.

11 James A. Winans, *Public Speaking: Principles and Practice* (New York: Sewell, 1915): 27; guidebooks also cited in Winans's *Notes on Public Speaking* (Ithaca, NY: Journal Print, 1911). See Sproule, "Inventing Public Speaking," 578–590; William Keith, "On the Origins of Speech as a Discipline," *Rhetoric Society Quarterly* 38 (2008): 239–258.

12 Laurence R. Veysey, *The Emergence of the American University* (Chicago: University of Chicago Press, 1965): 320–324.

13 James M. O'Neill, Craven Laycock, and Robert L. Scales, *Argumentation and Debate* (New York: Macmillan, 1917): 11.

14 Malcolm M. Willey and Stuart A. Rice, "The Agencies of Communication," in *Recent Social Trends in the United States* (3 vols., New York: McGraw-Hill, 1933): 1:209, 215; J. Michael Sproule, *Propaganda and Democracy* (New York: Cambridge University Press, 1997).

15 A.M. Lee, letter to author, February 19, 1985.

16 Earl J. McGrath, ed., *Communication in General Education* (Dubuque, IA: Wm. C. Brown, 1949); Carl H. Weaver, "A History of the International Communication Association," in *Communication Yearbook I*, ed. Brent D. Reuben (New Brunswick, NJ: Transaction, 1977): 607–618; J. Michael

Sproule, "'Communication': From Concept to Field to Discipline," in *The History of Media and Communication Research*, ed. David W. Park and Jefferson Pooley (New York: Peter Lang, 2008): 163–178.

17 Wilbur Schramm, "The Beginnings of Communication Study in the United States," in *Communication Yearbook 4*, ed. Dan Nimmo (New Brunswick, NJ: Transaction, 1980): 73–82; Schramm in "Conference on Research on Public Communication," 31 May–1 June 1954, Box 8, Folder 41, Hovland Papers; Everett M. Rogers and Steven Chaffee, "Communication as an Academic Discipline: A Dialogue," *Journal of Communication* 33, no. 3 (1983): 27.

18 Cf. Frederic Hudson, *Journalism in the United States* (1873; Repr., New York: Haskell, 1968) and Michael Schudson, *Discovering the News* (New York: Basic Books, 1978); Charles C. Fries, *American English Grammar* (New York: D. Appleton-Century, 1940).

19 Joseph T. Klapper, *The Effects of Mass Communication* (Glencoe, IL: Free Press, 1960): 27.

20 Thomas S. Kuhn, *The Structure of Scientific Revolutions* (2nd ed. Chicago: University of Chicago Press, 1970): 167; Stuart Hall, "Ideology and Communication Theory," in *Rethinking Communication, Volume 1, Paradigm Issues*, ed. Brenda Dervin et al. (Newbury Park, CA: Sage, 1989): 40, 42.

21 Robert C. Jeffrey, "A History of the Speech Association of America, 1914–1964," in *The Past Is Prologue*, ed. William Work and Robert C. Jeffrey (Annandale, VA: Speech Communication Association, 1989): 30; Weaver, "A History of the International Communication Association," 607; James J. Murphy, "Rhetoric Studies Twenty-Five Years Ago and the Origins of ASHR," *Advances in the History of Rhetoric* 6 (2001): 2.

References

Austin, Gilbert. *Chironomia*. 1806. Reprint edited by Margaret M. Robb and Lester Thonssen. Carbondale, IL: Southern Illinois University Press, 1966.

Bautain, M. *The Art of Extempore Speaking*. New ed. New York: McDevitt-Wilson's, 1916 [1859].

Berkeley, George. *The Principles of Human Knowledge*. 1710. Reprint, *Great Books of the Western World*, general editor, Robert M. Hutchins, 52 vols., 35:401–444. Chicago: Encyclopaedia Britannica, 1952.

Bingham, Caleb. *The Columbian Orator*. 1797. Reprint edited by David W. Blight. New York: New York University Press, 1998.

Black, Edwin. *Rhetorical Criticism*. 1965. Reprint. Madison: University of Wisconsin Press, 1978.

Blair, Hugh. *Lectures on Rhetoric and Belles Lettres*. 2 vols. London: W. Strahan and T. Cadell, 1783.

Bryce, James. *The American Commonwealth*. 3rd ed. 2 vols. New York: Macmillan, 1899.

Burgh, James. *The Art of Speaking*. 1761. Reprint. Danbury, CT: Edmund and Ephraim Washburn, 1795.

——. *Thoughts on Education*. 1745. Reprint. Boston: Rogers and Fowle, 1749.

Campbell, George. *The Philosophy of Rhetoric*. New ed., 1850. Reprint edited by Lloyd F. Blitzer. Carbondale, IL: Southern Illinois University Press, 1963.

Cassell's New Latin Dictionary. New York: Funk and Wagnalls, 1960.

Cathcart, George R. *The Literary Reader*. New York: Ivison, Blakeman, Taylor, 1874.

Chamberlain, William B. *Principles of Vocal Expression . . . Together With Mental Technique and Literary Interpretation*, by Solomon H. Clark. Chicago: Scott, Foresman, 1897.

Channing, William E. "The Demands of the Age on the Ministry" [1824]. In *The Works of William E. Channing, D. D.* 8th ed. 6 vols., 3:137–162. Boston: James Munroe, 1841.

——. "The Present Age" [1841]. In *Works of Channing*, 6:147–182.

Chase, Stuart. *The Proper Study of Mankind*. New York: Harper, 1948.

The Compact Edition of the Oxford English Dictionary. 2 vols. Glasgow: Oxford University Press, 1971.

Cooley, Charles H. *Social Organization*. New York: Charles Scribner's Sons, 1909.

Curry, S.S. *Mind and Voice*. Boston: Expression Co., 1910.

Delia, Jesse G. "Communication Research: A History." In *Handbook of Communication Science*, ed. C.R. Burger and S.H. Chaffee, 20–98. Newbury Park, CA: Sage, 1987.

Dilworth, Thomas. *A New Guide to the English Tongue*. New ed. London: Dean and Munday [1740].

Douglass, Frederick. *Narrative of the Life of Frederick Douglass*. 1845. Reprint. New York: Signet, 1968.

Ehninger, Douglas. "Dominant Trends in English Rhetorical Thought, 1750–1800." *Southern Communication Journal* 18 (1952): 3–12.

Enfield, William. *The Speaker*. 1774. Reprint. London: I. Gold for J. Johnson, 1805.

Fisher, George. *The American Instructor*. 9th ed. Philadelphia: B. Franklin & D. Hall, 1748.

Fiske, John and John Hartley. *Reading Television*. London: Methuen, 1978.

Franklin, Benjamin. *Franklin's Proposals for the Education of Youth in Pennsylvania*. 1749. Reprint. Ann Arbor, MI: Clements Library, 1927.

Fries, Charles C. *American English Grammar*. New York: D. Appleton-Century, 1940.

Fulton, Robert I. and Thomas C. Trueblood. *Practical Elements of Elocution*. 3rd ed. Boston: Ginn, 1896.

Goffman, Erving. *The Presentation of Self in Everyday Life*. Garden City, NY: Doubleday, 1959.

Hall, Edward T. *The Silent Language*. New York: Fawcett, 1959.

Hall, Stuart. "Ideology and Communication Theory." In *Rethinking Communication, Volume 1, Paradigm Issues*, edited by Brenda Dervin, Larry Grossberg, Barbara J. O'Keefe, and Ellen A. Wartella, 40–52. Newbury Park, CA: Sage, 1989.

Higginson, Thomas W. "The American Lecture-System." *Macmillan's Magazine* 18 (May 1868): 48–56.

——. *Hints on Writing and Speech-Making*. Boston: Lee & Shepard, 1887.

Hill, Adams S. *The Principles of Rhetoric*. Rev. ed. New York: Harper, 1895.

Historical Statistics of the United States Millennial Edition Online. Database, San Jose State University, accessed April 21, 2009.

Holmes, John. *The Art of Rhetoric Made Easy*. London: Hitch and Hawks, 1755.

Holyoake, George J. *Rudiments of Public Speaking and Debate*. London: J. Watson, 1849.

Horkheimer, Max and Theodor Adorno. *Dialectic of Enlightenment*. Translated by John Cumming. 1944. Reprint, New York: Continuum, 1987.

Hovland, Carl I. Papers. Yale University Library.

Hovland, Carl I., Arthur A. Lumsdaine, and Fred Sheffield. *Experiments on Mass Communication*. Princeton, NJ: Princeton University Press, 1949.

Howell, Wilbur S. *Eighteenth-Century British Logic and Rhetoric*. Princeton, NJ: Princeton University Press, 1971.

Hudson, Frederic. *Journalism in the United States*. 1873. Reprint. New York: Haskell, 1968.

James, William. *Psychology [Briefer Course]*. New York: Henry Holt, 1892.

Jeffrey, Robert C. "A History of the Speech Association of America, 1914–1964." In *The Past Is Prologue*, edited by William Work and Robert C. Jeffrey, 24–37. Annandale, VA: Speech Communication Association, 1989.

Jowett, Garth S. "Toward a History of Communication." *Journalism History* 2 (summer 1975): 34–37.

Keith, William. "On the Origins of Speech as a Discipline." *Rhetoric Society Quarterly* 38 (2008): 239–258.

Klapper, Joseph T. *The Effects of Mass Communication*. Glencoe, IL: Free Press, 1960.

Knox, Samuel. *A Compendious System of Rhetoric*. Baltimore: Swain and Matchett, 1809.

——. "An Essay on the Best System of Liberal Education Adapted to the Genius of the Government of the United States." 1799. In *Essays on Education in the Early Republic*, edited by Frederick Rudolph, 271–372. Cambridge, MA: Harvard University Press, 1965.

Kuhn, Thomas S. *The Structure of Scientific Revolutions*. 2nd ed. Chicago: University of Chicago Press, 1970.

(Lamy, Bernard). *The Art of Speaking*. 1676. Reprint edited by John T. Harwood. Carbondale, IL: Southern Illinois University Press, 1986.

Lasswell, Harold D., Nathan Leites, Raymond Fadner, Joseph M. Goldsen, Alan Grey, Irving L. Janis, Abraham Kaplan, Alexander Mintz, Ithiel De Sola Pool, Sergius Yakobson, and David Kaplan. *Language of Politics*. Cambridge, MA: MIT Press, 1949.

Lawson, John. *Lectures Concerning Oratory*. 1758. Reprint edited by E. Neal Claussen and Karl R. Wallace. Carbondale, IL: Southern Illinois University Press, 1972.

Le Bon, Gustave. *The Crowd*. 1895. Reprint. New York: Viking, 1960.

Lippmann, Walter. *The Phantom Public*. New York: Harcourt Brace, 1925.

Locke, John. *An Essay Concerning Human Understanding*. 1690. Reprint, *Great Books of the Western World*, general editor, Robert M. Hutchins, 52 vols., 35:83–509. Chicago: Encyclopaedia Britannica, 1952.

——. *Some Thoughts Concerning Education*. 1692. Reprint. Cambridge: Cambridge University Press, 1895.

Mackey, Philip E., ed. *A Gentleman of Much Promise: The Diary of Isaac Mickle, 1837–1845*. 2 vols. Philadelphia: University of Pennsylvania Press, 1977.

Marcuse, Herbert. *One-Dimensional Man*. Boston: Beacon, 1964.

McElligott, James N. *The American Debater*. New York: Ivison, Blakeman, Taylor, 1855.

McGrath, Earl J., ed. *Communication in General Education*. Dubuque, IA: Wm. C. Brown, 1949.

McGuffey, William H. *McGuffey's New Sixth Eclectic Reader*. Cincinnati: Sargent, Wilson & Hinkle, 1857.

Metcalf, John C. *English Literature*. Richmond: B.F. Johnson, 1912.

Miller, Thomas P. *The Formation of College English*. Pittsburgh, PA: University of Pittsburgh Press, 1997.

Morley, Charles. *A Guide to Forming and Conducting Lyceums, Debating Societies, &c.* New York: A.E. Wright, 1841.

Murphy, James J. "Rhetoric Studies Twenty-Five Years Ago and the Origins of ASHR." *Advances in the History of Rhetoric* 6 (2001): 1–3.

Murray, Lindley. *The English Reader*. 1799. Reprint. Belfast, ME: White and Row, 1829.

Northrop, Henry D. *The Peerless Reciter*. n.p., 1894.

Oliver, Robert T. *Culture and Communication*. Springfield, IL: Charles Thomas, 1962.

O'Neill, James M., Craven Laycock, and Robert L. Scales. *Argumentation and Debate*. New York: Macmillan, 1917.

Park, Robert E. "The Natural History of the Newspaper." *American Journal of Sociology* 29 (1923): 273–289.

Peters, John D. *Speaking into the Air*. Chicago: University of Chicago Press, 1999.

Pittenger, William. *Extempore Speech*. Philadelphia: National School of Elocution and Oratory, 1883.

Porter, Ebenezer. *Analysis of the Principles of Rhetorical Delivery as Applied to Reading and Speaking*. 4th ed. Andover: Flagg & Gould, 1831.

Priestley, Joseph. *A Course of Lectures on Oratory and Criticism*. 1777. Reprint edited by Vincent M. Bevilacqua and Richard Murphy. Carbondale, IL: Southern Illinois University Press, 1965.

——. *Miscellaneous Observations Relating to Education*. 1st U.S. ed. New London: J. Springer, 1796.

Rogers, Everett M. *A History of Communication Study*. New York: Free Press, 1994.

Rogers, Everett M. and Steven Chaffee. "Communication as an Academic Discipline: A Dialogue." *Journal of Communication* 33, no. 3 (1983): 18–30.

Rush, James. *The Philosophy of the Human Voice*. 2nd ed. Philadelphia: Grigg & Elliott, 1833.

Schramm, Wilbur. "The Beginnings of Communication Study in the United States." In *Communication Yearbook 4*, edited by Dan Nimmo, 73–82. New Brunswick, NJ: Transaction, 1980.

Schudson, Michael. *Discovering the News*. New York: Basic Books, 1978.

Scott, Walter D. *The Psychology of Public Speaking*. Philadelphia: Hinds, Hayden & Eldredge, 1907.

Scott, William. *Lessons in Elocution*. 1779. Reprint. New York: Thomas Kirk, 1799.

Sheridan, Thomas. *British Education*. 1756. Reprint. New York: Garland, 1970.

——. *A Course of Lectures on Elocution*. 1762. Reprint. Menston, England: Scolar, 1968.

——. *A General Dictionary of the English Language*. 2 vols. 1780. Reprint. Menston, England: Scolar, 1967.

——. *A Plan of Education for the Young Nobility and Gentry of Great Britain*. 1769. Reprint. Ann Arbor, MI: Xerox University Microfilms, 1970.

——. *A Rhetorical Grammar of the English Language*. 1781. Reprint. Menston, England: Scolar, 1969.

Smith, John. *The Mysterie of Rhetoric Unvail'd*. 1657. Reprint. New York: Georg Olms, 1973.

Snow, Louis F. *The College Curriculum in the United States*. 1907. Reprint. New York: AMS Press, 1972.

Sproule, J. Michael. "'Communication': From Concept to Field to Discipline." In *The History of Media and Communication Research*, edited by David W. Park and Jefferson Pooley, 163–178. New York: Peter Lang, 2008.

——. "Inventing Public Speaking." *Rhetoric & Public Affairs* 15 (2012): 563–608.

——. *Propaganda and Democracy*. New York: Cambridge University Press, 1997.

Steele, Joshua. *Prosodia Rationalis*. 2nd ed. 1779. Reprint. New York: Georg Olms, 1971.

Stirling, John. *A System of Rhetoric*. London: Thomas Astley, 1733.

Veysey, Laurence R. *The Emergence of the American University*. Chicago: University of Chicago Press, 1965.

Walker, John. *A Critical Pronouncing Dictionary*. New ed. London: Caxton, 1834.

——. *Elements of Elocution*. 4th ed. London: J. Walker, et al., 1810.

——. *A Rhetorical Grammar*. 1785. Reprint. Menston, England: Scolar, 1971.

Wander, Philip. "The Ideological Turn in Modern Criticism." *Communication Studies* 34 (1983): 1–18.

Ward, John. *A System of Oratory*. 2 vols. London: John Ward, 1759.

Ware, Henry, Jr. *Hints on Extemporaneous Preaching*. Boston: Cummings, Hilliard, 1824.

Weaver, Carl H. "A History of the International Communication Association." In *Communication Yearbook I*, edited by Brent D. Reuben, 607–618. New Brunswick, NJ: Transaction, 1977.

Webster, Noah. *An American Selection of Lessons in Reading and Speaking*. New ed. Utica, NY: Asahel Seward, 1806.

——. "On the Education of Youth in America." 1790. In *Essays on Education in the Early Republic*, edited by Frederick Rudolph, 41–77. Cambridge, MA: Belknap Press of Harvard University Press, 1965.

Whately, Richard. *Elements of Rhetoric*. 7th ed. 1846. Reprint edited by Douglas Ehninger. Carbondale, IL: Southern Illinois University Press, 1963.

White, Hayden. "The Suppression of Rhetoric in the Nineteenth Century." In *The Rhetoric Canon*, edited by Brenda D. Schildgen, 21–31. Detroit: Wayne State University Press, 1997.

Willey, Malcolm M. and Stuart A. Rice. "The Agencies of Communication." In *Recent Social Trends in the United States*. 3 vols., 1:167–217. New York: McGraw-Hill, 1933.

Wilson, Thomas. *The Art of Rhetoric*. 1560. Reprint edited by Peter E. Medine. University Park, PA: Pennsylvania State University Press, 1994.

Winans, James A. *Notes on Public Speaking*. Ithaca, NY: Journal Print, 1911.

——. *Public Speaking: Principles and Practice*. New York: Sewell, 1915.

Woolley, Edwin C. *Handbook of Composition*. Boston: D.C. Heath, 1907.

2.

PAYING LIP SERVICE TO "SPEECH" IN DISCIPLINARY NAMING, 1914–1954

Gerry Philipsen

In the early part of the twentieth century there was a scattered array of people, schools, courses, and organizations devoted to the study and teaching of "public speaking," "expression," "oral English," "rhetoric," "oratory," and "elocution," in and around US colleges and universities. But as to anything resembling an academic discipline for such subjects, the landscape was, to exaggerate only slightly, "without form, and void."

In 1914 seventeen men, who were teachers of public speaking in US colleges and universities, conceived an association that would draw them and some like them together in the service of their pedagogy. The association was fully established in 1915 with a name, the National Association of Academic Teachers of Public Speaking. The association inaugurated a scholarly journal, the *Quarterly Journal of Public Speaking*, published under the auspices of the University of Chicago Press, and printed three issues in 1915. By November of that year, they held a national convention in Chicago with sixty in attendance, and their paid membership numbered 160.

In this chapter, I examine the rich history of the association's naming, and on occasion renaming, itself, its journals, and the "profession," "field," or "discipline" with whose history it is intertwined. I also examine data pertaining to the naming of college and university academic departments that were formally or informally linked to the association. I treat the period 1914 to 1954 here, with special attention to how the word "speech" fares in this history.

I use "the association" to refer to the organization that has, *seriatim*, been named the National Association of Academic Teachers of Public Speaking (1915–1917), the National Association of Teachers of Speech (1918–1945), the Speech Association of America (1946–1969), the Speech Communication Association (1970–1997), and the National Communication Association (1998–present).

"In speech we find the substance of a discipline"[1]

In the first issue of the *Quarterly*, J.M. O'Neill, the first president of the association, published an essay titled "The National Association."[2] In it he stated as the association's first purpose "to promote and encourage research work in various parts of the field of public speaking,"[3] the second "to serve the teacher of public speaking as other professional journals serve teachers in other fields,"[4] and the third to support other organizational efforts "which have to do with any kind of work in public speaking."[5] In the same issue, the association's newly-formed Research Committee published a paper under its byline titled "Research in Public Speaking."[6] The committee wrote that "public speaking ... now aspires to become a scholarly subject with a body of verified knowledge and a professional tradition and ethics."[7] These early acts of naming the association and its journal, and these public statements, of subject matter and purpose, leave little doubt of the professed commitment of the association to the academic study and teaching of public speaking.

Less than a year after the essays by the Research Committee and the president of the association proclaimed a commitment to the development of public speaking as a subject of teaching and research, there was a new terminological development in the pages of the *Quarterly*. Charles H. Woolbert of the University of Illinois, a founding member of the association and a member of the Research Committee, reported that the president of his university had asked him to prepare a proposal for the organization in the university of a department for "speech studies and arts," that would be separate from the department of English, where such studies, and Woolbert, were then housed. The *Quarterly* editor, O'Neill, had, Woolbert wrote, asked him "to put these ideas in shape" for the journal, "hence this article."[8] The title of the essay, "The Organization of Departments of Speech Science in Universities," presents an early, perhaps the first, published use of "speech" as a term for the naming of academic departments and as a covering term for what Woolbert referred to as a "discipline."[9] Woolbert's title uses "speech science," and he uses this term throughout the essay, but occasionally broadens the potential range of "speech" with the expression "speech science and arts."[10]

Early in the essay, Woolbert gives some sense of what he means by "speech science" with the statement that "the man who is rightly trained to teach speech science finds his greatest inspiration . . . helping men and women to make speeches, to interpret literature, and to present the drama for the profit and delight of others."[11] He defines "public speaking" by enumerating three different practices or arts—making speeches, interpreting literature, and presenting the drama—that were commonly studied under its name. But here Woolbert makes "speech science" the master term where, until now, the master term had been "public speaking."

O'Neill raised the question of terminology six months later, in an editorial in the July issue of the *Quarterly*. In "Wanted: An Accurate Label," he complained that making "reference" to "our work" with "the term 'public speaking'" typically "demands a special explanation as to what is meant or not meant by the term."[12] In terms of department nomenclature, he reports that the "great majority of our departments" are labeled "Public Speaking," a few "Oratory" or "Expression," one is "Oral English," one "Speech," and one or two "Elocution." He mentions the recent suggestion that university departments be named departments of "Speech Science, or Speech Science and Arts," an obvious reference to Woolbert's proposal six months earlier.

The diversity of department names was, the editor wrote, an "embarrassment," and he thereupon invited entries for a "department-naming contest,"[13] predicting that:

> If someone could devise a label that would accurately cover our field, and not a small section of it only, we believe such a label would be adopted by so many of the leading institutions all over the country that its use would, within a decade, be universal.[14]

Woolbert's proposal and the editor's "department-naming contest" suggest that at least two prominent members (and founders) of the association were not satisfied with "public speaking" as the label for the work they and their colleagues were doing. Their expressions of concern are remarkable in that "public speaking" had so recently been established as the name of the association, as the focus of the work of the Research Committee, and as a crucial part of the quarterly's name; and "public speaking" was, by the editor's own report, the name of "the great majority of our departments." Perhaps he hoped that all non-conforming department names, such as "elocution," "expression," "oratory," and "speech," would be changed to "public speaking." But he tipped his hand when, in another editorial following immediately below "Wanted," he used the expression "any of the branches of speech science or art"[15] to describe the range of interests of the *Quarterly*, echoing Woolbert, again. Here again "speech" appears in a discursive environment where, just a year before, "public speaking" had been firmly, and seemingly proudly, put into place.

Soon after the appearance of Woolbert's "speech science" essay and the editor's "wanted" editorial there was organized movement toward the word "speech" as a name for academic departments and for other disciplinary matters. There is no record that any departments were ever named "speech science" or "speech science and art," but, by 1917, there is a report of the naming of the "Department of Speech" at Grinnell College. In his discussion of the new department's name and mission, J.P. Ryan used the expression "problems in speech science" to refer to one of the concerns of this new undergraduate department and attributes those quoted words to "Professor Woolbert."[16] Ryan emphasized that the naming decision at Grinnell was the solution to "largely a local problem," insisting that he was not proposing a name for such a department elsewhere. But at the 1917 convention of the association and in print the following year, in "Terminology: The Department of Speech," Ryan presented a systematic brief for the use of the name by departments at other institutions.[17]

Ryan's terminology speech at the 1917 convention[18] apparently was influential in shaping an important series of votes taken and decisions made at that convention. First, the members approved, "almost unanimously," a resolution that it was "the sense of the Association that our departments should be called departments of speech."[19] It was then voted unanimously that the Executive Committee be given power to act to change the name of the association to the National Association of Teachers of Speech and of the journal to the *Quarterly Journal of Speech Education*. Of the five members of the Executive Committee who participated in that body's decision, two were initially opposed to the motion regarding department names, but in the end, the Committee unanimously approved the proposed new names.

"Speech" won important victories in 1918 by its use in the names of the association and its journal, and in 1928 by allowing it to stand alone as the sole content word in the name of the association's only journal, the *Quarterly Journal of Speech*. The editor of the journal wrote, about the 1918 changes, that they would remedy "the inconveniences, and sometimes the indignities, suffered because we have been going about our academic business handicapped by a variety of inaccurate and misleading labels."[20]

After the events of 1918, there was substantial movement toward the creation and naming of departments of "speech." The editor's comments in "Wanted" suggest that in 1916 "public speaking" was the dominant name of departments that were allied with the work of the association and that there was only one department of "speech," while several other names had a footing in a few places. A report published in 1935 provides some information on the names of departments in US colleges and universities from 1860 to 1930.[21] Based on a study of 118 institutions, it shows that in the period 1910–1920 there were thirty-one departments of public speaking, eight of expression, and none of speech. For the period 1920 to 1930, the same study shows thirty-three departments of public speaking, two of expression, and sixteen of speech. From the 1910–1920 to the 1920–1930 period, not only had speech increased dramatically, but expression had decreased dramatically, and elocution, oratory, and rhetoric had all been reduced to zero. "Speech" as a department name had gotten a toehold on the path and was on the march. These numbers are displayed in Table 2.1.

Table 2.1 Names of academic departments in US colleges and universities, based on 118 institutions[22]

	Public speaking	Expression	Oratory	Rhetoric	Speech
1910–1920	31	8	3	3	0
1920–1930	33	2	0	0	16

By 1918, there was evidence that a consensus had been built around "speech" as the most desirable term for the work allied with the association. The name of the association had been changed; "academic" was excised and "public speaking" was replaced by "speech." The journal was renamed, with "speech education" replacing "public speaking." By 1928, the journal was renamed again, this time excising "education" and leaving "speech" to stand alone as the sole expression of academic substance in the title. Departments of "speech" had been created or departments with other names were renamed with "speech." By 1928, the members of the association had found in "speech" a name for their association, their journal, and many of their departments in colleges and universities. In terms of disciplinary naming, "speech" had prevailed over "public speaking" and other terms.

As impressive as is the frequency and prominence of "speech" in disciplinary discourse by 1928, of equal importance is the concomitant decline of the prominence of "public speaking." The term had in 1918 been excised from the names of the association and the *Quarterly*. After 1915, although the Committee on Research continued to make reports in the *Quarterly*, there never again appeared such a report with "public speaking" in its title. Although there was a small increase by 1930 in the number of departments of "public speaking" (from thirty-one to thirty-three), the greater increase was for "speech" (from zero in 1920 to sixteen by 1930). By 1928, "public speaking" had lost its once predominant place in the disciplinary discourse.

In the same issue of the *Quarterly* in which the editor reported on the decision to change its name from the *Quarterly Journal of Speech Education* to the *Quarterly Journal of Speech*, thus giving "speech" a new pride of unshared space in the substance slot of the journal's name, there was also published an essay that strikes me as startling. The essay, "After Thirteen Years," was written by O'Neill, first president of the association and first editor of the *Quarterly*, and was based on a speech he had presented at the association's 1927 convention. The association president for that year had invited O'Neill to speak about "the reasons for the founding of our Association and to answer the question whether or not the Association is doing what it was planned to do."[23] In his speech, O'Neill presented his own views of the subject and furthermore quoted at length from the responses he received from others of the seventeen who had formed the association and whom he had invited to respond to the same questions he had been assigned. He reported and quoted from answers from ten of the other men.

The reflections by O'Neill and the ten others are striking in the way they do, and do not, use the words "public speaking," as well as the ways they do use the word "speech." More particularly, a careful examination of their material shows that "public speaking" is hardly used at all, even when there is reference to the association as it was first formed and named. O'Neill presents a five-paragraph introduction in which he gives his own "brief paragraph of history."[24] In it, eleven times he uses one of the following expressions: "the association," "the National Association," "the organization," "this association," "this Association," "a National Association in our own field," and "a national organization of our forces." In this introduction, he makes no use of either "public speaking" or "speech." After he presents the words of the other ten men, he concludes with three long paragraphs in which he makes nine further references to "the Association" or similar expressions. In the final paragraphs, he does use the words "public speaking" and "speech," and to those uses I now turn.

In his concluding three paragraphs, all his own words, O'Neill begins by saying: "We organized the National Association for the promotion of research and better teaching in speech."[25] Compare the statement above with O'Neill's words in the *Quarterly* of 1915 that the first purpose of the association was "to promote and encourage research work in various parts of the field of public speaking."[26] Where O'Neill's 1915 statement uses the expression "the field of public speaking," the 1928 statement reformulates O'Neill's (and the association's) statement by substituting "speech" for "public speaking." O'Neill continued:

> True, most of us at the time called what we were doing public speaking, but already in many places this had become an inaccurate label. The broader conception of the whole field of human speech was even at that time taking shape in our professional thinking.[27]

Of the other men whose words O'Neill quotes, the pattern is, with one exception, just as stark. Nine of the ten never use "public speaking" even in their expressions of the name of the association that they had formed (and named the National Association of Academic Teachers of Public Speaking). One man refers to it as the National Association of Speech Education; most use the National Association of Teachers of Speech or some form of it. In these letters, where one might expect "public speaking" to appear, it either does not or hardly does appear. It seems to have been replaced by "speech" even in direct reference to an entity whose name included "public speaking" and did not include "speech." These acts of elision and substitution suggest that "public speaking" had been crowded off the path by "speech," almost as if the former term was now unspeakable.

"Speech" had become the predominant term in disciplinary discourse. But of what significance to the participants in the discourse of this period did "speech" have? For some participants in the conversation, "speech" was the answer to the problem of how to represent their subject and themselves to administrators at their local campuses, colleagues in other disciplines, and prospective students. In this sense, it met perceived needs for naming and reference.[28] To some it was "the common [linguistic] ground upon which teachers of public speaking, oral expression, debate, rhetoric, dramatic art and interpretative reading, correction of speech defects, and voice science have found it convenient to associate themselves in an academic institution."[29] To yet others, "speech" was the crystallizing term for "the substance" of a new academic discipline, something suggested in O'Neill's previously quoted "the whole field of human speech."[30]

The changes in names were hard-won achievements for "speech," the product of extensive and difficult discussion and debate. Although the record shows that there was near unanimity in the advisory vote taken about the changes approved at the 1917 convention and implemented in 1918, it also shows that when in 1917 the Executive Committee made the eventual decision, two of the five committee members initially had reservations. As late as 1923, James A. Winans, a founder of the association, continued to express principled opposition to "speech." He proposed "that we add rhetoric to our names," thus providing *The National Association of Teachers of Speech and Rhetoric* and *The Quarterly Journal of Speech and Rhetoric*,"[31] a move that would have diminished "speech" in its prominence in these two important disciplinary naming slots. He proposed further that the title page of the *Quarterly* include the title described above with the following "subtitles" arrayed just below the main title: "Public Speaking," "Speech Correction," "Dramatic Art," "History of Oratory," "Voice Training," "Oral Reading," "Debate," and "Phonetics."[32]

Regarding "rhetoric," Winans said that "it refers primarily to spoken discourse" and that its addition to the existing names should "present a possible ground where 'speechers' and 'speechifiers' may meet in peace."[33] Notwithstanding Winans's objections, and the larger record of diversity of opinion among members of the association in this era, Woolbert's proposal won wide acceptance, and the decision, and other disciplinary discourse of 1928, suggests evidence of stasis in disciplinary naming practices. Woolbert's statement, "In speech we find the substance of a discipline,"[34] seems to embody a solution to at least three aspects of naming and reference: it selects, as it were, a word from what I call the *content*, *mission*, and *enterprise* contrast sets. The content set includes such terms as "public speaking," "speech," "rhetoric," and "communication." The mission set includes such terms as "substance," "science," "academic," "art," and "teaching." The enterprise set includes such terms as "profession," "field," and "discipline." Woolbert's statement here illustrates one solution to the problems of naming, reference, and identity— it draws "speech" from the content set, "substance" from the mission set, and "discipline" from the enterprise set.

Consider the following linkages of "speech" versus "public speaking" as they co-occur with "field" or "discipline" in such expressions as:

> the field of public speaking (O'Neill 1915);
> the field of speech (O'Neill 1928);
> the teaching of speech as an academic discipline (Woolbert 1923: 1);
> in speech we find the substance of a discipline (Woolbert 1923: 9).

Although I selected "In speech we find the substance of a discipline" for the section heading, and as the item for my content-mission-enterprise analysis in the previous paragraph, note that the title of the article from which that statement is drawn is "The *Teaching* of Speech as an Academic Discipline" (emphasis supplied). I found no evidence that "public speaking" and "discipline" occur together, as in the hypothetical "the discipline of public speaking."

"This Speech Age"[35]

For fifty-one years, from 1918 through 1969, "speech" was, arguably, the crucial substance term in the name of the association. In the earlier part of this period, 1918 through 1945, "speech" had not achieved quite the privileged position it would eventually occupy. It would, for thirty-one years, be the object of pedagogy, in "Teachers of Speech" and "Academic Teachers of Public Speaking." But in 1946, when the name was changed to "Speech Association of America," "speech" stood by itself, the singularly named subject, and sequentially the first word, in the association's name.

For twenty-four years, from 1946 through 1969, when "speech" was the single substance term in the name of the association, it occupied a similarly privileged position in the names of the association's journals. By 1918, the *Quarterly Journal of Public Speaking* had become the *Quarterly Journal of Speech Education* and in 1928 was renamed the *Quarterly Journal of Speech*. The name changes show, in three movements, the eventual achievement of a title in which there is a single "substance" word. That one word, "speech," stands alone, neither modifier nor something modified, and the object of no one's preposition. Seven years after "speech" achieved its singular and central status in the *Quarterly*, in 1935, the association established a second journal, *Speech Monographs*, which was devoted to research. "Speech" was the sole term for substance in that journal's title as well. A journal devoted exclusively to the study of teaching "speech" was established in 1952 as *The Speech Teacher*.

The name changes of 1918 through 1946 had chipped away words that had impeded "speech" taking pride of place in the name of the association and the names of its journals, and a parallel series of acts had installed "speech" in the predominant position.

There was a similar process during this time with regard to the creation and naming of academic departments. A study based on a 1948 survey[36] of 738 institutions reports that there were 256 autonomous departments of "speech," fifty-one departments of "speech and drama," eighteen departments of "public speaking," and five of "communication." At the same time that departments of "speech" were being created, there was a falling off of other names. This study of 738 institutions reports that in 1920 there were thirty-one departments of "public speaking," and by 1948 there were only eight. These data do not show whether the departments of public speaking, expression, elocution, and rhetoric had been eliminated altogether or had been replaced by departments of speech. Nonetheless, by the year 1948 there had been established a substantial number of departments of "speech" and a substantial decrease in departments with other names that might be rivals to "speech" (see Table 2.2).

Table 2.2 Naming of academic departments in US colleges and universities: 1920–1930 data based on 118 institutions,[37] 1948 data based on 738 institutions[38]

	Public speaking	Expression	Oratory	Rhetoric	Speech
1920–1930 (118 institutions)	33	2	0	0	16
1948 (738 institutions)	18	no data	no data	1	256

When, in 1953, Rupert L. Cortright's essay, "This Speech Age Makes New Demands Upon Education," was published as the lead essay in the January edition of *The Speech Teacher*, there was little doubt that "this" (1953) was the "Speech Age," in terms of disciplinary naming practices. The journal provides a brief informational statement about Cortright, stating that he was "Professor and Chairman of the Department of Speech at Wayne State University, a past Executive Secretary and a past President of the Speech Association of America." It would have been impossible when Woolbert's proposal for the establishment of "the teaching of speech as an academic discipline" was published in 1923 to set forth such a set of credentials as those presented in 1953 for Cortright: a "Professor of Speech," "Chairman" of a "Department of Speech," past Executive Secretary and past President (in 1948) of the "Speech Association of America."

The man who coined the phrase "this speech age" did so in an essay in the association's newly-formed journal devoted to the teaching of speech. When *The Speech Teacher* was established in 1952, it ended a twenty-three-year period in which the association had no journal with a pedagogical reference in its name. With "teacher" in the title of the new journal, one of the words that had been chipped away from the earlier names of the association and its founding journal had been picked up, given slightly different form (the "s" was dropped from "teachers"), and placed carefully into the name of this newest journal. The title of the new journal also reflected an emerging term for a role in society, "speech teacher." At the same time, the association was sponsoring another new initiative that would link the pedagogy and the scholarship of "speech," a development that was realized two years later in 1954, and to which I now turn.

In 1954, an edited volume was published with the title *History of Speech Education in America: Background Studies*.[39] It was prepared under the auspices of the Speech Association of America and edited by Karl R. Wallace, who was president of the association in 1953. Each of its twenty-eight chapters are authored by a different scholar (with two authors for some chapters). The volume is divided into three parts: "The Heritage" (five chapters), "Rhetoric, Elocution, and Speech" (seventeen chapters), and "The Educational Theatre" (six chapters). It was expressly designed to provide a record of "the history and tradition of the field of Speech as it unfolded in the United States" up to around 1920 (note Wallace's capital "s" in "Speech"). There are three important implications, for disciplinary naming, of the publication of the *History of Speech Education in America*.

One, *History of Speech Education in America* is an important work of collective scholarship that was commissioned, produced, and edited by, to use an expression that Wallace used elsewhere, "persons identified with the field of speech."[40] It is not the first collective work so published, but it might be the most impressive work of scholarship so produced to that time. It is thus an embodiment of the scholarly work of people in "the field of Speech."

Two, the volume is an ingredient in the mix of elements that contribute to the establishment of "speech" as an academic discipline. The contents of *History of Speech Education in America* establish that over several centuries there were men and women who had thought about, studied, and practiced some aspect of what the book refers to as "speech education." These chapters construct intellectual and scholarly histories of the various subjects the volume treats. Thus, it constitutes palpable evidence that there is a history and a tradition of the subject(s) of "speech education." Wallace pushes the point with his linkage of "history and tradition" to the terms "speech" and "speech education." In this way, the volume gives Wallace a warrant (the documented record of a "history and tradition") and a place (the editor's preface) to assert the linkage of the "tradition" to "the field of Speech" and thus to imply that there is "a field of Speech."

Three, *History of Speech Education in America* provides an occasion on and an instrument with which to do the work of disciplining. It presents separate chapters on the history of such subjects as rhetoric, elocution, debate, phonetics and pronunciation, teaching of the deaf, speech and hearing, and educational theater. But it not only presents these each on its own terms, it also presents these as contributions to a "history and tradition" (not "histories and traditions") that is linked to "the field of Speech" and to "speech education." Wallace does something very similar in his essay "The Field of Speech, 1953: An Overview," a much longer work than his Preface to *History of Speech Education in America*.

By 1954, a series of efforts beyond those of 1918–1928 had been successful in giving "speech" pride of place in the disciplinary discourse. Where old things, such as the association, were renamed, the new name better positioned "speech." Where new things were named, such as two new journals and hundreds of departments, "speech" predominated. Increasingly "speech" was found in such linguistic environments as "Professor of —," "Department of —," "Field of —," and "— teacher." By now, "speech" had not only these homes but had, in its capitalized form of spelling, been endowed with a "tradition," in the association's *History of Speech Education in America*. If Rupert L. Cortright had any doubt that his expression "this speech age" was an overstatement, he could know that his overstatement was published in a newly established journal whose principal content word was "speech."

Earlier I asked about the significance, to participants in the disciplinary discourse, of "speech" as a term of disciplinary naming, in the period 1914–1928. Now I ask about the significance of "speech" as a disciplinary term in the "age of speech." To answer the question, I consider extended statements about "speech" by three mid-century professors of speech, each educated in the discipline of speech, each a practicing scholar, and each an active teacher in US higher education. I am concerned with how "speech" fares in each of these essays.

The first is a printed and published version of the presidential address delivered at the 1950 convention of the Speech Association of America by Horace Rahskopf of the University of Washington. Rahskopf's title, "Speech at Mid-Century," places "speech" in the first grammatical position as unambiguously the subject of the expression of which it appears. "Speech" here is not the object of a preposition, not a modifier, not modified, not contained geographically, situated only in the flow of time, as it were, and situated there with an epochal ring.

Rahskopf's essay preserves in print the salutation that presumably he uttered orally on the occasion of the presidential address: "Mister Chairman, fellow-presidents, and colleagues in the teaching of speech." I draw attention here to "colleagues in the teaching of speech," remarkable for two reasons. First, "teaching of speech" echoes Rahskopf's teacher Charles Woolbert's "the teaching of speech as an academic discipline,"[41] surely no accident from Rahskopf. Second, not in the salutation, and nowhere else in the essay, does Rahskopf use the words "discipline," "field," or "profession." I suggest that for Rahskopf "speech" is more important than the mere discipline or field in which it finds itself at mid-century.

Here is a sampler of statements Rahskopf makes about speech in "Speech at Mid-Century."[42] "Speech," he writes, is a:

basic human process;
unique human function;
primary aspect of human life;
primary and unique aspect of life;
distinctive and unified process of human life.[43]

This is a remarkably rare specimen of disciplinary discourse about "speech," remarkable and rare in the degree to which it treats speech as something that is "basic," "unique," "primary," and a "distinctive and unified process in human life."

By 1950, "speech" had, in spite of its great success in disciplinary naming, some challenges from "communication," and Rahskopf, mindful of these challenges, acknowledged the importance of "communication."[44] Nonetheless, he took pains to insist that, in his view, "speech" is the basic and primary process that should be of concern to his "colleagues in the teaching of speech," and that "Speech is the primary form of communication."[45]

Perhaps no one in the "speech age" was more devoted than was Rahskopf to "speech," as it is formulated in "the whole field of human speech,"[46] a devotion Rahskopf extended to his Herculean, but ultimately unsuccessful, efforts to sustain in the Department of Speech that he chaired an ensemble of subjects, of the breadth mentioned by Winans[47] within that department.[48] Google Scholar Citations shows only four citations of "Speech at Mid-Century," one by the present author.

Three years later, an essay by Wallace, a Professor of Speech at the University of Illinois, and president of the Speech Association of America in 1953, was published in the *Quarterly*, and it provided a carefully argued case for demonstrating the capacity of "speech" to serve as a cover term for the diverse subjects that comprised the discipline. Wallace's title, "The Field of Speech, 1953: An Overview," puts "the field" in first position.[49] Like Rahskopf's, it situates "speech" in time and, unlike Rahskopf's, situates it spatially as "a field," with many areas in which the diverse parts of the field reside. The burden Wallace takes on in the essay is the argument that "speech" is a cover term that sensibly and happily integrates these parts.

Wallace's "Field of Speech" essay is a tour-de-force that delineates systematically "the field of speech and its boundaries" with special attention to the way all of the "parts of the field" that are "cultivated" by specialists have enough in common that it is possible to "see the unity among diversified interests."[50] He surveys the field, looking into each of five plots, and makes for each a principled argument that its concern with speech warrants its subsumption under the master term. These plots include those of rhetoric, communication of literature, face-to-face interaction (under which he subsumes the several strands of speech and hearing disorders and correction), speech science, and drama and theater. Like Rahskopf, Wallace was head of a Department of Speech that included all of these areas.

Rahskopf of Washington and Wallace of Illinois were similar in many ways—Rahskopf with a PhD in Speech and Dramatic Art from the State University of Iowa (now the University of Iowa) and Wallace with a PhD in Speech and Drama from Cornell University, each head of a large Department of Speech that contained all the varieties of speech that Winans had envisioned on his hypothetical masthead of the *Quarterly*, each a man trained in rhetoric and public address, each elected in the 1950s to the presidency of the Speech Association of America.

And yet there are crucial differences between the two men's treatment of "speech" in the essays they wrote, in their presidential year, about speech at mid-century. Rahskopf's title puts "speech" in the first position, and makes no mention of a "field" or "discipline." Wallace's begins with "The Field" making "speech" the object of a preposition. Rahskopf makes no mention of a "field" or "discipline," anywhere in his essay, although in his first paragraph he uses "our" six times and "we" seven times to refer to activities and achievements of "all of us in the Speech Association of America."[51] The first seven words of Wallace's essay are "Persons identified with the field of speech"[52] and there are within his first paragraph ten uses of "the field" (or "field of speech"), one of "our field," and two of "the farm," apparently used as a substitution for "the field." Rahskopf's essay embraces "speech," Wallace's plots it out.

What is most striking about the difference between the two essays, though, is how they place "speech" in relation to another term: "communication." Rahskopf uses a form of "communication" eight times in six pages, Wallace forty-five times in twelve, nearly three times the frequency per page with which Rahskopf uses it. The frequency provides a possible clue to a difference, a reason to look further, and having looked, this is what I found: where Rahskopf treats "speech" as "primary," "basic," and a "distinctive and unified process in human life," Wallace persistently and consistently justifies the study of speech, and separately justifies each of the five areas he identifies within "the field of speech" as important activities because they are concerned with improvement in *speech* as a *means*, to the *end* of *communication*. It seems to be no accident that where Rahskopf uses the word "colleagues" it is in the expression "colleagues in the teaching of speech," and that where Wallace uses it is in the expression "colleagues who are devoted to the improvement of communication."[53]

A different take on the meaning and functioning of "speech" for a mid-century professor of speech is found in an essay by Barnet Baskerville, of the University of Washington, a 1948 doctoral graduate in speech from Northwestern University and a scholar of the history of American public address. In "I Teach Speech," he complains that when he answers the question posed to him "what do you teach?" and he answers "speech," more often than not the responses from his interlocutors reveal what he takes to be serious misunderstandings of what he actually does when teaching the art of public speaking. The responses he mentions, from a lady sitting near him on the bus, from a salesperson who comes to his door at home, from fellow scholars at the university at which he professes, and from his students in the classroom, suggest they find in his utterance, "I teach speech," evidence that he teaches overwrought delivery, trivial content, and superficial tricks of self-presentation.[54] Baskerville sets the record straight in a lucid essay that elicited a job offer from a highly prestigious US university that had no professor of speech but that wanted the one who had written the essay in question. In the essay, Baskerville writes in the persona of speech teacher, and what he reports from the field is that "speech" did not relieve him of the need, once expressed by O'Neill, to provide "a special explanation as to what is meant or not meant by the term" he had used to describe his subject.[55] O'Neill's complaint had been lodged against "public speaking," but twenty-eight years later Professor Baskerville had found "speech" to be wanting in the service of immediate and effective reference to the work of the teacher of speech at mid-century.

In the "speech age," there is apparent hegemony of "speech" in disciplinary naming practices. Were there also, at mid-century, signs of linguistic fissure, breakdown, or incomplete resolution of the tensions that had been experienced in the five decades in which there had been something resembling an academic discipline of speech in US higher education?

One such sign can be found in the title (and subject) of the closest thing the mid-century discipline had to a history of it in US higher education. For all of the ways in which Wallace's *History of Speech Education in America* is useful for the purpose of signaling disciplinary status for the work being done by people and in institutions closely identified with the association, one can ask: Why did the association commission a history of "speech education" rather than, say, a history of "the broader conception of the whole field of human speech" to which O'Neill had referred in 1928? Arguably those are different projects, and not mutually exclusive, but why one and not the other? Why not a history of the study of speech, the subject Woolbert had proclaimed the "substance of a discipline"?[56] Whatever the explanation, the first extended work of disciplinary history, published in 1954, is a history not of "speech" but of "speech education."

Shortly after the publication of *History of Speech Education in America*, a trenchant essay review of it in the *Quarterly* asks, as an expression of disappointment that the provided history puts too singular an emphasis on the teaching of speech as a merely practical art, "What is the subject matter of speech, the intellectual continuum?"[57] The author of the review, a Professor of English at Columbia University and editor of the journal *American Speech*, pushes hard against not only what he takes to be the volume's valorization of the merely practical but also of its failure to demonstrate the professional and intellectual unity across the diverse range of subjects—public speaking, speech correction, theater, speech interpretation—displayed under the banner "speech education."

Another sign is the large number of "Departments of Speech and Drama" or "Speech and Theatre" mentioned in Donald K. Smith's report.[58] Some of these are probably a necessary organizational solution to groupings in a small college, but such names are also found in departments in large universities that offer doctoral study. In 1923, James A. Winans asked, in his critique of "speech" as a disciplinary term, "Would any outside our little group use the word ['speech'] to refer to reading or dramatics?"[59] Thirty-two years later W. Norwood Brigance professed to be disturbed by hybrid names for departments such as "Speech and Drama" that should, he wrote, be labeled with the single word "speech,"[60] but perhaps "speech" was not strong enough to assert itself, in many places, as the single-word term for the field. The question to ask here is whether and how long "speech" could continue to sustain itself as "the common linguistic ground"[61] upon which such diverse and maturing subjects as theater and speech correction would stand together under the name of "speech"?

A fissure starts to form around "rhetoric" in 1953, with Donald C. Bryant's essay, "Rhetoric: Its Function and Its Scope," in which he severs analytically "rhetoric" from any necessary connection to "speech" by proposing that "rhetoric must be understood to be the rationale of informative and suasory discourse, both spoken and written."[62] Perhaps even more importantly Bryant's essay provides, in the pages of the *Quarterly Journal of Speech*, a basis for thinking about rhetoric apart from the act of performance, whether spoken or written, and gives further strength to the movement, in the field of speech, to think of rhetoric as a theoretical topic that could, conceivably, stand on its own, not as a subdivision of "speech" but as a topic in its own right.

Although many mid-century academic speech teachers felt a sense of pride and satisfaction that speech had become "a dignified, academic discipline in its own right,"[63] they showed little interest in valorizing speech over other means of action as an efficacious resource in the conduct of human affairs. *Speech*, I suggest, was, in the common culture of the mid-century academic teacher of speech, considered a means, and one among other means, to a more valorized end, namely, *communication*. Rahskopf was an exception, Wallace the rule.

The first appearance that I found of the notion "speech as means, communication as end" is from Winans, one of the founders of the National Association of Academic Teachers of Public Speaking. In 1915, he recommends to the student of public speaking, "whatever else you do, you should make your speech genuine communication,"[64] "a genuine dealing with men,"[65] as distinct from a performance or an exhibition. Woolbert, the chief advocate for "speech" as the controlling term for disciplinary naming, wrote that "the very thing for which it [speech training] ought to exist, [is] the art of communicating ideas to listeners."[66]

Flemming (1920), Drummond (1923), Gray and Wise (1946), Thonssen and Baird (1948), Baskerville (1953), Wallace (1954), Bryant and Wallace (1960), Ronald Reid (1965), Loren Reid (1967), Blankenship (1970), and others provide instances of the principled, sometimes relentless, positioning of *speech* as a *means* to the *end* of *communication*.[67] The Speech Association of America in 1964 issued a statement prepared by its Committee on the Nature of the Field of Speech: Donald K. Smith, Andrew T. Weaver, Karl R. Wallace, Chairman, titled *The Field of Speech: Its Purposes and Scope in Education*. It was published in the *Quarterly* in 1964.[68] It closely resembles Wallace in its systematic use of the notion "speech as means, communication as end." Ronald Reid and Loren Reid follow closely the exposition in Wallace and the Speech Association of America. Ronald Reid's essay is titled "The Process of Speech Communication" and appears in a volume he edited titled *The Field of Communication*.[69] Loren Reid's essay is titled "The Discipline of Speech" and appears in *The Speech Teacher*.[70]

"Speech" was in a hegemonic position in disciplinary naming in 1954, but there were terminological fissures. Where once "the teaching of speech" and "speech education" had been replaced by "speech" unmodified, "speech education" emerged as once again a prominent symbol in the disciplinary discourse of the field of speech. Although "Department of Speech" was the modal name for departments associated with the work of the association, in a substantial minority of departments "Speech and Drama" (or a variant of it) were still in place. Although some prominent scholars believed that "speech" could justifiably subsume "drama" in such a linguistic environment, in many places such a subsumption had not been achieved. "Rhetoric" had recently been given a rationale in the pages of the *Quarterly* that made it easier to break its previous tethering, in the field of speech, to speech. By 1954, "communication," always a valorized term in the forty-year history of the field of speech in US higher education, had been systematically wired into prominent disciplinary statements as the ultimate purpose of "speech." And for at least one professor of speech, Baskerville, "speech" was a problematic answer to the question, "And what do you teach?" Given all of this, could "speech" endure as the hegemonic term for the academic discipline that had been established in the United States at mid-century?

Conclusion

When the association was conceived in 1914 and established in 1915 "speech" was not used in the naming of the association and its academic journal. For two years, "public speaking" held pride of such places, as well as in the first report of the association's research committee. But the members of the new association soon replaced "public speaking" with "speech" as a term of reference and disciplinary identity, and "the whole field of human speech" became a candidate for the substance of the work of the founding and development of an academic discipline.

By 1954, a state of terminological hegemony had been achieved with "speech," in the name of the association, in the names of its journals, and in the names of departments associated with the new academic discipline. And if one surveys the field of such studies in 1914, the accomplishment of the establishment of a hegemony of naming, and of the objects to be so named (an association, journals, academic departments), is an impressive one.

As impressive as was the establishment of terminological hegemony in the new discipline, I have hinted here that there were dispositions and forces, practical and intellectual, that might be examined to help explain why and how that hegemony, so obvious in 1954, eventually was broken. These dispositions and forces include: the persistence, although often *sotto voce*, of a desire to make "rhetoric" a master term or at least a more prominent one in the disciplinary discourse; the breaking off of theater, speech science, and speech pathology from departments of speech and the association; the tethering of "speech" to "education"; the conceptual untethering of rhetoric from orality; the decline in prestige of the word "speech"; the long-established discursive force, in the new discipline, of "communication," and the concomitant emergence of "communication" as a term in the American cultural conversation.

Notes

1. Charles H. Woolbert, "The Teaching of Speech as an Academic Discipline," *Quarterly Journal of Speech Education* 9, no. 1 (1923): 1–18.
2. J. M. O'Neill, "The National Association," *Quarterly Journal of Public Speaking* 1, no. 1 (1915): 51–58.
3. O'Neill, "National," 56–57.
4. O'Neill, "National," 57.
5. O'Neill, "National," 57.
6. The Research Committee, "Research in Public Speaking," *Quarterly Journal of Public Speaking* 1, no. 1(1915): 24.
7. Research Committee, "Research," 24.
8. Charles H. Woolbert, "The Organization of Departments of Speech Science in Universities," *Quarterly Journal of Public Speaking* 2, no. 1 (1916): 64.
9. Woolbert, "Organization," 65.
10. Woolbert, "Organization," 64.
11. Woolbert, "Organization," 66.
12. J.M. O'Neill, "Wanted: An Accurate Label," *Quarterly Journal of Public Speaking* 2, no. 3 (1916): 294.
13. O'Neill, "Wanted," 294–295.

14 O'Neill, "Wanted," 295.

15 O'Neill, "Wanted," 295.

16 J.P. Ryan, "The Department of Speech at Grinnell," *Quarterly Journal of Public Speaking* 3, no. 2 (1917): 203–209.

17 J.P. Ryan, "Terminology: The Department of Speech." *Quarterly Journal of Speech Education* 4, no. 1 (1918): 1–11.

18 Ryan, "Terminology."

19 "Changes in Names," *Quarterly Journal of Speech Education* 4, no. 1 (1918): 114.

20 "Changes in Names," 113.

21 Thomas E. Coulton, *Trends in Speech Education in American Colleges*, unpublished PhD dissertation, New York University, 1935.

22 Coulton, *Trends*.

23 J.M. O'Neill, "After Thirteen Years," *Quarterly Journal of Speech Education* 14, no. 2 (1928): 242.

24 O'Neill, "After," 243. It is 290 words.

25 O'Neill, "After," 251.

26 O'Neill, "National," 56–57.

27 O'Neill, "After," 251–252.

28 Ryan, "Department," and "Terminology."

29 E.C. Mabie, "'Speech' from another Angle," *Quarterly Journal of Speech* 9, no. 4 (1923): 333.

30 O'Neill, "After," 251–252.

31 James Albert Winans, "Speech," *Quarterly Journal of Speech Education* 9, no. 3 (1923): 231.

32 Winans, "Speech," 230.

33 Winans, "Speech," 231.

34 Woolbert, "Teaching," 9.

35 Rupert L. Cortright, "This Speech Age Makes New Demands Upon Education," *The Speech Teacher* 2, no. 1 (1953): 1–6.

36 A.J. Braumbaugh, ed., *American Colleges and Universities* (Menasha, WI: American Council on Education, 1948).

37 Coulton, *Trends*.

38 Braumbaugh, *American Colleges*.

39 Karl R. Wallace, ed., *History of Speech Education in America* (New York: Appleton-Century-Crofts, 1954).

40 Wallace, *History*, 1.

41 Woolbert, "Teaching," 1.

42 Horace G. Rahskopf, "Speech at Mid-Century," *Quarterly Journal of Speech* 37, no. 2 (1951): 147–152.

43 Rahskopf, "Speech," 150–151.

44 Rahskopf, "Speech," 149.

45 Rahskopf, "Speech," 149.

46 O'Neill, "After," 251–252.

47 Winans, "Speech," 230.

48 See Thomas R. Nilsen, *Speech Communication at the University of Washington: An Informal History* (Seattle: Department of Speech Communication, University of Washington, 1991).

49 Karl R. Wallace, "The Field of Speech, 1953: An Overview," *Quarterly Journal of Speech* 40, no. 2 (1954): 117–129.

50 Wallace, "Field," 117.

51 Rahskopf, "Speech," 147.

52 Wallace, "Field," 117.

53 Wallace, "Field," 121.

54 Barnet Baskerville, "I Teach Speech," *Bulletin of the American Association of University Professors* 39 (1953): 58–69.

55 O'Neill, "Wanted," 294.

56 Woolbert, "Teaching," 1.

57   W. Cabell Greet, "Review of Karl R. Wallace (ed.) *History of Speech Education in America*," *Quarterly Journal of Speech* 41, no. 2 (1955): 176.

58   Donald K. Smith, "Origin and Development of Departments of Speech," in *History of Speech Education in America*, ed. Karl R. Wallace (New York: Appleton-Century-Crofts, 1954): 447–470.

59   Winans, "Speech," 224.

60   Henry L. Ewbank Sr., A. Craig Baird, W. Norwood Brigance, Wayland M. Parrish, and Andrew T. Weaver, "What is Speech? A Symposium," *Quarterly Journal of Speech* 41, no. 2 (1955): 148.

61   Mabie, "Speech," 331.

62   Donald C. Bryant, "Rhetoric: Its Function and Its Scope," *Quarterly Journal of Speech* 39, no. 4 (1953): 401–424.

63   Giles Wilkeson Gray, "Some Teachers and the Transition to Twentieth-Century Speech Education," in *History of Speech Education in America*, ed. Karl R. Wallace (New York: Appleton-Century-Crofts, 1954): 423.

64   James Albert Winans, *Public Speaking* (New York: The Century Company, 1915): 27.

65   Winans, *Public Speaking*, 28.

66   Woolbert, "Teaching," 9.

67   See Edwin Flemming, "A Lively Sense of Communication," *Quarterly Journal of Speech Education* 6, no. 3 (1920): 73–78; Alexander M. Drummond, "Graduate Work in Public Speaking," *Quarterly Journal of Speech Education* 9, no. 2 (1923): 136–146; Baskerville, "I Teach Speech"; Wallace, "Field"; Giles Wilkeson Gray and Claude Merton Wise, *The Bases of Speech* (New York: Harper & Brothers, 1946 [1934]); Lester Thonssen and A. Craig Baird, *Speech Criticism: The Development of Standards for Rhetorical Appraisal* (New York: The Ronald Press Company, 1948); Donald C. Bryant and Karl R. Wallace, *Fundamentals of Public Speaking* (New York: Appleton-Century Crofts, 1960); Ronald F. Reid, "The Process of Speech Communication," in *Introduction to the Field of Speech*, ed. Ronald F. Reid (Chicago: Scott, Foresman, 1965): 2–13; Loren Reid, "The Discipline of Speech," *The Speech Teacher* 16, no. 1 (1967): 1–10; Jane Blankenship, "Review of John R. Searle, *Speech Acts: An Essay in the Philosophy of Language*," *The Speech Teacher* 9 (1970): 85.

68   Speech Association of America, "The Field of Speech: Its Purposes and Scope in Education," *Quarterly Journal of Speech* 50, no. 1 (1964): 66–69.

69   Reid, "The Process of Speech Communication," 2–13.

70   Reid, "The Discipline of Speech," 1–10.

References

Baskerville, Barnet. "I Teach Speech." *Bulletin of the American Association of University Professors* 39 (1953): 58–69.

Blankenship, Jane. "Review of John R. Searle, *Speech Acts: An Essay in the Philosophy of Language*." *The Speech Teacher* 9 (1970): 85.

Braumbaugh, A.J., ed. *American Colleges and Universities*. Menasha, WI: American Council on Education, 1948.

Bryant, Donald C. "Rhetoric: Its Function and Its Scope." *Quarterly Journal of Speech* 39, no. 4 (1953): 401–424.

Bryant, Donald C. and Karl R. Wallace. *Fundamentals of Public Speaking*. New York: Appleton-Century-Crofts, 1960.

"Changes in Names." *Quarterly Journal of Speech Education* 4, no. 1 (1918): 113–114.

Cortright, Rupert L. "This Speech Age Makes New Demands Upon Education." *The Speech Teacher* 2, no. 1 (1953): 1–6.

Coulton, Thomas E. *Trends in Speech Education in American Colleges*. Unpublished PhD dissertation, New York University, 1935.

Drummond, Alexander M. "Graduate Work in Public Speaking." *Quarterly Journal of Speech Education* 9, no. 2 (1923): 136–146.

Ewbank Sr., Henry L., A. Craig Baird, W. Norwood Brigance, Wayland M. Parrish, and Andrew T. Weaver. "What Is Speech? A Symposium." *Quarterly Journal of Speech* 41, no. 2 (1955): 145–153.

Flemming, Edwin. "A Lively Sense of Communication." *Quarterly Journal of Speech Education* 6, no. 3 (1920): 73–78.

Gray, Giles Wilkeson. "Some Teachers and the Transition to Twentieth-Century Speech Education." In *History of Speech Education in America*, edited by Karl R. Wallace, 422–446. New York: Appleton-Century-Crofts, 1954.

Gray, Giles Wilkeson and Claude Merton Wise. *The Bases of Speech*. New York: Harper & Brothers, 1946 [1934].

Greet, W. Cabell. "Review of Karl R. Wallace (ed.) *History of Speech Education in America*." *Quarterly Journal of Speech* 41, no. 2 (1955): 174–178.

Mabie, E.C. "'Speech' from another Angle." *Quarterly Journal of Speech* 9, no. 4 (1923): 330–333.

Nilsen, Thomas R. *Speech Communication at the University of Washington: An Informal History*. Seattle: Department of Speech Communication, University of Washington, 1991.

O'Neill, J.M. "After Thirteen Years." *Quarterly Journal of Speech Education* 14, no. 2 (1928): 242–253.

———. "The National Association." *Quarterly Journal of Public Speaking* 1, no. 1 (1915): 51–58.

———. "Wanted: An Accurate Label." *Quarterly Journal of Public Speaking* 2, no. 3 (1916): 294–295.

Rahskopf, Horace G. "Speech at Mid-Century." *Quarterly Journal of Speech* 37, no. 2 (1951): 147–152.

Reid, Loren. "The Discipline of Speech." *The Speech Teacher* 16, no. 1 (1967): 1–10.

Reid, Ronald F. "The Process of Speech Communication." In *Introduction to the Field of Speech*, edited by Ronald F. Reid, 2–13. Chicago: Scott, Foresman, 1965.

The Research Committee. "Research in Public Speaking." *Quarterly Journal of Public Speaking* 1, no. 1 (1915): 24–32.

Ryan, J.P. "The Department of Speech at Grinnell." *Quarterly Journal of Public Speaking* 3, no. 2 (1917): 203–209.

———. "Terminology: The Department of Speech." *Quarterly Journal of Speech Education* 4, no. 1 (1918): 1–11.

Smith, Donald K. "Origin and Development of Departments of Speech." In *History of Speech Education in America*, edited by Karl R. Wallace, 447–470. New York: Appleton-Century-Crofts, 1954.

Speech Association of America. "The Field of Speech: Its Purposes and Scope in Education." *Quarterly Journal of Speech* 50, no. 1 (1964): 66–69.

Thonssen, Lester and A. Craig Baird. *Speech Criticism: The Development of Standards for Rhetorical Appraisal*. New York: The Ronald Press Company, 1948.

Wallace, Karl R. "The Field of Speech, 1953: An Overview." *Quarterly Journal of Speech* 40, no. 2 (1954): 117–129.

———, ed. *History of Speech Education in America*. New York: Appleton-Century-Crofts, 1954.

Winans, James Albert. *Public Speaking*. New York: The Century Company, 1915.

———. "Speech." *Quarterly Journal of Speech Education* 9, no. 3 (1923): 223–231.

Woolbert, Charles H. "The Organization of Departments of Speech Science in Universities." *Quarterly Journal of Public Speaking* 2, no. 1 (1916): 64–77.

———. "The Teaching of Speech as an Academic Discipline." *Quarterly Journal of Speech Education* 9, no. 1 (1923): 1–18.

3.

THE SILENCING OF SPEECH IN THE LATE TWENTIETH CENTURY

Joshua Gunn and Frank E.X. Dance

I do not suppose the younger generation . . . can realize how great a change has come over us. Any time back of twenty-five years ago each teacher stayed in his own little corner, hugging his own pet "system," and believing all the other fellows were nitwits and freaks . . . His extreme insistence upon his own little system of eternal truth was probably due to the fact that he had an inferiority complex.

James Winans, 1934[1]

Although it is tempting to joke that, in general, our common academic enterprise consists of finding one's own corner and believing those who do not join you there are "nitwits and freaks," the acerbic remarks of James Winans in 1934 referenced a moment decades prior in which the teachers of public speaking were in need of conferencing for a shared sense of disciplinary coherence and academic respectability. Along with Paul Pearson and Wilbur Jones Kay, Winans helped to establish the Eastern Public Speaking Conference, which in turn contributed to the formation of what we know today as the National Communication Association.[2] As a number of chapters in this volume detail,[3] the field that would come to be known as "speech"—along with its sibling "composition"— was *perceived* to be hastened by the growth of the "industrial classes" and the different kinds of students who were coming to the newly established Land Grant colleges and universities during reconstruction.[4] If the contents of new textbooks written for the emerging field in the late nineteenth and early twentieth centuries are any measure,[5] from its inception those affiliated with communication studies have imagined their mission as a response to the oral and written English literacy needs of the new student seeking a public education after the Civil War.[6]

Unquestionably, part of the struggle of early speech teachers for academic respectability involved forging a wedge between the "popular" and "academic," and this was most notably achieved with the call for the production of "research."[7] Concurrent with a growing disciplinary consciousness about teaching the literacies of writing and "Oral English" was an older, often itinerant and private pedagogy of elocution rooted in centuries-old European approaches to acting and platform speaking.[8] Strongly affiliated in the United States with the baffling, taxonomic excesses and complex systems of "delivery" and gesture promulgated by quasi-spiritualist figures like Francoise Delsarte, the US elocutionists formed a professional organization in the 1890s, which eventually emerged as the National Speech Arts Association in 1906.[9] As William M. Keith notes, many public speaking teachers who attended the elocutionists' conventions found them pompous affairs devoid of scholarly substance, focused as they were on the kind of speaking that we associate with the "inspirational," or the "motivational speakers" and "TED talkers" of our time.[10] Herman Cohen observes that composition teachers were no less unkind to the elocutionists, whom they regarded as "superficial and trivial" and "as perverters of rhetoric who stressed all that was offensive to rational discourse."[11] By the time a number of teachers of Oral English decided to forge a disciplinary independence from their composition colleagues and departments of English in 1914, a distinction between "elocution" or "expression" and "public speaking" or "speech" as objects of academic study was well underway. For decades after, the elocutionists would function as a foil for disciplinary self-fashioning.[12]

Although the object of *rhetoric* has been claimed and shared by scholars identified with English composition and communication studies alike for over a century, by the 1920s, many teachers of public speaking and oral interpretation (a precursor to performance studies) who were affiliated with academic institutions understood their object of study was "speech," and this in distinction from "Oratory and Expression," "Speech arts," and "Elocution," which J.P. Ryan forcefully argued should be "passed over and rejected because of their connotations" in 1918.[13]

In this chapter we are concerned principally with the shifting connotations of *speech*, and what the term came to mean for many in our organization by the end of the twentieth century. As a complement to the historical trajectory of "speech" carefully traced by Gerry Philipsen in this volume, here we attend primarily to the abandonment of speech as an object of disciplinary identity in the 1990s. We recognize that there remains much to be studied and said about the arguments about the term speech over the course of the twentieth century, including the major debates and discussions that occurred in the post-war period through the 1980s. Although we will describe these debates and discussions, our purpose is to show how the "death" of speech in the 1990s was the consequence of (1) an instability of disciplinary objects in general; and (2) the instability of speech as "our" titular object in particular. The latter unquestionably includes conceptions of speech from the field's earliest days; however, our argument is that the term takes on an increasingly *gendered* connotation in the 1980s. In short, in addition to a number of practical considerations, we think that speech was silenced because it betokened the unmanly or adolescent.[14]

To this end, we first briefly sketch the challenge "objects" pose for academic fields, noting that arguments and debates about what a field studies are actually formative and central to a sense of disciplinary coherence; apocalyptic proclamations about the dying, erosion, or incoherence of a given field, for example, are frequently measures of its robust perseverance. Then, we focus more narrowly on how the use of the term "speech" to mean everything from physiology to reasoned argument led to a widespread dissatisfaction with the term in the 1970s and two failed votes of the membership of our organization to replace it in the 1980s. Finally, we describe in detail the arguments for and against getting rid of "speech" as *the* disciplinary object in the 1990s and its eclipse with "communication" in 1997. We conclude with a discussion of what our field gained and lost with speech's silencing.

Speech as a Disciplined Object

Traditionally conceived, an object is a material thing that can be observed. And arguably, the history of human thought is the history of a failure to agree about the reality or existence of "the object" (ontology) or how we can know it, if at all (epistemology). Writing as a philosopher, librarian Henry E. Bliss captured the anxiety inspired by the uncertain status of the object in the early twentieth century: "In seeking a sane and consistent account of human experience . . . human science and philosophy are ever dealing with subjective perceptions of objective phenomena with concepts developed from subjective perceptions."[15] For Bliss, to fail to properly fix the object is to tempt "insanity," or as René Descartes famously meditated, to be like a lunatic, "befogged by the black vapors of the bile."[16] More measured minds have argued that the failures of observation are not as drastic as all that, and have deftly demolished any tidy distinction between subject and object because their "separation" is "both real and illusory."[17] Basically, to get on in the world everyone behaves as if they know the "object," but many of our professional thinkers are quick to remind us that—in the history of human thinking, at least—we don't.

Traditionally conceived, academic "fields"—or, considering the inevitable policing of nitwits and freaks, "disciplines"[18]—are in the orbit of an object of study, even if that object is a "practice" (such a medicine). Yet inasmuch as the subject–object relation is troubled, so too are our commonplace assumptions about disciplinarity. To use seemingly easy examples, we might assume that the object of philosophy is wisdom; that the object of biology is the living organism; that the object of anthropology is human kind; that the object of mathematics is number; and so on. Yet any cursory study of each of these discipline's published self-descriptions reveals widespread disagreement about their respective objects. Such disagreement is often coupled with repeated apocalyptic calls to stabilize a field's object to stave off its imminent demise, from Immanuel Kant's weird defense of the "faculty of reason" as a tonal object of philosophy, to Florian Znaniecki's strident insistence that sociology be rescued from "chaos" with a clearly defined "class of data . . . such as to allow a rational body of knowledge to be constructed about them."[19] To borrow a concept from developmental psychology, academic disciplines are plagued with the problem of object permanence or constancy—that objects persist independent of observation—as a condition of their own continuance.[20] This is to suggest that the definitional work of disciplines is both inevitable and central to their labor.[21] Whatever anyone assumes is the object domain of a given field, we think that knowing the arguments and debates over this domain in the context of institutional histories provides the most useful map of a discipline.

Although the instability of the disciplinary object is fettered to the inescapable and problematic construct of subject/object, our concern is the foundational assertion of the stability of a field's object, or what we can refer to as the primary political gesture of referential plenitude: "we study X!" Of course, *how* a given academic teaches or studies her object—the vexing question of method—is closely related to the foundational gesture, especially to fields of study that have decidedly disavowed methodological "purity" in favor of a hard-won, social science/humanities hybridity. As Dilip Parameshwar Gaonkar observed of rhetorical studies, object and method are locked into a mutually defining dialectic.[22] Nevertheless, at least conceptually, before that familiar disciplinary proclamation that Robert Lee Scott intones as "in the beginning was the error!" is the foundational gesture to an object,[23] however unstable or mistaken that gesture may be. For US communication studies, that object was originally declared as "speech!"

Gerald Philipsen has demonstrated that after the formation of the National Association of Academic Teachers of Public Speaking (NAATPS) in the 1914/1915 academic year, the ascent of speech as a "master term" was rather swift.[24] Discussion in the NAATPS' national organ, the *Quarterly Journal of Public Speaking*, urged dumping the formative discipline's object as a practice in favor of an object that better encompassed the variety of the interests of its membership, especially those with more scientific aspirations. Ryan's widely read argument in favor of the term "speech" over terms like "public speaking" clearly hinged on a perception of academic inferiority:

> The title public speaking hinders rather than helps towards a right recognition of the department in the curriculum. The hindrance comes out of an attitude in the mind of the teacher of speech . . . and the other members of the faculty toward the subject of speech . . . The teachers of speech must more and more take an intellectual attitude toward their work . . . In the minds of those who control the curricula the phrase public speaking means the practice of an art. To a man looking for graduate work in an eastern university the head of the graduate school replied that there was no work offered because speaking was merely a bit of technique.[25]

Ryan's arguments and anecdotes proved persuasive, or at the very least representative of a growing consensus. By 1923 the national organization changed its name to the "National Association of Teachers of Speech," and by 1946, simply the "Speech Association of America" (SAA). In the 1940s "Speech" was finally given "pride of unshared space," notes Philipsen, as it had become "the preponderant term in [the] names of academic departments, where the rival 'public speaking' was all but extinguished."[26]

Although we believe that all disciplines struggle with the instability of their objects, the pickle with the preponderance of "speech" was the assumption of an obvious and stable referent. Ryan argued that "speech" was the best title for a department (and by extension, the fomenting field) because it "is old, short, simple, stable, well-known, accurate, common, learned, definite, extensive, and academically acceptable because it connotes the art and denotes the science, or just as well it denotes the art, and connotes the science."[27] Such remarks make the foundational gesture of the field, and perhaps a grounding gaff, inaugurating decades of debate over scientific aspirations and artful connotations. The most heated, formative exchange occurred between Charles H. Woolbert and Everett Lee Hunt on whether "speech" is a science in the tradition of psychology, or a practice-centered art rooted in the humanities, respectively.[28] As the struggle over object and method continued for the next two decades, references to the object of speech were far from stable: "for some speech concerned the act of speaking, while for others it included the whole of human expression, including gesture. Some scholars treated speech as a synonym for oratory, while others used the term as a reference for physical voice."[29] After years of start-up, "speech" failed to be fixed. Woolbert's opening remarks in a posthumously published essay from 1930 helpfully relays the anxiety over the instability: "Speech is a term with many meanings, from elemental vocal sounds to a public address or even the language habits of a people. The term is used here to include 'Communication by voice and by total bodily action.'" Insofar as Woolbert consistently pushed for the "speech sciences," such an opening also conveys the nascent appeal and ascent of "communication" in the decades to come.[30]

Aside from the instability of what "speech" *denoted*, by the 1950s it was clear that the early efforts to define speech in opposition to the connotations of elocution or "expression" had, more or less, failed. In a 1953 essay reflecting on his profession as a speech teacher, Barnet Baskerville describes an encounter with an "old lady on the bus," who asks him the dreaded question, "And what do you teach at the University?"

> If only I could answer that I teach physics or history or English literature we might continue on our way with harmonious talk of books or atomic bombs . . . As it is, I might have said with equal effectiveness, "I teach Sxmpthx," for no meaning has been conceived. This, I hasten to add, is not always the case. More commonly, the rejoinder "I teach speech" evokes such a variety of comments revealing such amazing associations that one would gladly settle for an uncomprehending "Oh" and a well-intentioned "That's nice." . . . "I teach speech" is almost invariably met, as in the case of the old lady on the bus, with what may be termed the Long Pregnant Pause, which is then followed by The Comment.[31]

What are the amazing associations that so troubled Baskerville in 1953? He mentions many, but the most troubling come from an academic friend in English who associated speech with "burgeoning Toastmaster's Clubs, Dale Carnegie groups, and evening classes in public speaking," which produced "maximum talk with a minimum of thought."[32] Baskerville suggested that speech courses in "oral interpretation" only deepened the association with elocution, "with its inevitable connotations of simpering adolescents 'speaking pieces,' affected females rapturously declaiming 'The Little Brown House Under the Apple Tree,' and grown men with orotund voices intoning 'The Bells' or thundering the 'Call to Arms.'"[33] Although he declared that elocution "fell victim decades ago to its own excesses," Baskerville underscores and denounces a common and continued association.[34]

The attachment of speech to everything from public speaking teachers and debate coaches, to "pathologists and clinicians, the audiologists, the phoneticians," to those who taught "voice, oral reading, radio, argumentation, and group discussion," continued to bedevil those laboring under its name for decades hence.[35] Disagreement about the content of the "basic course" further exacerbated the problem, creating the impression for some that the field was dominated by the study of rhetoric and public address at the expense of "basic communication." At the behest of Elwood Murray, the National Society for the Study of Communication would emerge to counter a perceived dominance of rhetoric and public address in the 1950s, later becoming the International Communication

Association and circulating a successful scholarly journal, *The Journal of Communication*.[36] In the context of an emerging, competing organization, the SAA convened a special, February conference on research and instruction, co-sponsored by the US Office of Education, in New Orleans.[37] Rather than exclude anyone along the frequently discussed divide between the "communication arts and sciences," speech was amended to "speech communication," with a reportedly spirited debate on whether to hyphenate the term. John W. Bowers recalls that the

> debate on punctuation followed the crucial debate, the debate on labeling what we do, in which "communication" lost to "speech (-)(:) communication" by two votes, as I recall . . . The conference ended up with "speech-communication." I tried to signal my displeasure with that name later, during the SAA Summer Research Conference, by pronouncing the hyphen with a straining grunt: "ugh!"[38]

With or without a hyphen, for many "speech" represented the discipline's focus on the humanities and the oral arts, while "communication" denoted the sciences and a widening focus on an empirically driven journalism, media studies, or mass communication.[39] Like the early discussions of the discipline's founders in the 1910s, the push for "speech communication" was one in the service of inclusion, but it came with the cost of losing an assumed stability—an assumed stability that, arguably, it never really had.

In 1970 the organization officially became the Speech Communication Association (SCA), but the instability of speech, combined with an ever-expanding roster of methods and objects of study, made it an untenable unifying term for many. In 1976 the "SCA Committee to Consider a Name Change" was formed to discuss alternative terms, but the decision of the committee was "no immediate action."[40] Discussion and debate about dropping the term "speech" and establishing a national identity continued through the 1980s, leading to a constitutional amendment to change the name to the American Communication Association in 1984, and again in 1989, both of which were defeated by a vote of the membership.[41] While many recognized the need to return to a nation-state designator, some members objected to the term "America," while others objected to the loss of "speech." As we detail below, however, the instability of speech and an association of the term with academic timidity—to put matters kindly—led to its ultimate demise.

From the Bus to the Cocktail Party: The 1990s Debate over Speech

We have rehearsed a condensed history of the struggle over our field's titular object in order to underscore it was never a "stable" one. The notion of a disciplinary object is vexing for most academic disciplines, however, and arguments about what it should and should not be comprise a field's self-conception. "Speech" appeared to early field pioneers as a relatively straightforward object, but an examination of published arguments about the meaning of the term then reveals *no* consensus. Speech simply meant different things to different people, a thing for some and a practice for others. "Speech" was finally, officially retired by a vote of the membership in 1997, but not before a decade of debate and discussion that became increasingly tense—and sometimes angry. Although many of the arguments advanced against and in favor of keeping "speech" recalled those of the previous seventy years, debate over the term's final decade differs substantially in character, and principally because of a *tonal* shift hastened by the increasingly influential communication technology and medium: the Internet.[42]

Argumentative foment for changing the name of the SCA in the 1990s began in 1988, when the governing Legislative Council adopted a resolution to vote on changing the name to the American Communication Association, with a special balloting in April the following year. In the official March 1989 national newsletter of the association, *Spectra*, Bruce E. Gronbeck penned an essay urging the change, and one of the present authors of this chapter—Frank E.X. Dance—was invited to pen the opposition. The claims Gronbeck advanced for supporting a change reduce to four, all in the key of professional pragmatics:

(1) the field needs a national designator to participate better in national conversations and to lobby politically;
(2) "speech communication" is a "semantic compromise" that is more confusing than helpful;
(3) shifting to "communication" is more inclusive of the research and teaching currently conducted in the field; and
(4) a name change will help the national organization "blend" more seamlessly with the four regional organizations, all of which had dropped "speech" from their names.[43]

Dance's arguments were framed as a refutation of common arguments, and not necessarily those of Gronbeck. For example, one claim that Dance refutes is that "speech" creates a "negative image" that "hampers the Association in its quest for grant monies from outside agencies." While more intellectually complex, all of Dance's claims hinged on the fact that, "in its inception and earliest stages, human language is **spoken**" (boldface in original). At least from Joshua Gunn's perspective, Dance is among the most consistently outspoken advocates for "speech" in the field. Dance has repeatedly argued that speech is fundamentally concerned with "the causes and consequences of the phylo-genetic and ontogenetic spoken roots of human communication."[44] Dance's position for more than fifty years has been that speech should be in the name of the field because it is the basis of all forms of human communication.

The 1989 exchange in *Spectra* advanced arguments in a measured manner, but perhaps did not reflect a number of conversations actually occurring in conference halls and department hallways; few scholars were willing to commit their more divisive views to print. Michael Burgoon, who is widely regarded as one of the most prolific social science communication scholars, published what are perhaps the most acerbic arguments for "divorcing dame speech" in an odd essay appearing in a special issue of *Communication Education*. Ostensibly, the special issue concerns the state of "instruction" in the field, however, Burgoon uses his contribution as an opportunity to argue for "selected depart-ments to secede from the 'Speech' community" and "get on with forming a different discipline," as well as defend his participation in the decision to eliminate the "Department of Speech Communication" at the University of Arizona.[45] After repeating the established view that "SPEECH has historically been rooted in a tradition of a pedagogy of performance" that "retrodictively" determined scholarly endeavor, Burgoon argues that "extant theory and research must dictate what is taught and how it is to be taught." For Burgoon, speech is synonymous with "performance" and, consequently, does not connote "research." Moreover, as an administrator Burgoon bemoans the common association of speech with "some basic freshman-level service course," which he believed hampered scholarship and compromised disciplinary "integrity."[46] In an endnote Burgoon avers his critique of "speech" is not an "attack on rhetorical theory/scholarship or the development of critical theory," although he stresses that "a social-scientific orientation is a most appropriate approach to develop a discipline of communication" and that speech-side research, implicitly associated with rhetorical and performance studies, is of dubious quality.[47]

Burgoon's argument reflects in many respects the debate between Woolbert and Hunt in the 1920s, as well as the 1960s compromise of "speech communication." His stress of speech as a "dame," however, underscores a tacit connotation for speech bemoaned by Baskerville in the image of the "affected females" and "grown men with orotund voices": speech is *feminine* or *unmanly* and consequently not academically respectable. The gendered character of speech for Burgoon is clear in an argument offered against teaching the basic course: "Too often, Speech departments are campus whores who truly live in fear of not being loved enough by others to ensure their existence, even on meager resources."[48] In light of this language, the elaboration of the misogyny of such a sentiment is unnecessary.

Although the 1989 discussions and debates over the name change did not result in a successful vote, the argument that "speech" was a weak designator with unfavorable academic connotations persisted. Importantly, the forum created for email-based announcements and discussions by Thomas Benson on July 14, 1985 was a growing and increasingly dominant locus of disciplinary disputation.[49] Called the Communication, Research, and Theory Network or "CRTNET," the online forum gradually expanded to become the dominant and most widely read locus of discipline-related news and discussion. Until the 1990s, the newsletter *Spectra* had been the primary venue for issues concerning the professional organization. As more academics embraced email as a principal means of communication, CRTNET's largely un-moderated forum democratized access to the disciplinary imagination and by the mid-1990s played a significant role for the arguments that shifted the SCA's membership toward a name change.

Following an exploratory survey distributed by the national organization in the summer of 1996, Thomas Benson initiated a discussion on CRTNET on Wednesday, August 21, 1996 with a question:

Would anyone on CRTNET be willing to engage in an online discussion? If so, whether or not you are a member of SCA, please feel free to join the conversation. I'll assume that any replies sent to me are meant for publication in CRTNET unless the author tells me otherwise.

Benson's catholic invitation invited a lengthy, at times contentious, discussion. Among the first to respond was David L. Sutton, who brought the issue of institutional viability to the forefront: "College administrators across the country are looking for places to trim their budgets, and they are setting their sights on departments of communication. The latest round of oh-dear-what-shall-we-call-ourselves surveys is analogous to rearranging the chairs on the Titanic."[50] Sutton's sentiment was certainly shared, however, most of the discussions orbited the connotations of "speech" and how these helped or hindered recognition external to the field. "'Speech' comes with some baggage," wrote Robert Ivie, "that makes it difficult sometimes for us to be taken seriously as a scholarly discipline, especially within a college of arts and sciences."[51] Baskerville's 1950s bus ride anecdote was eclipsed by the scene of an imagined cocktail party. George Cheney wrote:

> Despite its inevitable ambiguities, "communication" is a more useful and appropriate term today than is "speech." At cocktail parties—as the favorite example goes—I'd rather explain what KIND of communication I "do" than say something like: "Studying public address is really a fairly small (but nevertheless significant) part of the larger field of communication studies today. We also do all these other things."[52]

James F. Klumpp's party, however, was a little different:

> If our need is to be comfortable with our identity, ["communication" names] imply an identity so broad that I do not feel [an] identity at all. Identification with my cable box and the folks in engineering who design it, with my local newscaster and his/her make-up artist, and with James Earl Jones and his Yellow Pages will dominate response to my use of the term at a cocktail party.[53]

Peter DeCaro and Bill Scarborough also partied differently, recommending the association change its name to the "International Babel Association" and "Yak Attack!" respectively.[54]

For the one of us active in the field at the time, however—again, that would be Frank—the name change was no laughing matter. Dance took the opportunity of the online discussion on CRTNET to remind participants of the history of the association's name change, stretching back to the formation of the National Association of Elocutionists in 1892, in addition to disclosing personal experiences that were absent from his previous, published defenses of "speech":

> In keeping with Pavlov's law of neuronal excitation and habituation the SCA voting membership may be becoming insensitive to the issue since the support in 1992 . . . In 1950, 42 years ago, I joined what was then the Speech Association of America . . . Since joining I seem to have been continuously engaged in a series of academic skirmishes designed to define and redefine our discipline, our field, our subject matter. I do not believe that these skirmishes have always been caused by substantive conceptual issues. Over the past 42 years there has been a sustained and persistent effort to remove any reference to speech or spoken language from our disciplinary association's name . . . How have we come to the point of a disciplinary historical revisionism which now even labels Aristotle, not as a philosopher or rhetorician, but as a *communication* scholar. Really![55]

In a manner reflecting his exchange with Gronbeck in 1989, Dance underscores that the dominant arguments for embracing "communication" have more to do with pragmatic, professional anxieties and less to do with conceptual or intellectual rationales in favor of "communication" or against "speech."[56]

The discussion on CRTNET was formative and influential: after reviewing "relevant exchanges on CRTNET" and the discussions of focus groups formed at the 1995 national convention, the elected leaders of the organization sent a letter and "straw ballot" to the membership asking if there should be a vote, once again, to change the name. Dated October 7, 1996, the paid membership was addressed by James W. Chesebro, SCA President, as well as officers of various positions: Judith S. Trent, John A. Daly, Sharon Ratliffe, Roderick Hart, Jo Sprague, Martha Watson, and Isa Engleberg. The letter announced the SCA administration "voted unanimously to recommend a change . . . [to] the National Communication Association" for five reasons:

(1) they believed "the majority of the membership supports a change";
(2) the majority no longer believed speech was an "adequate descriptor of the work performed by the majority of its members";
(3) a national designator is necessary to "explain ourselves" and to "represent our field to academic and non-academic audiences";
(4) while the term "American" was misguided, "National" is a better and important designator; and
(5) the new name does "not invade the semantic space occupied by existing communication associations."

Although discussion about the name change on CRTNET never seemed to wane over the summer and fall of 1996, the letter predictably inspired a new wave of discussion on CRTNET that, again, focused on the external perceptions. Paul B. Turpin's comments are representative of the general tenor of the discussions: "From my first exposure to the field, the history of 'speech' has been associated with Grand Speech—with Oratory." From his own reading of disciplinary history, Turpin concludes that arguments about the professional association's name "tend to boil down to one significant problem: we have to continuously justify ourselves."[57] Arguments about external representation were common in CRTNET discussions and likely influenced the success of the "straw vote," which in turn put an *official*, widespread vote of the membership on the agenda after the 1996 convention. In an effort to influence change, SCA President James W. Chesebro published an editorial in the November *Spectra* titled, "Why We Need to Change Our Name to the National Communication Association." Chesebro stressed anxiety over disciplinary reputation: "We are constantly asked to explain and justify our 'place at the table.' . . . We don't know how many times we're not even asked to participate in relevant discussions because others involved don't know who or what we are."[58] Chesebro framed the need for a name change as fundamentally one of public relations:

> [P]erhaps most importantly, the purpose of our name is to represent the organization externally as well as internally. We have, for example, complained for years that our scholarship is not

well represented publically. We dislike it when a political scientist is selected, and we are not, to provide televised comments on the Presidential Debates. We feel underrepresented in public policy discussions about our national communication policies, or even distance learning decisions on our campuses.[59]

In personal interviews with a number of elected officials in office during 1996 and 1997, the issue of external reputation was confirmed as paramount.[60]

As we recall what Dance reported in his 1989 *Spectra* editorial, a *major* point of concern in the 1990s was institutional and economic: in addition to the challenges posed by university and college administrations to speech departments in the 1990s (a number of departments were dissolved or reconfigured to exclude speech-related courses), many argued that the pursuit of external funding was hampered by the term "speech" and enhanced by "communication." Most of the former SCA officers we interviewed echoed Burgoon's published sentiment that "speech" was associated with "performance" and not considered by colleagues in other fields, as well as the general public, as an object of serious academic study. For some, John Daly observed, that "speech" also connoted forensics (competitive debate and oral interpretation), which was becoming an increasingly autonomous and independent activity in the 1990s. For decades many of the elected leaders of SCA were former debaters and competitive public speakers, but those individuals were either moving toward retirement or increasingly disinterested in administrative office. Finally, although external reputation seemed to be the dominant rationale for the name change, many former SCA officers were careful to note that, by the 1990s, the SCA had become a welcoming, professional home to a number of constituencies that did not draw a lineage to the speech departments of the 1930s: for example, scholars from empirically-driven media effects and mass communication subfields, social psychology, and the US "cultural studies" movement that synthesized the approaches to "communication" from Canada (e.g., media ecology) and Great Britain (the Birmingham School) did not identify with "speech."[61]

The "big tent" appeal of "communication" thus proved alluring to a majority of SCA members, and the early 1997 vote to change the name was, after almost eighty years of discussion and debate, finally successful. Associate Director Bill Eadie crafted a press release that announced as of Friday, March 21, 1997, "The Speech Communication Association officially changed its name to the National Communication Association," based on "[s]ixty nine percent of the 3,437 members who voted" for the amendment to the "association's constitution."[62] Response in department hallways and on CRTNET was swift and registered many complaints, to which an exasperated Ed Schiappa asked:

> Can we stop griping about the name change? More than 2/3rds of the membership approved, mostly (I suspect) because we shared a strong commitment to moving toward a more accurate label than "speech communication." We accomplished an important goal. Let's move on.[63]

Eventually, the field did.

Concluding Observations: The Body Speaks Back

In this chapter we have advanced a description of the 1990s debates and discussions over our national organization's name, which resulted in the retirement of "speech" in favor of "communication." In the many attempts to change the name over the past century, arguments premised on external perceptions of the field have dominated the discussion. Tensions originally voiced in the exchanges of Woolbert and Hunt between those who advocate social scientific approaches and those who center their studies in the humanities persist. Perhaps, in an amusing sense, the understanding of disciplinary history evinces the lyrical wisdom of the Talking Heads front man David Byrne: "same as it ever was!" We have also suggested that the arguments in favor of retiring "speech" in the 1990s reflect and repeat those of the early twentieth century for two reasons: the inevitable instability of disciplinary objects in general, and the variety of meanings, especially connotations, of "speech" in particular. If the unstable life of "speech" is any measure, "communication" will similarly endure debate and discussion over its meaning in the century to come.[64]

In closing, we acknowledge that there is little to no possibility of returning to speech as a titular object, however, we would do well to acknowledge William M. Keith's observation that communication scholars in the NCA "began, crucially, as the *speech teachers*."[65] Arguments against such an identity over the past century have been obsessed with the *perceptions* of our colleagues in academia as well as that of the general public. Because few are willing to commit their more candid views of the connotations of speech in print or "on the record"—they are often mentioned as "connotations" but rarely elaborated—our suspicion that speech connoted the feminine or the unmanly for many is difficult to confirm. Even so, such a connotation comports with the sadly common viewpoint that a field's "feminization" can lead to a decrease in prestige.[66]

That speech has been associated with the feminine, however, is not a new story and can be traced to the somatophobia of Plato. Adriana Cavarero explains:

> Symptomatically, the symbolic patriarchal order that identifies the masculine with reason and the feminine with the body is precisely an order that privileges the semantic with respect to the vocal. In other words, even the androcentric tradition knows that the voice comes from "the vibration of a throat of flesh" and, precisely, because it knows this, it catalogs the voice with the body. This voice becomes secondary, ephemeral, and inessential—reserved for women. Feminized from the start, the vocal aspect of speech and, furthermore, of song appear together as antagonistic elements in a rational, masculine sphere that centers itself, instead, on the semantic. To put it formulaically: woman sings, man thinks.[67]

Such a view certainly comports with Burgoon's suggestion that "speech" is fundamentally concerned with "performance"—bodily arts (inclusive of *teaching*) unsuited for rigorous scholarly interrogation.[68] The unstable, bodily aspect of speech must yield to the number or some form of measurement to become a proper academic object. The term "communication" deliberately disembodies in its hazy, semantic indeterminacy, but no more clearly reflects conceptual consensus than did speech. As Mladen Dolar has said of the field of linguistics, "the voice is the impending element" that linguists had "to get rid of in order to initiate a new science of language" based on abstract measure: "*the phoneme.* Beyond the voice . . . lies the fleshless and boneless entity defined purely by its function—*the silent sound, the soundless voice.*"[69] The gradual, widespread acceptance of Jacques Derrida's critique of phonocentrism in the theoretical humanities in the 1970s and 1980s only served to seal the deal.[70]

Even so, in the past two decades there has been resurgence in the interest of "voice" and "speech" as an object, both among communication studies scholars and in the wider humanities.[71] In part, this is because scholars are starting to realize that the silencing of speech, either by the critique of phonocentrism or with the shift to "the text" or number, "foreclosed" a number of intriguing questions about the sound or acoustic character of speech.[72] Both of us have advocated, in print and in person, for a revival of the study of speech as an object, not only because it is foundational to human communication— we cry before we write—but also *precisely* because there is an element of the human voice that is at once bodily, affective, and eludes the capture of language. As a field over the last century, we have responded to that elusive bodily character of speech as if it were histrionic and undisciplinable, a perception that has troubled our colleagues in performance studies more than most.[73] Somewhat in concert with Kendall R. Phillips, however, we wonder if the "general confusion concerning the term 'speech' among those not in our field" is simply a failure of the field to embrace the body and its affects, not necessarily a "failure of the term."[74]

Notes

1 From a letter addressed to Wayland Maxfield Parrish, April 4, 1934; in William M. Keith, *Democracy as Discussion: Civic Education and the American Forum Movement* (Lanham, MI: Lexington Books, 2007): 39.

2 Herman Cohen, *The History of Speech Communication: The Emergence of a Discipline, 1914–1945* (Annandale, VA: Speech Communication Association, 1994): 29–30. Keith, *Democracy*, 38–40.

3 See Introduction and Chapters 1 and 2, this volume.

4 Cohen, *History*, 13–28. We should stress at the outset that the commonly accepted narrative that the arrival of the public university was in response to the rise of the working classes is a touch romantic, at least based on high school graduation rates and college enrollment data—including the standards of proficiency exams—from the late nineteenth and early twentieth centuries. Across the board, college enrollment was limited to the "upper" classes until well into the twentieth century. See Thomas D. Snyder, ed., *120 Years of American Education: A Statistical Portrait* (Washington, DC: U.S. Department of Education, 1993).

5 See J. Michael Sproule, "Inventing Public Speaking: Rhetoric and the Speech Book, 1790–1930," *Rhetoric and Public Affairs* 15 (2012): 563–608.

6 See Cohen, *History*, 13.

7 Winans' 1915 call to better the status of public speaking as a field was widely heeded. See J.A. Winans, "The Need for Research," *Quarterly Journal of Speech* 1 (1915): 17–23.

8 The teaching of "expression" was the early twentieth-century term for what passed as "elocution" a century prior, which the Irish stage actor Thomas Sheridan popularized in his *Lectures on Elocution* in 1762. The core belief behind elocution and, later, expression was that written communication failed to convey the complexity of the human "passions" and only a scientifically based study of human voice and gesture could disclose the "infinite variety of the emotions of the mind." Such a study could then be formalized into delivery techniques that could be taught to actors and public speakers. Over the nineteenth century the study of elocution was further popularized by Irishman

Gilbert Austin's complex notational system for gesture, and later, Francoise Delsarte, a French acting teacher who linked the "Art of Oratory" to an exceedingly complex taxonomy of gesture that aimed toward spiritual awakening. See Thomas Sheridan, *A Course of Lectures on Elocution*, in *The Rhetorical Tradition: Readings from the Classical Times to the Classical Times to the Present*, ed. Patricia Bizzell and Bruce Herzberg (Boston: Bedford/St. Martin's, 1990): 732; and Cohen, *History*, 2–8.

9 See Cohen, *History*, 1–12.

10 Keith, *Democracy*, 38.

11 Cohen, *History*, 28.

12 See for example, Barnet Baskerville, "I Teach Speech," *Bulletin of the American Association of University Professors* 39 (1953): 58–69; and W.M. Parrish, "Elocution—A Definition and a Challenge," *Quarterly Journal of Speech* 43 (1957): 1–11.

13 J.P. Ryan, "Terminology: The Department of Speech," *Quarterly Journal of Speech Education* 4 (1918): 6.

14 These claims are not new, we recognize. "The search for . . . intellectual respectability unavoidably," argues Bruce E. Gronbeck, "had serious gender and class implications." Bruce E. Gronbeck, *Paradigms of Speech Communication Studies: Looking Back Toward the Future*, The Carroll C. Arnold Distinguished Lecture, National Communication Association, New York, November 21, 1998.

15 Henry E. Bliss, "The Subject-Object Relation," *The Philosophical Review* 26 (1917): 395–408.

16 Rene Descartes, *Philosophical Essays*, trans. Laurence J. Lafleur (New York: Macmillan, 1964): 76.

17 Theodor W. Adorno, "Subject and Object," in *The Essential Frankfurt School Reader*, ed. Andrew Arato and Eike Gebhardt (New York: Continuum, 2002): 498.

18 See Bryan S. Turner, "Discipline," *Theory, Culture & Society* 23 (2006): 183–186.

19 Immanuel Kant, "On a Newly Arisen Superior Tone in Philosophy," trans. Peter Fenves, in *Raising the Tone of Philosophy*, ed. Peter Fenves (Baltimore: Johns Hopkins University Press, 1993): 51–81; Florian Znaniecki, "The Object Matter of Sociology," *The American Journal of Sociology* 32 (1927): 529.

20 Jean Piaget introduced the idea of "object permanence" as one of the most important cognitive developments of infants; it refers to the moment a child realizes that external objects have a separate identity or existence independent of her, which occurs in concert with motor development, and which is central to the emergence of self-conscious subjectivity. "Object constancy," as developed by thinkers in the Object Relations school of psychoanalysis—and most notably by Margaret Mahler—refers to the realization that the primary parent or "other" is a separate individual. Permanence concerns inanimate objects, whereas constancy refers to people. When referring to academic fields, we prefer to discuss the never-ending discussion of their objects as a problem of "object constancy" because of the emphasis on—if not obsession with—paternal metaphors in regard to legacy and work of a field's pioneers, advisors, mentors, and so forth. See Jay R. Greenberg and Stephen A. Mitchell, *Object Relations in Psychoanalytic Theory* (Cambridge, MA: Harvard University Press, 1983): esp. 270–303.

21 One of us has developed this argument more fully in respect to the object of "rhetoric." See Joshua Gunn, "Size Matters: Polytoning Rhetoric's Perverse Apocalypse," *Rhetoric Society Quarterly* 38 (2008): 82–108.

22 Dilip Parameshwar Gaonkar, "Object and Method in Rhetorical Criticism: From Wichelns to Leff and McGee," *Western Journal of Speech Communication* 54 (1990): 290–316.

23 Scott was fond of saying this in his graduate seminars at the University of Minnesota. In personal communication, he remembered he borrowed the phrase from his late friend and philosopher H.E. Mason, who often said that "every philosophy department should inscribe 'In the beginning is the error' over the door, because until we catch someone making an error, we cannot say anything at all."

24 Gerry Philipsen, "The Early Career of Rise of 'Speech' in Some Disciplinary Discourse, 1914–1946," *Quarterly Journal of Speech* 93 (2007): 352–354.

25 Ryan, "Terminology," 9.

26 Philipsen, "The Early Career," 353.

27 Ryan, "Terminology," 9.

28 See E.L. Hunt, "The Scientific Spirit in Public Speaking," *Quarterly Journal of Public Speaking* 1 (1915): 185–193; and C.H. Woolbert, "The Organization of Departments of Speech Science in Universities," *Quarterly Journal of Public Speaking* 2 (1916): 64–67.

29 Joshua Gunn and Jenny Edbauer Rice, "About Face/Stuttering Discipline," *Communication and Critical/Cultural Studies* 6 (2009): 216.

30 Charles Henry Woolbert, "Psychology from the Standpoint of a Speech Teacher," *Quarterly Journal of Speech* 16 (1930): 9.

31 Baskerville, "I Teach Speech," 58–59.

32 Baskerville, "I Teach Speech," 60.

33 Baskerville, "I Teach Speech," 68.

34 Baskerville, "I Teach Speech," 69.

35 Baskerville, "I Teach Speech," 60.

36 Carl H. Weaver, "A History of the International Communication Association," *Communication Yearbook* 1 (1977): 607–618.

37 The description is from Baskerville, "I Teach Speech," 60. For a careful overview of the discussions at this conference, see David Zarefsky, "On Defining the Communication Discipline," in *Toward the 21st Century: The Future of Speech Communication*, ed. Julia T. Wood and Richard B. Gregg (Cresskill, NJ: Hampton Press, 1995): 102–112.

38 John W. Bowers, "The World Will Never Believe This!" Email post to CRTNET, August 21, 1996. CRTNET is an electronic discussion and announcement service sponsored by the National Communication Association.

39 See William F. Eadie, "Stories We Tell: Fragmentation and Convergence in Communication Disciplinary History," *The Review of Communication* 11 (2011): 161–176.

40 Frank E.X. Dance, "Name Change Once Again," Email post to CRTNET, August 22, 1996.

41 Dance, "Name Change."

42 The shift in norms of discourse, including tone and issues of formality, has been widely discussed. Drawing on the theories of Jacques Lacan and Slavoj Zizek, Jodi Dean describes the increasing informality of online discourse and trend toward righteousness (and rudeness) as a consequence of the "decline of symbolic efficiency," which is inclusive of a mistrust of authority. See Jodi Dean, *Blog Theory: Feedback and Capture in the Circuits of Drive* (Boston: Polity Press, 2010).

43 Bruce E. Gronbeck, "Supporting a Change," *Spectra* 25 (March, 1989): 3.

44 Frank E.X. Dance, "Opposing a Change," *Spectra* 25 (March, 1989): 4.

45 Michael Burgoon, "Instruction About Communication: On Divorcing Dame Speech," *Communication Education* 28 (1989): 303–304.

46 Burgoon, "Instruction," 305.

47 Burgoon, "Instruction," 308, n. 2.

48 Burgoon, "Instruction," 305.

49 Benson ran CRTNET independently via email, and then with listserv software and computer support from Penn State. He gifted the National Communication Association the service in 1997. For a discussion of the most controversial CRTNET discussion, see Thomas W. Benson, "A Scandal in Academia: Sextext and CRTNET," *Western Journal of Communication* 76 (2012): 2–16.

50 David L. Sutton, "Rearranging the Deck Chairs," CRTNET, August 21, 1996.

51 Robert Ivie, "What Would a Name Change Mean?" CRTNET, August 21, 1996.

52 George Cheney, "Nomenclature," CRTNET, August 22, 1996.

53 James F. Klumpp, "SCA Name Change," CRTNET, August 22, 1996.

54 P. DeCaro, "IBA," CRTNET, August 22, 1996; Bill Scarborough, "Name of Organization," CRTNET, August 22, 1996.

55 Dance, "Name Change."

56 Also see Frank E.X. Dance, "Swift, Slow, Sweet, Sour, Adazzle, Dim: What Makes Human Communication Human," *Western Journal of Speech Communication* 44 (1980): 60–63.

57 Paul Turpin, "SCA/NCA Name Change," CRTNET, October 31, 1996.

58 James W. Chesebro, "Why We Need to Change Our Name to the National Communication Association," *Spectra* 32 (1996): 2.

59 Chesebro, "Why," 22.

60 In-person interviews were held with 1996 straw ballot letter signatories Roderick Hart, the SCA Finance Board Chair, and John A. Daly, the SCA Second Vice President. Email interviews and discussions were conducted with then president James W. Chesebro, Jo Sprague, Educational Policies Board Chair, and Isa Engleberg, SCA Research Board Chair.

61 James Hay's introduction to his first edited issue of *Communication and Critical/Cultural Studies* is suggestive of such antipathy; see James Hay, "Introduction," *Communication and Critical/Cultural Studies* 10 (2013): 1–9.

62 Bill Eadie, "Name Change," CRTNET, March 21, 1997.

63 Anthony E. Schiappa, "Can We Stop Griping?" CRTNET, March 28, 1997.

64 Dance has predicted as much: "Those interested in the study and practice of human communication may be wise to cease concentrating so much into a single term for a single concept and to move towards the construction of a taxonomy of terms for a family of concepts. Such a taxonomy and its conceptual family should provide a matrix of greater flexibility and richness than that which follows upon our stuffing everything we are interested in thinking about or doing about into a single box labeled 'communication.'" Dance, "Swift Slow, Sweet," 60. Also see Frank E.X. Dance, "The Concept of Communication," *Journal of Communication* 20 (1970): 201–210.

65 William M. Keith, "We are the Speech Teachers," *The Review of Communication* 11 (2011): 83.

66 See Barbara F. Reskin and Patricia A. Roos, "Feminization of Fields a Result of Several Factors," *The Chronicle of Higher Education,* September 25, 1991; Robin Wilson, "The Feminization of Anthropology," *The Chronicle of Education*, April 18, 2003. Studies on the perceived "feminization" of a discipline are based on the increasing number of female teachers and scholars, not the objects of study. There is little empirical evidence to demonstrate a strong correlation between prestige and the number of women in a given field; however, there does seem to be some correlation with salaries. Reskin and Roos explain a decline in prestige is more a consequence of the perception of a field's decline before the issue of female representation.

67 Adriana Cavarero, *For More than One Voice: Toward a Philosophy of Vocal Expression*, trans. Paul A. Kottman (Stanford: Stanford University Press, 2005), 6. Also see Joshua Gunn, "Gimme Some Tongue (On Recovering Speech)," *Quarterly Journal of Speech* 93 (2007): 361–364; and Joshua Gunn, "Speech is Dead; Long Live Speech," *Quarterly Journal of Speech* 94 (2008): 343–364.

68 One of us has also written about the underlying misogyny of calls for "rigor" in rhetorical studies. See Gunn, "Size Matters," 97–100. Also see Carole Blair, Julie R. Brown, and Leslie A. Baxter, "Disciplining the Feminine," *Quarterly Journal of Speech* 80 (1994): 383–409.

69 Mladen Dolar, *A Voice and Nothing More* (Cambridge, MA: MIT Press, 2006): 17.

70 See John Mowitt, *Radio: Essays in Bad Reception* (Berkeley, CA: University of California Press, 2011): esp. 21–47.

71 In the humanities, the resurgence of interest in voice has been under the aegis of "sound studies." In communication studies, see for example, Joshua Gunn, "On Speech and Public Release," *Rhetoric & Public Affairs* 13 (2010): 1–41; and Samuel McCormick and Mary Stuckey, "Presidential Disfluency: Literacy, Legibility, and Vocal Aesthetics in the Rhetorical Presidency," *Review of Communication* 13 (2013): 3–22.

72 Mowitt, *Radio*, 24.

73 Owing to their common history and rootedness in the body/speech, we would agree with Phaedra Pezzullo when she confesses she is "often not sure where performance 'ends' and rhetoric 'begins' or vice versa." In the service of resurrecting the kinds of questions that the disciplinary silencing of speech seemed to banish, we urge more and continued collaboration between rhetorical and performance studies scholars and a renewed reckoning with their shared origin. Phaedra C. Pezzullo, "Deterritorializing," *Text and Performance Quarterly* 34 (2014): 98. The entire first issue of the 34th volume (2014) of *Text and Performance Quarterly,* guest edited by Mindy Fenske and Dustin

Bradley Goltz, is devoted to identifying points of intersection between rhetorical and performance studies. Also see Stephen Olbrys Gencarella and Phaedra C. Pezzullo, *Readings on Rhetoric and Performance* (State College, PA: Strata Publishing, 2010).

74 Kendal R. Phillips, "A Rose by Any Other Name," CRTNET, August 21, 1996.

References

Adorno, Theodor W. "Subject and Object." In *The Essential Frankfurt School Reader*, edited by Andrew Arato and Eike Gebhardt, 497–511. New York: Continuum, 2002.

Baskerville, Barnet. "I Teach Speech." *Bulletin of the American Association of University Professors* 39 (1953): 58–69.

Benson, Thomas W. "A Scandal in Academia: Sextext and CRTNET." *Western Journal of Communication* 76, no. 1 (2012): 2–16.

Blair, Carole, Julie R. Brown, and Leslie A. Baxter, "Disciplining the Feminine." *Quarterly Journal of Speech* 80, no. 4 (1994): 383–409.

Bliss, Henry E. "The Subject-Object Relation." *The Philosophical Review* 26 (1917): 395–408.

Bowers, John W. "The World Will Never Believe This!" Email post to CRTNET, August 21, 1996.

Burgoon, Michael. "Instruction about Communication: On Divorcing Dame Speech." *Communication Education* 38, no. 4 (1989): 303–308.

Cavarero, Adriana. *For More than One Voice: Toward a Philosophy of Vocal Expression.* Translated by Paul A. Kottman. Stanford: Stanford University Press, 2005.

Cheney, George. "Nomenclature." CRTNET, August 22, 1996.

Chesebro, James W. "Why We Need to Change Our Name to the National Communication Association." *Spectra* 32 (1996): 2.

Cohen, Herman. *The History of Speech Communication: The Emergence of a Discipline, 1914–1945.* Annandale, VA: Speech Communication Association, 1994.

Dance, Frank E.X. "The Concept of Communication." *Journal of Communication* 20 (1970): 201–210.

——. "Name Change Once Again." Email post to CRTNET, August 22, 1996.

——. "Opposing a Change." *Spectra* 25 (March 1989).

——. "Swift, Slow, Sweet, Sour, Adazzle, Dim: What Makes Human Communication Human." *Western Journal of Speech Communication* 44, no. 1 (1980): 60–63.

Dean, Jodi. *Blog Theory: Feedback and Capture in the Circuits of Drive.* Boston: Polity Press, 2010.

DeCaro, P. "IBA." Email post to CRTNET, August 22, 1996.

Descartes, Rene. *Philosophical Essays.* Translated by Laurence J. Lafleur. New York: Macmillan, 1964.

Dolar, Mladen. *A Voice and Nothing More.* Cambridge, MA: MIT Press, 2006.

Eadie, Bill. "Name Change." Email post to CRTNET, March 21, 1997.

Eadie, William F. "Stories We Tell: Fragmentation and Convergence in Communication Disciplinary History." *The Review of Communication* 11, no. 3 (2011): 161–176.

Gaonkar, Dilip Parameshwar. "Object and Method in Rhetorical Criticism: From Wichelns to Leff and McGee." *Western Journal of Speech Communication* 54 (1990): 290–316.

Gencarella, Stephen Olbrys and Phaedra C. Pezzullo. *Readings on Rhetoric and Performance.* State College, PA: Strata Publishing, 2010.

Greenberg, Jay R. and Stephen A. Mitchell. *Object Relations in Psychoanalytic Theory.* Cambridge, MA: Harvard University Press, 1983.

Gronbeck, Bruce E. *Paradigms of Speech Communication Studies: Looking Back Toward the Future.* The Carroll C. Arnold Distinguished Lecture, National Communication Association, New York, November 21, 1998.

——. "Supporting a Change." *Spectra* 25 (March 1989): 3.

Gunn, Joshua. "Gimme Some Tongue (On Recovering Speech)." *Quarterly Journal of Speech* 93, no. 3 (2007): 361–364.

——. "On Speech and Public Release." *Rhetoric & Public Affairs* 13, no. 2 (2010): 1–41.

——. "Size Matters: Polytoning Rhetoric's Perverse Apocalypse." *Rhetoric Society Quarterly* 38 (2008): 82–108.

————. "Speech is Dead; Long Live Speech." *Quarterly Journal of Speech* 94, no. 3 (2008): 343–364.

Gunn, Joshua and Jenny Edbauer Rice. "About Face/Stuttering Discipline." *Communication and Critical/Cultural Studies* 6, no. 2 (2009): 215–219.

Hay, James. "Introduction." *Communication and Critical/Cultural Studies* 10, no. 1 (2013): 1–9.

Hunt, E.L. "The Scientific Spirit in Public Speaking." *Quarterly Journal of Public Speaking* 1 (1915): 185–193.

Ivie, Robert. "What Would a Name Change Mean?" Email post to CRTNET, August 21, 1996.

Kant, Immanuel. "On a Newly Arisen Superior Tone in Philosophy," translated by Peter Fenves. In *Raising the Tone of Philosophy*, edited by Peter Fenves, 51–81. Baltimore: Johns Hopkins University Press, 1993.

Keith, William M. *Democracy as Discussion: Civic Education and the American Forum Movement*. Lanham, MD: Lexington Books, 2007.

————. "We are the Speech Teachers." *The Review of Communication* 11, no. 2 (2011): 83–92.

Klumpp, James F. "SCA Name Change." Email post to CRTNET, August 22, 1996.

McCormick, Samuel and Mary Stuckey. "Presidential Disfluency: Literacy, Legibility, and Vocal Aesthetics in the Rhetorical Presidency." *Review of Communication* 13, no. 1 (2013): 3–22.

Mowitt, John. *Radio: Essays in Bad Reception*. Berkeley, CA: University of California Press, 2011.

Parrish, W.M. "Elocution—A Definition and a Challenge." *Quarterly Journal of Speech* 43, no. 1 (1957): 1–11.

Pezzullo, Phaedra C. "Deterritorializing." *Text and Performance Quarterly* 34, no. 1 (2014): 97–98.

Philipsen, Gerry. "The Early Career of Rise of 'Speech' in Some Disciplinary Discourse, 1914–1946." *Quarterly Journal of Speech* 93 (2007): 352–354.

Phillips, Kendal R. "A Rose By Any Other Name." Email post to CRTNET, August 21, 1996.

Reskin, Barbara F. and Patricia A. Roos. "Feminization of Fields a Result of Several Factors," *The Chronicle of Higher Education,* September 25, 1991.

Ryan, J.P. "Terminology: The Department of Speech." *Quarterly Journal of Speech Education* 4, no. 1 (1918): 1–11.

Scarborough, Bill. "Name of Organization." Email post to CRTNET, August 22, 1996.

Schiappa, Anthony E. "Can We Stop Griping?" Email post to CRTNET, March 28, 1997.

Sheridan, Thomas. *A Course of Lectures on Elocution*. In *The Rhetorical Tradition: Readings from the Classical Times to the Classical Times to the Present,* edited by Patricia Bizzell and Bruce Herzberg, 881–888. Boston: Bedford/St. Martin's, 1990.

Snyder, Thomas D., ed. *120 Years of American Education: A Statistical Portrait*. Washington, DC: U.S. Department of Education, 1993.

Sproule, J. Michael. "Inventing Public Speaking: Rhetoric and the Speech Book, 1790–1930." *Rhetoric and Public Affairs* 15, no. 4 (2012): 563–608.

Sutton, David L. "Rearranging the Deck Chairs." Email post to CRTNET, August 21, 1996.

Turner, Bryan S. "Discipline." *Theory, Culture & Society* 23 (2006): 183–186.

Turpin, Paul. "SCA/NCA Name Change." Email post to CRTNET, October 31, 1996.

Weaver, Carl H. "A History of the International Communication Association." *Communication Yearbook* 1 (1977): 607–618.

Wilson, Robin. "The 'Feminization of Anthropology." *The Chronicle of Education*, April 18, 2003.

Winans, J.A. "The Need for Research." *Quarterly Journal of Speech* 1 (1915): 17–23.

Woolbert, C.H. "The Organization of Departments of Speech Science in Universities." *Quarterly Journal of Public Speaking* 2, no. 1 (1916): 64–67.

————. "Psychology from the Standpoint of a Speech Teacher." *Quarterly Journal of Speech* 16, no. 1 (1930): 9–18.

Zarefsky, David. "On Defining the Communication Discipline." In *Toward the 21st Century: The Future of Speech Communication,* edited by Julia T. Wood and Richard B. Gregg, 102–112. Cresskill, NJ: Hampton Press, 1995.

Znaniecki, Florian. "The Object Matter of Sociology." *The American Journal of Sociology* 32 (1927): 529–584.

4.

EPISTEMOLOGICAL MOVEMENTS IN COMMUNICATION

An Analysis of Empirical and Rhetorical/Critical Scholarship

James A. Anderson and Michael K. Middleton

Introduction

This study analyzes one hundred years of empirical and rhetorical/critical scholarship in communication. The project traces the epistemological movements within the discipline's history as developed in its scholarly publications. Such an undertaking is no easy task; as Eadie (2011) notes, communication lacks a "unified history" which requires some boundary setting from the outset. While, like Eadie, one could divide the discipline into "the speech story," "the communication story," and "the journalism story," we believe that assessing the history of the discipline over a century of its development requires a contextualization made possible only when one looks at these stories in combination. Accordingly, while we recognize that journalism has a varied history of inclusion in and independence from the communication discipline proper, the archive we examined includes the major (i.e., flagship) journals that have sustained each of these threads of communications studies in its broadest sense.

Accordingly, our history of the discipline starts with the *Quarterly Journal of Public Speaking* first published by the National Association of Academic Teachers of Public Speaking in 1915 and the *Journalism Bulletin* first published by the American Association of Teachers of Journalism in 1924. We added *Speech Monographs*, which the Speech Association of America began publishing in 1934, and the *Journal of Communication*, inaugurated in 1951, by the National Society for the Study of Communication. Some may better recognize them by their contemporary names: the *Quarterly Journal of Speech* (*QJS*) and *Communication Monographs* (*CM*), published by the National Communication Association, *Journalism & Mass Communication Quarterly* (*J&MCQ*), published by the Association for Education in Journalism and Mass Communication, and the *Journal of Communication* (*JOC*), published by the International Communication Association.

Data for this study were selected from our repository of every article published by the journals during their publication history—9,182 total articles. The present study compares three time periods—1951–1960, 1975–1985, and 2001–2010. They are the earliest decade for which all four publications were active, more or less the middle, and the most recent span of publication.

Our analysis had a fourfold focus: criticism, rhetoric, metric empiricism, and interpretive empiricism.[1] We excluded articles that were historical in focus, policy essays, theater focused, or speech pathology oriented; but we included reviews, meta-analyses, methodological analyses, theory development—all of the support work, if you will. Studies outside those general boundaries were set aside for another day. Table 4.1 presents the total number of articles examined for each period by journal.

Finally, this chapter presents the heart of the data analysis within the space allotted. We refer the reader to a more extensive presentation of the data in *Epistemological Movements in Communication: Reference Tables* (referred to hereafter as "reference article") available at http://content.lib.utah.edu/cdm/ref/collection/uspace/id/8832.[2]

Table 4.1 Number of articles for each time period, type of scholarship, and journal of publication

Period	Type	CM	JOC	J&MCQ	QJS	All
1950s	Empirical	73	132	134	15	360
	Rhet/Crit	18	5	7	247	277
1975–1985	Empirical	211	382	438	37	1068
	Rhet/Crit	71	61	12	224	368
2000s	Empirical	218	413	425	1	1057
	Rhet/Crit	24	12	15	173	224

Note: As this table makes apparent, empirical articles outpace rhetorical/critical articles by a ratio of nearly 3:1. This ratio matches the rate of publication in our journals.

Theoretical Position

Our study is based roughly on Foucault's notion of the *episteme*.[3] For Foucault, human thought is supported by a prevailing Zeitgeist or set of underlying beliefs about the character of claim, evidence, and the argument that connects them. Scholarship within an episteme has a normative form relative to how certain kinds of claims are supported by certain kinds of argument. Over the course of a disciplinary history, beliefs and argument forms change. What constitutes evidence or discovery in one era can be considered misguided or foolish in another.

As with Foucault's development in *The Order of Things*, this project is not a history of ideas, a catalogue of contributions, or a genealogy of thought explaining how we got to the present.[4] Rather, we are looking at the flow of scholarly practice. Our level of engagement is much more "on the ground" than Foucault's archeology or even Kuhn's scientific paradigms.[5] This is a history of ordinary research and scholarly practice.[6]

It considers research as part of society's epistemological-industrial complex and publications as its industrial product. Good, bad, sustained, or dismissed, these articles are each the product of multiple hands (authors, reviewers, editors, colleagues, and readers).

Analysis

Our analysis involved a two-part process: first, we used a combination of a priori and emergent coding to classify the articles according to their epistemological location, theoretical lineage, the presence or absence of a specified theory within the argument, scholarly intention, form of argument, and topical focus. All but *specified theory* were a priori classifications. Subcategories for each of the other classifications were developed after the initial reading of the articles and added to, consolidated, and refined in the course of coding. Attributes were added at the point where the need for an addition was recognized. Once all articles had been coded and final code sets determined, all the articles were again coded with the final set. In that manner, all articles were read against the same code set. Code sets are available in the tables of the reference article.

Second, we used computer-based textual analysis to identify the major themes, concepts, and topics that were included in the articles. This process starts with simple word frequency lists that document the character of research practice, the concepts in use, and the most common topics. These lists were then compared over time to explore shifts in research foci. Finally, individual terms were "chased" through their references to explore their evolution. For example, the concept of frame stands as a necessary part of a presentation through the mid-1980s, but then becomes a deliberate bias of media outlets in the 2000s as if a presentation could be "unframed." Given the constraints of space, we highlight a significant selection of the thousands of terms available in the present study.

Classification of Sources

Epistemological Location

We used (co-author) Anderson's approach to defining the epistemological communities of the discipline.[7] There are four components in this approach to defining community boundaries. They are: the relative privilege accorded to observation and to reason, the presence or absence of a claim of generalizability, the material versus the social construction of knowledge (reality), and modern versus post-modern character of claim. The boundary setting functions of these components are shown in Figure 4.1.

Clockwise from the left in Figure 4.1, quadrant 1 represents covering law empirical research; quadrant 2 interpretive empirical research; quadrant 3 standpoint rhetorical/critical analysis and quadrant 4 formal, universal rhetorical/critical analysis. Experience-based and narrative-based arguments are located in North–South hemispheres in Figures 4.1 and 4.2. The East–West hemispheres further divide research according to modernist and post-modernist proclivities. Without belaboring the nuances of the

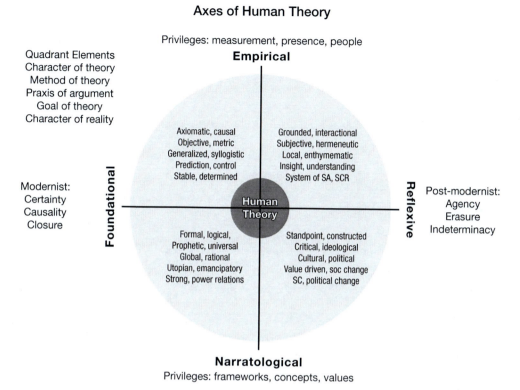

Figure 4.1 Epistemological quadrants by characteristics.

differences, it may suffice to say that modernist theories are foundational; they are seen as discoveries that provide a universal, transcendental, "final" statement about the nature of things. Post-modern theories are reflexive; they provide a contextualized narrative that captures a resonating understanding of things. Foundational theories are considered truthful; reflexive theories are considered to be standpoint-driven. Figure 4.2 locates the communities of practice in their typical quadrant locations.

EMPIRICAL ARTICLES

Over the sixty years, most work was taken from quadrant 1—the location for foundational, transcendental, truth claims, reaching 90% of all articles in the 2000s. There has been a doubling of interpretive work from one time period to the next, but it currently represents a little more than 5% of the total.

RHETORICAL/CRITICAL ARTICLES

Most rhetorical work occupied quadrants 3 and 4, reaching a combined 82% of all articles in the 2000s. Paralleling the growth of theoretical complexity in rhetorical research, interpretive empirical research has waned while marked increases in standpoint rhetorical and formal, universal rhetorical analysis has filled these gaps.

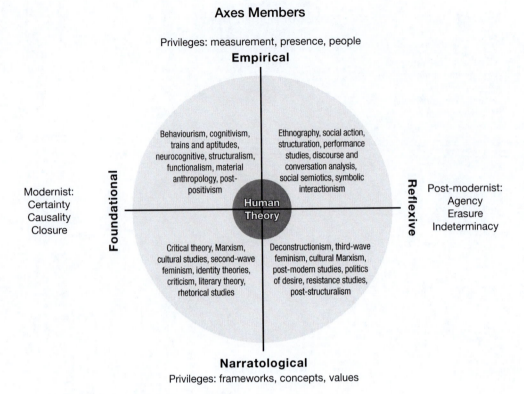

Figure 4.2 Epistemological quadrants by characteristic theories.

Theoretical Lineage

The large epistemologies depicted in the epistemological quadrants of Figure 4.1 direct disciplinarily-wide programs of work and would include multiple theories or theory-like claims. These theories and claims are themselves contained within theory families or perspectives that use common epistemological foundations and axiomatic positions. Cognitivism, for example, makes use of cognitive structures to predict behavior. Those cognitive structures, in turn, are developed through engagement with the world and through social processes. Similarly, criticism that depends on classical schema or an Aristotelian framework would have common elements. This section takes a step toward the particular from grand epistemology by examining the appearance of these theory families.

EMPIRICAL ARTICLES

The majority of the empirical work from the 1950s (63%) across all journals was produced from an unspecified, general empirical position. Given the historical moment, that position would represent a confluence of behaviorism and descriptive empiricism. Corresponding to the frequency of the general empirical position, 81% of the articles made use of no specific theory in their argument. Cognitivism was the next highest position. The very low report of social theories indicates that most work was psychological rather than sociological and based in methodological individualism.

Looking at specific journals, *CM*'s high report for cognitivism is the result of the emphasis on audiences' cognitive responses to messages signaled by words such as "perceptions," "attitudes," and the like. *JOC* shows the greatest diversity of positions, and, as might be expected, *J&MCQ* shows the highest proportion of "effects" studies. Nearly all of the effects studies from any journal or any time period could have also been coded as cognitivist.

Fifteen years later, cognitivism had eroded the lead of the general empirical position but was itself being siphoned by the rising popularity of social psychology. Social psychology uses nearly all the same terms as cognitivism, but is more specific in attributing the mechanisms of cognitive development to social practices. It is quite possible that most researchers would not distinguish among the three positions of cognitivism, social psychology, and effects except by name. Our coding followed their naming practices.

There is a slight increase in the diversity of theoretical positions during the 1975–1985 period, but not by much. In the 1950s, 91% of the articles came from the big four (general empiricism, cognitivism, social psychology, and effects); in 1975–1985, it is 87%. That 4% decline gets distributed in some way across ten other theory families. Despite much concern with a fermenting field, significant changes in the run of the scholarship mill seem to be much slower in their appearance within major journals.

The 2000s show a microscopic decline of the dominance of the big four, slipping to 86% of all articles. Yet cognitivism takes the top spot now, accounting for 40% of the articles, while general empiricism is second, followed by social psychology and effects. The rise of effects studies—by more than double—appears to be generated by a moral panic about video games. Social action, social justice, and critical issue arguments appear to have benefited most from the trickle down.

RHETORICAL/CRITICAL ARTICLES

On the rhetorical side of the ledger, the indelible influence of Classical/Aristotelian rhetorical perspectives dominates the disciplinary history of rhetorical study (i.e., it accounts for half the research examined in the 1950s and holds a top three position across all time periods). Alongside Aristotelian influences, the ascendancy of Burkean perspectives (expanding from 3% in the 1950s to 32% in the 1970s) and ideological/critical theories (over 40% in the 2000s) energized rhetorical/critical scholarship during the second half of the last century and into the new one.

Examining specific journals more closely, however, rhetorical scholarship's restive disposition toward a heavily public address-focused, Critical/Aristotelian perspective can be glimpsed. In the 1950s, the generously applied Classical/Aristotelian perspective informed over half the research occurring in mainstream journals. While a smaller portion of these articles overtly invoke Aristotle, the topical focus during the 1950s on public address (38%) underscores the dominant influence of classical Greco-Roman foundations on rhetorical study.

A decade and a half later, the contours of rhetorical scholarship reflected its encounters with theoretical foment, a proliferation of new scholars, and a decade of political turmoil. Equally, the emergence or coming debut of a broad array of regional journals and specialty journals (*Philosophy & Rhetoric, Rhetoric & Public Affairs*, etc.) opened space in the discipline's publishing flagships for marginal, insurgent, and critical voices to find an audience. And, the increasing appearance of rhetorically-oriented research in *JOC* and *J&MCQ* suggests a branching out of rhetorical scholars' interest and research foci.

Specifically, during the 1975–1985 period, an Aristotelian focus is surpassed by two theories that continue to dominate rhetoric into the twenty-first century: Burkean and ideological theories. This shift away from a narrow focus on rhetoric-as-(rational) persuasion is announced in the nearly 50% of publications from the period utilizing a non-Aristotelian framework. A forty-two-point drop in the influence of Classical perspectives on rhetoric that is distributed across a host of new theories, including fantasy theme, genre, metaphoric, movements/social change, "new rhetoric," and performance theories, reveals a tumultuous period of redefinition for rhetorical scholars.

The 2000s reveal the effects of the ascendancy of new perspectives in the 1975–1985 period; Burkean and ideological approaches still claim top five status and Classical/ Aristotelian theories fail to make up much of the ground lost during the middle period. Critical theories, theories reflecting a rethinking of the role of rhetoric (constitutive rhetoric), and standpoint theories (feminist, critical race, post-colonial, etc.) also move into the top ten most common approaches. Most significant, however, is the diminishing concentration of perspectives in rhetorical research. Whereas, in the 1950s, five theories accounted for over 80% of research conducted in the examined journals, by the 2000s that same proportion of the "run of the mill" was spread over ten theories, with no single theory enjoying the dominance of its Classical/Aristotelian predecessors.

For both empirical and rhetorical/critical scholarship, it is important to consider that by the time the middle period (1975–1985) ends, many new outlets were emerging. By the 2000s, these outlets are well-established scholarly publications. The effect on scholarly practice seems to be different across these two realms of scholarship; for the empiricist, the very slow growth of alternative theories in the mainline journals may be explained by the flight of such work to other publications.

For the rhetorician and critic, the story is a bit different. Over time one can glimpse a reversal. Marginal and novel theories begin moving toward the disciplinary center (i.e., its flagship publications) as "traditional" approaches gravitate toward niche publications. For example, during the earlier periods, theoretical innovation by rhetoricians was often distributed across many journals, both the flagship journals we examine, as well as regional outlets. As the discipline's history moves forward, however, flagship journals increasingly become the home for cutting-edge theoretical developments (e.g., *critical rhetoric* and the focus on *vernacular discourse* are coined in *CM*; a turn toward *counterpublics* and the study of *in situ* rhetorical performances are championed in *QJS*). Paralleling this increasing concentration of theoretical foment in flagship journals, the rise of specialty journals begins to sustain more traditional perspectives (e.g., *Rhetoric*

Society Quarterly, Rhetoric & Public Affairs, etc.). As such, with the passage of time, mainstream, flagship journals appear to increasingly become a magnet for "new" perspectives on rhetorical action, while traditionalists form communities around journals that foster a particular approach in rhetorical criticism.

Specific Theories

In the course of reading several thousand articles, it became clear that one of the processes the discipline was involved in was creating or appropriating particular named theories (e.g., agenda setting) and inserting them into the argument form. This practice seemed to be worth following; consequently, articles were tagged with this attribute.

EMPIRICAL ARTICLES

Because authors are quite liberal in their use of the term "theory," we were quite liberal in coding a theory present. A phrase like "management theory" with or without a specific reference would be coded as theory present. Despite that liberal application, most of the articles in the first two periods did not reference a particular theory (only 19% and 39% respectively), but by the 2000s the greater majority (71%) explicitly deployed theory. The denomination of explanation as theory seems to be a major work of empiricists during the time between 1985 and 2012. We searched all the articles from all sources during the 2000s time period on the word *theory* and alternate forms propagating across a ten-word context window: 972 (out of 1,057) sources with the word theory generated 11,180 references to theory. We examined those references and identified 311 unique theories. The same analysis run over the 1950s found sixty unique theories mostly imported from other disciplines. Only six of those theories move forward to the list of the 2000s. This is a staggering development of 305 theories in sixty years.

RHETORICAL/CRITICAL ARTICLES

Our treatment of rhetorical research was also quite liberal in assigning a theoretical position. While outright citation of, for example, Aristotle, Cicero, and others is far rarer than the coding would suggest, we chose to apply the Classical/Aristotelian label to articles that adopted a critical lens informed by the "rhetoric as the means of persuasion" perspective. This broad application of theoretical labels for our research purposes and the narrow range of types of rhetorical scholarship in the discipline's early years caused rhetorical scholarship, unlike its empirical fellow travelers, to reflect a strong connection to theories of persuasion, influence, and argumentation from the initial time period we examine (95% in 1950s). However, by the 2000s, what becomes apparent is that rhetoric embraces a culture of theory proliferation as readily, if not more so, as its empirical counterparts. For example, by the 2000s, twelve theories (Marxist, critical, Foucaultian, Queer, organizational, psychoanalytic, constitutive, feminist, narrative, hermeneutics, effects, New Rhetoric), largely unexplored in the 1975–1985 period, account for nearly 40% of rhetorical research during the most recent decade, and not one of those twelve claims greater than a 7% share of the total number of articles published in the 2000s.

Scholarly Intention

We used Boyer's (1990) fourfold classification of scholarship (with post-modern clari-
fications in parentheses)—discovery (invention), integration (consolidation), application
(engaged), and teaching—to begin to identify the scholarly intention and predominant
contribution of the articles we examined from each time period.

EMPIRICAL ARTICLES

In all time periods, empirical researchers were out to discover something, with *discovery*
accounting for 53% of all 1950s articles, 83% of 1975–1985, and 90% of all 2000s articles.
The 1950s showed a notable representation of articles that were applied or about teaching.
By the 2000s, these had all but disappeared. The primary non-discovery scholarship of
the later years was *integration*, which denotes reviews and meta-analyses.

RHETORICAL/CRITICAL ARTICLES

Utilizing theoretical knowledge to uncover better insights about rhetorical practice is
the most durable commitment in rhetorical scholarship. While the discovery of new
theoretical insights played a significant role in the 1950s (37%) and likely laid the
foundation for the aggressive exploration of new theories that could better illuminate
rhetorical practice that defined later periods, rhetorical scholarship has, in the main, been
defined as an enterprise of locating, "discovering," or poaching theoretical developments
to further refine disciplinary understanding of rhetoric. By the 1975–1985 time period,
a majority of research (56%) engaged in the work of applying these new perspectives to
extant rhetorical problems. And, by 2000, an explosion of imported theorizing from
psychoanalysis, continental philosophy, and elsewhere contributed to increasing this
trend (77%) within the rhetorical quarters of our discipline.

Form of Argument

Every epistemology has to have its praxeology and every theory its method. This
combination constitutes a particular form of argument. For example, the family of
cognitivism has an affinity for experiments and surveys while the social action theory
family exhibits an affinity for observation and participation. Similarly, traditional criticism
with its foundational coda of principles would approach the analysis of particular works
from those principles. The form of argument was identified by referencing each article's
resident theory and methodology combination.

EMPIRICAL ARTICLES

Forms of argument varied widely across the empirical articles we examined. In the 1950s,
CM was almost entirely filled with experimental work; *JOC* was quite self-conscious with
essays and analysis; *J&MCQ* showed a balance across surveys (always number one in
this journal), experiments, content analysis, and essay types.

By the 2000s, survey arguments are the dominant form in all (three) journals with
experiments and/or content analysis following second. We see a glimmering of quadrant

2 forms in case studies, ethnographies, qualitative surveys, as well as text, discourse, and conversation analysis. All of these alternative forms together, however, represent less than 15% of the total publications reviewed.

In the 1950s, rhetorical and critical analyses reflected the greatest diversity of argumentative forms, including a nearly even distribution of argument types in *QJS* during the period. However, the following two periods show a significant concentration toward criticism as the coin of the realm in rhetorical/critical scholarship.

Equally unsurprising given the theoretical foment in the rhetorical quarters of the discipline, theory building sustains second place by a large margin over case studies, histories, reviews, or other forms of scholarly argument. Indeed by the 2000s, all but 15% of the scholarship being performed by rhetorical and critical scholars is done so in the rubric of criticism or theory building/explication.

Topical Foci

We used a set of broadly defined topical attributes to sort the subject matter of the articles. The purpose was to be able to generate useful subgroupings of articles that had good separation from one another while still maintaining substantive differences between them. The coding goal here was:

(1) to use global topics that would house a large number of specific topics;
(2) to code only the central idea of the article; and
(3) to use only one code for the entire article.

The purpose of this coding approach was to be sensitive to large-scale topic changes over the sixty years rather than to code every individual topic.

An example of the difference can be seen with the empirical variable of "framing." The variable is absent in the 1950s but appears in 358 sources in the 2000s. It is coded, however, as a "communication variable" topic. Specific topics such as framing are easily accessed in the database, but there are potentially hundreds of them, making them nearly useless for comparison. It does mean, however, that all topics have considerable internal variation.

Twenty-two fairly broad topics provided coverage of the content (see Table 7 of the reference article). The top three for the 1950s were communication variables, business/policy/regulation, and instruction/teaching. For the middle period, the top three were communication variables, message characteristics/effects, and communication practices. The top three of the 2000s were media praxis/consequences, communication variables, and message characteristics effects. Communication variables signal a variable/analytical approach in which variables are the subject of an experiment or the topic of a survey. The focus on business is almost entirely related to media and becomes an "also ran" topic in the 2000s. And, as noted before, instruction and teaching all but disappear by the 2000s.

Message characteristics/effects show the continuing interest in message construction and its consequences. Most of this work is done from a "who says what to whom with what effect" approach appropriate to a perspective that assumes unproblematic content and audience interpretation. Media praxis and consequences adopt much the same position but shift the emphasis to the medium of presentation. Most of these articles fail to problematize content, audience, or medium. Television, for example, is simply television regardless of technology, practices of engagement, or contexts of use.

Communication practices of the 1975–1985 period are best understood when coupled with audience (number four in those charts). Together they would top the chart at 21% of the articles. There was a flurry of studies published concerning communication strategies and uses of technology. By the 2000s, the pair had declined to 11% of the total—despite the explosion of social media—whether absent as an interest or simply gone elsewhere.

The fifty years intervening between the three time periods saw the demise of listening, communication skills, and speech and hearing from the topic list and the introduction of organizational, gender, race identity, campaigns, and politics. But there are considerable differences across the three journals, which is to say that the communication discipline is not well represented in any of them. Rather each journal appeals to particular subsets of the discipline. For example, the top three topics of the 1950s account for 36% of all content but the top three of the 2000s account for 48% of all content, indicating an increased concentration.

RHETORICAL/CRITICAL ARTICLES

Thirty-eight broad topics captured the content foci of the articles examined across the journals and time periods we selected, which, given the nearly 900 articles that were examined, indicates a significant amount of consolidation during the coding process. Unlike its empirical counterparts, rhetorical criticism continues to be populated by many of the same topical foci across all the time periods. New critical and theoretical perspectives, however, provided the means to cast a broader net when identifying communicative activity worthy of research within the domain of rhetoric (e.g., visual rhetoric, organizational rhetoric, etc.), and a proliferation of topics paralleled the discipline's perspectival expansion. For example, in the 1950s, the three most common topics (public address, theater, language) accounted for 62% of the articles reviewed, while in the 2000s the top three topics accounted for only half as much (36%) of scholarship (public address, media, movements/social change). Likewise, newcomers in the 2000s reflected the critical shifts within rhetorical study, including the introduction of cultural studies, performance, gender/sexuality, race, citizenship, health, visual rhetoric, and engaged scholarship, which combined account for nearly 40% of the topical foci of research in the last decade.

Epistemological Character

Examination of the epistemological positioning of the articles has to proceed inferentially. Communication scholars, both empirical and rhetorical/critical, apparently consider their epistemological positioning "taken for granted" and not worthy of concern or comment. Only two empirical articles in the 1950s, twenty-four articles from 1975–1985, and forty-nine articles in the 2000s directly reference or explore epistemology. The remaining 2,410 articles are written from an "of course it's true" standpoint. Within the rhetorical/critical tradition, only four articles in the 1950s, fifty-nine in the 1975–1985 period (influenced largely by Scott's 1967 statement on epistemic rhetoric), and twenty-five articles in the 2000s directly reference or explore epistemology. The remaining 780 articles leave such determinations to be made by their reading audiences.

Empirical Articles

Fortunately, it is fairly easy to determine what the empirical standpoint might be, with 90% of the 1950s articles and 86% of the 2000s articles using a cognitivist, social psychological, general empirical, or effects theoretical stance and the majority from each time period using an experiment, survey, or content analysis form of argument. The cross tabulations of these categories showed 98% of the 1950s articles, 79% of the 1975–1985 articles, and 81% of the 2000s articles that met one of the classification requirements met one of the other classification requirements. Overall, 51% of all 1950s articles fell into the matrix; 69% of 1975–1985, and 68% of all 2000s articles were so classified. These journals focused early and have sustained that focus.

The implications of these findings would hold that, first, methodological individualism is the standpoint of choice. Methodological individualism holds that all argument must stem from the characteristics of the individual. In this body of work it appears as a psychological perspective generally hostile to or indifferent toward cultural, sociological, interactionist, and semiotic perspectives as well as critical issue standpoints, action research, social justice initiatives, and engaged scholarship. It is clearly modernist with causality being the gold standard of argument, a belief in the certainty of knowledge, and that questions can ultimately be fully answered, thereby reaching closure.

Second, an interrelated set of characteristics of this position provides the support for a typical methodology. Language is considered unproblematic, referentially secure, and ideationally representational. One can write a declarative sentence, and it will reliably mean the same to thousands of individuals in different situations and contexts (the practice of measurement scales). Ordinary behavior is considered to be self-produced formulations of possible acts under the governance of internal intentions (independent actors). And, of course, the foundational belief is that we are all the product of cognitive structures that develop with the engagement of the environment and common social practices. These structures will be reliably the same across individuals engaging similar environments (the "effects" position).

Given their belief in prior cognitive structures that initiate behavior, our authors would have difficulty with integrating agency into their formulations. Agency is a self-caused cause; it does not require a prior state. Acts without causes pose a deep challenge to cognitivism. Our authors do not, however, have the same problem with rationality—also presented as a sui generis, human capability. Rational thought is the unmarked standard against which all other cognitive processes are measured.

Third, evidence typically takes a metric form (even though empiricism does not have to deal with numbers), which brings in all the assumptions of quantification, operationalism, the relationship between theory and method, measurement, sampling, and statistical analysis. Along with these assumptions there are the usual slippages: self-fulfilling claims, solipsistic instrumentation, convenience sampling, use of improper error terms, the reach for causation from coincidence, positing individual change from group means, and so on. Statistical analysis has become increasingly robust over the sixty years (or arcane, depending on one's point of view). Nowhere was this more evident than in *CM* where the number of sources using some form of statistical argument rose from 44% in the 1950s to 78% in the 2000s.

Rhetorical/Critical Articles

Unlike their empirically oriented colleagues, grand claims about a dominant epistem-ological mooring are difficult to support in critical/rhetorical scholarship. In fact, over all but the earliest period we examine, no combination of theory family and form of argument, or even related theories, manages to claim more than a small plurality of published scholarly efforts. For example, in the 2000s, after a large uptake of critical theories into rhetorical projects, theoretical perspectives assuming a rational agent of communication remained nearly tied (26% of all articles surveyed) with research adopting critical approaches (33% of all articles surveyed) that challenged the privileged, rational rhetor that is the trademark of early rhetorical scholarship.

The picture of the discipline in the most recent decade also highlights a dramatic shift in scholarly activity. While empirical research in the 2000s continued to use the theoretical perspectives dominant in the 1950s, rhetorical scholarship eroded the 94% majority held by Classical/Aristotelian by nearly 70% (down to 26%) in the 2000s. Interestingly, all but 10% of this slide in prominence by Aristotelianism would appear to have occurred during the first twenty-five years of the span of time we examine (1950–2000): that is, by 1975–1985, Classical/Aristotelian and related theoretical foundations had already been reduced to accounting for only 37% of research in the discipline.

Thus, rhetorical scholarship has been carried forward by a much more restive cadre of scholars and has been erected on much more rapidly shifting epistemological foundations. These shifting foundations that underpin the rhetorical scholarship in our discipline organize around a few central questions that point to the contested (and evolving) commitments that shaped and continue to shape the rhetorical enterprise as defined by our flagship journals.

First, scholars operating within the rhetorical tradition struggle with an effort to satisfyingly conceptualize the nature of the rhetor. The prevailing trend suggests increasing dissatisfaction with the rhetor when conceived of as a rational agent. In other words, the notion that language is unproblematically deployed or referentially secure for an agent engaged in rhetorical action appears to become an increasingly less tenable position for scholars in the field. However, the remarkable endurance of this perspective (a quarter of research in the last decade) also suggests that the vestiges of early approaches to rhetorical study remain hard to fully dispense with despite the prevailing trend toward more critical, contextually-bounded standpoint-specific theories.

Second, the nature of language, the nuts and bolts of rhetorical practice, is increasingly problematized by scholars in the rhetorical tradition. The influx of critical, feminist, ideological, Marxist, and other perspectives undoes any unproblematic belief that language and its (in)effectiveness is within the agency of its practitioner/rhetorician. Rather, rhetoricians increasingly grapple with how representational systems, individual actions (through or in response to symbolic action), and the ability to participate in meaning-making are influenced by power dynamics defined by race, gender, class, and other axes of inequality.

Third, however, the rhetorical enterprise does cling to one common epistemological foundation: criticism is the undisputed coin of the realm in rhetorical research. The predominant form of evidence is the example(s), or more properly the exemplar(s). And, knowledge is built based on the critic's (hopefully) well-informed inferences made from the example. The downside is that methodology becomes a question of personality, individual perspective, and the amount of interpretive license one chooses to assume. As a consequence, the ability to verify or falsify rhetorical claims remains fuzzy across the sixty years examined. The production of knowledge takes on a horizontal character, expanding by adding to the breadth of perspectives on an ever-expanding range of rhetorical situations. Lost in this approach is a cultivation of depth of knowledge: that is, a sustained engagement or prolonged study of a particular rhetorical situation, strategy, or act.

Analysis of Central Concepts

We can demonstrate the effect of this epistemological positioning by examining the "tag clouds" that can be generated from the individual journals within a period, across periods, and over all journals across time periods. Tag clouds are visual representations of word frequency lists that highlight important concepts in play. In generating these word displays, we used the following rule: display the top hundred words comprised of four characters or more and not on the "excluded words" list (see Appendix A, reference article, for the list and an explanation of its artifacts). To support the interpretation of the tag clouds, we explored the terms on that list by examining the content units in which they appeared and their positioning within a cluster analysis.[8] This analysis generates thirty tag clouds, an equal number of cluster analyses, and 3,000 terms—far more data than we can present in this space. Consequently, we provide the tag clouds across all sources combined across the three time periods and explore a few critical terms. The reference article provides a more complete set of tag clouds.

Empirical Themes, Concepts, and Topics

Figure 4.3 presents the tag clouds drawn for all empirical articles from all sources across the three time periods.[9] The figure documents a remarkable change across the discipline. We lost most of our "Dame Speech" heritage[10] and traditional newspaper journalism.

1950s

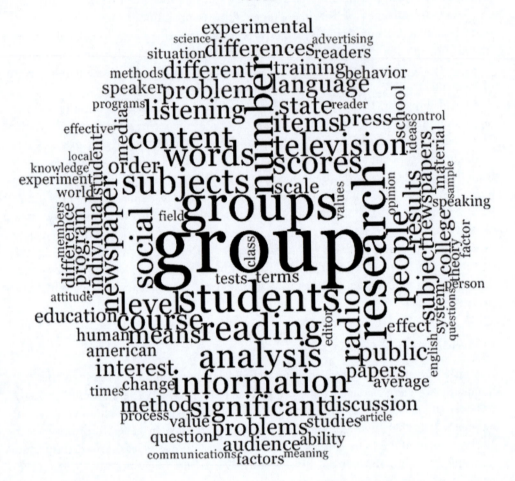

4.3(a) 1950s

Figure 4.3 Empirical tag clouds for all journals over the three time periods.

1975–1985

4.3(b) 1975–1985

2000s

4.3(c) 2000s

We are much more concerned about effects and media. In looking at the three graphics *media, effects, political*, and *public* indicate lively topical interests. *Research information* and *social* are less topical and more about language in use.

One has to be careful in drawing conclusions as to these common topics because terms change over time and across journals. The term *television* of the 1950s is not the television of the middle period or of the 2000s. Within journals, the term *women* is more likely to refer to a variable in *CM*, a cultural object in *JOC*, and a target group in *J&MCQ*. These differences correspond to the differences across journals with *CM* being variable-analytic, *JOC* being more open to alternative arguments, and *J&MCQ* having a concern for civic matters.

The terms for the 1950s show little topical convergence across the journals. The top ten terms *group, groups, research, students, number, reading, subjects, analysis, words*, and *information* are all indicators of language in use. Even *reading* is not a study of reading but rather a description of an activity. The current topical focus begins to emerge in the 1975–1985 period. The terms there—*media, television, research, social, information, group(s), public, analysis, children*, and *content*—show media, television, public, and children to be topics.[11] Finally, the 2000s show the terms *media, research, social, information, public, political, effects, analysis, content*, and *group*. Of these, *media, public, political*, and *effects* point to topics.

The tag clouds lead the authors to wonder if empirical researchers (and editors) are simply picking the low-hanging fruit. There are over 36,000 references to media in the 2000s but only 8,763 references to organization (in any of its variants) and just 5,182 to family. Both organizations and families are much more difficult to empirically study than media, but we spend much more time in those than we do with media. Apparently, a virtual world is to be preferred.

Rhetorical/Critical Themes, Concepts, and Topics

Figure 4.4 includes the tag clouds for the combination of all sources for each of the three time periods.

In surveying the clouds, each period highlights the importance of *public* rhetoric, as well as a focus on *rhetorical* criticism and history. Critical research will become more relevant as time passes. Likewise, topical interests that disappear and emerge, as well as become larger (more prominent), highlight the topical shifts and concentrations that emerge. *Stage, speeches*, and *theater* disappear; *women, culture, authority*, and *language* come to the forefront.

Analysis of the leading terms also provides the simple insight that *QJS* is the hegemonic center of rhetorical scholarship in the four flagship journals we examine. The top ten topics identified when all four journals are examined in combination are 93% identical with the top ten topics one uncovers when examining only *QJS*. This remains true across all three time periods, as well as within each individual period, with only slight changes in the order of topics. It would appear that, at least insofar as one is concerned with the subset of flagship journals we examined, if one wants to identify the trends of rhetorical study or find the data to predict the next phase in the discipline's dominant

1950s

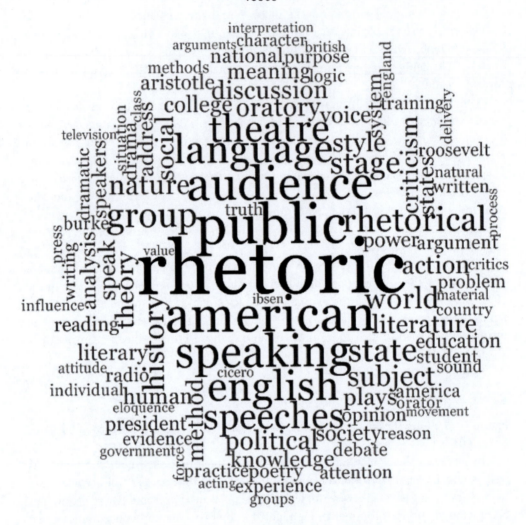

4.4(a) 1950s

Figure 4.4 Rhetorical/critical tag clouds for all journals over the three time periods.

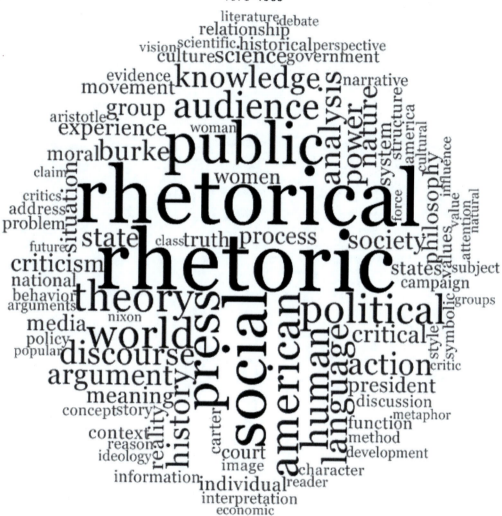

4.4(b) 1975–1985

4.4(c) 2000s

journals, one need not look beyond the rhetorical perspective's flagship publication to find the dominant guidance that is required. Nonetheless, it is important to consider that while *QJS* clearly sets the tone for the four journals we examine, a bevy of specialty and regional journals depart from, challenge, and (sometimes) help shift the foci of scholarship in *QJS* and that this broader tapestry of scholarly foment is beyond the scope of our present analysis.

Synthesis

Across all sources and all periods, an interesting trend becomes apparent in the discipline. Many of the topics that concern us, whether we are empiricists or rhetoricians, remain a constant topic of concern, and often they take on new meanings as the discipline evolves. For example, both "sides" of the discipline demonstrate a long-standing concern with the "political." However, what is more interesting is that for both sides of the discipline, the political shifts from a topical area (i.e., political speech) to a research vocation (i.e., politically-engaged research). Perhaps, this is simply explained by a shift in the way in which academics and the academy understand the ethics of research. It underlines, however, that communication researchers of every stripe seem committed to exerting socio-political influence on their domains of study.

Perhaps this suggests something that our examination of theory proliferation in both arenas does not. While we seem to be a restless discipline, importing ideas, adopting new perspectives, and trying out new research strategies, we seem to maintain a few consistent guiding commitments. The commitment to practical knowledge seems enduring through time and omnipresent across journals. The focus on political forums and politicized research seems to be consistent and similarly framed across domains, time periods, and journals in our study. And, the impulse toward inclusivity of marginalized standpoints, identities, and communicative/rhetorical actions seems to occur in similar density across time periods and publication outlets.

Absences

In the early stages of this project a reviewer recommended that we be particularly attentive to what was absent from the core literature. And, like the analysis of the *present* central concepts, the *absent* central concepts are interesting both in their diversity and in the points of synthesis between the two data sets.

Empirical Absences

The empirical mill has been addressing relatively particular questions while eschewing the search for large answers. It operates like a mosaic tile factory churning out bits and pieces (mostly red, white, and blue) with no big picture in mind. There is virtually no *theory* of the media, no narrative theory, no theory of reception, no theory of interpretation, no theory of the audience – though much study of these things. There is little *theory* of relationships, interaction, social practices, structurations, or emotions. The

Internet and social media have a cautionary, slight presence, as if the entire discipline had not been paying attention for the last ten years. And, as we have seen in the overview, there is scant cultural theory, social theory, social action theory, critical issue theory, psychoanalytic theory, or semiotic theory (and dare we even think of phenomenology?).

None of this is to claim that these topics were not addressed (even phenomenology) in these four journals or even extensively elsewhere. It is to say that they were not theorized. Studies of relationships, for example, used ipsative definitions for the relationship being studied, asking respondents to "recall their present or most recent" relationship. With that relationship salient, the respondent would be asked to complete a set of scales on, say, goals, styles, maintenance strategies, values, influence, and/or the like. In these sorts of studies, we learn about correlated characteristics of relationships but nothing of what a relationship is. Uncertainty reduction theory, for example, does not theorize the nature of the relationship in which uncertainty might develop.

We can see Weber's (among others) epistemological concept of *Verstehen* at work in this approach.[12] In this German philosophic principle, humans are privileged interpreters of human experience. We experience relationship, and, from this experience, we can understand the relationships of others: no need to speak of it.

All of these absences are quite predictable given the historical precedent and current zeitgeist of these journals. We have seen from the 1950s that communication scholars are not afraid to rush in despite an absence of theoretical foundation, collecting data on the basis of available measurement alone. The ruler precedes the concept of dimension in this approach. As general empiricism resolved itself into a dominant cognitivism in these journals, all other positions have the extra burden of justification and the extra work of creating the space for their presence. Both authors and readers who might not sustain the cognitivist position, therefore, migrate away from these journals, and associations tend to appoint editors of them who support that position. The result is that there is most likely no place where an empirically minded student of the discipline can go to engage the discipline writ large. The cost is that we, and our students, are no longer communication scholars but are rather one of the multiple kinds of communication scholars.

There are a number of speculations that can be raised in comment: the low threshold of evidence required to claim a theory from an empirical result leads to the ready development of particular theory. At the same time, large theory may well require a fulsome resource of particular theory—have to have the pieces before the big picture can be formed. We may be too young to have large theory. The fractionalization of the discipline plays its part in gathering congregations of scholars who write like-mindedly to each other and in controlling access to content. Finally, ours is the first meta-analysis, of which we are aware, that has searched across the discipline without topic limitation. Other meta-analyses are directed toward particular domains (e.g., media violence). Consequently, this may be the first empirical notice of these absences.

Rhetorical Absences

For the rhetoricians among us, our discipline is also consistently focused on the effective message, the great oratory, the influential movement, and the practiced rhetorician.

From beginning to end, the time periods we examined lack a sustained theory of the rhetoric of the everyday: an effort to make sense of rhetorical failures/ineffectiveness is absent despite being woefully too common in our lived experiences. Rhetorical scholars seem to have little patience for critiquing the experiences many of us are more likely to have had or the situations in which many of us are more likely to encounter rhetoric.

This may suggest a fundamental flaw. Rhetorical research, as our analysis suggests, is criticism driven, and criticism requires texts. Perhaps this reveals rhetoric's most troubling failure: its effort to capture rhetoric in a stable, (entirely) analyzable form defined as the exemplar text leaves it unequipped to engage with the reality of "live" and lived rhetorical phenomena. It is not difficult to advance the argument that rhetoric is aimed at identifying and improving the way we "do things with words" in both the halls of political power and the back-alleys of everyday life. If accepted as true, then what remains underdeveloped in rhetorical study is a deliberate, sustained engagement with the question of how we might come to understand rhetorical practice in the more mundane and common of these two venues. To maximize what is possible for a rhetorical research program with an orientation toward the everyday requires that the absences found in this study increasingly become the foci of a new wave of rhetorical theorizing.[13] Glimmers of these efforts emerge in the articles we examine as rhetoricians begin to focus their critical lens on vernacular texts and embark on efforts to map the terrain of everyday rhetorical practice. Nonetheless, we remain cautious in our optimism, at least insofar as mainstream journals represent trends in the discipline, because such developments remain remarkably inadequate to the influence exerted by everyday rhetorics.

Some Observations

As the mill is still running, we cannot offer conclusions; our disciplinary project continues. Nonetheless, after spending nearly a year on this research, some profitable observations can be made. We start by noting two cautions: Our study does not take into account the proliferation of alternative venues for publications within the discipline, as well as the increasing number of more specialized journals with more or less direct links to the communication discipline. It is certainly true that different search techniques would produce modified results, but they would also lack the historical perspective provided by these journals, and, as well-read scholars, we do not believe there is a hidden cache of the "good stuff" somewhere that would markedly change our conclusions. Second, one should not take from our analysis that rhetoric is the space of creativity and inventiveness, and empiricism is the space of repetition and dullness. It's both more encouraging and more depressing than that as the following comments will point out.

In general, our analysis reveals a fairly narrow range of focus and a limited amount of expansion in disciplinary scholarship, especially in empirical research. The discipline has chased changing technology and forums of rhetorical practice while asking the same questions. Empiricists have, for example, reprised the concern over violence in the media for every new medium since the penny arcade. Rhetoricians have, by the same token, applied Aristotle's rhetorical proofs to every rhetorical situation imaginable. At the same time we have neither arrived at a compelling argument of how the engagement of violent narratives translates into violent behavior, nor found a way to reliably prevent audiences from being hoodwinked by the wily rhetorician peddling false *ethos*.

Similarly, there is nothing in our theoretical tool kit that would have predicted social media, its influence on our political discourses and deliberative practices, or that can predict the directions it will take. And as technology changes and the forums of our rhetorical engagements shift, some of our best beloved theories show their limitations—four functions of the press, agenda setting, on the one hand, and Aristotelian rhetoric, rational argumentation on the other; all are at risk.

And, as the discipline has matured, the contours of our arguments reflect both its growth and the increasing integration of our disciplinary community. For example, while constructing the tag cloud graphics for the 2000s set, dates began to appear as part of the top 150 occurring words in the word frequency lists. Analysis of this phenomenon showed that it was a function of the greatly enlarged use of citations and references. This result indicates that the discipline has moved from using a few strategic references to advance a claim to wholesale lists in the constitution of its arguments. It may well be profitable to investigate this change, perhaps as a form of academic social networking. Apparently, it takes a village to write an article.

Finally, some food for thought for the empirically minded: Four years ago, Erik Timmerman introduced a forum in *Communication Monographs* that addressed the question "Has communication research made a difference?"[14] It is the sort of question that if it can be legitimately asked, the answer may not be one we like. One cannot imagine a similar question appearing in the *Journal of Organic Chemistry*. Equally concerning, Celeste Condit, in the same journal, reminds us that for scholars in the rhetorical camp, "original theories of [and epistemological positions in] communication [are] underwhelming."[15] As a community that is seemingly "rotten with imperfection" and "goaded by the negative," she suggests rhetorical scholars have become locked into criticism and have failed, by and large, to take up the challenge to invent new concepts, new modes of inquiry, and new habits of thinking and knowing about rhetoric.

Our analysis confirms the position of both scholars and expands it. Communication research (both empirical and rhetorical), while significantly more sophisticated than at the beginning of the sixty years our study examines, remains an unduly staid undertaking. Let's hope Timmerman's question can't be asked, and that Condit's critique can't be levied as strongly, in the next sixty years.

Notes

1 Metric empiricism depends on the processes of quantification for its arguments, resulting in statistical evidence; interpretive empiricism depends on the processes of interpretation, resulting in narrative evidence. Likewise, we distinguish criticism/rhetoric from empiricism based on whether claims are derived from the treatment of text(s) versus claims derived from the examination of metric or observational data. While recent trends that mix rhetorical and ethnographic approaches blur these lines, we believe it provides a useful distinction for organizing our present analysis.

2 The data tables follow the order of the chapter narrative.

3 Michel Foucault, *The Order of Things* (New York: Vintage, 1966/1994).

4 Foucault, *The Order of Things*.

5 Michel Foucault, *The Archeology of Knowledge* (New York: Vintage, 1969/2010); Thomas S. Kuhn, *The Structure of Scientific Revolutions* (Chicago: University of Chicago Press, 1962).

6 James A. Henretta, "Social History as Lived and Written," *The American Historical Review* 84, no. 5 (1979): 1293–1322; Raymond Williams, "Base and Superstructure in Marxist Cultural Theory," *New Left Review* 82 (1973): 3–16.

7 James A. Anderson, *Communication Theory: Epistemological Foundations* (New York: Guilford, 1996); James A. Anderson, *Media Research Method: Understanding Metric and Interpretive Approaches* (Los Angeles: Sage, 2012); James A. Anderson and Geoff Baym, "Philosophies and Philosophic Issues in Communication, 1995–2004," *Journal of Communication* 54, no. 4 (2004): 589–615.

8 Word frequency lists and tag clouds both depend on effective "excluded word" lists, otherwise artifacts of syntax, grammar, and the publication venues would overwhelm their explanatory value. This, of course, creates situations where concepts like "speech" and "communication" are absent in the tag clouds even though central to the discipline because their use as concepts is conflated with their use as publication identifiers. Our excluded word list is available in the reference article. It should also be noted that within empirical articles, *QJS* effectively disappears as an influence in empirical research by the 2000s, and from the rhetorical side, *J&MCQ* has a limited presence in rhetorical/critical scholarship.

9 Readers are cautioned not to connect words—all words are individual.

10 Michael Burgoon, "Instruction about Communication: On Divorcing Dame Speech," *Communication Education* 38 (1989): 305–308.

11 In this period and in the 2000s only about 10% of the references to content are explained in the conjoint term of content analysis.

12 A.M. Henderson, T. Parsons, and M. Weber, *The Theory of Social and Economic Organization* (New York: Oxford University Press, 1947).

13 M.K. Middleton, S. Senda-Cook, and D. Endres, "Articulating Rhetorical Field Methods: Challenges and Tensions," *Western Journal of Communication* 75 (2011): 386–406.

14 C.E. Timmerman, "Forum Introduction: Has Communication Research Made a Difference?" *Communication Monographs* 76, no. 1 (2009): 1–19.

15 C.M. Condit, "You Can't Study and Improve Communication with a Telescope," *Communication Monographs* 76, no. 1 (2009): 4.

References

Anderson, James A. *Communication Theory: Epistemological Foundations.* New York: Guilford, 1996.
——. *Media Research Method: Understanding Metric and Interpretive Approaches.* Los Angeles: Sage, 2012.

Anderson, James A. and Geoff Baym. "Philosophies and Philosophic Issues in Communication, 1995–2004." *Journal of Communication* 54, no. 4 (2004): 589–615.

Anderson, James A. and Michael K. Middleton. "Epistemological Movements in Communication: Reference Tables." Salt Lake City: University of Utah, 2014. Accessed April 14, 2014 from: http://content.lib.utah.edu/cdm/ref/collection/uspace/id/8832.

Boyer, Ernest L. *Scholarship Reconsidered: Priorities of the Professoriate.* Princeton, NJ: Princeton University Press, 1990.

Burgoon, Michael. "Instruction about Communication: On Divorcing Dame Speech." *Communication Education* 38 (1989): 305–308.

Condit, Celeste M. "You Can't Study and Improve Communication with a Telescope." *Communication Monographs* 76, no. 1 (2009): 3–12.

Eadie, William F. "Stories We Tell: Fragmentation and Convergence in Communication Disciplinary History." *Review of Communication* 11, no. 3 (2011): 161–176.

Foucault Michel. *The Archeology of Knowledge.* New York: Vintage, 1969/2010.
——. *The Order of Things.* New York: Vintage, 1966/1994.

Henderson, A.M., Talcott Parsons and Max Weber. *The Theory of Social and Economic Organization.* New York: Oxford University Press, 1947.

Henretta, James A. "Social History as Lived and Written." *The American Historical Review* 84, no. 5 (1979): 1293–1322.

Kuhn, Thomas S. *The Structure of Scientific Revolutions.* Chicago: University of Chicago Press, 1962.

Middleton, Michael K., Samantha Senda-Cook, and Danielle Endres. "Articulating Rhetorical Field Methods: Challenges and Tensions." *Western Journal of Communication* 75 (2011): 386–406.

Scott, Robert L. "On Viewing Rhetoric as Epistemic." *Communication Studies* 18, no. 1 (1967): 9–17.

Timmerman, C. Erik. "Forum Introduction: Has Communication Research Made a Difference?" *Communication Monographs* 76, no. 1 (2009): 1–19.

Williams, Raymond. "Base and Superstructure in Marxist Cultural Theory." *New Left Review* 82 (1973): 3–16.

5.

THE SCHOLARLY COMMUNICATION
OF COMMUNICATION SCHOLARS

Centennial Trends in a Surging Conversation

Timothy D. Stephen

The periodical literature of the academic field of human communication studies is now one hundred years old and is constituted of more than 65,000 articles, each of which comprises a formal contribution in a consequential, ongoing process of self-definitional discourse within the global community of communication scholars. The recent rapid multiplication of the number of articles published and the number of journals serving the field as well as changes in topical focus of the field's directions of interest provide a challenge for tracking this process of discourse, historically and in the present. In recent years the pace and extent of change has been so great as to likely leave many communication scholars unaware of evolving currents in scholarly conversation occurring beyond the boundaries of their own specialties. As Wolfgang Donsbach has asserted, "the field grows faster than the capacity of the average scholar to process and digest information."[1] This dynamic promotes fragmentation in the field. Tracking the field's trends in scholarly discourse is useful not only in the problem of tracing the historical roots of the field's topics of engagement, but also in efforts to identify significant areas in the field's current focus, which, as Pat Gehrke asserts, serves as a primary frame for all discussion of what comprises valid and consequential contribution.[2]

The study of the formal communication of communication scholars is useful not only to individual scholars attempting to position their contributions within a rapidly diversifying stream of professional discourse, but such study is also useful to practical problems of department planning and disciplinary self study. Dale Bertelsen and Alan Goodboy, for example, have noted the importance of understanding the shifting trends of emphasis within the discipline so that departments can assess the extent to which curriculum is keeping pace with the changing focus of the field's discourse.[3] Indeed, Thomas Hollihan documented significant controversy during the design of the most recent NCA doctoral program reputational study over the question of the discipline's main areas of intellectual engagement.[4] In dispute was the question of whether the nine areas identified validly represented the field's significant current interests. Disagreement was strong enough that some departments chose to withdraw from the study. As the field has expanded and diversified and as its rate of change has accelerated, there is increasing value in systematic study of the directions of the field's engagement of ideas as manifest in its formal scholarly communication.

Perhaps more than most academic disciplines, the modern field of human communication studies has multiple points of origin and permeable boundaries so that there will likely be exceptions to any attempt to characterize its current status or its history in simple terms.[5] Indeed, controversy over where the field's boundaries lie may be inevitable. As Robert Craig has pointed out, communication is a "variable-oriented" field, rather than a "levels-oriented" field, which means that its subject matter may cross disciplinary boundaries more often than some of its sister disciplines.[6] Beyond this, at least in the United States, the field retains, among other sources, deeply rooted interests in humanistic scholarship, applied practice, and in areas of performance and critique. Yet, while the discipline may encompass a sufficiently diverse range of concepts, perspectives, and organizational tributaries to be difficult to formulate neatly or in economical terms, it can be defined in practical terms. Many contemporary scholars working in academic communication departments—departments of communication, telecommunication, speech, mass communication, rhetoric, and derivative names—recognize the field in its current manifestation as comprised of that body of scholars who, for the most part, tend to associate underneath the organizational umbrellas of the International Communication Association (ICA), the National Communication Association (NCA), the Association for Education in Journalism and Mass Communication (AEJMC), and the four US regional associations (the Western, Eastern, Southern, and Central communication associations). There are of course other communication-related professional societies, but membership in many of them tends to overlap this core set, and, indisputably, this core group of organizations has the longest and broadest history of influence in the field in its scholarly publication programs. The NCA and the AEJMC are the most deeply rooted among the larger of these organizations, and, while the field traces its origins through multiple influences both in the United States and abroad (including, according to William Keith, nineteenth-century organizations of teachers of elocution[7]), a strong central component in that history is the founding in 1910 of the Eastern Communication Association, in 1912 of the AEJMC, then known as the American Association of Teachers of Journalism, and in 1914 of the NCA, then known as the National Association of Academic Teachers of Public Speaking (NAATPS). Thus defined, the field, now at its centennial mark, has been predominantly centered in the United States, Canada, and Europe and there are signs of active international expansion, particularly, but not exclusively, in Asia.

The communication field's first scholarly journal, the NAATPS's *Quarterly Journal of Public Speaking* (now, following other name changes, the *Quarterly Journal of Speech*), released its inaugural issue in April of 1915. In the following five decades, the emerging communication field was served by a small number of academic journals and the core of the field's scholarship was dominated by a humanities, education, and performance focus. Teachers of speech were concerned with formal public address as a practice, and scholarship in the area often addressed classical and historical reviews of writing about public speaking, trends in speech education, reviews of teaching techniques, and, occasionally, forays into theater performance, theatrical training, and topics in speech pathology and the physiology of speech production (e.g., stuttering). For the most part, this was not a research literature in the modern sense. Herman Cohen's history of the speech communication discipline elaborates this aspect of the evolution of the field through 1945.[8] Simultaneously, in the area of public opinion, propaganda studies, political communication, attitude change, and mass communication, prominent centers of study and traditions of research were taking shape independent of the NAATPS tradition.[9] However, as William Eadie has summarized, by the third quarter of the twentieth century, administratively, the field was well along in coalescing into its modern configuration.[10] At this time, the rate of its scholarly output began to accelerate significantly.

By the 1970s, the communication field had evolved into one whose divisions of research focus were gaining steam and diversifying rapidly. While retaining a core interest in rhetorical studies with ties to other humanities fields, the broad adoption of social science theoretical perspectives and research methodologies permitted scientifically inclined communication scholars to better integrate their own research and theory with relevant lines of inquiry in fields such as sociology, psychology, and anthropology.[11] There were as well by then securely established associated applied fields including broadcasting, theater, audiology, and public relations, and for the most part these applied fields had become autonomous. At present, according to the NCA's research, the primary divisions of emphasis in communication doctoral education are interpersonal communication, organizational communication, health communication, mass communication, critical/cultural studies, rhetoric, political communication, intercultural communication, and communication technology.[12]

The list of the changing circumstances of communication that have impacted potently up and down the spectrum of societal contexts in the last one hundred years is lengthy. It is difficult to think of any other academic field whose subject focus has evolved as rapidly or to any similar extent in this period of time. Keeping up with these changes presents a significant challenge, and, according to Robert Craig and David Carlone, "there continues to be a surprising lack of systematic data on the recent history of communication studies in U. S. higher education."[13] Now that the field, at least in its journal publication programs, has been visible for one hundred years, there are signs of interest in getting the story of the field's evolution sorted before time creates even more distance and renders the threads more difficult to gather. Many historical accounts have been offered in recent years. All these accounts are of value in elaborating and preserving the field's complicated history of professional discourse, but as a body they constitute a fragmented corpus of work. And as Keith has complained, "much of the historical materials we have so far ... tend toward reminiscence and anecdote."[14] There are exceptions to this in the body of work that has examined publication practices in the field at large and the history of publication in particular journals, and in some cases in particular areas of research. Such studies often employ some form of content analysis. However, when an author asserts that a tradition of thought was historically influential, it is common for the account to be grounded in authority, case example, and subjective impression.

To be sure, for a field so complexly comprised whose interests have shifted rapidly with changing technologies of communication and with the changing social, political, and economic circumstances of the modernizing world, it is possibly more challenging than in other academic fields to conduct any type of non-fragmented data-driven assessment of the evolution of the focus of the communication field's intellectual dialogue, yet, as Eadie complains, "the disciplinary status of communication is hindered by the lack of a unified history."[15] Of course, it isn't certain how to credit such a complaint; perhaps in actuality the field's history is multilayered. Either way, in fact, the situation as regards data sources has recently improved in result of two factors:

(1) the creation of comprehensive databases representing the field's scholarly literature; and
(2) advances in techniques and tools for the analysis of digitized texts.

Thus, at this centennial moment in the field's history, a study was conducted capitalizing on these new resources, using techniques of automated textual analysis to track the shifting emphasis across time of particular key areas of focus in the field's legacy of scholarly publication: its formal scholarly communication. This study addressed the following research questions:

RQ1:   What changes have been evident in the communication field's rate and extent of journal publication productivity since the inauguration of its first continuing journal in 1915?
RQ2:   What changes have been evident in the communication field's scholarly focus as represented in its serial literature over the course of its history?
RQ3:   What are the divisions and interrelationships of the field's areas of scholarly focus as revealed by analysis of current journal-published scholarship in communication?

Answers to these questions may inform current professional practice, contribute to the development of a unified history of the field, and provide data that can serve as a baseline for future studies of the evolution of scholarly communication in the communication field.

Method

Data for the study were journal article records from the ComAbstracts database maintained by the Communication Institute for Online Scholarship (CIOS).[16] This database covers approximately 130 academic journals and annuals from the core literature of the communication discipline.[17] Coverage tends to be deep with the oldest records going to the original issue of the *Quarterly Journal of Public Speaking* in 1915. Coverage is restricted to contributions comprising original and significant scholarship, omitting, for example, book reviews (but not review essays), teaching materials, poll reports, impressions of conferences, course syllabi, bibliographies, and brief editorial statements. As of the time of this study, the ComAbstracts database contained approximately 70,000 records. However, about 3,000 of the records are for academic books in communication and these were excluded from analysis since ComAbstracts' coverage of books tends to be no deeper than the last twenty years.

The majority of records in the ComAbstracts database are coded using a closed dictionary of classification terms developed by the CIOS. This system was derived from statistical study of word usage in the titles of articles in the core communication literature as described by Timothy Stephen.[18] Within the communication discipline, article titles are predominantly constructed within the tradition of APA style so that a title tends to function as a mini-abstract of the article, usually containing the important concepts that the article addresses. This is not always the case, but it is so for a great majority of the field's articles.[19] Thus, to develop the coding system, all significant title words were reduced to their linguistic roots using Martin Porter's stemming algorithm.[20] High frequency phrases (e.g., "spiral of silence," "third person effect") were collapsed to single tokens (e.g., "spiralofsilence," "thirdpersoneffect"), and low frequency terms/tokens were eliminated. The remaining set of terms was cluster analyzed and the resulting groups of terms were assigned a classification category usually named for the cluster's most central term or phrase. Thus, the category "conflict" represents a range of terms/tokens whose components include such concepts as "aggression," "coercion," "abuse," "violence," "bargaining," and "compromise." Added to the high-level classification system were a set of geographical labels representing world regions such as "Africa," "Asia," "Europe," "Middle East," "Central America," etc. This procedure produced a total of 104 classification categories. Since the deployment of this system in the late 1990s one additional category has been added, "studies of the field," which identifies articles reporting the field's norms, history, and professional practices. Thus, in total there are 105 coding categories, the labels for which are referred to as "metaterms." CIOS staff code each article with as many metaterms as applicable. The ComAbstracts database and its metaterm data has been the basis for studies of the structure of specific subsets of the communication literature,[21] for studies of career productivity of the field's scholars,[22] for studies of the impact and prestige of the field's journals,[23] and for studies of the productivity and centrality of the field's graduate programs.[24]

Results

RQ1: Changes in the Field's Publication Productivity

The question of change in the communication field's scope of academic publication productivity was addressed through examination of the number of journals in print throughout the field's history and the number of articles published. Figure 5.1 displays the number of academic journals in communication in production since 1915 based on data from the ComAbstracts database.

The figure illustrates a significant discontinuity between the period 1915 to 1970 and the years following. In the fifty-five years between 1915 and 1970 the rate of launch of communication journals was approximately one new journal every two years. However, in the forty years between 1970 and 2010, the overall rate increased by 600%, accelerating to a rate of approximately three new journals launched each year.

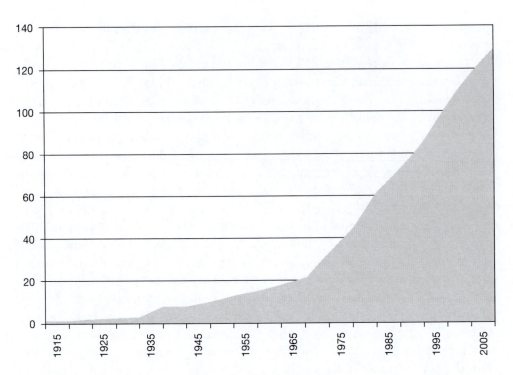

Figure 5.1 Cumulative number of mainline academic communication journals in print 1915–2010.

Figure 5.2 displays the number of scholarly articles published within the field's literature in five-year intervals between 1915 and 2010. Here again is illustrated the sea change for the field that began in the 1970s. In the decade of the 1960s, the field's scholars collectively published within the field's journals at a rate of approximately 200 articles per year; however, in 1970 the field published 672 articles, in 1980 1,020 articles, in 1990 1,469 articles, in 2000 1,596 articles, and in 2010 the field produced 2,702 articles. Indeed, the communication field published more scholarly articles in its core literature in the five-year period 2006–2010 than it did in the fifty-nine years between 1915 and 1974.

RQ2: Changes in the Focus of Communication Scholarship

Detailed changes in the focus of communication scholarship were examined by tallying the number of occurrences of each of the metaterm codes by year. The range of years was restricted to 1970 through 2010. The start year selected was 1970 because of indications that the decade of the 1970s was the beginning of the modern era for the communication field when a majority of scholars began to practice and be educated within the framework of a modern model of scholarly productivity. As will be shown, there was a steady and dramatic increase in the number of journals serving the field beginning about 1970. 2010 was selected as the last year for analysis since the ComAbstracts database is lagged for some of the journals covered.

Time effects were assessed for each of the metaterms using partial correlation procedures where the total number of metaterm-coded articles published per year for

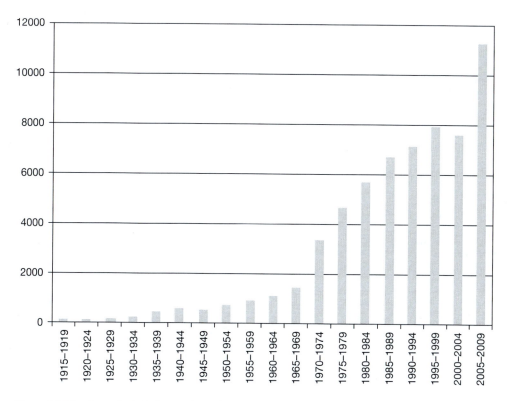

Figure 5.2 Number of scholarly articles published in communication journals in five-year intervals, 1915–2009.

the field was used as the control variable in assessing the relationship between time (year of publication) and total occurrence of each of the metaterms. It was necessary to control for the amount of publication in each year because, as seen, the rate of publication has been consistently on the rise since 1970. Thus in most cases the simple bivariate correlation between time and frequency of any metaterm would be positive and significant for no other reason than that more articles have appeared in the communication literature each year. Partial correlation renders this effect neutral allowing examination of the relationship of time to changes in frequency of occurrence of the metaterms. Results of these analyses are detailed in Table 5.1.

In all, twenty-six categories of scholarship showed significant linear change with time. Twelve gained significantly and fourteen declined significantly (i.e., at $p < 0.05$). The trends seemed particularly consistent in the case of the declining categories. Rhetorical scholarship, represented by the metaterms "Rhetoric" and "Classical Rhetoric," has shown significant decline in frequency, as have the "Public Speaking," "Biography," "Religion," and "Debate" categories, which are often associated with the rhetorical studies side of the field. Studies of language acquisition and production and language in use (e.g., heckling, sexist language, English as a second language, linguistics, sign language, etc.) declined, as did studies of the education process. Scholarship treating small group roles (e.g., leadership, group facilitation, gatekeeping) and group processes (e.g., brainstorming,

Table 5.1 Receding and gaining metaterms 1970–2010

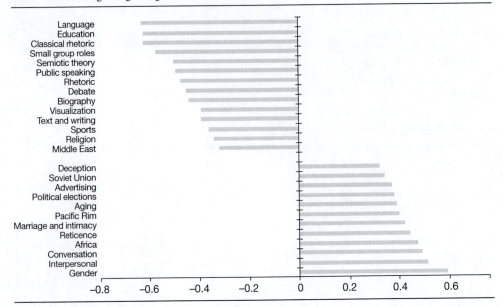

group dynamics, "groupthink," group development and stages, group decision-making) has also been in decline, as has scholarship related to studies of text and writing, semiotic theory, and visualization (as represented in studies concerned with graphics, photography, and multimedia), and studies addressing events in the Middle East and sports.

There is greater diversity among the gaining areas, but a trend is revealed in the substantial proportion of gaining areas that relate to the interpersonal side of the field. In addition to gains in the appearance of the "Interpersonal" code, six of the eleven other gaining codes reflect issues of psychological or social psychological focus: "Gender" (including research with a focus on issues in women and communication, gender differences, sexism, and feminist theory), "Conversation" (which includes research on conversation analysis, narrative, discourse analysis, ethnomethodology, and storytelling), "Reticence" (this category reflects research on shyness and communication anxiety and apprehension), "Marriage and Intimacy" (the "Family" category gained too but narrowly missed achieving statistical significance ($r = 0.31$, $p < 0.06$)), "Aging," and "Deception." Other changes reflect the expanding geographical focus of communication research. Gains were shown in the frequencies with which studies related to Africa, the Soviet Union (including its satellite states), and the Pacific Rim nations (this code is primarily used to reference Australia/New Zealand, China, and other Asian countries). The "Asia" category also showed gains ($r = 0.29$), but only at the 0.07 level of significance. Gains were also evident in scholarship touching on advertising and political elections.

Although it is possible to identify areas of advance and decline in the field's serial literature, the question of change in relative frequency of a category of scholarship is different from the question of the absolute proportion of a category of scholarship within the literature. A category may be in a significant growth spurt but still constitute a small area of the field's research focus, or it may be in decline but still account for a substantial proportion of the published literature. Table 5.2 details the top categories of the communication literature over the five-year period 2006 through 2010.

Table 5.2 displays those thirty-three metaterm coding categories that occurred in the five-year period in at least 5% of the 12,607 articles incorporated into the ComAbstracts

Table 5.2 Metaterms with frequency of occurrence in more than 5% of articles published between 2006 and 2010

Metaterm	Frequency	Percent
Interpersonal	2,274	18
Computer	2,079	17
Print journalism	1,987	16
Technologies	1,956	16
Broadcasting and media	1,955	16
Theory	1,825	15
News	1,814	14
Politics and government	1,750	14
Rhetoric	1,605	13
Television	1,309	10
Organizational	1,292	10
Cognition	1,209	10
Health	1,190	9
Europe	1,079	9
Gender	1,019	8
Persuasion	979	8
Democracy	929	7
Education	885	7
Text and writing	837	7
Economics	796	6
Visualization	749	6
Methodology	749	8
Race and ethnicity	732	6
History	729	6
Critical theory	695	6
Higher education	690	5
Language	652	5
Asia	652	5
Children	639	5
Pacific Rim	630	5
International development	627	5
Semiotic theory	609	5
Conflict	595	5

database during that time period. In each case, these terms were used in classification of approximately 600 journal articles. Although no single term was present in greater than 18% of the articles, metaterm use is not mutually exclusive so that it is not only possible but common for some of those listed to have been used in conjunction with each other. For example, the categories "Computer" and "Interpersonal" frequently co-occur as do many other pairs (e.g., "Economics" and "Broadcasting and Media," "Children" and "Health," "Print Journalism" and "News"). The list references most of the primary divisions of the field's emphases in graduate education identified by the NCA in its study of trends in graduate education in the field: interpersonal communication, organizational communication, health communication, mass communication, critical/cultural studies, rhetoric, political communication, and communication technology.[25] Metaterms serving as primary identifiers of these areas are prominent in Table 5.2. The one top area from the NCA study not included was intercultural communication. The "Intercultural" metaterm referenced only 4% of the coded articles, on par with terms such as "China," "Ethics," "Marriage and Intimacy," and "Nonverbal." Of the terms referencing geographic regions, "Europe," "Asia," and "Pacific Rim" (which includes Australia) occurred as areas of prominent attention. These are among the few areas outside of the United States served by journals publishing scholarship of regional focus. In Europe, these journals include the *Central European Journal of Communication, European Journal of Communication, Communications: The European Journal of Communication Research, Javnost: The Public, Nordicom Review, International Journal on Media Management*, and *British Journalism Review*. In Asia/Pacific Rim, these include the *Australian Journal of Communication, Chinese Journal of Communication, Mass Communication Research*, and *Asian Journal of Communication*.

RQ3: Structure of Current Scholarship in Communication

Cluster analysis of the metaterm classifications was performed to explore interrelatedness within the set of high frequency terms. In this use, cluster analysis can be regarded as a statistically-assisted interpretive technique providing insight into the structure of the communication literature based on co-occurring patterns of article classification. Two of the metaterms—"Theory" and "Methodology"—stand apart from the others because they reference the type of content an articles addresses rather than the actual content focus and thus they were excluded from this analysis. The result of the cluster analysis, exploring co-occurrence patterns within the remaining thirty-one metaterms, is presented in Figure 5.3.

The cluster dendrogram in Figure 5.3 provides a roadmap of recent directions in the published scholarship of the communication field. Two clusters stand apart from the others: the cluster consisting of "Asia" and "Pacific Rim" and the cluster consisting of "Computer" and "Technologies." The "Computer/Technologies" cluster is more closely connected to the remaining body of clustered metaterms than the "Asia/Pacific Rim" cluster, but both these small clusters are generally associated across the divisions of scholarship indicated among the remaining clusters. This suggests that publications addressing "Computer/Technologies" or "Asia/Pacific Rim" may occur anywhere within

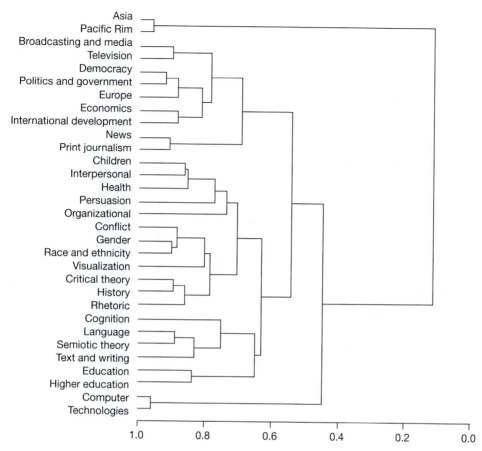

Figure 5.3 Cluster analysis of high frequency metaterms.

the context of the other, thematically segmented areas of research focus. At the center of the analysis can be seen a set of clusters that represent primary divisions of scholarship. A mass communication/political communication cluster with an international focus incorporates a sub-cluster that identifies studies related to journalism and news. The next large grouping identifies interpersonal communication research in connection with research on health communication, and children. Research in the areas of persuasion and organizational communication connect to this cluster, though they appear more loosely coupled. The next broad cluster consists of a grouping relating research on gender to research on conflict, likely representing a stream of studies appearing in the literature during the time frame covered in this analysis that address spouse abuse and issues of violence against women. This group stands in association with a small cluster consisting of "Critical Theory," "History," and "Rhetoric." Two additional groups are apparent, one with a focus that might be captured by the label "language in use" and the other references scholarship related to the educational process.

Discussion

This study traced broad changes in the communication field's scholarly communication during its first hundred years as an academic discipline. The data indicate that there was a significant discontinuity between the field's scholarly output prior to and following the decade of the 1970s. Since the 1970s, the number of journals introduced per year and the annual volume of articles published have increased steadily and dramatically. There can be little doubt that this has constituted a mounting problem for communication scholars struggling to keep abreast of the directions of their rapidly growing and diversifying literature. Because of the pace and extent of change, routine and systematic assessments of the field's evolving productivity norms and shifting intellectual directions may be increasingly useful.

The study reveals systematic declines in the proportion of scholarly articles addressing some areas related to the traditions of rhetoric, debate, and public address, which are areas linked to the field's historically deep roots in speech communication. Proportionally, studies in the small group area are also in decline as are studies related to the educational process. Strong gaining areas appear to be related to the interpersonal side of the field, although the Gender classifier, the strongest gaining area, may not be exclusively assigned to articles examining gender as a factor in interpersonal phenomena. The classifier may also represent feminist theory and research and may connect with the rhetorical area (as in the cluster analysis) or with other areas entirely. Within the ComAbstracts database, Gender co-occurs with Interpersonal as a classifier twice as often as it does with Rhetoric, but Gender also has substantial co-occurrence with other classifiers such as Computer, Technologies, and Television.

It is worth reiterating that an area that has shown declining or advancing representation in the literature does not reflect the area's importance in the field. While the proportion of articles receiving the Rhetoric classifier has dropped since the 1970s, Rhetoric remains within the top ten classification terms in absolute frequency (they were, in order, Interpersonal at 2,274 articles, Computer at 2,079, Print Journalism at 1,987, Technology at 1,956, Broadcasting and Media at 1,955, Theory at 1,825, News at 1,814, Politics and Government at 1,750, Rhetoric at 1,605, and Television at 1,309). Similarly, while the Conversation classifier stands among those with the strongest growth, it was applied to less than 5% of the field's articles in recent years.

As for the cluster analysis, it is important to note that clustering procedures don't yield definitive solutions. What emerges is dependent on the algorithm and as well on the particular mix of variables included in the analysis. The standard for judging a solution is not the achievement of statistical significance but the interpretive plausibility and heuristic value of the solution. Both are evident in the present case. As for the heuristic value, one might assume that the reasonably clear structure of the current analysis will pave the way for future comparative studies. As regards interpretive plausibility, in the main, the structures revealed are consistent with the divisions of the field as represented in NCA and ICA divisions.

It had been planned to compare the cluster structure of the field's current conceptual engagement with that of the decade of the 1970s. However, that analysis was abandoned because the data from the 1970s are so dissimilar to the data from our current period as to render detailed comparison incomprehensible. For the decade of the 1970s, the most frequent occurring metaterm was "Rhetoric" with 1,049 occurrences, followed by "Education" at 721 occurrences. Nothing else came close. "Interpersonal" was only coded for 390 articles and "Television" for only 358. Only a handful of terms accounted for as much as 5% of the literature of the decade. In that ten-year period, the literature was spread more or less evenly across virtually the entire 105-category coding system. Thus, except for the predominance of "Rhetoric" and "Education," the 1970s was a time where the field's literature was comparatively ungrouped, suggesting that the discipline was exploring a range of directions before settling into its present, more concentrated configuration.

Some caution about the conclusions of this study should be raised as there are aspects of the methodology that are less than optimal. It is a strength that the coding system was constructed as a closed dictionary based on statistical study of concept appearance in the same basis of data to which the coding system was then applied. However, once fixed, a closed coding system may become insensitive to emerging areas of focus or to shifts within an area of study and this coding system has now been in use for nearly fifteen years. On the other hand, there is practically no value at all in a completely open coding system such as that comprised by the sets of author-supplied keywords that now conventionally accompany scholarship published in the field's literature. From the standpoint of data retrieval, an open coding system is simply reiterative of the particular linguistic conventions of article authors. That the present coding dictionary is closed is a significant strength for the purpose of data retrieval, but a better system might be developed with benefit to the field in a number of applications, especially future efforts in discipline-wide self study.

There has been no formal assessment of reliability as the coding was not performed within the context of scientific research but as a practical application. CIOS coders are trained and monitored for consistency, but in classifying hundreds of studies per year, coders occasionally confront articles difficult to describe within the confines of the coding dictionary and in such cases judgment may be ad hoc. At the same time, a significant strength of these data lies in the extraordinarily high volume and the use of a large group of coders. Any particular coder's drift toward idiosyncratic coding is unlikely to register significantly in a data set that encompasses scores of thousands of articles.

As for the validity of the system, Bertelsen and Goodboy recently analyzed change between 1999 and 2009 in curricular offerings in departments of communication at US universities and four-year colleges noting discipline-wide trends in pedagogy that are consistent with the trends discovered here.[26] While there are some points of departure, in the main Bertelsen and Goodboy's research mirrors this study, reporting, for example, a ten-year decline in course offerings in debate, advanced public speaking, oral interpretation, rhetorical criticism, coaching forensics, voice and diction, public address history, instructional communication, and teaching methods. And Bertelsen and Goodboy report an increasing frequency of course offerings in interpersonal communication, communication and gender, and communication and aging, among other areas. The directions of changing focus in the field's scholarship seem to be reflected in concomitant change in the field's pedagogy.

As well, the cluster analysis reveals correspondence between the structure of the field's scholarship and common perceptions of the field's primary divisions of interest. Consistent with many accounts of the field's history that suggest the field has two major roots, one in mass communication and journalism and the other in speech communication,[27] the cluster analysis of the field's scholarship reflected these two large divisions. Beyond this, however, the speech communication division appears to consist of three significant subdivisions: one comprised of interpersonal, health, persuasion, and organizational scholarship; one of rhetorical/critical/historical scholarship; and one comprised of scholarship on cognition, language, and semiotic theory. The cluster analysis does provide intriguing suggestions about the positioning of some emerging areas of focus. In particular, there is an indication that studies carrying an Asia/Pacific Rim focus may eventually coalesce into an independent division of scholarship, as has already happened with communication technology. Both areas are served by multiple special-focus journals, a hallmark of a strongly emerging area within a field of study.

The creation of new journals is also a hallmark of the recent history of the field as a whole. But the rapid launch of so many new journals creates difficulty for anyone attempting to track trends in the field's literature and even more so for academic libraries that must provide access to it. Just as it has become virtually impossible for individual scholars to keep abreast of the field's intellectual directions outside of their own specialties, it has become critically difficult for library budgets to expand to keep up with the pace at which new journals have been introduced. Adding to this crisis, the rate of annual price increases for communication journals is among the highest in the academy. Lisa Romero tracked pricing for communication journals over a recent ten-year period, finding that price increases for communication journals outpaced price increases for academic journals in all other fields, tripling during the period of her study.[28]

The recent extraordinary growth in the volume of article output in the communication field suggests the benefit of further research into the circumstances under which this has occurred. It is not clear that the number of practicing communication scholars has grown proportionately to the growth of the field's journal literature. Part of the explanation may lie in increasing rates of multiply-authored articles. While the single-authored article published in the field's core journals has often been regarded as a centerpiece of academic merit, Stephen and Geel found that the proportion of single-authored articles had dropped over the period 1970 to 2000 from a rate of two to three times the number of multi-authored articles in the 1970s to only one to two times the number of multi-authored articles by 2000.[29] Thus, increasingly, scholars may be collaborating in their publication output with teams, generating a higher volume of articles. This possibility is only speculative because, unfortunately, there is no source of historical data on the number of faculty in the field, making it difficult to validly estimate long-term per-capita output. Understanding this issue is important for forecasting additional growth in the volume of publication based on future changes in the size of the field (e.g., due to factors such as changes in retirement ages of communication researchers, the conversion of tenure-track positions that carry research responsibilities to non-tenure track positions without them, or due to the expansion of the field internationally).

Looking ahead to the communication field's bicentennial about 2114, one would hope that long before that point the field's professional societies will have begun to execute regular studies of the field's organization and membership, its shifting intellectual and pedagogical foci, and its normative professional practices. As the significant controversy surrounding the recent NRC study has demonstrated,[30] no outside agency is likely to do the job adequately for the communication field. If the discipline of communication studies continues its present rate of change, the dimensions of the profession in 2114 will be wholly unfamiliar to any communication scholar alive today. However, one predicable aspect of the future is this: should the field sustain its present rate of increase in the volume and diversity of scholarly communication, without a fundamental revamping of the traditional model for formal contribution, it will create problems of significant proportion for the coherence of the field itself. Scholars must devote attention to tracking the field's fast-changing intellectual geography so that the communication discipline's process of scholarly communication may be more effectively accessed and documented, uniting scholars rather than risking their division into increasingly separated areas of research focus.

Many authors have chosen to describe the evolution of the field in terms of the ebb and flow of the influence of particular sets of people, ideas, theories, and methodologies that are argued to have inspired the discipline from various institutional locations and points in time. For the most part these accounts are not accompanied by particularly hard data. But at this time, tools permitting the systematic analysis of large databases of unstructured text have grown in sophistication and have been incorporated into accessible analytic software programs. With the field's literature increasingly available in digital form, it is now possible for scholars exploring the field's history of ideas to begin to make use of text analysis techniques to potential benefit. As one possible example among many, Craig has characterized the communication field as comprised of works stemming from seven distinct theoretical traditions: the rhetorical, semiotic, phenomenological, cybernetic, socio-psychological, socio-cultural, and critical.[31] Electronic access to the field's formal scholarly communication permits the possibility of developing markers for the areas of such category systems and empirically testing the classification, the interdependencies of its categories, and tracing their shifting influence and socio-geographic representation over long spans of time.

The systematic study of the evolution of the field's engagement of ideas is critical for understanding the sources underlying the changing directions of discussion that characterize communication scholarship from one period in its history to the next. As Gehrke notes, the stories told about the structure and evolution of the discipline's intellectual agenda, historically and in the present, are consequential because "they not only provide descriptive accounts of what happened, they also generate criteria for evaluating, locating, and displacing forms of scholarship."[32] Indeed, the field would benefit from studies making transparent the factors responsible for its change. Systematic study of the ongoing scholarly communication of the communication field would serve the need for a grounded history of the field and test ideas about the relative influence of individuals, networks, gatekeeping processes, intellectual trends and movements, factors promoting or inhibiting the creation and diffusion of new ideas, and other communication dynamics that influence the overall excellence and impact of the profession.

At one hundred years, the field is still young enough for some senior scholars of long experience to masterfully characterize the tributaries and currents of the field's century-long flow of intellectual engagement. However, it will not be much more time before those who experienced the profession before the radicalization of its rate of change in the 1970s will be gone, rendering the communication field's roots more obscure to this type of recounting. Fortunately, techniques for textual data mining and for linking texts to people, places, and times are now able to assist, potentially placing more of the field's history in a framework suited to independent verification. This type of work should not displace other approaches to the study of the field's evolution as a community of professionals who, year-to-year, engage and influence each other through their formal communication. Hopefully, the outcomes of the present study can serve as a baseline for the future for some types of data-driven approaches to the field's historiography.

Notes

1 Wolfgang Donsbach, "The Identity of Communication Research," *Journal of Communication* 53, (2006): 437.

2 Pat J. Gehrke, "Historical Study as Ethical and Political Action," *Quarterly Journal of Speech* 93 (2007): 355–357.

3 Dale A. Bertelsen and Alan K. Goodboy, "Curriculum Planning: Trends in Communication Studies, Workplace Competencies, and Current Programs at 4-Year Colleges and Universities," *Communication Education* 58 (2009): 262–275.

4 T. Hollihan, "NCA Doctoral Reputational Study, 2004," *National Communication Association*, 2004, www.natcom.org/nca/files/ccLibraryFiles/FILENAME/000000000318/Doc%20Study%20Report.pdf.

5 Cf. Jesse G. Delia, "Communication Research: A History," in *Handbook of Communication Science*, ed. C.R. Berger and S.H. Chaffee (Newbury Park, CA: Sage Publications, 1987): 20–98.

6 Robert T. Craig, "Communication as a Field and Discipline," in the *International Encyclopedia of Communication*, Vol. II, ed. W. Donsbach (Oxford, UK and Malden, MA: Blackwell Publishing, 2008): 675–688.

7 William Keith, "On the Origins of Speech as a Discipline: James A. Winans and Public Speaking as Practical Democracy," *Rhetoric Society Quarterly* 38 (2008): 239–258.

8 Herman Cohen, *The History of Speech Communication: The Emergence of a Discipline, 1914–1945* (Annendale, VA: Speech Communication Association, 1994).

9 For example, Everett Rogers, *History of Communication Study: A Biographical Approach* (New York: Free Press, 1994).

10 William Eadie, "Stories We Tell: Fragmentation and Convergence in Communication Disciplinary History," *The Review of Communication* 11, no. 3 (2011): 161–176.

11 John M. Wiemann, Robert P. Hawkins, and Suzanne Pingree, "Fragmentation in the Field and the Movement Toward Integration in Communication Science," *Human Communication Research* 15 (1988): 304–310.

12 Hollihan, "NCA Doctoral Reputational Study, 2004."

13 Robert T. Craig and David A. Carlone, "Growth and Transformation of Communication Studies in U.S. Higher Education: Towards Reinterpretation," *Communication Education* 47 (1998): 68.

14 William Keith, "Crafting a Usable History," *Quarterly Journal of Speech* 93 (2007): 345.

15 Eadie, "Stories We Tell," 161.

16 The author is executive director of the CIOS.

17 See www.cios.org/www/aboutcomabstracts.htm.

18 Timothy D. Stephen, "Computer Assisted Concept Analysis of HCR's First 25 Years," *Human Communication Research* 25 (1999): 498–513; in the early 1970s a group of scholars within the Speech Communication Association undertook to build a similar coding system for classifying the communication field's literature, but these pioneers found it difficult to do so with the technologies of the times. They noted that, "we do not yet have an artificial intelligence system that has the ability to determine relationships [between concepts] from real language input." Within fifteen years that was no longer the case and it became possible to submit digitized text of original scholarly articles to classificatory analysis. This permits a statistical approach that reins in some of the subjectivity that Borden et al. complained about in their own classification; George A. Borden, Susan M. Jenkins, and John D. Stone, "Computer Aided Thesaurus Construction: The Speech Communication Association Information Retrieval System," *Today's Speech* 20 (1972): 14.

19 As the field's literature has become diverse and indeed massive in size, it is increasingly important for authors and journal editors to consider the problem of future access, imagining perhaps a time another hundred years out where the discipline's literature has grown in excess of 500,000 articles and memory of the significant early contributors has faded. To enhance the ability of future scholars to locate historical resources and to trace the work of particular authors, three practices are recommended: (1) journal editors should require that all article titles signal their conceptual focus by including key concepts (thus, avoiding titles such as "Another shooting in cowtown"); (2) all journals should publish article abstracts along with the full article and the abstract should state the article's purpose and essential findings; and (3) all author attributions should include middle initial or full middle name whenever possible so that authors with similar names can be distinguished.

20 M.F. Porter, "An Algorithm for Suffix Stripping," *Program* 14 (1980): 130–137.

21 Stephen, "Computer Assisted Concept Analysis of HCR's First 25 Years"; Timothy D. Stephen, "Concept Analysis of Gender, Feminist, and Women's Studies Research in the Communication Literature," *Communication Monographs* 67 (2000): 193–214; Timothy D. Stephen, "Concept Analysis of the Communication Literature on Marriage and Family," *Journal of Family Communication* 1 (2001): 91–110.

22 Timothy Stephen and R. Geel, "Normative Publication Productivity of Communication Scholars at Selected Career Milestones," *Human Communication Research* 33 (2007): 103–118; Timothy D. Stephen, "The Quest for Practical Benchmark Indicators of Communication Doctoral Program Quality and Reputation: Relating Data from the NCA, CIOS, and NRC," *Electronic Journal of Communication* 22 (2012).

23 Timothy D. Stephen, "A Methodology for Calculating Prestige Ranks of Academic Journals in Communication: A More Inclusive Alternative to Citation Metrics," *Behavioral and Social Science Librarian* 30 (2011): 63–71; Stephen, "The Quest for Practical Benchmark Indicators."

24 T.H. Feeley and G.A. Barnett, "Comparing the NRC and the Faculty Hiring Network Methods of Ranking Doctoral Programs in Communication," *Communication Education* 60 (2011): 362–370; Timothy D. Stephen, "Measuring Reputation and Productivity of Communication Programs," *Communication Education* 57 (2008): 297–311; Timothy D. Stephen, "Clustering Research Activity in Communication Doctoral Programs: Relationship of Publication Productivity and Department Size," *Journal of Communication* 59 (2009): 824–843; Timothy D. Stephen, "Helping Communication Programs Represent Their Strengths: Toward an Endogenous Measure of Article Publication Productivity in Communication Serials," *Electronic Journal of Communication* 22 (2012).

25 Hollihan, "NCA Doctoral Reputational Study, 2004."

26 Bertelsen and Goodboy, "Curriculum Planning."

27 For example, Delia, "Communication Research."

28 Lisa Romero, "Confirming Suspicions: An Analysis of Original Communication Studies Journal Price Data," *Collection Management* 33 (2008): 189–218.

29 Stephen and Geel, "Normative Publication Productivity."

30 Feeley and Barnett, "Comparing the NRC"; E.L. Fink, M.S. Poole, and S. Chai, Comments on "A Data-Based Assessment of Research-Doctorate Programs in the United States" as applied to Communication, 2010, retrieved from www.nap.edu/rdp; Stephen, "The Quest for Practical Benchmark Indicators."

31 Robert T. Craig, "Communication Theory as a Field," *Communication Theory* 9 (1999): 119–161.
32 Gehrke, "Historical Study as Ethical and Political Action," 355.

References

Bertelsen, Dale A. and Alan K. Goodboy. "Curriculum Planning: Trends in Communication Studies, Workplace Competencies, and Current Programs at 4-Year Colleges and Universities." *Communication Education* 58 (2009): 262–275.

Borden, George A., Susan M. Jenkins, and John D. Stone. "Computer Aided Thesaurus Construction: The Speech Communication Association Information Retrieval System." *Today's Speech* 20 (1972): 11–16.

Cohen, Herman. *The History of Speech Communication: The Emergence of a Discipline, 1914–1945.* Annendale, VA: Speech Communication Association, 1994.

Craig, Robert T. "Communication Theory as a Field." *Communication Theory* 9 (1999): 119–161.

——. "Communication as a Field and Discipline." In *International Encyclopedia of Communication*, Vol. II, edited by W. Donsbach, 675–688. Oxford, UK and Malden, MA: Blackwell Publishing, 2008.

Craig, Robert T. and David A. Carlone. "Growth and Transformation of Communication Studies in U.S. Higher Education: Towards Reinterpretation." *Communication Education* 47 (1998): 67–81.

Delia, Jesse G. "Communication Research: A History." In *Handbook of Communication Science*, edited by C.R. Berger and S.H. Chaffee, 20–98. Newbury Park, CA: Sage Publications, 1987.

Donsbach, Wolfgang. "The Identity of Communication Research." *Journal of Communication* 53 (2006): 437–448.

Eadie, William. "Stories We Tell: Fragmentation and Convergence in Communication Disciplinary History." *The Review of Communication* 11, no. 3 (2011): 161–176.

Feeley, T.H. and G.A. Barnett. "Comparing the NRC and the Faculty Hiring Network Methods of Ranking Doctoral Programs in Communication." *Communication Education* 60 (2011): 362–370.

Fink, E.L., M.S. Poole, and S. Chai. Comments on "A Data-Based Assessment of Research-Doctorate Programs in the United States" as applied to Communication. 2010. Retrieved from www.nap.edu/rdp.

Gehrke, Pat J. "Historical Study as Ethical and Political Action." *Quarterly Journal of Speech* 93 (2007): 355–357.

Hollihan, T. "NCA Doctoral Reputational Study, 2004." *National Communication Association.* 2004. Retrieved from www.natcom.org/nca/files/ccLibraryFiles/FILENAME/000000000318/Doc%20Study%20Report.pdf.

Keith, William. "Crafting a Usable History." *Quarterly Journal of Speech* 93 (2007): 345–348.

——. "On the Origins of Speech as a Discipline: James A. Winans and Public Speaking as Practical Democracy." *Rhetoric Society Quarterly* 38 (2008): 239–258.

Porter, M.F. "An Algorithm for Suffix Stripping." *Program* 14 (1980): 130–137.

Rogers, Everett. *History of Communication Study: A Biographical Approach.* New York: Free Press, 1994.

Romero, Lisa. "Confirming Suspicions: An Analysis of Original Communication Studies Journal Price Data." *Collection Management* 33 (2008): 189–218.

Stephen, Timothy D. "Computer Assisted Concept Analysis of HCR's First 25 Years." *Human Communication Research* 25 (1999): 498–513.

——. "Concept Analysis of Gender, Feminist, and Women's Studies Research in the Communication Literature." *Communication Monographs* 67 (2000): 193–214.

——. "Concept Analysis of the Communication Literature on Marriage and Family." *Journal of Family Communication* 1 (2001): 91–110.

——. "Measuring Reputation and Productivity of Communication Programs." *Communication Education* 57 (2008): 297–311.

——. "Clustering Research Activity in Communication Doctoral Programs: Relationship of Publication Productivity and Department Size." *Journal of Communication* 59 (2009): 824–843.

——. "A Methodology for Calculating Prestige Ranks of Academic Journals in Communication: A More Inclusive Alternative to Citation Metrics." *Behavioral and Social Science Librarian* 30 (2011): 63–71.

——. "The Quest for Practical Benchmark Indicators of Communication Doctoral Program Quality and Reputation: Relating Data from the NCA, CIOS, and NRC." *Electronic Journal of Communication* 22 (2012).

——. "Helping Communication Programs Represent Their Strengths: Toward an Endogenous Measure of Article Publication Productivity in Communication Serials." *Electronic Journal of Communication* 22 (2012).

Stephen, Timothy and R. Geel. "Normative Publication Productivity of Communication Scholars at Selected Career Milestones." *Human Communication Research* 33 (2007): 103–118.

Wiemann, John M., Robert P. Hawkins, and Suzanne Pingree. "Fragmentation in the Field and the Movement Toward Integration in Communication Science." *Human Communication Research* 15 (1988): 304–310.

6.

SEXING COMMUNICATION

*Hearing, Feeling, Remembering Sex/Gender and
Sexuality in the NCA[1]*

Charles E. Morris III and Catherine Helen Palczewski

Even before sex/gender and sexuality were overtly thematized as subjects and objects of study (and before diverse bodies of sexes, genders, and sexualities visibly and audibly populated the Association), they were present in the history of the discipline of speech because rhetoric, itself, is sexed, gendered, and sexualized. The Greeks worshipped Peitho, the goddess who personifies persuasion *and* seduction—and one should not underestimate either's import. Peitho was "utterly essential in democratic states, where persuasion, rather than violence, was the ideal," yet in "vase painting she has overwhelmingly erotic implications."[2] And the distance between sex, sexuality, and sexualized violence was not far. In a casual aside, the *Theoi Greek Mythology* website explains, "Peitho was usually depicted as a woman with her hand lifted in persuasion or fleeing from the scene of a rape" as though these two are parallel.[3]

Rhetoric's sexualizing would go even farther with the designation of eloquence as the "harlot of the arts," a phrase that appears to find its origin in the writings of first-century historian Tacitus.[4] In the Middle Ages, Peitho would transform from a goddess to Rhetorica, Dame Rhetoric,[5] who would then revert to the harlot, as "The noble and beautiful Lady Rhetoric of the twelfth and thirteenth centuries has become a whore, a mother of harlots and lies."[6] Writing in 1690, John Locke would compare the deceptive power of rhetoric to the deceptive power of the "fair sex," noting that both play on men's desire to be deceived: "*Eloquence*, like the fair sex, has too prevailing beauties in it, to suffer itself ever to be spoken against. And it is vain to find fault with those arts of deceiving, wherein men find pleasure to be deceived."[7] Earl Stanley Baldwin, in his 1926 book *On England, and Other Addresses*, meditates on speech's seduction: "I was greatly struck when I was about eighteen, at coming across a phrase in Froude [a Victorian historian], 'Oratory is the harlot of the arts,' illustrated, as Froude could illustrate it, with a wealth of eloquence."[8] Writing in 1972, Wayne Brockriede theorized the ethics of argument by describing arguers as lovers, seducers, and rapists.[9] Time and again, rhetoric has been sexed and sexualized: in the fourth century B.C.E., in the first century C.E., in the middle ages, in Georgian England, and in the present.

In a 1989 issue of the Association journal *Communication Education*, Michael Burgoon called for the discipline to divorce "Dame Speech."[10] Referencing "recently published indices of productivity," he proclaimed: "It is clear that *most* Speech teachers do not do scholarship and would have to be relegated to the role of spectators in their field."[11] Arguing against a model in which communication departments offer a general education course in speech "for the masses," Burgoon declared "Speech departments are campus whores who truly live in fear of not being loved enough by others."[12] Playing with this sexed/gendered sexualizing, Celeste Condit mused about the fact that "rhetoric (the harlot of the arts) and the social science of communication (the sanctimoniously chaste youth) have been pressed up against each other for something around forty years now."[13]

Not only has the discipline been sexed/gendered and sexualized, but so too have the people whom the discipline thinks it teaches. Lest contemporary readers conclude that the use of the (falsely) universal male pronoun was merely a stylistic foible, consider Samuel Becker's description of the "communication environment in which any man in a modern or highly industrialized society lives," as offered in 1971 in *The Prospect of Rhetoric*:

> This man lives in a veritable pressure cooker of communication; everyone and everything is pushing him. The media are pushing him to buy . . . His children are pushing him to play with them or given them money for the movies or to buy them a car. And his wife is telling him to mow the lawn and take it easy and fix his tie. And those above him at the plant or office are pushing him to work harder, and those below him are pushing him to stop making *them* work so hard . . . He cannot escape this barrage of communication, and his wife wonders why he is not more communicative in the evening when she demands, "Talk to me. Why don't you ever talk to me?"[14]

That this quotation is from Becker is important, given that he is one of the men identified as "good enough to be a woman" because "he didn't have the tools"[15] to be unfair. Even coming from a man known to not be patronizing, the vision of the male speaker was present.

As this time-warped jaunt through the discipline demonstrates, even if confined to the last hundred years, providing a comprehensive history of the field and the Association is an impossibility given the complexity of sex/gender and sexuality. If we tried to identify all of the significant individuals or scholarly works, we would inevitably leave many out. If we tried to tell a story of clear progress, we would mislead. History is never a simple linear progression: moments and people are interwoven and reflexive in complex ways. Particularly in relation to sex/gender and sexuality, histories are collections of fits and starts, episodes, and moments whose significance is often not recognized at the time or whose significance may be lost to the vagaries and vicissitudes of time. Then, there are those instances that should have constituted a historical moment, but because of silences—personal, institutional, professional—they vanish into the mists of memory. Finally, we recognize here our own shortcomings in a genealogical project still calling for ever deeper intersectional analysis and engagement. Gender, sex, and sexuality never exist separate from race, class, nationality, ability, ethnicity, religion, and other enabling and constraining identity ingredients. Yet, the way scholars are asked to conduct, and do conduct, history seems to reinforce the separability of ingredients even after the complexity of identity has been baked.

Because there is not a unitary history, this chapter will not speak with a unitary voice. We want readers to hear us as a chorus: sometimes discordant, sometimes making clear the power of harmonizing goals, practices, praxis, politics, and peoples. Thus, what we offer are a series of parallel moments, explored through the modes of rhetorical abridgment, allusion, and anecdote, where women and feminist scholarship and Lesbian, Gay, Bisexual, Transgender, and Queer (LGBTQ) people and queer scholarship made visible the scholarly politics involved in sex/gender and sexuality. These moments make manifest the challenges presented when navigating the boundaries between the personal, public, and professional, boundaries that scholars of sex/gender and sexuality question, disturb, blur, and redraw as a central part of their work. In this chapter, we identify and narrate moments of structural change in the Association (the creation of the Women's and LGBTQ Caucuses), extended scholarly conversations (about "Disciplining the Feminine" and "Sextext"), and instances when the politics of the personal challenged the institution (the debates over 1978 and 2008 convention siting). We realize many other organizational moments, scholarly debates, and professional ruptures made manifest the politics of the personal. Such omissions do not indicate lack of interest or import. Instead, they offer an invitation to flesh out our history even more, to add blocks to the pattern as we collectively sew together the crazy quilt that is the Association's history of sex/gender and sexuality and the diverse bodies who populate it.

Institutional Structures

The field of communication may be defined by its ideas and practices, but as part of the modern university, it also operates as an institution. When people who taught at the post-secondary level came together and organized themselves under the banner of Speech, they discussed and formalized intellectual ideas, pedagogical practices, and institutional structures that defined relationships of gender/sex and sexuality as part of the new field. Our task is both to notice this gendering/sexing and sexualizing and to trace the moments of reflexivity when the organization became aware of itself relative to these dimensions, or demonstrated its ignorance or willful obtuseness. Those moments, for the Association as well as the larger society, have not come without struggle over the boundaries of the personal, professional, and political.

The Women's Caucus

The decade leading up to the formation of the Women's Caucus represents years of social foment, personal empowerment, and political change, particularly for women. In 1960, the Food and Drug Administration approved birth control pills. In 1963, Betty Friedan published *The Feminine Mystique*, the President's Commission on the Status of Women issued its report documenting widespread workplace discrimination against women, and Congress passed the Equal Pay Act. In 1964, Title VII of the Civil Rights Act outlawed employment discrimination on the basis of sex and race. In 1965, *Griswold* v. *Connecticut* declared it unconstitutional for state laws to prohibit the use of contraceptives by married couples. In 1966, the National Organization for Women was founded. In 1968, the Equal Employment Opportunity Commission (EEOC) ruled that sex-segregated help-wanted advertisements were illegal (a rule the Supreme Court would uphold in 1973). In 1969, the phrase "the personal is political" appeared in print.[16] In 1972, Congress passed the Equal Rights Amendment (ERA) (sending it to the states for ratification) and Title IX (outlawing sex discrimination in education); *Ms.* magazine was first published; Shirley Chisholm was the first African American woman to run for president; in *Eisenstadt* v. *Baird* the Supreme Court found the right to privacy guaranteed an unmarried person's right to use contraceptives; and the Association's Women's Caucus officially formed.

As histories of women's movements make clear, feminist activism occurred both in terms of political action aimed at institutional change and discursive politics that enabled women to define, for themselves, their identity, interests, and needs.[17] When the personal is political, change occurs at the personal and political levels simultaneously. And communication is central to this process.

Women coming together, to discuss their lives, made evident the relationship between the personal and the political. As Carol Hanisch made clear about the consciousness-raising process, "One of the first things we discover in these groups is that personal problems are political problems. There are no personal solutions at this time. There is only collective action for a collective solution."[18] The Association's women engaged in their own groups, coming to similar conclusions.

The first informal meeting of what would become the Women's Caucus occurred in 1970. In this moment, the power of talk enabled women to identify the way their personal experience could inform their professional politics. Bonnie Ritter, first Caucus chairperson, remembered one instance of consciousness raising that was essential to the creation of the Woman's Caucus and that, in and of itself, may have constituted the Women's Caucus as such (even prior to institutional recognition):

> "This is who I am" . . . for an hour and a half we just unzipped ourselves, and each person told her story and it might be an hour and a half a person: "This is what I remember about everything that mattered that happened to me, or that I did, that brought me to this point." And there was pain and there was glory, egregious errors, you know every kind of thing, and then we just went out and organized the next day, but that went on all night . . . We really had to be known by someone and we were just learning to know ourselves and that's surely more useful than any of the specific things we accomplished.[19]

Before a professional presence could be articulated, women had to see themselves as whole people, whose value was not determined by their treatment by others in the profession. Women's personal stories formed the foundation of their political and professional organizing.

The genesis of the Women's Caucus, according to both the oral histories and the letter sent to the Association informing it of the Caucus's formation, made clear the link between women's personal experience as professionals in the field and the political choices of the Association. The nascent Women's Caucus had interviewed women as they exited the convention placement center and uncovered the bizarre and "soul-killing questions" women were asked, where "every interview was an occasion to violate yourself or lose the chance to teach."[20] To spread the word about their research, the Women's Caucus asked if they could put up a poster outside placement announcing a meeting. They were told not to. They did it anyway.[21]

Because jobs were not identified by institution, applicants did not know to where they had applied, and when they received no response to their application, they did not know who had not replied. This meant it was virtually impossible to gather data about which schools were interviewing which people and who was being hired.[22] In response, the Women's Caucus created an alternative: a Women's Caucus Placement Service staffed by a coordinator from the Women's Caucus.[23]

The concern with job placement was articulated in the founding charter letter sent to the Association's then-president, Theodore Clevenger, announcing the Caucus's formation. To be clear, these founding mothers quite consciously did not ask for permission to form the caucus,[24] nor does there appear to have been debate in the Legislative Assembly. Instead, the women declared their existence as a caucus and, in so doing, constituted themselves as a political entity within the Association. In the letter, Caucus Chairperson Bonnie Ritter provided a list of the forty-one charter members (all preceded by the honorific "Ms.") and outlined the Caucus's goals:

(1) More active participation by women in all phases of the organization . . .
(2) Increased convention attention to programs concerning women . . .
(3) Careful survey and sharing of the professional interests, abilities, activities, and wishes of women members of the SCA.
(4) Revision of current SCA placement practices particularly the unidentified employer in correspondence . . .
(5) A separate placement service by the SCA or by the Caucus for women who wish to be so listed.[25]

In the responding letter, the Association president focused less on the content, and more on the signature line and honorifics even though the charter contained no demand for linguistic changes:

> You will encounter the greatest difficulties, I think, in your efforts to change the language behavior of the English speaking community. Moreover, I think you should know that I do not believe you should be successful in this particular effort. It is perhaps impolitic of me to call attention to this difference in our viewpoints, but since I am supporting so strongly some of your goals, I do feel it important to not [be] misleading with regard to this particular point. I shall not use the title Ms. but will continue to refer to my colleagues as Dr., Prof., Miss, or Mrs. Moreover, I shall not refer to you as chairperson but rather by the accepted title chairman. I believe these attempts to meddle with the language are unwarranted and I will not support them either now, or at any time in the future. I trust that this refusal on my part to succumb to the efforts of the women's liberation movement to manipulate my language behavior will not render suspect my willingness to support worthwhile changes along other dimensions.[26]

Ritter, in remembering the response, noted how the most detailed reaction had little to do with the substance of the Caucus charter. Yet, even the response makes clear how personal the political was, both in the sense that women were not accorded the right to name themselves as they saw fit and in the sense that personal umbrage was a sufficient reason to resist a political statement.

The founding mothers' strategy of proclaiming their status, rather than asking permission, seems to have had the desired effect. The first official meeting of the Caucus occurred at the 1972 convention, at which it had requested two panel slots, and in 1973 representatives of the Women's Caucus appear in minutes of the Legislative Council making motions, which would pass, concerning the placement center.[27] And here is one of the interesting places of silence: In response to a question about whether the Caucus faced opposition to its creation, Ritter remembered "I never heard any, but we wouldn't have because it wouldn't be said directly."[28]

The role of the Caucus was not only to advance the professional concerns of women, but also to create a personal space in which the professional identity of women scholars could develop. The significance of this development of agency was foregrounded by Ritter. In the early meetings, which were characterized by talk and wine, Ritter recalls that the

> Feelings, the interdependence . . . the love . . . was so powerful. There weren't so many of us, but there was so much love and so little judging. And I would want anybody who participated now to know about that love. And, it wasn't just general for all women, it was that, but it was people that we had found ourselves with and we had found *ourselves* while we were with them.[29]

She believed that:

> Probably none of the [original charter] goals that were achieved were as significant as being together was because a lot of times individuals can do things that they believe can't be done if they notice they're not the only ones saying anything about it. And women were particularly isolated from one another and we certainly wanted to be reasonable and we had to be reasonable, or appear to be . . . because the reaction was so unreasonable and so crazy.[30]

The enclaved space of the Women's Caucus offered (and continues to offer) a space relatively free of surveillance in which women, as women, can articulate their identities, interests, and needs in preparation for oscillating outward to the larger Association and voicing their demands.

The need for continued attention to the role of women in the Association is clear when looking at the leadership records. According to the Association's own "Women's Leadership Project" website, in the twentieth century, women represent thirteen of the eighty journal editors and eleven of the eighty-seven Association presidents.[31] Prior to the 1970s, only two women had edited a journal and only five had been Association president.

The LGBTQ Caucus

This or any story of the LGBTQ Caucus is less an origin story than a foundational configuration. Queer archival work to excavate, interpret, and narrate a longer genealogy of sexuality in/of/through this Association (for example, the life, pedagogy, and leadership of Maude May Babcock, University of Utah professor and 1932 president of the National Association of Teachers of Speech) is beyond the limits of this chapter. Currently no LGBTQ equivalent to the Association's "Women's Leadership Project" exists (and only limited intersectional focus on sexuality appears within that group[32]). The events of November 1978 at the Association convention in Minneapolis, which culminated in the Caucus on Gay and Lesbian Concerns, constitute an official beginning. However, they should also be understood as a historically significant and formative critical interruption,[33] produced and performed in the coalescence of multiple and diverse, inchoate and emergent, intersectional queer affects, identifications, whisperings, assignations, relationships, alliances, utterances, publications, and confrontations across the entire lifespan of the field. Such a deeper genealogy must also account for the organization's history of heteronormativity and homophobia.

Though these historical traces are elusive, it is important to evoke, however imperfectly, the scene of that first meeting on Thursday, November 2, 1978. James Darsey, then a University of Wisconsin graduate student and one of the key organizers, remembered there being "so much excitement in that room in Minneapolis as men and women gathered for the first time in NCA (then SCA) history as gays, lesbians and friends—it was dangerous and exhilarating."[34] Sally Miller Gearhart of San Francisco State University, who had also been involved in the formation of the Women's Caucus, and Temple University professor James W. Chesebro, convened and chaired the meeting. Gearhart attributed the mobilization effort to Fred Jandt, a visiting Instructor at SFSU, Darsey, tenured professors Chesebro and Joseph DeVito of Queens College, and two Indiana University graduate students, Jan Carl Park and Randy Majors.[35] We do not know with certainty all those who planned and attended that meeting (numbers range, in participants' memories, from ten to thirty).[36] Surely it is not hagiographic to label these people a coalition of the vulnerable and brave, or to conjure the manic murmuring, streaked countenances, and whiff of perspiration as evidencing the stakes—the sights and sounds of profound queer risk and hope as that meeting commenced.

This gathering must also be understood within a broader nexus of animating contextual events. The years 1977–1978 had been by tumultuous turns two of the most demoralizing, triumphant, and tragic years in LGBT/US history. Minor celebrity, singer, and occasional orange juice shill Anita Bryant had gained national prominence for her homophobic "Save Our Children" campaign, which resulted on June 7, 1977 in the repeal of an anti-discrimination ordinance in Dade County, Florida, which had been heralded as the harbinger of "gay rights" transformation. San Francisco community organizer Harvey Milk proclaimed in the aftermath of "Orange Tuesday" that the resulting national visibility and discourse, as well as movement mobilization among activist organizations throughout the country, should be understood as a victory for LGBT people, even though homophobic hate speech and violence simultaneously proliferated. Milk's election that fall to the San Francisco Board of Supervisors marked a significant political achievement, one harassed by the emergent campaign of California state senator John Briggs, what would officially be called Proposition 6, the "School Employees Homosexual Initiative," which intended to remove gay and lesbian teachers, and anyone who affirmed them, from California schools. Throughout 1978, despite anti-discrimination legislative victories in San Francisco and California, high-profile fights over existing ordinances protecting LGBT people ended in repeal: St. Paul, MN in April, Wichita, KS and Eugene, OR in May. In June 1978, Sally Miller Gearhart and Harvey Milk formed the United Fund to Defeat the Briggs Initiative. Throughout the summer and fall, a fierce battle to save the careers and lives of LGBT teachers flared throughout California; as late as September, the first poll suggested a 2 : 1 margin in favor of Prop 6. On November 2, just as the Action Caucus on Gay Issues/Communication meeting came to order at the Speech Communication Association convention, Milk was debating Briggs in Los Angeles (live on KABC TV and KABC radio) amid the frenzied eleventh-hour effort and heightened anticipation of the vote the following Tuesday, November 7. Gearhart no doubt understood the work at the Association's convention in Minneapolis (punctuated by the recent gay rights defeat in St. Paul) in relation to the struggle at home. How could the Caucus not be understood, felt, wagered by all those in that room except as inextricably bound to the larger drama playing out materially and symbolically?[37]

Owing to the archive preserved by those who forged the Caucus, key portions of which were published in the January 1979 inaugural issue of *Alternative Communications: Bulletin of The Caucus of Gay and Lesbian Concerns of the Speech Communication Association*, we have a detailed account of what Robert Asen might call the "rhetorical life of public policy,"[38] as the Caucus mission, value, and timing were deliberated, advocated, and legislated by different groups and committees during the Association's convention. In her eloquent "Proposal" delivered to the meeting, Gearhart situated the Caucus plan within a broader vision of Robert M. Hutchins's "Learning Society," an environment of full becoming, which requires cultural change, especially on behalf of "less powerful people." She declared:

> For the SCA at this time and place in history to establish an action caucus on gay issues/communication is to merge the increasing needs of gay people for their civil rights and the sense of intellectual and social responsibility on the part of this academic discipline.

The Caucus would facilitate "professional and social" support for "gay people" and their heterosexual allies within the Association, and address the lag, measurable against other professional scholarly associations, in published "research and analysis of gay phenomena" and in organizational recognition and support of "the civil rights of the nation's gay citizens." In framing her vision and appeal in organizational terms, Gearhart praised the Association's "strong stand on the issue of the ERA" (which had resulted in the convention site being moved from Chicago to Minneapolis) and formation of the Women's and Black Caucuses, and argued that this new action caucus "could only strengthen the association's reputation for responsible advocacy of social reform." "From the perspective of gay persons," Gearhart concluded, "there seems [no] agency more historically or morally equipped to provide an atmosphere for learning and creative change on this matter than that professional group whose expertise is communication and whose traditional concern has been the freedom of public discourse."[39]

Although inevitably and thoroughly political, what politics (and "politicization") meant to advocates and opponents alike must have varied. According to Chesebro's account, those at the November 2 meeting largely favored a caucus agenda devoted to promoting research concerning how "affectional and sexual preference affect the communication process theoretically, methodologically, and in applied areas." Chesebro himself argued that "ultimately . . . research justifies the existence of a permanent gay caucus and the caucus justifies gay and lesbian communication research." Twelve of the fifteen suggestions for Caucus activities that emerged during the meeting concerned research topics, distribution and legitimation of scholarship, and interdivisional and interdisciplinary connections (only one suggestion explicitly named the organizational guarantee of gay rights—"as women's rights are"—and relationship to convention site selection).[40] Nine months later, as its official existence was being hotly contested and defended in the pages of *Spectra*, the Caucus in its "Statement" emphatically asserted that:

> *The Resolutions were not designed and were not intended to promote any particular moral, religious, political, cultural, life-style, or sexual set of preferences beyond those which are inherent to SCA . . . it is illogical to have formulated the gay caucus primarily to promote gay rights, for a host of political vehicles far more effective than SCA now exist which are designed to achieve political objectives.[41]*

And yet, the four resolutions (M–P) crafted by the newly-formed Steering Committee, which would be taken up by the Divisions, General Legislative Assembly, and Legislative Council throughout the weekend of the convention, undoubtedly premised gay and lesbian research on political grounds:

> *M*   WHEREAS, other professional associations such as the Modern Language Association, The American Anthropological Association, The American Sociological Association, The American Political Science Association, The Folklore Association, the American Psychological Association, etc., have acknowledged the contributions of Gay men and Lesbians to their professions; WHEREAS, the Speech Communication has affirmed the value of other minority groups including Blacks and Women; therefore, BE IT RESOLVED that the Speech Communication Association affirms and supports the contributions of Gay men and Lesbians as educators and scholars in the Speech Communication discipline.

> *N*   WHEREAS, the Speech Communication Association has consistently supported research into communication patterns of subcultures and minority groups; WHEREAS, Gay men and Lesbians are among the most misunderstood, discriminated against, and least studied of subcultures in the United States and throughout the world; and WHEREAS, affectional preference influences communication processes and outcomes; therefore, BE IT RESOLVED that the Speech Communication Association encourages research into the area of Gay men and Lesbian communications.

> *O*   WHEREAS, the Speech Communication Association has consistently opposed any attempt to abridge human rights; therefore, BE IT RESOLVED that the Legislative Council of the Speech Communication Association deplores any legislation which uses affectional preference as the basis for infringing upon these rights.

P BE IT RESOLVED that the Caucus on Gay and Lesbian Concerns of the Speech
Communication Association be recognized as a caucus with the Speech Communication
Association.[42]

The Steering Committee's second meeting on November 4 also committed to a
Caucus newsletter that would publish bibliographies and articles, promote programming
at future conventions, and press for published statements from Second Vice-President
candidates; plan a "no-host cocktail party"; and pursue an Association-sponsored summer
conference.

We should not underestimate the effort required to circulate and advocate these
resolutions in the Resolutions Committee, Division meetings, General Legislative
Assembly, and Legislative Council, what Darsey characterized as "a logistical triumph
since we had arrived at the conference with no plan, had met as an action caucus once
(many of us meeting one another for the first time) the first night of the conference, and
quickly mobilized as a group."[43] Absent Divisional minutes, we may nevertheless take
as representative those arguments that emerged in the Legislative Council. It is important
to note that leading caucus advocates remembered this deliberation and debate on their
behalf as a coalitional effort *sine qua non*, with indispensable solidarity and strategy
provided by feminist stalwarts Bonnie Ritter of the University of Kansas, San José State
University's Jo Sprague, and Anita Taylor of Missouri's Florissant State Community
College.[44]

The informal minutes which record the exchange of the Legislative Council
convey rather conventional legislative maneuvering in the context of reported strong
organizational support (Chesebro later wrote that every Division and Interest Group
passed the Resolutions; Darsey's minutes reported unanimous, if in one instance qualified,
support among reporting Divisional and Caucus representatives but noted that several
divisional representatives were absent or did not report). Across discussions of the four
Resolutions, opponents argued for deferral until the 1979 calendar of business; questioned
the Council's jurisdiction and argued for delegation to the Referenda Committee;
noted that members would view Resolution O as an "endorsement of immorality";
expressed concern about increased organizational cost; queried whether there would
be sufficient program time for additional meetings and panels; and raised the bogey of
the previous ERA fight and its contractual impositions. Perhaps surprisingly, Resolution
O caused the greatest discomfort among those who believed it "external to the operations
of the organization." Despite Jo Sprague's argument that the Association takes political
stands and "sticks to them," O was first separated from the other resolutions, then tabled
until 1979 (when an amended version passed). Supporters of Resolutions M, N, and
P seemed to have relatively less struggle overcoming objections, though arguably the
important articulated warrants for M and N (comparisons to the Women's and
Black caucuses, description of the oppression of gay and lesbian people, respectively)
were excised by amendment after objection by the Black Caucus representative and
others. Resolutions M, N, and P passed, and the Caucus on Gay and Lesbian Concerns
was born.[45]

Institutionalizing Sex/Gender and Sexuality

During the span of a decade, an organization that was structured on the pretense that its members were White, male, and heterosexual became institutionally aware of the scholarly and professional needs and concerns of women, LGBTQ people, and people of color (as the chapter on race in this volume details). It is one thing to say that women and LGBT people belong to a scholarly organization, but it is another to make good on the promises of that membership by supporting scholarship, offering professional recognition, and changing institutional practices (e.g., placement center practices and job description content). We now consider some moments in scholarship, looking specifically at "Disciplining the Feminine" and "Sextext" as points of reflexive articulation of gendered/sexed and sexualized scholarship and scholars.

Scholarship

The following two moments of scholarly controversy share much: both (eventually) generated substantial CRTNET discussions and both have been framed as examples of "disciplinary scandal,"[46] with *scandal* having its connotations of moral or legal wrongdoing, offense to propriety, and general distastefulness. As Thomas Benson observed:

> "Sextext" and "Disciplining the Feminine" and their discussion in CRTNET make useful companions, since both involve issues of disciplinary boundary policing, in one case involving allegations that editor and referees were too permissive ("Sextext") and in the other ("Disciplining") that editor and referees were too dismissive, or even abusive.[47]

Disciplines discipline. They draw boundaries, sometimes explicitly, sometimes invisibly, around appropriate topics of discussion, appropriate discussants, appropriate locations to discuss approved topics, and even the tone appropriate to discuss approved topics. A history of sex/gender and sexuality in the Association would not be complete without recognition of the disciplinary power involved in the publication of the Association's journals. Although what follows is not hagiography, neither is it mere diplomatic equivocation (all history, being rhetoric, is partisan; but not all history is pardonable).

Sex/Gender in/and Scholarship

The power of the discipline of communication studies to discipline the female/feminine was first made evident in an institutionally empowered moment when Marie Hochmuth Nichols (the first elected female president of the Association and the first female editor of the *Quarterly Journal of Speech*)[48] critiqued the Wingspread Conference for a conspicuous absence that produced an audible (at least to her ears) silence. The Association's National Development Project on Rhetoric was meant to "outline and amplify a theory of rhetoric suitable to twentieth-century concepts and needs."[49] The Project included two conferences: Wingspread, held in January 1970, and Pheasant Run, held in May 1970. Conference planners selected participants as a result of nomination from their departments or from Association members. Conference planners selected no women. This absence was made visible by Nichols, who wrote in her review of the conference report, *The Prospect of Rhetoric*:

> More than forty males presented their wisdom about rhetoric for the 70's and beyond. This reviewer, in something of a huff, would like to ask the question: Would the inclusion of four or five females have greatly lowered the quality of the discussions? Such a distribution would probably have been more in line with the realities of the present.[50]

Capping her request at the level of 10% (the percentage usually occurring when women are added to an existing canon) should have appeared as reasonable. Instead, it generated a disciplining. In her retrospective on Nichols, Jane Blankenship provided a taste of the response:

> A male colleague could and did refer publicly to her as "our menopausal scholar." And the very issue of *Spectra* carrying her presidential photo on the front page titled the call for papers for the 1969 convention program: "One Man—One Paper (and women too)."[51]

The point of remembering this historical moment is to note that when Association members call for women's scholarly presence to be recognized, often the initial (defensive) response is to discipline the request by feminizing the scholar making the demand—as menopausal, as feline, as ball bashing, as lesbian.

Carole Blair, Julie R. Brown, and Leslie A. Baxter's "Disciplining the Feminine" essay overtly named and challenged the way women were disciplined. Published in 1994, the early version of their essay was a critique of Hickson, Stacks, and Amsbary's 1992 essay, "Active Prolific Female Scholars in Communication," published in *Communication Quarterly*. Blair, Brown, and Baxter submitted their essay to Virginia P. Richmond, then editor of *Communication Quarterly* (and #2 on the Hickson et al. list). They argued that the "Prolific" study was a form of discipline that impacted the professional lives of women in distinctive ways. Their goal with the essay was "to point to and critique a constellation of practices" which took the form of "particular themes and enabling mechanisms of a masculinist disciplinary ideology, whose professionalized and seemingly liberal thematic motifs serve as a benign cover for a selectively hostile and exclusionary disciplinary practice" in the hopes of discouraging others from using the "Prolific" study in any "professional/institutional/authoritative" way.[52]

The reviews commissioned by the editor would then perform an additional level of disciplining, operating as "unusually explicit manifestations of the apparatuses that sustain and enable" masculinist disciplinary ideology.[53] The reviewers offered the following comments: "there are too many feline, petty attacks in this manuscript and too much ball-bashing to be a scholarly article"; it is "anti-intellectual"; the paper is "the single worst piece of 'scholarship'"; and it contains "a political harangue against so-called 'male paradigm,' which is nothing more than the typical male-bashing brought forth by Marxist writers."[54] Unsurprisingly, the conflation of sex/gender and sexuality was enacted by one reviewer who declared Blair, Brown, and Baxter sought "a whole new field that was off limits to males and heterosexual females."[55] Blair, Brown, and Baxter's analysis of the reviews of their essay makes clear how these disciplining moves seek to re-personalize political critiques, reducing their critique to merely a complaint by those who did not "make the list."

Unfazed by this attempt at discipline, Blair, Brown, and Baxter used the reviews to provide further evidence of how the female/feminine is disciplined. They recognized that the texts they had in their hands were precious, "a rare find, tangible and unusually explicit fragments of what is almost certainly a larger, intolerant disciplinary text that typically remains implicit, unreadable, and deniable,"[56] giving insight to a form of discipline that often occurred outside of view and hearing. Given this, even if they could not find a publication outlet, they committed themselves to distributing photocopies of the reviews. However, they did not need to resort to self-distribution.

Treating the reviewers' comments as "explicit objects of analysis," they brought "them into the public conversation of scholarly discourse,"[57] conducting a deft rhetorical criticism combining their original analysis of the study with a new analysis of the reviews. As Blair, Brown, and Baxter explain, they "found the reviews to be overt displays of ideological mechanisms that not only approve the themes of the masculinist paradigm, but which seek to ensure that the masculinist paradigm represents the exclusive thematic directive for professional work in the discipline."[58] They then submitted the essay to the *Quarterly Journal of Speech*. Robert Ivie, editor of the journal, published the essay as the lead article in volume 80, issue 4, timing the publication of the essay so that it would arrive in people's mailboxes before the Association's national convention.[59]

Evidencing that sex and gender are always already present in scholarship published in the Association's journals, Blair, Brown, and Baxter made clear that:

> the focal work of both these reviews is the designation of approved and disapproved identities; that is, articulation of the range of what one is able to say and how, as well as who one can be as an acceptable member of a group, in this case the discipline.[60]

Blair, Brown, and Baxter spoke gender/sex into existence in a place where typically it was made absent by "the ideological apparatuses that approve a very narrow range of identities and readings and that force a politics of exclusion" and they declared such apparatuses "must not be allowed to silence other voices."[61] Just because maleness/masculinity is not overt in scholarship does not mean it is absent. In fact, it is the secured center that makes clear "the rules for writing the field's scholarship . . . demand personae of singular, neutral, authoritative, observers who are detached from or ambivalent about their own histories and contexts."[62] Yet, how can one overtly speak/write of sex/gender and not make present the sexed/gendered body from which one communicates?

The publication process faced by the essay also offers an interesting moment for considering the politics of scholarship a question of intellectual power: What is speakable and hearable? Prior to publication, Blair, Brown, and Baxter had to struggle to make audible the reviewers' comments. *CQ* editor Richmond sought to block publication of the reviews, arguing that they were the property of the Eastern Communication Association. Relying on existing case law and legal advice, Blair, Brown, and Baxter believed that letters' recipients are the legal owners. After consultation with Association lawyers, *QJS* editor Ivie published the essay even with its extensive quoting of the reviews. As explained in footnote 32 of the essay, the reviews were quoted almost entirely, but not as whole pieces—a concession to the Association lawyers.[63] Ivie also was willing to allow the original reviewers to respond to the essay published in *QJS*. Through the new *CQ* editor, Raymie McKerrow, they declined.

As with opposition to the formation of the Women's Caucus, silence stifled what should have been a scholarly and professional exchange, making it virtually impossible to address an amorphous resistance. Three years after its publication, one scholar noted the essay was "met with silence in scholarly journals."[64] But, this silence is a complex one. Informal discussions of the essay did occur, in communication and other disciplines. Email conversations with the authors were plenty. But, little overt debate over the merits of the criticism had appeared in print (whether in journals or in the field's online bulletin board and town hall CRTNET), although Hickson and his colleagues' mischaracterization and dismissal of the critique made clear that more discussion would be helpful. Virtually no discussion occurred in the institutionally sanctioned location of Association journals even if voices rebounded off the hallways at the national convention and in other reviews.[65]

Although the essay was cited, it was not really discussed, or those citing it often missed its point.[66] For example, Hickson and his colleagues characterized Blair, Brown, and Baxter's critique this way: "Some opposed listing women separately from men,"[67] and declared that their "main concern" had to be that women had been "singled out" because they had not offered any critique of previous prolific scholars' essays.[68] Or, instead of a specific answer to the specific critiques of the essay, people offered "vigorous reassertions that the field of communication is progressive, enlightened, and essentially unassailable in its treatment of women and scholarship."[69]

The eerie silence, however, was broken as part of the discussion of "Sextext" when, as that conversation on CRTNET was winding down, Bill Eadie posted Omar Swartz's essay from the *Southern Communication Journal* that noted the dearth of published discussion of the "Disciplining" essay. The posting of Swartz's essay generated twelve issues of CRTNET across two months devoted to the "Disciplining" essay, with many of the same contributors to the "Sextext" discussion articulating similar issues about the "Disciplining" essay.[70] "Disciplining" is an instance where the theories used to guide study in the discipline were applied to texts produced by members of the discipline. And, it appears it was this meshing of the professional and personal that generated such controversy, here—the case of holding particular individuals accountable to professional critique. As Swartz noted:

> As long as the scholar stays in the realm of feminist or Marxist theory, then he/she is okay. The problem arises when scholars try to apply their theory to affect the lives and material practices of people in a direct way . . . To take theory seriously is to invite praxis, and therein lies the conflict with established authority.[71]

This is the unique challenge. The implications of sexed/gendered criticism is that we *all* might need to change our practices.

For many CRTNET commenters, however, there was no need to change anything. Two critiques were written as dismissive satires, one starring (and authored by) Theodore Wendt and a dog named Macduff and another penned by David Sutton who cast Michael McGee as a character in an *X-Files* conspiracy. Summarizing the reasons for dismissal, Steve Corman explained away the non-reaction by saying:

(1) Most scholarly articles are not discussed (though we would point out to him that most articles are not critiques of the discipline itself);
(2) "This is just not a burning issue for people in our field" because "women, feminists, and critics get lots of papers published" (but—why would the disciplining of the feminine not be a concern for most *people?*);
(3) "Some people, me included, perceived the article as so much whining" (reducing a systematic critique of professional practices to a personalized complaint); and
(4) Most everyone has received a nasty review (which, perhaps, leads to the questions: why has the profession tolerated nasty reviews for so long and why did it take scholars with a feminist orientation to critique such a practice?).[72]

Despite this dismissal, the essay had staying power. The essay won the Association's Woolbert Award in 2006 (only the second instance in which an essay authored by only women had won). One of us (CEM) had this to say about one of the essay's authors:

> Carole Blair is anything but provincial; indeed as a self-proclaimed disturber—one of the field's most influential—she has taught us again and again the value in being on the move, traversing time and space, querying all that is taken for granted and imagining the unforeseen, the unspoken, the yet-to-be-realized. She is queer in this regard, provoking disquiet and dissonance, a restlessness that begets rhetorical and critical innovation. With Blair's essay my sense of critical value in disorientation is restored through a refusal of the business as usual of entrenchment and diffusion.[73]

We valorize the authors of "Disciplining" for their refusal to accept the taken-for-granted boundaries, norms, and dictates of the discipline. And, we note that the points of resistance to the essay's critique, the resistance to its full assimilation by the field, is part of a still-unfolding history. A history brought to the fore again with "Sextext" which provided ample opportunity for enfolding the queer into the scholarly.

Sexuality in/and Scholarship

Since the formation of the Caucus on Gay and Lesbian Concerns, research on communication and homosexuality had been understood as its means and ends of organizational contribution and legitimation, its *raison d'être*.[74] Generating, publishing, and circulating scholarship became a primary focus of *Alternative Communications*, the Caucus bulletin, which devoted its second issue in May 1979 to an annotated bibliography of relevant scholarship (what would become a regular feature), as well as calls for and listings of panels on gay and lesbian themes at the annual convention (early on slated only by the Caucus itself, with its two panels, and the Commission on Freedom of Speech). During the Caucus's first decade, *Alternative Communications* also published research by its members, a practice that must be understood within the daunting challenges these scholars faced in getting published in Association journals. Though of course the bigotries of academic gatekeeping are very often archivally absent (except in the discredited modes of preservation such as gossip), we can discern much in the paltry statistics on representative publications during this period: only two articles in communication journals at the Caucus's founding, eight by the time of its ten-year anniversary (Association panel listings and citations from outside the field provide useful comparative context for surmising plausible explanations). There must have been a sense of arrival, even triumphalism, when twenty-five essays (by twenty-seven scholars) appeared in James Chesebro's 1981 edited volume, *Gayspeak: Gay Male and Lesbian Communication*, essays that amply demonstrated the relevancy of such research through rhetorical, interpersonal, discourse, media, and ethnographic methods, cases, and analyses.[75] Although Gay Rights/Liberation occupied and influenced LGBT scholars in the field, and though the very existence of the Caucus and its scholarship was essentially political, it appears that no one inside or outside the Caucus *politicized*, i.e., exposed as ideological or made a political issue, LGBT communication research as a matter of public organizational concern (nevertheless, that unrecorded, off the record, and other quotidian heteronormative and homophobic discourse and discrimination undoubtedly and materially affected the lives of LGBT Association members is a bedrock assumption of this history).

Yet throughout the 1990s, LGBT scholarship proliferated in the field's journals, perhaps owing to the coming of age for one generation of scholars and the emergence of another, both encouraged and equipped by the now established domain of inquiry called Gay and Lesbian Studies, which itself was quickly being transformed by the emergence of Queer Theory. In a single decade, journals in the field published nearly six times the LGBT articles as they had in their entire history, a statistical and symbolic boom; every journal in the field except *Communication Monographs* published at least one essay. Singular in its commitment to LGBT scholarship, however, was the performance studies flagship, *Text & Performance Quarterly* (*TPQ*), publishing sixteen articles across the decade, more than twice that of its nearest peers, *Quarterly Journal of Speech* and *Critical Studies in Mass Communication*, combined.[76] *TPQ*'s visibility in cultivating and circulating LGBT research was such that some scholars worried aloud about queer ghettoization.[77]

Given its investments in post-modern theory, embodiment, ethnography, and personal narrative, *TPQ* might seem in hindsight just the right platform for a dramatic and transformational exhibition of Queer Theory's disruption of sanctioned research production and performance, which queer theorist Michael Warner called a "regime of the normal." Warner had written in his pathbreaking *Fear of a Queer Planet* (1993):

> For academics, being interested in queer theory is a way to mess up the desexualized spaces of the academy, exude some rut, reimagine the publics from and for which academic intellectuals write, dress, and perform ... For both academics and activists, "queer" gets a

critical edge by defining itself against the normal rather than the heterosexual, and normal includes normal business in the academy.[78]

In the January 1997 special issue of *TPQ*, devoted to "pushing the perceived boundaries" of the "genre of scholarly discourse," Frederick Corey and Thomas Nakayama queered the field in an explosive critical interruption titled simply, provocatively, "Sextext."[79]

One really has to read "Sextext" to understand it: no mere précis can do it justice. Yet many who contributed to the fierce battle over its meaning, legitimacy, and consequences didn't bother or appeared to have merely skimmed it. "Sextext" is a piece of experimental performative writing that explores the relationship among desire, theory, gay male sexuality, and the conventions, pleasure, politics, and representations of porn and academe. "To be a fulcrum subject, to be between the study and the experience," Corey and Nakayama wrote, "How is it possible to write in the fulcrum between the language of academia and the language of sex?" Their fictive pro/antagonist "Mark Stark," the graduate student-cum-porn actor whose cowboy hat and mischievous grin, orifices and appendages, groping and sucking, configured the movements of the essay across registers, embodied Corey and Nakayama's aim to "*write aloud* desire in an elaborate performance that indexes the fleeting nature of desire in the context of academic discourse that attempts (never successfully) to capture and ground that flight."[80] As they recollected in 2003:

> "Sextext" played in the borderlands. The essay was written in first-person singular narrative, but it was co-authored. It was identified as fiction but published in a journal not designed for fiction. The narrative conjoined the politics of pornography with the politics of academia. The ideas were derived from French psychoanalytic theory but focused on U.S. American sexual identities. The central ideas of the text included eroticism and melancholia, liberation and repression, whiteness and marginality, males and subjection.[81]

Others evidently thought the essay was something else, dangerously so, leading Corey and Nakayama to this understatement: "the commotion following the publication of the manuscript indicated the authors of 'Sextext' entered unauthorized territory."[82]

Indeed, as Susan Owen observed, "Few essays under the aegis of the National Communication Association (NCA) have provoked more energized responses"; Thomas Benson, in accounting for those responses, concluded that "'Sextext' comes, in memory, to represent the sense in which the discussion implicitly was about a scandal—the scandal of unorthodox publication."[83] What Craig Gingrich-Philbrook astutely called "heated contestatory attempts to refunction, on the one hand, and reassert, on the other, the recognized grammar of communication scholarship"[84] flared across the pages of *Spectra* and a number of journals but especially through CRTNET, where 148 messages were posted over two years beginning on January 31, 1997, the majority of which appeared in the first two months after the essay's publication. Although it is impossible to do justice here to the nuances and complexities of the manifold positions that unfolded across this body of discourse, it will suffice to say that myriad assertions, arguments, exhibition(ism)s, apologias, rebuttals, rejoinders, and non-sequiturs explicitly and implicitly constituted referenda on what is and is not scholarship; what the field's journals should and should not be publishing; the broader reputation of the discipline; how membership dues ought to be spent; the disciplinary definition, value, and status of autoethnography, of performance studies, of *Text & Performance Quarterly*; the (de)merits of post-modern theory; language decorum in research; pornography; and corporate sponsorship of research. Though ranging in perspective and judgment, the discourse was dominated and flamboyantly performed by a small cadre of putatively or self-identified straight males, exuding privilege and authority across their denigrating philippics and harsh satires, some from elevated positions within the field (Robert Craig, Brant Burleson, Theodore Wendt, Malcolm Parks, Don Ellis, Gary Kreps, John Hollwitz), some enjoying their proverbial fifteen minutes (David Sutton), all collectively transforming CRTNET into a bully pulpit—notwithstanding its democratic design and invitation or the counterarguments by Carole Blair, Bryan Taylor, Carolyn Ellis, Robert Drew, Bruce Gronbeck, Ann Gravel, Lesa Lockford, Michael McGee, and others. From our perspective, the true scandal of the "Sextext" battle was that, ostensibly an open debate, much of the sanctimonious, self-indulgent, ungenerous (if not mean-spirited), and prejudiced discourse amounted to a public tarring and feathering. Corey and Nakayama themselves were more gracious: "Academia is not short on disciplinarians. Academics demonstrate their mastery of the field by carefully guarding its boundaries and the proper production of knowledge."[85]

Owen and Gingrich-Philbrook have offered masterful critical readings of the "Sextext" battle, key documents in this archive that explicate and emphasize Corey and Nakayama's groundbreaking intervention by "turning the subjective gaze of queer theory on rational paradigms … seriously destabiliz[ing] the privileged, disembodied voice and vision of masculinist authority and entitlement"; by clarifying the "inverse relations of scholarship and discipline, visuality and privilege, and obscenity and decorum"; by "*embody*[ing] the academic/intellectual voice, constituting *as* visible and, therefore, as a potential object for investigation"; by "invert[ing] the constructed gaze of academic scrutiny, thereby exposing gendered norms of spectatorial power"; by exposing the "homophobic dimensions of masculinist research ideology"; by modeling reflexivity and revealing its profound lack in the discipline.[86] In addition, we would argue that the "achievement" of "Sextext" was precisely in what Corey and Nakayama more modestly describe as its function as "a perlocutionary act, initiating consequences temporally removed from the utterance of the text."[87]

Scholarship and/in the Association

We offer two consequences stemming from these two episodes. One largely unrecognized perlocutionary effect-as-benefit was the disciplinary uncovering generated by both "Disciplining" and "Sextext." As in extracting venom from a wound, the responses to the essays exposed the field's deeply rooted hegemonic masculinity, heteronormativity, and homophobia. Taking the reviews seriously as evidence, Blair, Brown, and Baxter noted:

By casting us as lesbians ... this reviewer invokes the approved politics of exclusion and silencing accomplished via segregation. To be different, especially to be vocal about one's differences, is simply unacceptable, and action must be taken to silence those who would express their differences so openly.[88]

Blair, Brown, and Baxter were not calling for separatism but, instead, were calling attention to the already functional separatism effected by privileging masculinist disciplinary norms—a separatism effected by the exclusion of others not-male/not-masculine. If readers were not convinced by arguments against the Hickson *et al.* essay, the proof offered by the reviews (and later responses or lack thereof to the essay), made Blair, Brown, and Baxter's argument stronger. The same is true with "Sextext"; the responses are as informative as the original essay.

Most were more politic than Donald K. Smith (notably the man who decades before had co-authored "The Rhetoric of Confrontation"):

["Sextext" is] faddish as an entry into the current enthusiasm of many universities to establish programs of "queer," or "gay and lesbian studies," not because of demonstrable need for advancing knowledge through scholarly inquiry, but in order to bring comfort to yet another group allegedly suffering from historical victimage.[89]

However, it was in fact those, like Smith, who ridiculed and denied the charge through their ironically unself-reflexive, "exuberantly narcissistic," and camp performances (hungrily swallowing Corey and Nakayama's bait), who enacted the broad superficial understanding of heteronormativity and homophobia and the need for its multi-methodological reflexive engagement.[90] Gingrich-Philbrook gets at the heart of it in observing:

Whereas Wendt and company do not explicitly stigmatize the bodies of gay men and performance studies theorists, their maintenance of the male research economy implicitly participates in a masculinist suspicion of the body as a site of knowing, as well as a reading of gay sex, bodily acts, as more or less inherently pornographic.[91]

Such exposure arguably changed the field's relationship to sexuality and its embodied academic performances.

The second consequence, never overtly mentioned in the "Sextext" and "Disciplining" battles, was the public muting of the Association's LGBT community and of women in any collective sense. Blair, Baxter, Brown, Corey, and Nakayama all remember many private expressions of support by email or in person, chatter in the hallways and social gatherings at conferences. But not a single self-identified LGBT person or member of the Caucus on Gay and Lesbian Concerns (CEM included) can be found among the hundreds of CRTNET postings on "Sextext" and very few women (or self-identified feminists, author CHP included) contributed to the discussion of the merits of the "Disciplining" essay (some women did comment, but not really about the substance of the original essay: Martha Watson offered an institutional response to questions concerning the role of the Publications Board, Mari Boor Tonn commented on whether reviews should be signed, and Naomi Rockler commented on the general societal use of *ad hominems* as a feminist issue; only Jane Banks commented on the essay itself, noting her faculty women's discussion group had read the article and the women's reactions within the group were split on its merits).

Like the eerie silence that met "Disciplining," there is no evidence of individual or collective response to "Sextext" in *Alternative Communications*, as an agenda item at the 1997 Caucus business meeting, or as a thematic conference panel, even when "Sextext" partially factored in the whispered reasons for Thomas Nakayama's 1999 rejection by the University of Texas administration despite being the candidate of choice to direct the Asian American Studies Program. Only Gingrich-Philbrook published a scholarly analysis. The rest was expected, conspicuous, though unremarked upon silence.

No doubt there are multiple and complex dimensions of any coherent explanation for the dearth of scholarly engagement with these essays. But one important possibility is that, for all the brave early political struggle to create the LGBT and Women's Caucuses, for all the proliferating LGBTQ and feminist scholarship, for all the activist work outside the field, "Sextext" and "Disciplining" revealed an undeveloped vision and praxis among LGBT and feminist Communication scholars regarding the professional and political, women's bodies and feminist work, queer bodies and queer work. "Sextext" and "Disciplining" may both mark, in other words, an important LGBT and feminist disciplinary loss of innocence.

Finally, critically significant though we believe these publications and their responses to have been, other interruptions could be nominated here which challenge and extend these exemplified notions of innocence, discipline, and transformation. For instance, though not touted or thrashed on CRTNET (nor across multiple Association Divisions or journals), E. Patrick Johnson's 2001 essay, "'Quare' Studies or (Almost) Everything I Know about Queer Studies I Learned from My Grandmother," published in *Text & Performance Quarterly*, constituted, or more precisely *should* have constituted (beyond performance studies—does this sound familiar?), a crucial turn toward intersectionality within the field. In critiquing erasure of (especially racial) difference in queer theory, Johnson proposed a "quare" perspective that "not only speaks across identities, it articulates identities as well. 'Quare' offers a way to critique stable notions of identity and, at the same time, to locate racialized and class knowledges." Characterized as a "theory of the flesh," quare "emphasize[s] diversity within and among gays, bisexuals, lesbians, and transgendered people of color . . . conjoin[ing] theory and practice through an embodied politic of resistance."[92] Johnson's essay by implication shone a spotlight on racial erasures in landmarks of the field's LGBTQ history—*Gayspeak* (1981); *Queer Words, Queer Images* (1994); "The Future of Gay and Lesbian Studies," NCA Annual Convention (1999)—as well as helped to inaugurate, outside the discipline, "black queer studies" and what would come to be known as "queer of color critique," described by fellow progenitor Roderick Ferguson as:

> an interrogat[ion] of social formations as the intersections of race, gender, sexuality, and class, with particular interest in how those formations correspond with and diverge from nationalist ideals and practices. Queer of color analysis is a heterogeneous enterprise made up of women of color feminism, materialist analysis, poststructuralist theory, and queer critique.[93]

Johnson's quare influence among LGBTQ scholars in the field was immediate and all the more apparent in this centennial generation.[94] Communication writ large, and the Association, perhaps not coincidentally absent in Johnson and Henderson's Queer Black Studies project,[95] is still in great need of the quare lessons in/among differences, reflexivity, and praxis taught by Johnson's grandmother.

Conventions

In a reflection on the 2008 conference site boycott and the alternative protest conference, called the UnConvention, Anna M. Young, Adria Battaglia, and Dana L. Cloud note: "No academic organization exists in a vacuum, but rather, all are party to larger cultural struggles—and histories."[96] The NCA (under its many names) is no exception, and in its history, the Association has tried to identify its role in larger historical struggles, even as it wrote its own history. Whether in debates about civil rights or about moving the convention in the wake of the 1968 police riot at the Democratic National Convention, the Association has debated about what its role should be in the political struggles of various times, struggles over sex/gender and sexuality included. Yet, it seems that these struggles do not become part of the remembered history of the association—or when they do, they become misremembered.[97]

Sex/Gender Politics and/in the Association

As soon as women won the right to vote in 1920 with the passage of the 19th Amendment, Alice Paul shifted activist attention to the passage of the Equal Rights Amendment (ERA), which declared: "Equality of rights under the law shall not be denied or abridged by the United States or by any state on account of sex."[98] The ERA was introduced in every session of Congress since 1923, finally passing Congress in 1972 after which it was sent to the states for ratification. Thirty-eight of the fifty states would need to ratify the ERA for it to become the law of the land. In 1972, twenty-two states ratified the ERA; in 1973, eight more; in 1974, three more; in 1975, only one; in 1976, no states ratified. Illinois was one of the states that had failed to ratify, a failure made more painful by the approaching ratification deadline of 1979 (a deadline that would be extended in 1978 to June 30, 1982).

When Illinois failed to ratify the ERA, debate ensued in the Association's 1977 Legislative Council over the following resolution: "If SCA believes that all of its members should be equal under the law, then it should not hold conventions in states that fail to ratify the Equal Rights Amendment."[99] The actual vote on the resolution was delayed until divisions and sections had a chance to discuss it so that Legislative Council members would be representing their respective area's position.[100] The resolution passed in a show of hands vote after an "extended discussion,"[101] resulting in the cancellation of "bookings for four future SCA conventions scheduled in states that have not ratified the Equal Rights Amendment,"[102] including the convention slated to be held in Chicago in 1978.[103] (As an example of the interweaving of moments, in this same issue of Spectra, a new publication was announced: Women's Studies in Communication.)

The Legislative Council vote was not the end of the debate. Over *Spectra* issues from February 1978 to October 1978, debate ensued in the form of letters to the editors. The vote's characterization deserves remembering. In a letter from New Orleans Director of Convention Sales (New Orleans being a scheduled city site that also was cancelled), the vote was characterized as the breaking of a contract on "the whim of a select group of individuals."[104] Over the next four issues of *Spectra*, fifteen letters were published in support of the vote (including letters by Francine Merritt, Carol Taylor, and Karlyn Kohrs Campbell) and thirty opposed (written almost all by men, with at least three threatening non-renewal of SCA dues). The key themes of the opposed letters, as rightly identified by Campbell, were that the act politicized the Association and was undemocratic (which the process clearly was not). In response, one supporter clarified: "I do not believe that the SCA is 'politicized' by taking action to defend the rights of its members as professionals."[105]

Opponents' accusations of an undemocratic process pointed not only to the vote, but also to the boycotts, which were cast as unethical means of persuasion; supporters of the resolution were accused of using "irrational means" and "coercion."[106] The vote was an example of "economic blackmail rather than persuasion"[107] and the Association had "lowered itself into the battleground of pressure politics, of bribery . . . For shame that S.C.A. should ever put force above reason."[108] In addition, opponents of the vote worried for the very professionalism of the organization, and described the vote as evidence of a "politicizing trend"[109] that "smacks of 'McCarthyism'."[110] One opponent declared: "I cannot support with my money and my name an organization that is so easily influenced by politics . . . I am surprised that SCA has the audacity to call itself professional. You insult real professionals."[111] Another writer asked "By what right are you changing this professional academic association into an arm of political coercion?" and proceeded to cancel his membership "until such time as your policy and procedures reflect a professional educational and academic association and not those of a two year-old having a tantrum because he hasn't gotten his own way as quickly as he desired it."[112] The slippery slope argument reared its head, with the first example making visible the interweaving of issues of sex/gender and sexuality: "Who will draw the line on such issues? Will we not convene in Dade County, Florida, because of recent votes re the rights of homosexuals?"[113] Another questioned if the Association will "be an auxiliary for every tin-pot crusade which comes along."[114] One letter writer demanded "we should expect to receive a public apology at the November Convention by those whose action at the 1977 Convention has caused the integrity of the organization to be questioned."[115]

The August 1978 issue of *Spectra* offered a straw poll, the results of which were not quite as imbalanced as the letters: Approve, 444; Disapprove, 547; No strong opinion, 31. This same issue announced that Anita Taylor had been added to the ballot as candidate for second vice-president.[116] Taylor—an "outsider" as someone *not* from a Big 10 institution and who also happened to be a woman—was elected as a result of a write-in ballot as second vice-president of the Association. Taylor identified a notable motivating factor in her decision to run: when Marie Hochmuth Nichols made a speech as part of a national conference awards ceremony, she "said something to the effect that she knew some people claimed women were discriminated against in the Association, but she didn't believe it. For one thing, [Hochmuth Nichols] said, she'd never experienced discrimination in all her years with SCA."[117]

By October, *Spectra* had published forty-five letters (not including ones from state and city officials). An Editor's Note made clear the significance of this exchange: "Since the inception of *Spectra* in 1965, no issue has stirred more member response than the SCA action on ERA." The October 1978 *Spectra* would be the end of the letter barrage given the editor explained that because the issue had "been thoroughly aired" no new letters would be published unless they added "substantively to the dialogue about SCA and 'controversial' issues."[118] The recognition that the Association, as a professional and intellectual enterprise, was shot through with politics, would not come without a struggle.

Remarkably, this moment, for many, is not part of the Association's collective history. Neither of us knew of this moment before beginning this project and, even when researching it, contradictory accounts arose. Also odd, even though repeated intersections and interconnections appeared between histories of the caucuses' formation, and with the "Disciplining" and "Sextext" essays, virtually no reference was made in the debates about the UnConvention to the move occasioned by the ERA votes.

Sexuality Politics and/in the Association

This is not a story of radical transformation, but what radically happened in San Diego, in some senses, changed everything that followed. Grumblings in the spring of 2008 about the annual conference registration policy (an earlier mandated deadline and its financial impositions on the membership) took the form on CRTNET of a few angry calls for boycotting that year's convention. Few likely considered seriously the possibility of such action; it had been decades since political intervention of this magnitude occurred, and the Association, constitutionally and temperamentally, as evidenced comparatively among other national academic associations, preferred studies over stands where social justice is concerned. No member of the Association, from the most conservative to the most radical, would have predicted that a different boycott was soon to organize, occupying the membership through November's convention in San Diego.

In May 2008 the California state Supreme Court ruled unconstitutional (in *In re Marriage Cases*) an existing statute prohibiting same-sex marriage. As gay and lesbian couples throughout the state flocked to city halls to exchange vows or planned their dream weddings, opponents quickly mounted a protest campaign in the form of a proposed ballot initiative and constitutional amendment called the "California Marriage Protection Act," what would become familiarly known in media and popular culture as "Prop 8."[119] The Association immediately became implicated because the primary hotel for the November annual convention was the Manchester Grand Hyatt, co-owned by and named for Doug Manchester, real estate and hotel magnate who as a self-identified devout Catholic contributed $125,000 to the Prop 8 cause. That the statewide vote would occur just weeks before the convention only heightened the material stakes and symbolic capital of the controversy.

NCA Executive Director Roger Smitter, apparently having fielded correspondence expressing concern over the Manchester Grand Hyatt, issued a statement on behalf of the Executive Committee on May 7, a document that demonstrated and foreshadowed the limited rhetorical capacity of organizational leadership lacking vision amidst a political crisis:

> NCA opposes efforts to eliminate or restrict diversity. Diversity enriches life's experiences and is essential to help people to communicate effectively in an increasingly complex and pluralistic world. Disenfranchisement of any group threatens and destroys the framework of open and free communication to which NCA is committed. NCA seeks to ensure, protect, nurture, and encourage the broadest range of participations for public discourse ... NCA believes dialogue provides the first and best vehicle to address social issues.[120]

That said, Smitter flatly stated that the NCA would honor its contract by holding the convention at the Manchester Grand Hyatt. The NCA would mitigate the institutional dissonance by hosting open forums on same-sex marriage; spotlighting GLBTQ panels; "send[ing] an open letter to Mr. Manchester further explaining the NCA's views on diversity and the importance of communication"; inviting Mr. Manchester to participate in the convention; facilitating forums to educate California voters; encouraging media outreach by communication experts; and disseminating the NCA's published GLBTQ research.[121] Smitter also solicited a letter from the general manager of the Manchester Grand Hyatt who asserted that the Hyatt Corporation did not share Manchester's views and had a long track record of lauded support for GLBT employees and guests.[122] This public stance would remain virtually unaltered across a number of official statements between May and November, though as pressure mounted during those increasingly turbulent months, Smitter and the Executive Committee deployed less seemly tactics and discourse to maintain control.

Some irony attended one of the first two prominent public responses to the NCA statement. Former president Martha Solomon Watson ridiculed it by questioning the appropriateness of organizational politicization and the claim of "diversity as an unqualified good"; while insisting on her "liberal" *bona fides*, Watson also embarrassingly and inappropriately compared same-sex marriage to honor killings, child pornography, and polygamy.[123] Overshadowed by this spectacle was the birth of the boycott, a letter from Georgia State University assistant professor Jeffrey Bennett and Indiana University assistant professor Phaedra Pezzullo asking readers, in coalition against Manchester's homophobic bigotry, to divest, confront, and publicize.[124] Bennett and Pezzullo's significant "founding," as it were, accompanied later in the summer by their shared research on alternate hotels for lodging and departmental parties (as well as organizing behind the scenes by email, exchanges with the NCA, pro and con arguments on CRTNET by a few publicly identified GLBTQ scholars, and the cancellation of the University of Wisconsin reception), is less prominent in public memory because of a developing shift in the disposition of the boycott.[125]

On July 10, San Diego GLBTQ activist and community organizations forged a coalition with the local labor movement to call for a boycott of the Manchester Grand

Hyatt. Hotel employees and their advocates had claimed at least since 2006 unfair and injurious working conditions; as a representative of the Raza Rights Coalition said to then-University of New Mexico assistant professor and boycotter Karma Chávez, "The Hyatt is one of the most, if not the most anti-union, anti-worker hotel in San Diego ... what we can tell you for sure based on the communication that we have with the housekeepers is that the abuses in the work place continue."[126] In keeping with this coalitional effort in San Diego, Pezzullo, by way of introducing UNITE HERE Local 30 (hospitality and hotel union) spokesperson and liaison Powell DeGange to the NCA community via CRTNET, averred, "as with many people who do not believe in justice for one, Manchester appears not to believe in justice for all: the boycott has expanded to include the complaints of women and workers."[127] This expansion of the ground of protest by September had two particular effects that would shape the boycott's mobilization and adversarial escalation throughout the fall. First, University of Texas associate professor Dana Cloud threw herself into the boycott and quickly would emerge as its most vocal leader and, as Indiana University associate professor Jon Simons described her, a "lightning rod." Cloud wrote on CRTNET, "When the hotel workers call for a boycott, that holds great significance for me. I will not cross a picket line, and my ambivalent stand regarding the boycott is now a firm one in favor of it."[128] Ten days later Roger Smitter issued a second official statement reaffirming earlier themes of disappointment and dialogue, but with a new tactic of discrediting the boycott by denouncing what he described as UNITE HERE's parasitic and opportunistic use of the Prop 8 fight, what Cloud assailed as NCA's "union busting rhetoric."[129]

During the fall of 2008, the public debate exploded on CRTNET, on blogs (such as Josh Gunn's *Rosewater Chronicles*), and in departments, over what began to be called the boycott "UnConvention" (the Association's official conference theme was "unCON-VENTIONal!"). Proponents shared a common foundation that financial and symbolic support of the Manchester Grand Hyatt (bodily presence, rooms, food, bar tabs) constituted complicity that should be resisted. When the NCA in late September announced that it absolutely would not move the convention site, boycotter arguments shifted to pressuring the Executive Committee to accommodate those participants and departments wishing to move panels, division and caucus meetings, job search related activities, and parties outside the hotel, appeals always rejected by the NCA (though limited refunds were granted).[130] Some supporters and organizers, more sympathetic than others to the NCA's dilemma and its manifestations, were willing to enter, stay, and/or keep convention business in the Manchester Grand Hyatt. Fearing acquiescence by his GLBTQ colleagues, for example, Charles E. Morris III issued "An Appeal to Members of the GLBTQ Division, the Caucus on GLBTQ Concerns, and Our Allies" to "respect and love ourselves and each other to say: Not Here, Not Now: Never Compromise with Homophobia and Exploitation."[131] Those GLBTQ bodies would by November issue a strong joint statement categorically rejecting Manchester's homophobia while accommodating pragmatic contingencies that would take some conferees into the Hyatt.[132] Through moving statements of solidarity and quieter action, dozens of departments and divisions relocated meetings, panels, parties, and pre-conference seminars, and offered alternate arrangements to job or student applicants.[133] At the same time, Pezzullo was working to craft a resolution for the Legislative Assembly that would strengthen social justice criteria for convention site selection; her engagement with Association leadership undoubtedly led to President Arthur Bochner's formation of a Task Force on Site Selection, for which he appointed Pezzullo as co-chair and key boycott organizers as members.[134]

There was, of course, fierce resistance to the boycott, some principled and eloquent, and some petty and hostile. Arguments ranged from stances against organizational engagement in politics as violation of the NCA's mission; rejection of elite boycotter "bullying" on the grounds of personal choice and free speech; and predictions that the boycott would be disruptive while having no meaningful effect. Two unrelenting important objections concerned disability and protection of graduate students. Laura Ellingson of Santa Clara University and Janis Edwards of University of Alabama, both avowedly supportive of GLBTQ and workers' rights, passionately challenged the boycotters to understand the unreasonable and insensitive extent of the sacrifice being demanded in requiring movement outside of the Hyatt. "I am not convinced that a boycott is the only or best response ... the realities of my life are now that ... I cannot always act according to the plans laid out by people who wish to persuade us to take the righteous path."[135] These principled opponents categorically were unmoved by boycotters' consistently stated acknowledgement of disability's extraordinary challenge, insistence that non-participation would not nullify solidarity, and concerted efforts to create accommodations. The ways in which the UnConvention positioned graduate students and young professors, for whom the NCA convention mattered in ways keenly lived, felt, and imagined, also was fraught. Mari Yandall wrote:

> I gladly advocate for same-sex marriage and will personally speak out against this ridiculous injustice until we are all able to enjoy the same rights. However, I do not have freedom to stand on principle here and I am slightly troubled by the lack of responsibility for those of us who have worked very hard to attend this convention and are in no position to withdraw.[136]

These dissenting voices ultimately deepened the intersectionality of the boycott vision and expressed its inevitable limitations.

What the majority of the Association's membership, friend and foe alike, couldn't see because it occurred off CRTNET through countless phone calls and emails was the remarkable coalitional, grassroots effort to bring the UnConvention into being, against long odds. Some of that effort is documented in postings on the boycott's Facebook page, which Pezzullo launched on September 14, with its more than 300 members (including the core of tireless planning team members) by the time of the convention: the labor of finding an alternate site with adequate rooms (finally the Embassy Suites near the Hyatt); fundraising to pay for the relocation; lobbying divisions and departments to stand in solidarity; creating t-shirts and publicity; drafting the resolution and open letters; scheduling the calendar of presentations and printing programs. Nor did the vast majority of those in the mainstream of the NCA who opted for business as usual inside the Manchester Hyatt (or those who, for good reasons and glaring rationalizations, stayed home) see, except perhaps later in Angela Aguayo's video documentary coverage, the electric intellectual, affective, and political work—consummatory, constitutive, catalytic—that took place at the well-attended UnConvention panels; at the registration table in the lobby cheerfully operated for hours and hours by UnConvention volunteers; at the two protest events in front of the Manchester Grand Hyatt; and in social gatherings populated by those diverse boycotters who dared to stand with workers and GLBTQ people in San Diego.

Certainly partisan and competing accounts of the UnConvention's effects exist. The Association claimed the boycott had no discernible impact on what it touted as a wildly successful convention and some of its leaders insisted on besmirching the credibility of the UnConventioneers long after the NCA had left San Diego.[137] By contrast, on Facebook and through email exchange and on a reunion panel at the Association convention in Chicago the following year, boycotters generally expressed what University of Alabama assistant professor Jason Edward Black posted:

> Thank you for organizing the UNconvention. It flowed so well, and the unity, solidarity and love that underscored the whole weekend were incredibly empowering. I've never had such a great experience at a convention/conference. I left SD rejuvenated and re/centered.[138]

More importantly, less empirically verifiable, measured along the arc spanning from the Caucus formation in the 1970s and through the growing pains across subsequent decades, the UnConvention constituted a coming of age, a maturation of praxis, an intersectional awakening—collectively speaking—that brought into full stride the pathbreaking steps of those of previous GLBTQ generations within the Association. The relationship between the center and the margin was also irrevocably altered by this turn toward differential belonging and queer worldmaking.

Politics and/in the Association

At the heart of these debates is a particular understanding of identity: Who are Association members? Are we scholars and teachers who inhabit particular bodies? How do our bodies, and what we do with them, interact with our scholarship and practices as a scholarly association? Articulating this stance, the Women's Caucus and the Feminist and Women's Studies Division explained their position on the 2008 UnConvention:

> As members of the Feminist & Women Studies Division and Women's Caucus, our identity as scholars and teachers is inseparable from our commitment to social justice in its myriad forms and contexts. This commitment is what brings us together as a division and caucus. In our teaching, research, writing, and in our daily lives, we consciously engage in practices that aim to generate and foster more equitable, knowledgeable, and humane communities and societies.[139]

The ideology debates of the 1970s and 1980s made clear that simple objectivity was impossible, and that (personal) politics play a role in scholarly conversations. However, we (as a discipline) do not seem to have figured out the flip side of that: that once our subjectivities are introduced into scholarship, then we are responsible for what we, as subjects, do.

Conclusion: To Be Continued

We hope we have offered important moments of sexed/gendered and sexualized reflexivity, moments when the discipline's members were made, or became, aware as professionals, scholars, and citizens of the ways in which sex/gender and sexuality are imbricated in the Association's structures, scholarship, and conventional practices. We cannot end this chapter without making clear that many other moments deserve remembrance, moments when gender/sex and sexuality became visible and audible, and when intersections of race, class, nationality, and other identity ingredients complicated understandings of sex, gender, and sexuality. We hope this chapter has engendered a desire to reconstruct, recover, and remember those moments.

Equally important, we encourage recognition that those moments are not only the history of *some* members of the Association, but are a history of *all* members of the Association. Every member possesses sex/gender and sexuality and every action of the Association has woven throughout its warp and weft the effects of hegemonic masculinity and heteronormativity. We recounted moments of struggle over the role of sex/gender and sexuality in the discipline that exposed how the scholarly and professional is always already the personal and political. These moments should make clear that none of the Association members can, or should, pretend these intersections are not always present. Existing histories of rhetoric and of the Association tend to be *a* history of White, heterosexual maleness presented as *the* history of rhetoric and the Association. To account for a full history of the discipline, one must account for the full range of bodies that populate its institutions, scholarship, and gatherings.

Notes

1 The authors are grateful to Bill Keith and Pat Gehrke for their generous invitation. They owe thanks to a number of people who helped them remember: Anita Taylor, Cynthia Lont, Trevor Parry-Giles, Bruce Gronbeck, James Darsey, Tom Dunn, Tom Nakayama, and Fred Corey. Cate would also like to thank her students, Alexandria Chase and Erik Walker, for their research assistance. Chuck would like to thank Scott Rose, who helps make all this work possible.

2 Helen F. North, "Emblems of Eloquence," *Proceedings of the American Philosophical Society* 137, no. 3 (1993): 408. See also Amy C. Smith, "Athenian Political Art from the Fifth and Fourth Centuries BCE: Images of Political Personifications," in *Dēmos: Classical Athenian Democracy*, ed. C.W. Blackwell, 1–26. January 18, 2003.

3 "Peitho," par. 2. *Theoi Greek Mythology*. Last updated 2011. www.theoi.com/Daimon/Peitho.html.

4 Most likely from Tacitus's "Eloquence, the harlot of the arts" as cited in Donald C. Bryant, *The Rhetorical Idiom* (Ithaca, NY: Cornell University Press, 1958): 130; John Louis Lucaites and Celeste Michelle Condit, "Introduction," in *Contemporary Rhetorical Theory*, ed. John Louis Lucaites, Celeste Michelle Condit, and Sally Caudill (New York: The Guilford Press, 1999): 6; Martin J. Medhust, "Editor's Welcome," *Rhetoric & Public Affairs* 1, no. 1 (Spring 1998): iii.

5 Ernest J. Enchelmayer, "Rhetoric in the Visual Arts," *Conference of the International Journal of Arts and Sciences* 1, no. 19 (2009): 59–79.

6 C. Jan Swearingen, *Rhetoric and Irony: Western Literacy and Western Lies* (New York: Oxford University Press, 1991): 228.

7 John Locke, *An Essay Concerning Human Understanding* (Edinburgh: Mundell & Son, 1801): 247.

8 Stanley Baldwin, *On England, and Other Addresses* (London: Books for Libraries Press, 1926): 93.

9 Wayne Brockriede, "Arguers as Lovers," *Philosophy & Rhetoric* 5, no. 1 (Winter 1972): 1–11.

10   Michael Burgoon, "Instruction About Communication: On Divorcing Dame Speech," *Communica-tion Education* 38, no. 4 (1989): 303–308.

11   Burgoon, "Instruction," 304–305.

12   Burgoon, "Instruction," 305.

13   Celeste Michelle Condit, "The Birth of Understanding: Chaste Science and the Harlot of the Arts," *Communication Monographs* 57 (1990): 323.

14   Samuel L. Becker, "Rhetorical Studies for the Contemporary World," in *The Prospect of Rhetoric*, ed. Lloyd F. Bitzer and Edwin Black (Englewood Cliffs, NJ: Prentice-Hall, Inc., 1971): 26.

15   Bonnie Ritter, Videotaped Interview with Cindy Lont, National Communication Association, Chicago, November 1997, at 29.00.

16   General consensus is that the phrase first appears in print in February or March 1969 in *Feminist Revolution*, although the concept had been generally circulating in the ether for decades, and for years specifically in relation to women. Carol Hanisch's essay in *Notes from the Second Year* (1970) was likely given the title "The Personal is Political" by editors Shulamith Firestone and Anne Koedt.

17   See Barbara Ryan, *Feminism and the Women's Movement* (New York: Routledge, 1992); Rita Felski, *Beyond Feminist Aesthetics* (Cambridge, MA: Harvard University Press, 1989); and Nancy Fraser, "Rethinking the Public Sphere," in *Habermas and the Public Sphere*, ed. Criag Calhoun (Cambridge, MA: MIT Press, 1992): 109–142.

18   Carol Hanisch, "The Personal is Political." February 1969. www.carolhanisch.org/CHwritings/PIP.html.

19   Ritter at 26.40

20   Ritter interview, at 5.28, 5.08. See also Taylor, "Interview"; and Marlene Fine, "Telling Our Herstory: 2007 NCA Convention Program." www.iupui.edu/~ncafws/2008/herstory08.htm.

21   Ritter interview at 2.39.

22   Ritter interview, at 6.50. See also Taylor "Interview," and Fine, "Telling Our Herstory."

23   Ritter interview, at 5.40.

24   Anita Taylor, email message to Catherine H. Palczewski, September 4, 2013.

25   Bonnie E. Patton (Ritter), chairperson, letter to Theodore Clevenger, February 20, 1972.

26   Paragraph of two-page letter as read by Ritter, in her interview, at 8.55.

27   "1973 SCA Legislative Council Summary Minutes," *Spectra* 10, no. 1 (February 1974): 11–12.

28   Ritter interview at 12.40.

29   Ritter interview at 21.00.

30   Ritter interview at 24.50.

31   National Communication Association. "Women's Leadership Project," par. 1. (2013) www.natcom.org/womensleadership/.

32   Issues of sexuality were attended to in Chapter 14, "Reading Between the Lines" by Patti P. Gillespie and Janette Kenner Muir in *Our Stories: Twentieth-Century Women Presidents of NCA*. The chapter notes the early presidents did not marry and most had no children, "two remarked specifically on the nontraditional nature of their marriages ... And throughout the twentieth century, many people in committed relationships were not allowed, by law, to marry" (p. 125). In Blankenship's essay, she writes that "I usually tell inquisitive inquirers that my long-time partner and I 'live in a very large English Cocker Spaniel dog house in which humans are permitted' ... inquiries beyond that have been on a need-to-know basis, as we were both brought up to be circumspect about our private lives in workplaces" (p. 76).

33   Phaedra Pezzullo, "Performing Critical Interruptions: Stories, Invention, and the Environmental Justice Movement," *Western Journal of Communication* 65 (2001): 1–25.

34   James Darsey, "Randall Majors, a Memorial," *Alternative Communications* 17 (September 1997): 3.

35   Sally Miller Gearhart, "Foreword: My Trip to Queer," in *Queer Theory and Communication: From Disciplining Queers to Queering the Discipline(s)*, ed. Gust A. Yep, Karen E. Lovaas, and John P. Elia (New York: Harrington Park Press, 2003): xxiv.

36 Estimates from James Darsey, Fred Jandt, and James Chesebro, all of whom were present. Personal correspondence from James Darsey to Charles E. Morris III, September 4, 2013.

37 For the events of 1977–1978, see Charles E. Morris III and Jason Edward Black, "Harvey Milk's Political Archive and Archival Politics," in *An Archive of Hope: Harvey Milk's Speeches and Writings*, ed. Jason Edward Black and Charles E. Morris III (Berkeley, CA: University of California Press, 2013): 1–59; Dudley Clendinen and Adam Nagourney, *Out for Good: The Struggle to Build a Gay Rights Movement in America* (New York: Simon & Schuster, 1999).

38 Robert Asen, *Invoking the Invisible Hand: Social Security and the Privatization Debates* (East Lansing, MI: Michigan State University Press, 2009): 16.

39 Sally Miller Gearhart, "Proposal for an Action Caucus on Gay Issues/Communication for the 1978 Convention of the Speech Communication Association (abridged)," *Alternative Communications* 1 (January 1979): 3–6.

40 James W. Chesebro, "The 1978 SCA Convention and the Gay Action Caucus," *Alternative Communications* 1 (January 1979): 1–3.

41 "Statement of the SCA Caucus on Gay and Lesbian Concern," *Spectra* 15, no. 4 (August 1979): 10–12; reprinted in *Alternative Communications* 1 (November 1979): 7.

42 "Resolutions," *Alternative Communications* 1 (January 1979): 6–7.

43 James Darsey, "An Introduction to Alternative Communications," unpublished essay, n.d.

44 James Darsey, "Notes from the SCA Legislative Council's Debate over Resolution M, N, O, & P Submitted by the Action Caucus of Gay and Lesbian Concerns," *Alternative Communications* 1 (January 1979): 7; Gearhart, "Foreword," xxiv–xxv.

45 Darsey, "Notes," 7–10.

46 Thomas W. Benson, "A Scandal in Academia: Sextext and *CRTNET*," *Western Journal of Communication* 76, no. 1 (January–February 2012): 11.

47 Benson, "Scandal," 12.

48 Herein lies one of the complexities of histories of sex/gender and sexuality. Even champions of one identity ingredient may not see themselves in that role, and, in fact, may participate in the very privileges that exclude peoples. Hochmuth Nichols is no exception. From her comment that she did not believe women were discriminated against (which in turn motivated Anita Taylor to run for Association president), to her speech "The Tyranny of Relevance," which motivated the entire Black membership of the Association to walk out on her presidential address, Nichols reminds us that progress is never linear and liberatory politics are not necessarily coalitional.

49 Lloyd F. Bitzer and Edwin Black, eds., *The Prospect of Rhetoric* (Englewood Cliffs, NJ: Prentice-Hall, 1971): v.

50 Marie Hochmuth Nichols, "Two Windows on *The Prospect of Rhetoric*," *Quarterly Journal of Speech* 58, no. 1 (1972): 96.

51 Jane Blankenship, "Marie Hochmuth Nichols (1908–1978): A Retrospective," *The Review of Communication* 4, no. 1/2 (2004): 82.

52 Carole Blair, Julie R. Brown, and Leslie A. Baxter, "Disciplining the Feminine," *Quarterly Journal of Speech* 80, no. 4 (1994): 383–384.

53 Blair et al., "Disciplining the Feminine," 384.

54 As quoted in Blair et al., "Disciplining the Feminine," 398.

55 As quoted in Blair et al., "Disciplining the Feminine," 399.

56 Blair et al., "Disciplining the Feminine," 384.

57 Blair et al., "Disciplining the Feminine," 397.

58 Blair et al., "Disciplining the Feminine," 397.

59 Robert L. Ivie, email message to Catherine H. Palczewski, August 20, 2013.

60 Blair et al., "Disciplining the Feminine," 397.

61 Blair et al., "Disciplining the Feminine," 401.

62 Blair et al., "Disciplining the Feminine," 402.

63 For a more detailed discussion of this, see a post by Carole Blair on CRTNET, #2273: Discussion of "Disciplining the Feminine," September 18, 1997.

64 Roy Schwartzman, "The Forum: Peer Review as the Enforcement of Disciplinary Orthodoxy," *Southern Communication Journal* 63 (1997): 69–75; Omar Swartz, "Disciplining the 'Other': Engaging Blair, Brown, and Baxter," *Southern Communication Journal* 62, no. 3 (1997): 253.

65 Joshua Gunn recounts how, in response to his use of the essay, one reviewer commented "Blair et al., despite the circulation their essay has gotten, struck me as simply whining, and generalizing on the basis of a highly limited sample." Personal communication.

66 The essay has fifty-six citations in the CMMC database. Twenty of those citations have occurred in the six years since the essay won the Woolbert award.

67 Mark Hickson III, Don W. Stacks, and Jonathan H. Amsbary, "Active Prolific Female Scholars in Communication: An Analysis of Research Productivity, II," *Communication Quarterly* 40 (1992): 338

68 Mark Hickson III, Don W. Stacks, and Jean Bodon, "The Status of Research Productivity in Communication: 1915–1995," *Communication Monographs* 66, no. 2 (1999): 180.

69 Schwartzman, "The Forum," 69.

70 Benson, "Scandal," 12.

71 Swartz, "Disciplining the 'Other'," 253.

72 Steve Corman, "Eerie Silence?" *CRTNET* 2215 (August 27, 1997).

73 Charles E. Morris III, "(Self-)Portrait of Prof. R.C.: A Retrospective," *Western Journal of Communication* 74, no. 1 (2010): 30.

74 Chesebro, "1978"; Gearhart, "Proposal."

75 James W. Chesebro, ed., *Gayspeak: Gay Male and Lesbian Communication* (New York: Pilgrim Press, 1981).

76 Frederick C. Corey, Ralph R. Smith, and Thomas K. Nakayama, "Bibliography of Articles and Books of Relevance to G/L/B/T Communication Studies," NCA Caucus on LGBTQ Concerns and GLBTQ Communication Studies Division, 2002: http://glbtqcaucus.wordpress.com/resources/.

77 Charles E. Morris III, "Precious Enclaves and Academic Tricks: Prospects for the Future of Queer Studies in Communication," Spotlight on Scholarship panel: *The Future of Gay & Lesbian Studies*, National Communication Association, Chicago, 1999.

78 Michael Warner, ed., *Fear of a Queer Planet: Queer Politics and Social Theory* (Minneapolis: University of Minnesota Press, 1993): xxvi.

79 Frederick C. Corey and Thomas K. Nakayama, "Sextext," *Text and Performance Quarterly* 17, no. 1 (January 1997): 58–68.

80 Corey and Nakayama, "Sextext," 58, 59.

81 Thomas K. Nakayama and Frederick C. Corey, "Nextext," in *Queer Theory and Communication: From Disciplining Queers to Queering the Discipline(s)*, ed. Gust A. Yep, Karen E. Lovaas, and John P. Elia (New York: Harrington Park Press, 2003): 331.

82 Nakayama and Corey, "Nextext," 331.

83 A. Susan Owen, "Disciplining 'Sextext': Queers, Fears, and Communication Studies," in *Queer Theory and Communication: From Disciplining Queers to Queering the Discipline(s)*, ed. Gust A. Yep, Karen E. Lovaas, and John P. Elia (New York: Harrington Park Press, 2003): 298; Benson, "Scandal," 2.

84 Craig Gingrich-Philbrook, "Revenge of the Dead Subject: The Contexts of Michael Bowman's Killing Dillinger," *Text and Performance Quarterly* 20, no. 4 (October 2000): 380.

85 Nakayama and Corey, "Nextext," 328.

86 Owen, "Disciplining," 298, 300–301, 305; Craig Gingrich-Philbrook, "Disciplinary Violation as Gender Violation: The Stigmatized Masculine Voice of Performance Studies," *Communication Theory* 8, no. 2 (1998): 210, 218.

87 Nakayama and Corey, "Nextext," 332.

88 Blair et al., "Disciplining the Feminine," 399.

89 Donald K. Smith, "Letter to the Editor," *Spectra* 33, no. 9 (September 1997): 8.

90 See for example Brant Burleson, "Advancing the Discipline?" *CRTNET* 1688 (February 2, 1997); David Sutton, "Read It for Yourself," *CRTNET* 1714 (February 6, 1997); Ted Wendt, "Confessions of a Long-Time TPQ Reader," *CRTNET* 1719 (February 7, 1997); David Sutton, "Rumpole and

the Professor's Goldfish," *CRTNET* 1724 (February 8, 1997); Ted Wendt, "Standard Forms," *CRTNET* 1759 (February 14, 1997); David Sutton "A Letter from Goldfish," *CRTNET* 1779 (February 23, 1997); Ted Wendt, "The Macduff Dialogues II," *CRTNET* 1786 (February 24, 1997); Ted Wendt, "The Ways and Means of Knowing: The 'Problem' of Scholarship in a Postmodern World," *American Communication Journal* 1 (February 1998): 3–4, 5. Craig used the phrase "exuberantly narcissistic" to describe the original post, his parodic "nightmare" fantasy that "Sextext" would become the new norm for publishing in the field. Robert Craig, "Textual Harassment/Autoethnography," *CRTNET* 1705 (February 4, 1997); Robert Craig, "Textual Harassment," *CRTNET* 1681 (January 31, 1997).

91 Gingrich-Philbrook, "Disciplinary," 215.

92 E. Patrick Johnson, "'Quare' Studies or (Almost) Everything I Know about Queer Studies I Learned from My Grandmother," *Text & Performance Quarterly* 21, no. 1 (2001): 3.

93 Roderick A. Ferguson, *Aberrations in Black: Toward a Queer of Color Critique* (Minneapolis: University of Minnesota Press, 2003): 149.

94 See Gust A. Yep, Karen E. Lovaas, and John P. Elia, eds., *Queer Theory and Communication: From Disciplining Queers to Queering the Discipline(s)* (New York: Harrington Park Press, 2003); Charles E. Morris III, *Queering Public Address: Sexualities in American Historical Discourse* (Columbia, SC: University of South Carolina Press, 2007); Karma Chávez, "Pushing Boundaries: Queer Intercultural Communication," *Journal of International and Intercultural Communication* 6, no. 2 (2013): 83–95; Karma Chávez, *Queer Migration Politics: Activist Rhetoric and Coalitional Possibilities* (Urbana, IL: University of Illinois Press, 2013); Isaac West, *Transforming Citizenships: Transgender Articulations of the Law* (New York: New York University Press, 2014).

95 E. Patrick Johnson and Mae G. Henderson, eds., *Black Queer Studies: A Critical Anthology* (Durham, NC: Duke University Press, 2005).

96 Anna M. Young, Adria Battaglia, and Dana L. Cloud, "(Un)Disciplining the Scholar Activist: Policing the Boundaries of Political Engagement," *Quarterly Journal of Speech* 96, no. 4 (November 2010): 431.

97 Jane Blankenship wrote a retrospective in the *Review of Communication* as a past president of the Association. In it, she reminisces about the debates over convention siting in states that failed to ratify the ERA. "The second event occurred when the State of Illinois failed to ratify the ERA. Many members requested that our Association's convention be moved out of Chicago ... A long and passionate debate in the Legislative Assembly ensued. Those who opposed the move did so on the basis of possible legal consequences. Moreover, they argued that it was too late to make alternative arrangements. Other arguments focused on the very real economic consequences for the low-income wage earners who were typically hired for a major convention, on the ethics of breaking a contract, and on whether the Association should be taking stands on political issues. We did not move." Blankenship, who was vice-president at the time of the debates, and president at the time of the 1978 convention, misremembered. Jane Blankenship, "Jane Blankenship, 1978 President, National Communication Association," *The Review of Communication* 6, no. 3 (2006): 196.

98 "Equal Rights Amendment," www.now.org/issues/economic/eratext.html.

99 "Resolution on Equal Rights Amendment," *Spectra* 14, no. 1 (February 1978): 23.

100 Jane Blankenship, "To the Membership" and "Letters," *Spectra* 14, no. 3 (June 1978): 5.

101 "1977 SCA Legislative Council Summary Minutes 63rd Annual Meeting," *Spectra* 14, no. 1 (February 1978): 15.

102 "Minneapolis Selected for November 2–5, 1978 SCA Annual Meeting," *Spectra* 14, no. 1 (February 1978): 1.

103 According to Bonnie Ritter, Ronald Allen was president at the time of the ERA vote; 1978 was his convention to plan, and he could have said the move was impossible, but he did not. Part of the history highlighted by Ritter in her memory of this event was that five representatives from Chicago had cast the deciding ballots in the Illinois ERA ratification vote. Ritter interview at 32.10.

104 William C. Peeper, "Letter to Executive Secretary William Work," *Spectra* 14, no. 1 (February 1978): 23.

105   Karlyn Kohrs Campbell in "Letters," *Spectra* 14, no. 5 (October 1978): 4.

106   Charles Veenstra in "Letters," *Spectra* 14, no. 3 (June 1978): 4.

107   Carroll B. Ellis in "Letters," *Spectra* 14, no. 2 (April 1978): 13.

108   L. Day Hanks in "Letters," *Spectra* 14, no. 4 (August 1978):15.

109   Ronald F. Reid in "Letters," *Spectra* 14, no. 3 (June 1978): 10.

110   Karl B. Harris in "Letters," *Spectra* 14, no. 2 (April 1978): 11.

111   Carol A. Berthold in "Letters," *Spectra* 14, no. 5 (October 1978): 4.

112   Merlin D. Waite in "Letters," *Spectra* 14, no. 2 (April 1978): 13–14.

113   James Edward Sayer in "Letters," *Spectra* 14, no. 2 (April 1978): 12.

114   David W. Shepard in "Letters," *Spectra* 14, no. 5 (October 1978): 5.

115   L.E. Norton in "Letters," *Spectra* 14, no. 5 (October 1978): 5.

116   Perhaps it is no accident that Nichols, Blankenship, and Taylor all had a history with competitive debate, a location that enables women to learn to advocate—for others and themselves. See Carly Woods, "Women Debating Society: Negotiating Differences in Historical Argument Cultures," PhD dissertation, University of Pittsburgh, 2010.

117   Anita Taylor, "Anita Taylor, 1981 President of the National Communication Association," *Review of Communication* 6, no. 3 (July 2006): 210. In the version of this essay printed on the NCA website (www.natcom.org/womensleadership/), Taylor contextualizes these comments as part of "the many controversies at the time. This was, after all, the convention during which we debated the wisdom of holding our meetings in states that had not ratified the ERA, of which Illinois was one" (pp. 5–6).

118   "Editor's Note," *Spectra* 14, no. 5 (October 1978): 6.

119   See Linda Hirschman, *Victory: The Triumphant Gay Revolution* (New York: Harper Perennial, 2013).

120   Roger Smitter, "NCA Response to Mr. Manchester's Contribution to Support a Marriage Amendment," *CRTNET* 10397 (May 7, 2008).

121   Smitter, "NCA Response."

122   Ted Kanatas, "Hyatt's Response to Mr. Manchester's Contribution," *CRTNET* 10397 (May 7, 2008).

123   Martha Solomon Watson, "Doug Manchester," *CRTNET* 10399 (May 9, 2008).

124   Jeffrey Bennett, "NCA Hyatt Boycott," *CRTNET* 10399 (May 9, 2008).

125   Craig Gingrich-Philbrook, "Response to Dr. Watson," *CRTNET* 10402 (May 12, 2008); A. Susan Owen, "Non-Normative Marriage," *CRTNET* 10402 (May 12, 2008); Joe DeVito, "NCA's Letter," *CRTNET* 10402 (May 12, 2008); David Weiss, "Our 2008 Conference Hotel," *CRTNET* 10468 (July 18, 2008); Phaedra Pezzullo, "A Boycott of the NCA Hotel," *CRTNET* 10485 (August 4, 2008); Charles E. Morris III, "Manchester Boycott," *CRTNET* 10487 (August 5, 2008); Susan Zaeske, "UW-Madison Cancels Reception in Protest," *CRTNET* 10487 (August 5, 2008); Bill Eadie, "The Manchester Grand Hyatt Boycott," *CRTNET* 10490 (August 6, 2008).

126   Powell DeGange, "NCA Convention at the Manchester Grand Hyatt Boycott," *CRTNET* 10529 (August 28, 2008); Jon Simons, "Open Letter to NCA Executive Committee," *CRTNET* 10631 (October 31, 2008); Karma Chávez, "Response to Powell Lito," *Facebook* (October 13, 2008): www.facebook.com/groups/25023464067/.

127   Phaedra Pezzullo, "CRTNET Submission," *CRTNET* 10631 (August 28, 2008).

128   Dana Cloud, "Developments in Manchester Hotel Boycott," *CRTNET* 10532 (September 2, 2008); Jon Simons, *Facebook* (September 25, 2008): www.facebook.com/groups/25023464067/.

129   Roger Smitter, "Posting in Response to DeGange," *CRTNET* 10550 (September 12, 2008); Dana Cloud, "NCA's Union Busting Rhetoric," *CRTNET* 10551 (September 15, 2008).

130   Dana Cloud, "Now that NCA Has Decided . . .," *CRTNET* 10558 (September 18, 2008).

131   Charles E. Morris III, "An Appeal to the GLBT Division, Caucus on LGBTQ Concerns, and Our Allies," *CRTNET* 10581 (October 1, 2008).

132   Jeffrey Bennett, "Statement from the NCA GLBTQ Division and the Caucus for LGBTQ Concerns," *CRTNET* 10631 (October 31, 2008).

133 See for example, Kendall R. Phillips, "Rhetoric and Public Memory Preconference Relocating," *CRTNET* 10591 (October 7, 2008); Bryan Crable, "Villanova University Withdraws from the Manchester Hyatt," *CRTNET* 10591 (October 7, 2008); Dana Cloud, "FW: CCS Statement on San Diego," *CRTNET* 10598 (October 9, 2008).

134 Phaedra Pezzullo, "NCA Resolution," *Facebook* (September 22, 2008): www.facebook.com/groups/25023464067/; Art Bochner, "NCA Presidential Task Force on Hotel Site Selection," *CRTNET* 10585 (October 3, 2008).

135 For principled objections, see Richard E. Vatz, "Voices from the Margins: The Conservative Perspective: NCA's *De Facto* Ideological Discrimination," *Spectra* 45, no. 2 (February 2009): 3. For practical objections, see Janis Edwards, "Boycott at NCA," *CRTNET* 10560 (September 19, 2008). See also Laura Ellingson, "Shall I be an LGBTQ and Labor Advocate Today, or a Person with a Disability?" *CRTNET* 10558 (September 18, 2008), and "Response to Charles Morris," *CRTNET* 10583 (October 2, 2008).

136 Mari Yandall, "NCA Convention-Student Response," *CRTNET* 10555 (September 17, 2008).

137 Betsy Bach, "Engage All Voices," *Spectra* 45, no. 11 (December 2009): 3, and "On Practicing What We Preach." Presidential address, annual convention of the National Communication Association, Chicago, Illinois, November 14, 2009. www.natcom.org/NCA/files/ccLibraryFiles/Filename/000000002131/Pres%20Address202009.pdf; Young et al., "(Un)Disciplining the Scholar Activist."

138 Jason Black, *Facebook* (November 26, 2008): www.facebook.com/groups/25023464067/.

139 Karrin Anderson, Suzanne Enck-Wanzer, Radhika Gajjala, Kimberly Golombisky, Krista Hoffmann-Longtin, Sheena Malhotra, Vicky Newsom, Kristina Sheeler, and Helen Tate (Feminist & Women Studies Division and Women's Caucus leadership). [Letter]. October 10, 2008.

References

"1973 SCA Legislative Council Summary Minutes." *Spectra* 10, no. 1 (February 1974): 11–12.

"1977 SCA Legislative Council Summary Minutes 63rd Annual Meeting." *Spectra* 14, no. 1 (February 1978): 14–15.

Anderson, Karrin, Suzanne Enck-Wanzer, Radhika Gajjala, Kimberly Golombisky, Krista Hoffmann-Longtin, Sheena Malhotra, Vicky Newsom, Kristina Sheeler, and Helen Tate (Feminist & Women Studies Division and Women's Caucus leadership). [Letter]. October 10, 2008.

Asen, Robert. *Invoking the Invisible Hand: Social Security and the Privatization Debates*. East Lansing, MI: Michigan State University Press, 2009.

Bach, Betsy Wackernagel. "Engage All Voices." *Spectra* 45, no. 11 (December 2009): 3.

——. "On Practicing What We Preach." Presidential address, annual convention of the National Communication Association, Chicago, Illinois, November 14, 2009. www.natcom.org/NCA/files/ccLibraryFiles/Filename/000000002131/Pres%20Address202009.pdf.

Baldwin, Stanley. *On England, and Other Addresses*. London: Books for Libraries Press, 1926.

Becker, Samuel L. "Rhetorical Studies for the Contemporary World." In *The Prospect of Rhetoric*, edited by Lloyd F. Bitzer and Edwin Black, 21–43. Englewood Cliffs, NJ: Prentice-Hall, Inc., 1971.

Bennett, Jeffrey. "NCA Hyatt Boycott." *CRTNET* 10399 (May 9, 2008).

——. "Statement from the NCA GLBTQ Division and the Caucus for LGBTQ Concerns." *CRTNET* 10631 (October 31, 2008).

Benson, Thomas W. "A Scandal in Academia: Sextext and *CRTNET*." *Western Journal of Communication* 76, no. 1 (January–February 2012): 2–16.

Bitzer, Lloyd F. and Edwin Black, eds. *The Prospect of Rhetoric*. Englewood Cliffs, NJ: Prentice-Hall, Inc., 1971.

Black, Jason. *Facebook* (November 26, 2008): www.facebook.com/groups/25023464067/.

Blair, Carole, Julie R. Brown, and Leslie A. Baxter. "Disciplining the Feminine." *Quarterly Journal of Speech* 80, no. 4 (1994): 383–409.

Blankenship, Jane. "Jane Blankenship, 1978 President, National Communication Association." *The Review of Communication* 6, no. 3 (2006): 187–203.

———. "Marie Hochmuth Nichols (1908–1978): A Retrospective." *The Review of Communication* 4, no. 1/2 (2004): 75–85.

———. "To the Membership" and "Letters." *Spectra* 14, no. 3 (June 1978): 5.

Bochner, Art. "NCA Presidential Task Force on Hotel Site Selection." *CRTNET* 10585 (October 3, 2008).

Brockriede, Wayne. "Arguers as Lovers." *Philosophy & Rhetoric* 5, no. 1 (Winter 1972): 1–11.

Bryant, Donald C. *The Rhetorical Idiom.* Ithaca, NY: Cornell University Press, 1958.

Burgoon, Michael. "Instruction About Communication: On Divorcing Dame Speech." *Communication Education* 38, no. 4 (1989): 303–308.

Burleson, Brant. "Advancing the Discipline?" *CRTNET* 1688 (February 2, 1997).

Chávez, Karma. "Pushing Boundaries: Queer Intercultural Communication." *Journal of International and Intercultural Communication* 6, no. 2 (2013): 83–95.

———. *Queer Migration Politics: Activist Rhetoric and Coalitional Possibilities.* Urbana, IL: University of Illinois Press, 2013.

———. "Response to Powell Lito." *Facebook* (October 13, 2008): www.facebook.com/groups/250234 64067/.

Chesebro, James W., ed. *Gayspeak: Gay Male and Lesbian Communication.* New York: Pilgrim Press, 1981.

———. "The 1978 SCA Convention and the Gay Action Caucus." *Alternative Communications* 1 (January 1979): 1–3.

Clendinen, Dudley and Adam Nagourney. *Out for Good: The Struggle to Build a Gay Rights Movement in America.* New York: Simon & Schuster, 1999.

Cloud, Dana. "Developments in Manchester Hotel Boycott." *CRTNET* 10532 (September 2, 2008).

———. "FW: CCS Statement on San Diego." *CRTNET* 10598 (October 9, 2008).

———. "NCA's Union Busting Rhetoric." *CRTNET* 10551 (September 15, 2008).

———. "Now that NCA Has Decided . . ." *CRTNET* 10558 (September 18, 2008).

Condit, Celeste Michelle. "The Birth of Understanding: Chaste Science and the Harlot of the Arts." *Communication Monographs* 57 (1990): 323–327.

Corey, Frederick C., Ralph R. Smith, and Thomas K. Nakayama. "Bibliography of Articles and Books of Relevance to G/L/B/T Communication Studies." NCA Caucus on LGBTQ Concerns and GLBTQ Communication Studies Division, 2002: http://glbtqcaucus.wordpress.com/resources/.

Corey Frederick C. and Thomas K. Nakayama. "Sextext." *Text and Performance Quarterly* 17, no. 1 (January 1997): 58–68.

Corman, Steve. "Eerie Silence?" *CRTNET* 2215 (August 27, 1997).

Crable, Bryan. "Villanova University Withdraws from the Manchester Hyatt." *CRTNET* 10591 (October 7, 2008).

Craig, Robert. "Textual Harassment." *CRTNET* 1681 (January 31, 1997).

———. "Textual Harassment/Autoethnography." *CRTNET* 1705 (February 4, 1997).

Darsey, James. "An Introduction to Alternative Communications." Unpublished essay, n.d.

———. "Notes from the SCA Legislative Council's Debate over Resolution M, N, O, & P Submitted by the Action Caucus of Gay and Lesbian Concerns." *Alternative Communications* 1 (January 1979): 7

———. "Randall Majors, A Memorial." *Alternative Communications* 17 (September 1997): 3.

DeGange, Powell. "NCA Convention at the Manchester Grand Hyatt Boycott." *CRTNET* 10529 (August 28, 2008).

DeVito, Joe. "NCA's Letter." *CRTNET* 10402 (May 12, 2008).

Eadie, Bill. "The Manchester Grand Hyatt Boycott." *CRTNET* 10490 (August 6, 2008).

"Editor's Note." *Spectra* 14, no. 5 (October 1978): 6.

Edwards, Janis. "Boycott at NCA." *CRTNET* 10560 (September 19, 2008).

Ellingson, Laura. "Response to Charles Morris." *CRTNET* 10583 (October 2, 2008).

———. "Shall I be an LGBTQ and Labor Advocate Today, or a Person with a Disability?" *CRTNET* 10558 (September 18, 2008).

Enchelmayer, Ernest J. "Rhetoric in the Visual Arts." *Conference of the International Journal of Arts and Sciences* 1, no. 19 (2009): 59–79. http://openaccesslibrary.org/images/AUS182_Ernest_J._Enchelmayer.pdf.

"Equal Rights Amendment." www.now.org/issues/economic/eratext.html.

Felski, Rita. *Beyond Feminist Aesthetics*. Cambridge, MA: Harvard University Press, 1989.

Ferguson, Roderick A. *Aberrations in Black: Toward a Queer of Color Critique*. Minneapolis: University of Minnesota Press, 2003.

Fine, Marlene. "Telling Our Herstory: 2007 NCA Convention Program." www.iupui.edu/~ncafws/2008/herstory08.htm.

Fraser, Nancy. "Rethinking the Public Sphere." In *Habermas and the Public Sphere*, edited by Criag Calhoun, 109–142. Cambridge, MA: MIT Press, 1992.

Gearhart, Sally Miller. "Foreword: My Trip to Queer." In *Queer Theory and Communication: From Disciplining Queers to Queering the Discipline(s)*, edited by Gust A. Yep, Karen E. Lovaas, and John P. Elia, xxi–xxx. New York: Harrington Park Press, 2003.

——. "Proposal for an Action Caucus on Gay Issues/Communication for the 1978 Convention of the Speech Communication Association (abridged)." *Alternative Communications* 1 (January 1979): 3–6.

Gillespie, Patti P. and Janette Kenner Muir. "Reading Between the Lines." In *Our Stories: Twentieth-Century Women Presidents of NCA*, edited by Patti P. Gillespie, 123–132. Washington, DC: National Communication Association, 2010.

Gingrich-Philbrook, Craig. "Disciplinary Violation as Gender Violation: The Stigmatized Masculine Voice of Performance Studies." *Communication Theory* 8, no. 2 (1998): 203–220.

——. "Response to Dr. Watson." *CRTNET* 10402 (May 12, 2008).

——. "Revenge of the Dead Subject: The Contexts of Michael Bowman's Killing Dillinger." *Text and Performance Quarterly* 20, no. 4 (October 2000): 375–387.

Hanisch, Carol. "The Personal is Political." February 1969. www.carolhanisch.org/CHwritings/PIP.html.

Hickson, Mark III, William R. Self, Justin R. Johnston, Cynthia Peacock, and Jean Bodon. "Prolific Research in Communication Studies: Retrospective and Prospective Views." *Communication Research Reports* 26, no. 4 (2009): 337–346.

Hickson, Mark III, Don W. Stacks, and Jonathan H. Amsbary. "Active Prolific Female Scholars in Communication: An Analysis of Research Productivity, II." *Communication Quarterly* 40 (1992): 350–356.

Hickson, Mark III, Don W. Stacks, and Jean Bodon. "The Status of Research Productivity in Communication: 1915–1995." *Communication Monographs* 66, no. 2 (1999): 178–197.

Hirschman, Linda. *Victory: The Triumphant Gay Revolution*. New York: Harper Perennial, 2013.

Johnson, E. Patrick "'Quare' Studies or (Almost) Everything I Know about Queer Studies I Learned from My Grandmother." *Text & Performance Quarterly* 21, no. 1 (2001): 1–25.

Johnson, E. Patrick and Mae G. Henderson, eds. *Black Queer Studies: A Critical Anthology*. Durham, NC: Duke University Press, 2005.

Kanatas, Ted. "Hyatt's Response to Mr. Manchester's Contribution." *CRTNET* 10397 (May 7, 2008).

"Letters." *Spectra* 14, no. 2 (April 1978): 11–14.

"Letters." *Spectra* 14, no. 3 (June 1978): 4–5, 10–11.

"Letters." *Spectra* 14, no. 4 (August 1978): 15–17.

"Letters." *Spectra* 14, no. 5 (October 1978): 4–6.

Locke, John. *An Essay Concerning Human Understanding*. Edinburgh: Mundell & Son, 1801.

Lucaites, John Louis and Celeste Michelle Condit. "Introduction." In *Contemporary Rhetorical Theory*, edited by John Louis Lucaites, Celeste Michelle Condit, and Sally Caudill, 1–18. New York: The Guilford Press, 1999.

Medhust, Martin J. "Editor's Welcome." *Rhetoric & Public Affairs* 1, no. 1 (Spring 1998): iii–iv.

"Minneapolis Selected for November 2–5, 1978 SCA Annual Meeting." *Spectra* 14, no. 1 (February 1978): 1.

Morris III, Charles E. "An Appeal to the GLBT Division, Caucus on LGBTQ Concerns, and Our Allies." *CRTNET* 10581 (October 1, 2008).

——. "Manchester Boycott." *CRTNET* 10487 (August 5, 2008).

——. "Precious Enclaves and Academic Tricks: Prospects for the Future of Queer Studies in Communication." Spotlight on Scholarship panel: *The Future of Gay & Lesbian Studies*. National Communication Association, Chicago, 1999.

——. *Queering Public Address: Sexualities in American Historical Discourse*. Columbia, SC: University of South Carolina Press, 2007.

——. "(Self-)Portrait of Prof. R.C.: A Retrospective." *Western Journal of Communication* 74, no. 1 (2010): 4–42.

Morris III, Charles E. and Jason Edward Black. "Harvey Milk's Political Archive and Archival Politics." In *An Archive of Hope: Harvey Milk's Speeches and Writings*, edited by Jason Edward Black and Charles E. Morris III, 1–59. Berkeley, CA: University of California Press, 2013.

Nakayama, Thomas K. and Frederick C. Corey. "Nextext." In *Queer Theory and Communication: From Disciplining Queers to Queering the Discipline(s)*, edited by Gust A. Yep, Karen E. Lovaas, and John P. Elia, 319–334. New York: Harrington Park Press, 2003.

National Communication Association. "Women's Leadership Project." 2013. www.natcom.org/womensleadership/.

Nichols, Marie H. "Two Windows on *The Prospect of Rhetoric*." *Quarterly Journal of Speech* 58, no. 1 (1972): 92–96.

——. "The Tyranny of Relevance." *Spectra* 6, no. 1 (February 1970): 1, 9–10.

North, Helen F. "Emblems of Eloquence." *Proceedings of the American Philosophical Society* 137, no. 3 (1993): 406–430.

Owen, A. Susan. "Disciplining 'Sextext': Queers, Fears, and Communication Studies." In *Queer Theory and Communication: From Disciplining Queers to Queering the Discipline(s)*, edited by Gust A. Yep, Karen E. Lovaas, and John P. Elia, 297–318. New York: Harrington Park Press, 2003.

——. "Non-Normative Marriage." *CRTNET* 10402 (May 12, 2008).

Peeper, William C. "Letter to Executive Secretary William Work." *Spectra* 14, no. 1 (February 1978): 23.

"Peitho." *Theoi Greek Mythology*. Last updated 2011. www.theoi.com/Daimon/Peitho.html.

Pezzullo, Phaedra. "A Boycott of the NCA Hotel." *CRTNET* 10485 (August 4, 2008).

——. "CRTNET Submission." *CRTNET* 10631 (August 28, 2008).

——. "NCA Resolution." *Facebook* (September 22, 2008): www.facebook.com/groups/25023464067/.

——. "Performing Critical Interruptions: Stories, Invention, and the Environmental Justice Movement." *Western Journal of Communication* 65 (2001): 1–25.

Phillips, Kendall R. "Rhetoric and Public Memory Preconference Relocating." *CRTNET* 10591 (October 7, 2008).

"Resolution on Equal Rights Amendment." *Spectra* 14, no. 1 (February 1978): 23.

"Resolutions." *Alternative Communications* 1 (January 1979): 6–7.

Ritter, Bonnie. Videotaped Interview with Cindy Lont, National Communication Association, Chicago. November 1997.

Ryan, Barbara. *Feminism and the Women's Movement*. New York: Routledge, 1992.

Schwartzman, Roy. "The Forum: Peer Review as the Enforcement of Disciplinary Orthodoxy." *Southern Communication Journal* 63 (1997): 69–75.

Simons, Jon. *Facebook* (September 25, 2008): www.facebook.com/groups/25023464067/.

——. "Open Letter to NCA Executive Committee." *CRTNET* 10631 (October 31, 2008).

Smith, Amy C. "Athenian Political Art from the Fifth and Fourth Centuries BCE: Images of Political Personifications." In *Démos: Classical Athenian Democracy*, edited by C.W. Blackwell, 1–26. January 18, 2003. http://cwb@stoa.org.

Smith, Donald K. "Letter to the Editor." *Spectra* 33, no. 9 (September 1997): 8.

Smitter, Roger. "NCA Response to Mr. Manchester's Contribution to Support a Marriage Amendment." *CRTNET* 10397 (May 7, 2008).

——. "Posting in Response to DeGange." *CRTNET* 10550 (September 12, 2008).

"Statement of the SCA Caucus on Gay and Lesbian Concern." *Spectra* 15, no. 4 (August 1979): 10–12; reprinted in *Alternative Communications* 1 (November 1979): 7.

Sutton, David. "A Letter from Goldfish." *CRTNET* 1779 (February 23, 1997).
——. "Read It for Yourself." *CRTNET* 1714 (February 6, 1997).
——. "Rumpole and the Professor's Goldfish." *CRTNET* 1724 (February 8, 1997).
Swartz, Omar. "Disciplining the 'Other': Engaging Blair, Brown, and Baxter." *Southern Communication Journal* 62, no. 3 (1997): 253–256.
Swearingen, C. Jan. *Rhetoric and Irony: Western Literacy and Western Lies.* New York: Oxford University Press, 1991.
Taylor, Anita. "Anita Taylor, 1981 President of the National Communication Association." *Review of Communication* 6, no. 3 (July 2006): 204–216.
——. "Interview with Anita Taylor: A Look into NCA Women's Leadership." By Kristina Horn Sheeler and Matthew Lamb. September 13, 2006. www.iupui.edu/~ncafws/taylor06.htm.
Vatz, Richard E. "Voices from the Margins: The Conservative Perspective: NCA's *De Facto* Ideological Discrimination." *Spectra* 45, no. 2 (February 2009): 3.
Warner, Michael. "Introduction." In *Fear of a Queer Planet: Queer Politics and Social Theory,* edited by Michael Warner, vii–xxxi. Minneapolis: University of Minnesota Press, 1993.
Watson, Martha Solomon. "Doug Manchester." *CRTNET* 10399 (May 9, 2008).
Weiss, David. "Our 2008 Conference Hotel." *CRTNET* 10468 (July 18, 2008).
Wendt, Ted. "Confessions of a Long-Time TPQ Reader." *CRTNET* 1719 (February 7, 1997).
——. "The Macduff Dialogues II." *CRTNET* 1786 (February 24, 1997).
——. "Standard Forms." *CRTNET* 1759 (February 14, 1997).
——. "The Ways and Means of Knowing: The 'Problem' of Scholarship in a Postmodern World." *American Communication Journal* 1 (February 1998): 3–5.
West, Isaac. *Transforming Citizenships: Transgender Articulations of the Law.* New York: New York University Press, 2014.
Woods, Carly. "Women Debating Society: Negotiating Differences in Historical Argument Cultures." PhD dissertation, University of Pittsburgh, 2010.
Yandall, Mari. "NCA Convention-Student Response." *CRTNET* 10555 (September 17, 2008).
Yep, Gust A., Karen E. Lovaas, and John P. Elia, eds. *Queer Theory and Communication: From Disciplining Queers to Queering the Discipline(s).* New York: Harrington Park Press, 2003.
Young, Anna M., Adria Battaglia, and Dana L. Cloud. "(Un)Disciplining the Scholar Activist: Policing the Boundaries of Political Engagement." *Quarterly Journal of Speech* 96, no. 4 (November 2010): 427–435.
Zaeske, Susan. "UW-Madison Cancels Reception in Protest." *CRTNET* 10487 (August 5, 2008).

7.

LIBERALISM AND ITS DISCONTENTS

Black Rhetoric and the Cultural Transformation of Rhetorical Studies in the Twentieth Century

Reynaldo Anderson, Marnel Niles Goins, and Sheena Howard

Introduction

African American or Black rhetoric is a diverse field of research, which cannot be summed up in one article or monograph. Therefore, this chapter focuses on the relationship between some intersecting influences on the emergence of modern Black rhetoric. Specifically, this study looks at how the emergence of modern Black rhetoric engaged various ideological and socio-economic formations such as liberalism, the modern world system, and the digital turn early in the twenty-first century.

We begin with a political theory, rather than with African American theorists or rhetors, because the emergence of Black rhetoric was not a given, but was contingent on dismantling certain assumptions of liberalism. Contemporary liberalism is a set of values and ideas that emerged after World War I during the Great Depression, contributing to the development of the politics and policy of the New Deal that influenced an elite consensus around economic and social practices in American society.[1] Yet, beginning in the 1950s through the late 1960s and early 1970s, during the height of the Cold War and Vietnam War, and segregationist Jim Crow policies, African Americans and other minorities began to organize, argue, harangue, and fight for civil rights and human rights.

During this period, scholars began to focus communication research on the structure of discourse relative to social movements, identity, and culture. For example, at the Speech Association of America's annual convention held in Chicago in December of 1968, an ad hoc committee of African American scholars put forth *A Manifesto to the Speech Profession*, a document that lamented the social irrelevance of communication scholarship and noted the discipline needed to undergo an intellectual revolution with a society that is undergoing a social revolution.[2] Furthermore, in relation to that manifesto it is useful to ask the rhetorical question attributed to sociolinguist Richard Wright: "If communication can be defined as the universe of forms, processes, and structures that govern how we relate to the world, then aren't there forms, processes, and structures that are particular to African Americans?"[3] The authors of the manifesto argued for the relevance of research on the relationship between those structures and processes and how they inform the study of Black rhetoric.

This chapter will proceed by first examining, along a historical axis, how race and rhetoric have been always intertwined, though not always visibly so; then exploring how texts and scholarship have shaped each other, leading to an account of how institutional changes brought Black rhetoric into focus; and, finally, confronting the post-modern challenges that face Black rhetoric in the twenty-first century.

Race and Rhetoric

Historically, the study of classical Black rhetoric begins in antiquity with the framework found in Egyptian (Kemetic) texts such as the *mdw nfr* that focused on effective speech and ethical concerns, and preceded the Greco-Roman perspectives by some 3,000 to 4,000 years.[4] In addition, the Islamic influence on certain parts of the continent and on Black rhetoric, specifically, cannot be overestimated as a factor in communication or philosophical frameworks.[5] Moreover, African rhetoric is a contemporary phenomenon: one example (among many) of contemporary West African rhetorical analysis is the *Odu Ifa*, a sacred text of the Yoruba people of West Africa.[6] However, in the context of Western modernity, and particularly relevant to American communication studies, modern Black rhetoric emerged out of the nexus of the transatlantic slave trade, modern racialized capitalism, the emergence of the modern world system, the dialectical relationship between segregation and colonialism, neoliberalism and neocolonialism, and the internal contra-dictions of European philosophy and religion. Without understanding these historical streams, we cannot see how and why the possibility of a Black rhetoric emerged.

The twelfth to fifteenth centuries, preceding the emergence of modern geopolitics of the Atlantic basin, represented a period of Islamic expansion, trans-Saharan trade, the rise and fall of African empires, Meso-American nations, and the emergence of European hegemony by virtue of appropriating Asian and African technology, science, and resources.[7] Correspondingly, the modern Black rhetorical tradition arose from various sources, including the organized revolts of slave castles in West Africa, slave ships, maroon settlements, *palenques* and *quilombos* (places of refuge for runaway African slaves), plantations, Christian evangelical movements, abolition movements, Black women's club movements, segregated living conditions, and of course the agency of African men and women.[8] Moreover, during the period when Africans and the indigenous populations of the Western hemisphere were systematically exploited, the concepts of race, racism, and capitalism in the modern world system developed. The cultural institutions and scientific rationale emerged for dominating people of color with "race as its epistemology, its ordering principle, its organizing structure, its moral authority, its economy of justice, commerce, and power."[9] Therefore, in relation to the racialized formation of capital (as well as gender and sexuality), these processes were not only incorporated into the socio-cultural and psychological underlying patterns of European feudalism/mercantilism, but were intended to "extend these social relations into the larger tapestry of the modern world's political and economic relations."[10]

However, during the Haitian Revolution, African slaves appropriated the philo-sophical tools of European modernity in their own interests; these tools would serve as a leitmotif or underlying principle to the emergence of a modern Black rhetoric in the Western hemisphere and the rest of the Atlantic basin. The revolution revealed the internal contradictions of slavery, and "the emergence of a secular social philosophy that necessitated a redefinition of the place of human bondage in the rational order of being."[11] For example, although their ideas were not in support of abolition of "negro" slavery but against absolute power, secular philosophers of the European Enlightenment, such as John Locke, argued that in relation to the importance of natural liberty, slavery was "the state of War continued, between a lawful Conqueror, and a Captive."[12] Montesquieu similarly noted that slavery was against the principles or ideas that promoted the happiness of the individual.[13] A second source of secular impulse was Adam Smith's *The Theory of Moral Sentiments* and *The Wealth of Nations* and their impact on British Protestantism by not only attempting to resolve the tension between individual enterprise and sympathetic benevolence, but arguing that slavery was limiting human progress. Although most Christians (or Muslims or Jews, for that matter) saw no contradiction between the practice of their faith and slavery, the work of Christian evangelicals such as John Wesley and others concluded that slavery was a sin for which the world would soon be judged.[14]

In relation to the agency of the Africans themselves, Anthony Bogues has argued that it is commonly assumed that the ideas, philosophies, and practices of Black activists and intellectuals are primarily derivative of Europeans and should be critiqued mainly for their "experiences."[15] Bogues believes this assumption is mistaken on several counts, including:

(1) reducing the aforementioned "experiences" to a philosophically skewed interpretive approach, concerning the way political ideas and thought are studied, the relationship between knowledge, power, and discursive systems;
(2) theoretical frameworks that reject the privileged location of the Western episteme yet are rooted in the same conceptual protocols; and
(3) the way Africa and African peoples are represented in the Western intellectual tradition and popular culture.

Therefore, Black radicals seem to commit a form of heresy when generating a new critical discourse that questions the *doxa* of Western intellectual formations that themselves employ "systems of classifications that reproduce their own logic . . . imposing their own principles of social reality."[16] Additionally, "Black radical intellectual production engages in a double operation . . . an engagement with Western radical theory and then a critique of this theory . . . breaking the epistemic limits established by the Western intellectual tradition." Furthermore, "For the Black radical intellectual, 'heresy' means becoming human, not white or imitative of the colonial, but overturning white/European norm-ativity."[17] Thus, Cedric Robinson argues that the 1791 slave revolution in Haiti started under the leadership of people such as Dutty Boukman, using alternative epistemologies that drew upon African faith traditions such as *vodun* while also engaging the discourse of the Enlightenment and rearticulating an alternate conception of human freedom and agency. As the news of the successful slave revolution spread all over the Western hemisphere, throughout the Caribbean, South America, and North America, slave revolts began to spread and from that time Haiti was treated as a pariah state in the modern world.[18]

By the 1830s in North America, the abolition movement had grown into two primary rhetorical approaches, agitation and conversion. Ernest Bormann recounts that in the anti-slavery *evangelist* camp, largely represented by William Lloyd Garrison, Theodore Weld, and Frederick Douglass, the goal was to galvanize the audience to the cause and embrace immediate abolition of slavery, whereas the *agitator* approach sought to disturb or upset the listener.[19] Additionally, the unique African American contribution to the rhetorical field was the emergence of the "Black jeremiad." A uniquely American rhetorical form rooted in Anglo-American puritan Christianity, the Black jeremiad is composed of three elements, including "affirmation of society's promise, criticism of declension, or current retrogression from the promise, and a closing prophecy that society will shortly complete its mission and redeem the promise."[20] However, radical writings like David Walker's "Appeal to the Colored Citizens of the World," and orators such as Mariah Stewart, Henry Highland Garnet, Frederick Douglass, and other radical abolitionists extended the previous epistemic limits of the jeremiad and incorporated the fourth element of the denunciation of slavery that encouraged violent insurrection by the slaves themselves; thus, before and after the Civil War the Black jeremiad remained the dominant expression of Black oratory in the nineteenth century.[21]

Correspondingly, during the 1830s and 1840s, labor movements grew in Western countries and the issues of slavery and gender discrimination permeated their literature and organizing.[22] Many Europeans who had been exposed to the ideas of socialism and Marxism would eventually immigrate to the United States and spread their ideas.[23] Following the defeat of the socialist revolutions in 1848, a convention was organized in Seneca Falls, New York, for the empowerment of women.[24] Although initially mocked by the White female organizers of the convention, Sojourner Truth highlighted the intersections of race and gender in her speech, "Ain't I a Woman," pointing out the ideological and practical limitations of the suffragist position. During this historical period, tensions between the goals and ideas of these movements were largely repressed until the passage of the 13th, 14th, and 15th Amendments of the US Constitution following the end of the Civil War.[25] For example, women's rights leaders such as Elizabeth Cady Stanton would see the 14th Amendment as a setback because of the explicit insertion of "male" into the Constitution.[26]

The resulting schism between the women's movement and former abolitionists would last a generation, but not before elements of the suffragist cause would endorse racist politics, sometimes in the name of science, in the interests of suppressing the rights of immigrants and empowering the worst elements of segregation.[27] However, the Black jeremiad underwent a significant evolution during the period following Reconstruction and through the beginning of Jim Crow and the emergence of American and European imperialism, referred to by the historian Rayford Logan as the nadir in American race relations. The Black jeremiad moved away from the prophetic expression of Frederick Douglass upon his death in 1895 and into a conservative middle-class approach championed by Booker T. Washington in an address at the Atlanta Industrial Exposition. Washington promoted racial self-help and economic sufficiency based on an "interracial compromise."[28] However, other leaders such as Bishop Henry McNeal Turner of the African Methodist Episcopal Church and Dr. W.E.B. Du Bois would, in response to American and European imperialism, retranslate the Black jeremiad into a more international scope that coincided with the emergence of the modern Pan African movement, launched in 1900 in London by Trinidadian barrister Henry Sylvester Williams.[29] An example of the intersection of Black theology and the influence of Marxist social theory in the late nineteenth and early twentieth centuries was Reverend George Woodbey. Woodbey's rhetorical opposition to Booker T. Washington was exemplified in his 1903 work *What to Do and How to Do It or Socialism vs. Capitalism*. Also, the influence of the rhetoric of Mary Church Terrell and Ida B. Wells-Barnett was seminal in galvanizing the anti-lynching campaign as a moral critique of American society and civilization before and after World War I.[30] Yet Du Bois was the singular figure that reconfigured the Black jeremiad into a powerful political expression and international influence in the first decade of the twentieth century. In regard to the burgeoning Progressive movement, Du Bois "believed he was witnessing a neo-abolitionist revival of the true American spirit when he noted the participation of many leading white Progressive reformers that met with Blacks to organize the NAACP and commit themselves to achieving equality for all Americans."[31]

In the decade prior to World War I, Du Bois pointed out the relationship between racism and imperialism, expanding the Black jeremiad into a twentieth-century critique of the modern world system. Du Bois famously noted, in regard to American and European imperialism and colonialism, that the division of the world's people along racial categories was also a fight over control of resources; he noted in his seminal text, *The Souls of Black Folk*, "The problem of the twentieth century is the problem of the color line."[32]

Texts and Scholarship

Correspondingly, in relation to the scholarly expression of Black public oratory, E.M. Brawley's *The Negro Baptist Pulpit* in 1890 and, a generation later, Carter G. Woodson's book *Negro Orators and their Orations* in 1925 relied primarily upon Aristotelian classifications and Christian pulpit oratory.[33] However, in regards to scholarly and academic impact on the approach to elocution and Black rhetoric at the end of the nineteenth century and beginning of the twentieth, Hallie Quinn Brown was unsurpassed. Brown can probably be considered one of the great speech teachers in elocution and rhetoric to emerge in North America after the Civil War, making rhetorical studies "available to post-emancipation African Americans."[34] During her career Brown taught at plantation schools, later as Dean of Women at Wilberforce College, and lectured extensively in Europe and North America on issues ranging from the intellectual imperialism of Whites, to Black women's self-determination and sexual autonomy, Christian temperance, and the suffrage movement as a contemporary of Frances Watkins Harper, Anna Julia Cooper, Fannie Barrier Williams, and Fannie Jackson Coppin.[35]

Brown's approach to oratory is clearly influenced by the work of eighteenth-century elocutionist Thomas Sheridan who was an "advocate of the natural manner in delivery."[36] However, her contributions to the field of elocution and rhetorical studies extended Sheridan's through her belief in an "embodied rhetoric" reflected within the vernacular culture of African Americans and texts such as *Bits and Odds: A Choice Selection of Recitations for School Lyceum, and Parlor Entertainments* in 1880; *Elocution and Physical Culture: Training for Students, Teachers, Readers, and Public Speakers* in 1910; and *First Lessons in Public Speaking* in 1920.[37]

However, by the 1920s and the 1930s Black rhetorical practices and oratory were now influenced domestically and internationally by several events such as the Pan African-oriented Garvey movement, the Harlem Renaissance, the Italian invasion of Ethiopia, the Soviet Union and its advocacy of communism, the rising power of imperial Japan as a leader of the non-White world, the Socialist movement, Black women's club movements, and the growing influence of a young Civil Rights movement.[38] Conversely, seemingly unaware of these events, in the field of Speech in the first half of the twentieth century, the flagship journal the *Quarterly Journal of Speech* published two articles on Black oratory: "Negro Minstrelsy"[39] and "Old-Time Negro Preaching: An Interpretive Study."[40] Yet Black rhetoric even thrived in settings that operated at the presidential level. For example, during the Roosevelt administration Mary McLeod Bethune, leader of the National Council of Negro Women (NCNW), delivered a radio speech on the eve of World War II, *What Does American Democracy Mean to Me?*, that sought to reconcile the contradiction between Black inequality and American democracy.[41] However, after World War II rhetorical studies would be impacted by a series of domestic and international events that would also ultimately reorient the study of Black rhetoric.

Following World War II, there was a period of reassessment and development in rhetorical studies in relation to the Cold War and the emergence of the modern Civil Rights movement. For example, the appearance of Kenneth Burke's *A Grammar of Motives* in 1945[42] and *A Rhetoric of Motives* in 1950[43] was an intellectual response to the destruction and horrors of the fascism of World War II and sought to understand how "man" used symbols to make meaning. Additionally, Stephen Toulmin unwittingly made a major contribution to rhetorical studies with his text *The Uses of Argument*,[44] which served as a corrective to accounts of argument based on formal logic. However, during this period continental Africans would have a direct impact on the future ideological development of Black rhetoric in the West at the historic 1945 Fifth Pan African Congress in London where future leaders such as Kwame Nkrumah (Ghana), Jomo Kenyatta (Kenya), and Hastings Banda (Malawi) gathered. At this conference the participation of Amy Jacques Garvey, George Padmore, W.E.B. Du Bois, the aforementioned African leaders, and Caribbean leaders would link issues of colonialism, imperialism, racism, and exploitation, and the beginnings of the modern anti-colonial struggle.[45]

Correspondingly, after World War II, the integration of both the military and sports, the use of the GI Bill in higher education, federally subsidized home loans, growth of suburbia, birth control, McCarthyism, and the consequences of *Brown* v. *Board of Education* set into motion a series of events that would test the liberal principles of the American republic. Also, the modernization of southern agriculture over the course of the century signaled that the labor of African American agricultural workers was obsolete, forcing large numbers of them into urban centers seeking work.[46] For a decade, after the decision in *Brown* v. *Board of Education*, there were sit-ins, marches and protests, murders, and assassinations for the Civil Rights cause.

However, by the mid-1960s, nearing the zenith of the movement and the pending passage of the Civil Rights Act of 1964 and the Voting Rights Act of 1965, questions persisted about the direction of the country. A speech given by Dr. Benjamin Mays on February 11, 1964 at Livingstone College provides an illustration of these questions. Mays was the president of Morehouse College and mentor to Martin Luther King, Jr., and in a speech entitled "Desegregate and Integrate to What End?" Mays rebuked America:

> We spend millions upon millions ... to desegregate and integrate the United States. For what? To what end? ... Desegregate and integrate for what? Here we must distinguish between desegregation and integration. It is strange to me how learned people and scholars have been using "integration" since 1954 when they really meant "desegregation."[47]

The "Freedom Rides" of the early 1960s, along with the struggle against Bull Connor in Birmingham in 1963 and subsequent March on Washington, represented the peak of the Civil Rights movement. By the time of the march, the alliance with trade unionists, Christians, Jews, and others was already fragmenting and the perceived reliance of the Civil Rights movement on White democratic support in the Democratic Party, the Congress, and the Executive branch represented by the Kennedy administration exposed its bourgeois limitations.[48]

For example, several weeks after the march in a speech given in Detroit entitled "Message To the Grassroots," Nation of Islam spokesman Malcolm X mocked the Civil Rights movement and drew distinctions between a "Black Revolution," which was fought for "Land" and self-determination, and a "Negro Revolution," noting: "The only revolution based on loving your enemy is the Negro Revolution," scorning the "House Negro" who "was trying to crawl back on the plantation" and the "Field Negro" who should internationalize his struggle along with the world's anti-colonial movements.[49]

Therefore, by the mid-1960s, following Mississippi Freedom Summer 1964, the 1964 Democratic Party National Convention in Atlantic City, the Selma campaign of 1965, the assassinations of Malcolm X and other civil rights workers, and the 1965 Watts rebellion, the cultural and political stage was set for the emergence of Black Power. For example, Mississippi sharecropper Fannie Lou Hamer helped to organize the Mississippi Freedom Democratic Party attempting to unseat the all-White delegation from Mississippi and the Democratic National convention of 1964.[50] These afore-mentioned events called into question the traditional civil rights leadership and its orthodoxy of limited liberal reforms.

Therefore, by the middle of the decade of the 1960s, the Black Power movement, riots, rise of the New Left, and protest against the Vietnam War had begun to impact the field of rhetoric. Historically, studies of rhetoric and social movements had been restricted to a macro perspective examining strategic themes or the texts of individual speeches vis-à-vis local movements. Notable research included Leland Griffin's *The*

Rhetoric of Social Movements, Haig and Hamida Bosmajian's *The Rhetoric of the Civil Rights Movement*, Robert Scott and Wayne Brockriede's piece published in *The Rhetoric of Black Power*, and the 1971 classic by John Waite Bowers, Donovan Ochs, and Richard Jensen, *The Rhetoric of Agitation and Control*. Scott and Brockriede's *The Rhetoric of Black Power*, informed by exposure to the existentialist writings of Jean-Paul Sartre and Franz Fanon, noted the broader ramifications of the rise of Black power in relation to domestic unrest in their preface:

> Black Power may give that American power one of its more severe trials . . . The Establishment may be able to purge these tendencies. In rage at the revelation, eager for a righteous self-justification, it may contort democratic institutions in Orwellian molds long before 1984 . . . Black Power, no matter what shapes it assumes in the next few years, will remain vital as one starting point for the study of the American Ethos which is now developing and which will dominate lives for the last quarter of the twentieth century.[51]

Yet, these texts, along with those of other rhetoricians, largely constructed the emergence of African American rhetoric from a male Eurocentric perspective that viewed such rhetoric at worst as irrational or, at best, as oratory confined to either utopian impulses or unreasonable demands and ignored the structure of discourse in relation to the geo-culture of the modern world-system. Although there were attempts to historically situate the study of Black rhetoric, such as Lowell Moseberry's *An Historical Study of Negro Oratory in the United States to 1915*[52] and Marcus Boulware's *The Oratory of Negro Leaders; 1900–1968*,[53] these texts primarily examined distinction in eloquence and differences from White patterns of rhetoric and the nature and style of oratory.

Institutional Change Begins

As the 1960s witnessed the emergence of the modern Civil Rights movement, Black Power movement, women's rights movement and anti-colonial struggles, so the field of rhetoric experienced a period of re-assessment and change. By the end of the 1960s, the liberal consensus that had previously dominated American society was in crisis and this tension was reflected in the larger geo-culture of the modern world-system that had previously "proclaimed the inclusion of all as the definition of the good society."[54]

The political economic relations established during the 1945–1967 period that had stabilized the geo-culture of the modern world-system were shaken in 1968 by revolutions and anti-colonial movements on a global scale as the ideological hegemony of liberalism and the United States was challenged, along with the Soviet Union's acquiescence to that hegemony.[55] Furthermore, national minorities located within nation states had been making progress since the 1950s and sought to accelerate their claims through strategies ranging from non-violence to armed confrontation with the state; several varieties of movements broke with the previous orthodoxy represented by communism and, in particular, an American left that had been crushed a decade earlier was revitalized.[56] The structures of colonialism and segregation were coming to an end.

Yet by the summer of 1968, American universities and the field of rhetoric were in upheaval and there was a desire for social relevance following the assassinations of Martin

Luther King Jr. and Robert Kennedy, the unpopular Vietnam War, the insurgent Black Power movement, the war on poverty, the free speech movement, and the peace movement.[57] In response, members of the Speech Association of America (SAA) developed an ad hoc committee comprised of Jack Daniel (chair), John Condon Jr., Frank E.X. Dance, Rosa Lee Nash, Lyndrey Niles, Thomas Pace, Robley Rhine, Donald Smith, and Fredericka Williams.[58] The ad hoc committee would later transform into the Commission on the Profession and Social Problems, and circulated among the SAA membership a document entitled *A Manifesto to the Speech Profession* in preparation for a December 28, 1968 national meeting in Chicago. At the Chicago meeting, during the open meeting on Social Relevance, Charles Hurst, Chair of the Howard University Speech Department, followed by Arthur Smith (who later changed his name to Molefi Kete Asante), forcefully articulated the need for the profession to transform in relation to the atmosphere in the broader society and suddenly the "Black Agenda" was a central item in the agenda of the association.[59] At the same December meeting, the document, retitled *A Manifesto to the Speech Profession: From a Concerned Committee of Students and Teachers*, was circulated among the membership.[60] The document's key points focused on transforming the curriculum and textbooks, lack of minority participation in the profession, graduate student training, lack of relevance between older theoretical ideas and contemporary issues, political neutrality in a changing society, and whether the organization's professional structures adequately prepare scholars to implement the study of discourse and support programs of service, action, and research. In October 1969, several members, including Lyndrey Niles, Lucia Hawthorne, Arthur Smith (Molefi Asante), and Jack Daniel, initially known as the "Black Action Group" and later the "Black Caucus," attempted to secure funding from Dr. James Roever, the Speech Association of America Research Director, to facilitate the development of a Black Rhetoric Institute.[61] While facing difficulty getting the institute off the ground, nonetheless, the Black Caucus was able to hold an important Black Communication Conference on November 5–10, 1972 at the University of Pittsburgh.[62]

Over the next few years, under the leadership of its members, including Lucia Hawthorne, Melbourne Cummings, Jack Daniel, Molefi Asante, and Lyndrey Niles, the informal ad hoc gathering of Black scholars formally launched the Black Caucus of the Speech Communication Association with chairs such as Dorthy Pennington among its early leaders. Over the next generation its membership would rearticulate the study of rhetoric.[63]

Conversely, in the broader communication studies discipline scholars like Marshall McLuhan and Ernesto Grassi sought to reconcile Greco-Roman classical rhetoric with Italian humanism, Jürgen Habermas would rearticulate Marxism into a universal pragmatic, and finally, Michel Foucault attempted to address the epistemic knowledge formations of historical eras.[64] Correspondingly, the 1970s and 1980s would influence the study of identity, culture, and the construction of knowledge frameworks.

Yet, the newly formed Black Caucus was not immune to the rapid changes brought on by the local and international changes that emerged during the transition from Jim Crow segregation and colonialism that would bring its diverse scholars into intellectual tension around the advancement and development of Black rhetoric and communication.

This concern over issues of "development" was also reflected in formerly colonized societies and in domestic debates over the meaning of Black power, Black capitalism, revolutionary praxis, and the women's movement. These intellectual tensions had been steadily emerging since the passage of the civil rights bill of the mid-1960s and began to disturb the intellectual consensus that had held sway and were illustrated in Harold Cruse's *The Crisis of the Negro Intellectual.*[65]

Cruse argued that:

> the Constitution recognizes the rights, privileges and aspirations of the individual, but whose political institutions recognize the reality of ethnic groups only during election contests . . . Every four years the great fiction of the assimilated American ideal is put aside to deal with the pluralistic reality of the hyphenated-American vote.[66]

Cruse makes this argument in an essay within the text entitled "Individualism and the Open Society" that drew upon the political socio-historical circumstances of African Americans and developed an argument for a strategy of group identity in relation to pluralistic American politics. Furthermore, Cruse argued the United States was and is: "a nation dominated by the social power of groups, classes, in-groups and cliques . . . The individual in America has very few rights that are not backed up by the political, economic and social power of one group or another."[67]

A scholarly acknowledgment of this tension would emerge in Black rhetoric, as addressed in Mark McPhail's 2003 essay entitled "The Politics of (In)visibility in African American Rhetorical Scholarship: A Request for an African Worldview." In the essay, McPhail sought to compare and contrast two important essays considered foundational to the modern investigation of African American rhetorical scholarship: Molefi Asante's "Markings of an African Concept of Rhetoric"[68] and Chief Fela Sowande's "The Quest of an African Worldview."[69] More importantly, McPhail is concerned with the "politics of invisibility in African American scholarship" or why "the contributions of many scholars . . . remain unseen."[70]

First, according to McPhail, Asante's work and its emphasis on epistemological objectives and meta-theoretical approaches that place African values and ideals as a "framework" ultimately became "hallmarks of Afrocentric scholarship in the discipline of communication."[71] Unlike Sowande, Asante's rhetorical theory and practice overly relied on "culture as a primary determinant of consciousness," while Sowande "believed both culture and consciousness were subordinate to a more fundamental unity that transformed all forms of difference and identity."[72] Sowande's approach eschewed drawing a distinction between African-centered worldviews and European-centered worldviews, believing this move "undermines the value" of an African worldview and that this perspective augurs a move toward inclusiveness and self-reflexive critique that can avoid the politics of invisibility and move toward an "integrative vision of African American Scholarship."[73]

These concerns may be valid. However, setting aside the concerns of the institutional lack of exposure to Black rhetoric that McPhail raises, at first glance there are at least two reasons why the position developed by Asante gained pre-eminence, namely, global anti-systemic change and popular culture. For example, in 1974, Sowande's approach to an "African Worldview" was not prominent even among African diasporas or continental African intellectuals during the anti-colonial period, especially between 1955 and 1975. The intellectual debate that was raging globally among Black intellectuals and activists emerged at the 1974 sixth Pan African conference at Dar Es Salaam, Tanzania and largely surrounded the tension between Marxists and cultural nationalists.[74]

Correspondingly, philosophical works by Amilcar Cabral (*Return to The Source*, 1974),[75] Kwame Nkrumah (*Neo-Colonialism: The Last Stage of Capitalism*, 1965),[76] Franz Fanon (*Wretched of the Earth*, 1963),[77] Walter Rodney (*How Europe Underdeveloped Africa*, 1974),[78] and many others were widely read and applied in response to the assassinations of Black leaders throughout the diaspora and continent along with government coups sponsored by the West's military-industrial complex. For example, Jack Daniel asserts that one of the most popular texts read in the late 1960s and early 1970s by the newly formed caucus was Fanon's *Wretched of the Earth*.[79] Second, the "culturally conscious" version associated with Asante resonated with youth culture in the 1980s, especially with the emergence of rap and hip-hop culture as a dominant aesthetic among youth during the reactionary politics of the Reagan and Bush presidencies. The 1980s were a troubling time, witnessing the lack of a progressive social movement, the rise of neoliberalism (resulting in benign neglect in the United States), and the "War on Drugs" that would plant the seeds of the New Jim Crow and lead to roughly one-third of Black American males becoming entangled in the criminal justice system.[80] Thus, Sowande's important contribution, and others for that matter, to Black rhetoric were not rendered "invisible" due to some intentional bias. It is more probable that the cross currents of socio-political historical events and popular cultural consumption need to be re-examined in relation to the inclusive development of an African worldview. However, the view advanced by Sowande, McPhail, and others is indeed compatible with the cultural approach advanced by Asante in light of intergenerational and technologically urbanized populations of the early twenty-first century.

Correspondingly, the field of rhetoric would experience an ideological turn during the mid-1970s to late 1980s as several noted scholars produced important monographs that break with previous Aristotelian commitments like Aaron Gresson III's important monographs on rhetoric and race. *Minority Epistemology and the Rhetoric of Creation*[81] and *Phenomenology and the Rhetoric of Identification: A Neglected Dimension of Coalition Communication*[82] are excellent contributions to the discipline, as are Raymie McKerrow's "Critical Rhetoric: Theory and Praxis,"[83] Michael Calvin McGee's "In Search of 'The People': A Rhetorical Alternative"[84] and "The Ideograph: A Link between Rhetoric and Ideology,"[85] and Philip Wander's "The Ideological Turn in Modern Criticism."[86]

Furthermore, from the mid-1970s onward, scholars such as Audre Lorde,[87] Barbara Smith,[88] bell hooks,[89] Alice Walker,[90] and Angela Davis[91] developed organizations such as the Combahee River Collective, and scholarly works focused on the then emerging Womanist, Black Feminist, or Africana Womanist theoretical perspectives that would eventually begin to impact the field of Black rhetoric.

However, by the 1990s the field of Black rhetoric would transition again following the fall of the Berlin Wall on November 9, 1989, the release of Nelson Mandela from prison three months later, the invasion of Iraq in Operation Desert Storm in 1991, the Anita Hill and Clarence Thomas hearing surrounding sexual harassment, and President George Bush's speech on a "New World Order," as a new generation of scholars in Black rhetoric entered the profession. These events, along with others, would herald the rise of the culture wars in the last decade of the twentieth century.

The Post-Civil Rights Era and Race Inside and Outside the Academy

In the post-Civil Rights era, race became important both inside and outside the academy. As the Black Caucus and the study of Black rhetoric grew over the course of the 1980s and by the early 1990s, a younger generation began to make its presence felt in the discipline. An important scholar who served as an intellectual bridge between the senior members of the Black Caucus and the younger generation, whose ideas intersected race, sex, and class, was Marsha Houston. Houston not only served as a founding member of the Women's Studies Division, but helped found the African American Communication and Culture Division (the research arm of the Black Caucus) of the National Communication Association.[92] Houston's most widely used work over the 1990s was the text, *Our Voices: Essays in Culture, Ethnicity and Communication*, that she co-edited with Alberto Gonzalez and Victoria Chen.[93] However, during the latter part of the 1990s and early twenty-first century the cultural studies approach to communication, critical approaches, and Black feminist praxis, along with the Afrocentric approach in rhetoric and communication studies by scholars such as Mark McPhail, Brenda Allen, Ron Jackson, Eric Watts, Mark Orbe, and others, began to make their presence felt. Moreover, the exposure to cultural studies would begin to popularize the scholarly contribution of Stuart Hall. Although Stuart Hall was not a rhetorical scholar, his ideas explored the ways ethnicity, race, and racism intersected with concepts of hegemony, class, and power.[94] In the mid-1980s Hall published *Signification, Representation, Ideology: Althusser and the Post-Structuralist Debates* and asserted that diaspora scholars should not overly invest in *collective experience* in the course of their work.[95]

Post-modern Challenges

Similarly, during the "culture wars" of the 1990s, Afrocentric schools of thought received criticism from cultural studies, queer scholars, and gender scholars. For example, one enduring criticism within gender and queer studies is that the history of Black rhetoric, including Afrocentricity, is limited and restrictive in grasping the complexity of modern African identities. New schools of thought around gender and queer theory, which have directly and indirectly been influenced by Afrocentric thought, continue to emerge. This dialectic is bi-directional in that Afrocentric thought has been and continues to be a starting place for queers of color and Black feminist theoretical frameworks, but these conceptual structures have and will continue to transform the study of race and rhetorical communication. For instance, Patricia Collins places emphasis on an "Afrocentric feminist epistemology"[96] where she articulates the tensions of Black womanhood by addressing the multiple intersecting identities in which African American women, as members of two historically oppressed groups, find themselves. These challenges and developments within and around Black liberation rhetoric continue to shape and transform race and rhetorical studies. In addition, in relation to cultural studies, gender and queer studies have noted the relative silence of some Afrocentric scholars on same-sex relationships.[97]

The lack of Afrocentric scholarship on queer theory undermines claims of support for personal or collective liberation. For example, the Afrocentric idea, though historically heteronormative in its development, is not fundamentally homophobic.[98] Black queer theory emerged in the last quarter of the twentieth century during the final years of the Cold War and during the AIDS crisis. However, Black intellectual structures failed to build the relationships with Black queer theorists necessary to create an approach that would have expanded their scope and theoretical development.[99]

The aforementioned engagement and disengagement with the LGBTQ population within and outside of academia are *rhetorical acts* that have significant meaning as they relate to the progression and expansion of Black liberation rhetoric. For example, E. Patrick Johnson and Mae G. Henderson's edited volume, *Black Queer Studies: A Critical Anthology*,[100] acts as a critical intervention in the discourses of Black studies. This volume makes a statement as it relates to the inclusion of queer scholarship within Black studies and the ways in which rhetoric needs to be expanded beyond the confines of a narrow hegemonic masculinist lens. In other words, African identities are varied and the inclusion of queer of color theory widens the scope around what Black liberation rhetoric is and can be. This new emergence within Black studies has inevitably influenced the scope of Black liberation rhetoric. These emerging frameworks as related to gender and sexuality continue to ground themselves in Afrocentric thought and Black liberation rhetoric. For example, *Black Queer Identity Matrix: Towards An Integrated Queer of Color Framework*[101] specifically moves communication studies toward an Afrocentric queer epistemology, using Black liberation rhetoric and Afrocentricity as its foundation to developing a baseline of knowledge around queer rhetoric.

However, a current challenge facing Black rhetoric and Africana communication studies in general is the "digital turn" in contemporary communication and culture. The digital turn is reflected in the growing power and influence of networked software, database logic, deep remixability, technological interfaces, cultural analytics, and neurosciences that began to emerge in the 1970s and 1980s and accelerated at the turn of the twenty-first century with the explosion in social media that rapidly expanded globally and much of that culture is now written in computer software.[102] For example, Richard Lanham's 1992 text, *Digital Rhetoric: Theory, Practice, and Property*, forecast how computers were going to impact pedagogy and communication practices.[103] This phenomenon contributed to the idea of what would later be called the "digital divide," or the perceived shortcomings that minorities had in relation to access to technology.[104] Janell Hobson notes that this contemporary techno-rhetorical construction of minority or gendered subjects suggests that in the realm of the digital, "power dynamics that exist offline get reproduced online and in 'Big Media' in disturbing and retrogressive ways."[105] For example, within the realm of contemporary digital media, such as movies or gaming, the digital divide is recreated via works like *The Matrix* or *Avatar*; therefore, contrary to the cyborg manifesto of Donna Haraway,[106] with a focus on regeneration and possible reconstitution, "we instead witness in the sci-fi films re-inscriptions, not regenerations, of the same old meanings of race and gender in cyborg imagery."[107]

However, African American rhetoric may have the ability to engage the "Digital Turn." For example, an interface with Africanist perspectives on digital phenomena is represented by the rising number of technologically sophisticated members of Africa and its diaspora that are embracing a Black cultural signification of digital technology in the form of Afrofuturism.[108] Correspondingly, a re-examination of the theoretical approach developed by Sowande and advanced by McPhail concerning an African worldview in relation to metaphysics and technology may provide fruitful investigation to advance rhetorical praxis with respect to technogenesis or co-evolving of humans and technology. Although the theoretical expression of Afrofuturism is now emerging from its developmental phases, its ability to incorporate, interrogate, and capture this digitized historic moment, facing the destabilization of previous epistemological assumptions about knowledge, control, and the co-evolving of humans with respect to technology, remains to be seen.

Current work done by media scholars such as Anna Everett in her work *Digital Diaspora: A Race for Cyberspace* demonstrates an Africanist perspective engaging and extending Frankfurt theorist Walter Benjamin's concept of the *flaneur* into a "Black cyber-flaneur subjectivity."[109] Moreover, in relation to rhetorical studies, the current promising work by Adam Banks skillfully fuses together the African notion of "Griot" and the digital to examine the post-modern aesthetic assumptions of contemporary media and connects traditional African American rhetoric with a "remix" of values and technology to perform critical reflexive practice.[110]

Thus, the emergence of modern Black rhetoric and its relationship to the political philosophy of liberalism, its institutions, and its contradictory assumptions continues in relation to global societal transition early in the twenty-first century. Black rhetoric that has emerged in relation to processes in the modern world-system and the status of people of African descent will continue into the foreseeable future, contrary to the shallow sophistry or assertions of a post-racial era. Theoretically, Black rhetoric and Africanist communication scholarship in general will continue to refine methods and ideas that will lead to the development of new approaches to advance the knowledge of the discipline. The current ideological location of the Black Caucus and its challenges early in the twenty-first century are perhaps best summed up by one of its founders at the 99th annual NCA convention in 2013. At that convention's pre-conference meeting, founding member and former Black Caucus Chair Dr. Dorthy Pennington in her speech, "A Synoptic Early Social History of the SAA/SCA/NCA Black Caucus: From a Bedroom Community to Center Stage," addressed the several intellectual strands that grew out of the caucus's initial rhetorical focus, noting:

> We have ontologically moved from a collective focus on rhetoric in our formative years to now specializations in every conceivable area of communication . . . We now have the luxury and the challenge of divided loyalty among our numerous interest groups . . . we are conflicted,

at times. Which begs the essential questions of where does our primary allegiance lie? Our identity is continuously growing in complexity. Will we ever be able to put the "genie" back into the bottle called the NCA Black Caucus? Maybe, we can be symbolized by a helical diagram, a classical communication model authored by scholar Dr. Frank Dance. The helix is ever expanding at the top, while staying connected to, and informed by its base.[111]

Notes

1 Alan Brinkley, *Liberalism and its Discontents* (Cambridge, MA: Harvard University Press, 1998).
2 Jack L. Daniel, *Changing the Players and the Game: A Personal Account of the Speech Communication Association Black Caucus Origins* (Annandale, VA: Speech Communication Association, 1995).
3 Michael Hecht, Ronald L. Jackson, II, and Sidney Ribeau, *African American Communication: Exploring Identity and Culture* (Mahwah, NJ: Lawrence Erlbaum Associates, 2003): 1.
4 Maulana Karenga, "Nommo, Kawaida, and Communicative Practice: Bringing Good into the World," in *Understanding African American Rhetoric: Classical Origins to Contemporary Innovations*, ed. Ronald L. Jackson, II and Elaine B. Richardson (New York: Routledge, 2003): 3–22.
5 Edward Blyden, *Christianity, Islam and the Negro Race* (Baltimore: Black Classic Press, 1994).
6 Karenga, "Nommo, Kawaida, and Communicative Practice," 7.
7 Patricia Pearson, "The World of the Atlantic before the 'Atlantic World': Africa, Europe, and the Americas before 1450," in *The Atlantic World, 1450–2000*, ed. Toyin Falola and Kevin David Roberts (Bloomington, IN: Indiana University Press, 2008): 3–26.
8 Cedric Robinson, *Black Marxism: The Making of The Black Radical Tradition* (London: Zed Press, 1983); Ernest G. Bormann, ed., *Forerunners of Black Power: The Rhetoric of Abolition* (Englewood Cliffs, NJ: Prentice-Hall, 1971).
9 Robinson, *Black Marxism*, xxix.
10 Robinson, *Black Marxism*, 10.
11 David B. Davis, *The Problem of Slavery in the Age of Revolution, 1770–1823* (Annandale, VA: Oxford University Press, 1999): 45; Robinson, *Black Marxism*.
12 Davis, *The Problem of Slavery*, 45.
13 Davis, *The Problem of Slavery*, 45.
14 Davis, *The Problem of Slavery*, 47.
15 Anthony Bogues, *Black Heretics, Black Prophets: Radical Political Intellectuals* (New York: Routledge, 2003): 13.
16 Bogues, *Black Heretics, Black Prophets*, 12–13.
17 Bogues, *Black Heretics, Black Prophets*, 13.
18 Davis, *The Problem of Slavery*, 149.
19 Bormann, *Forerunners of Black Power*, 6.
20 David Howard-Pitney, "The Jeremiads of Frederick Douglass, Booker T. Washington, and W.E.B. Du Bois and Changing Patterns of Black Messianic Rhetoric, 1841–1920," *Journal of American Ethnic History* 6, no. 1 (1986): 49.
21 Willie J. Harrell Jr., "A Call to Political and Social Activism: The Jeremiadic Discourse of Maria Miller Stewart, 1831–1833," *Journal of International Women's Studies* 9, no. 3 (2013): 300–319; Howard-Pitney, "The Jeremiads"; James Jasinski, "Constituting Antebellum African American Identity: Resistance, Violence, and Masculinity in Henry Highland Garnet's (1843) 'Address to the Slaves,'" *Quarterly Journal of Speech* 93 no. 1 (2007): 27–57.
22 Immanuel M. Wallerstein, *Centrist Liberalism Triumphant, 1789–1914*, Vol. 4 (Berkeley, CA: University of California Press, 2011): 162.
23 Wallerstein, *Centrist Liberalism Triumphant*, 195.
24 Wallerstein, *Centrist Liberalism Triumphant*, 195.

25 Wallerstein, *Centrist Liberalism Triumphant*, 205.
26 Wallerstein, *Centrist Liberalism Triumphant*, 205.
27 Wallerstein, *Centrist Liberalism Triumphant*, 207.
28 Howard-Pitney, "The Jeremiads," 53.
29 Howard-Pitney, "The Jeremiads"; Marc S. Gallicchio, *The African American Encounter with Japan and China: Black Internationalism in Asia, 1895–1945* (Chapel Hill, NC: UNC Press, 2000): 8–11.
30 Deborah Atwater, *African American Women's Rhetoric: The Search for Dignity, Personhood, and Honor* (Lanham, MD: Lexington Books, 2009): 59.
31 Howard-Pitney, "The Jeremiads," 56.
32 William Edward Burghardt Du Bois, *The Souls of Black Folk* (New York and Oxford: Oxford University Press, 2007): 9.
33 Keith Gilyard, "Introduction: Aspects of African American Rhetoric as a Field," in *African American Rhetoric(s): Interdisciplinary Perspectives*, ed. Elaine B. Richardson and Ronald L. Jackson, II (Carbondale, IL: Southern Illinois University Press, 2007): 1–18.
34 Ronald L. Jackson, II and Sonja M. Brown Givens, *Black Pioneers in Communication Research* (Thousand Oaks, CA: Sage, 2006): 79.
35 Jackson and Brown Givens, *Black Pioneers in Communication Research*, 71.
36 Lester Thonssen and Albert Craig Baird, *Speech Criticism: The Development of Standards for Rhetorical Appraisal* (New York: Ronald Press, 1948): 128.
37 Jackson and Brown Givens, *Black Pioneers in Communication Research*, 70.
38 Gallicchio, *The African American Encounter*.
39 Richard Moody, "Negro Minstrelsy," *Quarterly Journal of Speech* 30, no. 3 (1944): 321–328.
40 William Harrison Pipes, "Old-Time Negro Preaching: An Interpretative Study," *Quarterly Journal of Speech* 31, no. 1 (1945): 15–21.
41 Atwater, *African American Women's Rhetoric*, 69.
42 Kenneth Burke, *A Grammar of Motives* (Englewood Cliffs, NJ: Prentice-Hall, 1945).
43 Kenneth Burke, *A Rhetoric of Motives* (New York: Prentice-Hall, 1950).
44 Stephen Toulmin, *The Uses of Argument* (Cambridge: Cambridge University Press, 1958).
45 Peter Olisanwuche Esedebe, *Pan-Africanism: The Idea and Movement, 1776–1991*, Vol. 2 (Washington, DC: Howard University Press, 1982): 161–164.
46 Cornell West, "The Paradox of the Afro-American Rebellion," *Social Text* 9/10 (1984): 44–58.
47 Benjamin Elijah Mays, "Desegregate and Integrate to What End?" (Founder's Day Speech, Livingstone College: Salisbury, NC, 1964).
48 West, "The Paradox."
49 George Breitman, ed., *Malcolm X Speaks: Selected Speeches and Statements* (New York: Pathfinder Press, 1989): 9–10.
50 Atwater, *African American Women's Rhetoric*, 52.
51 Robert Lee Scott, and Wayne Brockriede, eds., *The Rhetoric of Black Power* (New York: Harper & Row, 1969): 14.
52 Lowell Tillry Moseberry, "An Historical Study of Negro Oratory in the United States to 1915" (PhD dissertation, University of Southern California, 1955).
53 Marcus H. Boulware, *The Oratory of Negro Leaders, 1900–1968* (Westport, CT: Negro Universities Press, 1969).
54 Immanuel M.Wallerstein, *World-Systems Analysis: An Introduction* (Durham, NC: Duke University Press, 2004): 60.
55 Wallerstein, *World-Systems Analysis*, 60.
56 West, "The Paradox."
57 Daniel, *Changing the Players and the Game*, 1.
58 Daniel, *Changing the Players and the Game*, 2.
59 Daniel, *Changing the Players and the Game*, 7.
60 Daniel, *Changing the Players and the Game*, 3.

61   Daniel, *Changing the Players and the Game*, 11.

62   Daniel, *Changing the Players and the Game*, 13.

63   Daniel, *Changing the Players and the Game*, 13–14.

64   James L. Golden, ed., *Rhetoric of Western Thought* (Dubuque, IA: Kendall Hunt, 2003).

65   Harold Cruse, *The Crisis of the Negro Intellectual: A Historical Analysis of the Failure of Black Leadership* (New York: New York Review of Books, 1967).

66   Cruse, *The Crisis of the Negro Intellectual*, 6.

67   Cruse, *The Crisis of the Negro Intellectual*, 8.

68   Arthur L. Smith, "Markings of an African Concept of Rhetoric," *Communication Quarterly* 19, no. 2 (1971): 13–18.

69   Fela Sowande, "The Quest of an African Worldview: The Utilization of African Discourse," in *Black Communication: Dimensions of Research and Instruction*, ed. Jack L. Daniel (New York: Speech Communication Association, 1974): 67–117.

70   Mark Lawrence McPhail, "The Politics of (In)visibility in African American Rhetorical Scholarship: A (Re)quest for an African Worldview," in *Understanding African American Rhetoric: Classical Origins to Contemporary Innovations*, ed. Ronald L. Jackson, II, and Elaine B. Richardson (New York: Routledge, 2003): 100.

71   McPhail, "The Politics of (In)visibility," 102.

72   McPhail, "The Politics of (In)visibility," 105.

73   McPhail, "The Politics of (In)visibility," 105–106.

74   Horace Campbell, "Pan African Renewal in The 21st Century," in *Pan-Africanism: Politics, Economy, and Social Change in the Twenty-First Century*, ed. Tajudeen Abdul-Raheem (New York: New York Press, 1996): 212–228.

75   Amilcar Cabral, *Return to the Source: Selected Speeches* (New York: Monthly Review Press, 1974).

76   Kwame Nkrumah, *Neo-Colonialism, the Last Stage of Capitalism* (New York: International Publishers, 1965).

77   Frantz Fanon, *The Wretched of the Earth* (New York: Grove Press, 1963).

78   Walter Rodney, *How Europe Underdeveloped Africa* (Washington, DC: Howard University Press, 1974).

79   Daniel, *Changing the Players and the Game*, 35.

80   Patricia Hill Collins, *From Black Power to Hip Hop: Racism, Nationalism, and Feminism* (Philadelphia: Temple University Press, 2006).

81   Aaron D. Gresson III, "Minority Epistemology and the Rhetoric of Creation," *Philosophy and Rhetoric* 10, no. 4 (1977): 244–262.

82   Aaron D. Gresson III, "Phenomenology and the Rhetoric of Identification: A Neglected Dimension of Coalition Communication," *Communication Quarterly* 26, no. 4 (1978): 14–23.

83   Raymie McKerrow, "Critical Rhetoric: Theory and Praxis," *Communication Monographs* 56, no. 2 (1989): 91–111.

84   Michael C. McGee, "In Search of 'the People': A Rhetorical Alternative," *Quarterly Journal of Speech* 61, no. 3 (1975): 235–249.

85   Michael C. McGee, "The 'Ideograph': A Link between Rhetoric and Ideology," *Quarterly Journal of Speech* 66, no. 1 (1980): 1–16.

86   Phillip Wander, "The Ideological Turn in Modern Criticism," *Communication Studies* 34, no. 1 (1983): 1–18.

87   Audre Lorde, *Sister Outsider: Essays and Speeches* (Berkeley, CA: Crossing Press, 1984).

88   Barbara Smith, *Home Girls: A Black Feminist Anthology* (New Brunswick, NJ: Rutgers University Press, 1983).

89   bell hooks, *Ain't I a Woman: Black Women and Feminism*, Vol. 3 (Boston: South End Press, 1981).

90   Alice Walker, *In Search of Our Mothers' Gardens: Womanist Prose* (San Diego: Harcourt Brace, 1984).

91   Angela Davis, *Women, Race & Class* (London: Women's Press, 1981).

92   Jackson and Brown Givens, *Black Pioneers in Communication Research*, 173.

93   Alberto Gonzalez, Marsha Houston, and Victoria Chen, *Our Voices: Essays in Culture, Ethnicity, and Communication* (Oxford: Oxford University Press, 2011).

94   Jackson and Brown Givens, *Black Pioneers in Communication Research*, 166.

95   Jackson and Brown Givens, *Black Pioneers in Communication Research*, 167.

96   Patricia Hill Collins, *Black Feminist Thought: Knowledge, Consciousness, and the Politics of Empowerment* (New York: Routledge, 1991): 206.

97   Reynaldo Anderson, "Molefi Kete Asante: The Afrocentric Idea and the Cultural Turn in Intercultural Communication Studies," *International Journal of Intercultural Relations* 36, no. 6 (2012): 760–769.

98   Anderson, "Molefi Kete Asante," 7.

99   Kaila A. Story, "There's No Place Like Home: Mining the Theoretical Terrain of Black Women's Studies, Black Queer Studies and Black Studies," *The Journal of Pan African Studies* 2 (2008): 44–57, at 54.

100 E. Patrick Johnson and Mae G. Henderson, eds., *Black Queer Studies: A Critical Anthology* (Durham, NC: Duke University Press, 2005).

101 Sheena Howard, *Black Queer Identity Matrix: Towards an Integrated Queer of Color Framework* (New York: Peter Lang Publishing, 2014).

102 Lev Manovich, *Software Takes Command* (New York: Bloomsbury Academic, 2013); Nicholas Negroponte, *Being Digital* (New York: Alfred Knopf, 1995).

103 Richard A. Lanham, "Digital Rhetoric: Theory, Practice, and Property," in *Literacy Online: The Promise (and Peril) of Reading and Writing with Computers*, ed. Myron C. Tuman (Pittsburgh, PA: University of Pittsburgh Press, 1992): 221–224.

104 Janell Hobson, *Body as Evidence: Mediating Race, Globalizing Gender* (New York: SUNY Press, 2012): 96.

105 Hobson, *Body as Evidence*, 94.

106 Donna Haraway, *Simians, Cyborgs and Women: The Reinvention of Nature* (New York: Routledge, 1991): 149–181.

107 Hobson, *Body as Evidence*, 95.

108 Hobson, *Body as Evidence*, 109.

109 Anna Everett, *Digital Diaspora: A Race for Cyberspace* (Albany, NY: SUNY Press, 2009).

110 Adam Joel Banks, *Digital Griots: African American Rhetoric in a Multimedia Age* (Carbondale, IL: Southern Illinois University Press, 2011): 11.

111 Dorthy Pennington, "A Synoptic Early Social History of the SAA/SCA/NCA Black Caucus: From a Bedroom Community to Center Stage" (Black Caucus Pre-Conference of the National Communication Association Convention: Washington, DC, 2013).

References

Anderson, Reynaldo. "Molefi Kete Asante: The Afrocentric Idea and the Cultural Turn in Intercultural Communication Studies." *International Journal of Intercultural Relations* 36, no. 6 (2012): 760–769.

Asante, Molefi K. *The Afrocentric Idea*. Philadelphia: Temple University Press, 1987.

Atwater, Deborah F. *African American Women's Rhetoric: The Search for Dignity, Personhood, and Honor*. Lanham, MD: Lexington Books, 2009.

Banks, Adam Joel. *Digital Griots: African American Rhetoric in a Multimedia Age*. Carbondale, IL: Southern Illinois University Press, 2011.

Blyden, Edward. *Christianity, Islam and The Negro Race*. Baltimore: Black Classic Press, 1994.

Bogues, Anthony. *Black Heretics, Black Prophets: Radical Political Intellectuals*. New York: Routledge, 2003.

Bormann, Ernest G., ed. *Forerunners of Black Power: The Rhetoric of Abolition*. Englewood Cliffs, NJ: Prentice-Hall, 1971.

Bosmajian, Haig A. and Hamida Bosmajian, eds. *The Rhetoric of the Civil-Rights Movement*. New York: Random House, 1969.

Boulware, Marcus H. *The Oratory of Negro Leaders, 1900–1968*. Westport, CT: Negro Universities Press, 1969.

Bowers, John Waite, Donovan J. Ochs, and Richard J. Jensen. *The Rhetoric of Agitation and Control*. Reading, MA: Addison-Wesley, 1971.

Brawley, Edward M. *The Negro Baptist Pulpit*. Philadelphia: American Baptist Publication Society, 1890.

Breitman, George, ed. *Malcolm X Speaks: Selected Speeches and Statements*. New York: Pathfinder Press, 1989.

Brinkley, Alan. *Liberalism and its Discontents*. Cambridge, MA: Harvard University Press, 1998.

Brown, Hallie Quinn. *Bits and Odds: A Choice of Selection of Recitations for School, Lyceum and Parlor Entertainments*. Chew Printers: University Press, 1884.

——. *Elocution and Physical Culture: Training for Students, Teachers, Readers, Public Speakers*. Wilberforce, OH: Homewood Cottage, 1910.

Burke, Kenneth. *A Grammar of Motives*. Englewood Cliffs, NJ: Prentice-Hall, 1945.

——. *A Rhetoric of Motives*. New York: Prentice-Hall, 1950.

Cabral, Amilcar. *Return to the Source: Selected Speeches*. New York: Monthly Review Press, 1974.

Campbell, Horace. "Pan African Renewal in The 21st Century." In *Pan-Africanism: Politics, Economy, and Social Change in the Twenty-First Century*, edited by Tajudeen Abdul-Raheem, 212–228. New York: New York Press, 1996.

Cruse, Harold. *The Crisis of the Negro Intellectual: A Historical Analysis of the Failure of Black Leadership*. New York: New York Review of Books, 1967.

Daniel, Jack L. *Changing the Players and the Game: A Personal Account of the Speech Communication Association Black Caucus Origins*. Annandale, VA: Speech Communication Association, 1995.

Davis, Angela. *Women, Race & Class*. London: Women's Press, 1981.

Davis, David B. *The Problem of Slavery in the Age of Revolution, 1770–1823*. New York and Oxford: Oxford University Press, 1999.

Du Bois, William Edward Burghardt. *The Souls of Black Folk*. New York and Oxford: Oxford University Press, 2007.

Esedebe, Peter Olisanwuche. *Pan-Africanism: The Idea and Movement, 1776–1991*. Vol. 2. Washington, DC: Howard University Press, 1982.

Everett, Anna. *Digital Diaspora: A Race for Cyberspace*. Albany, NY: SUNY Press, 2009.

Fanon, Frantz. *The Wretched of the Earth*. New York: Grove Press, 1968 [1963].

Gallicchio, Marc S. *The African American Encounter with Japan and China: Black Internationalism in Asia, 1895–1945*. Chapel Hill, NC: University of North Carolina Press, 2000.

Gilyard, Keith. "Introduction: Aspects of African American Rhetoric as a Field." In *African American Rhetoric(s): Interdisciplinary Perspectives*, edited by Elaine B. Richardson and Ronald L. Jackson, II, 1–18. Carbondale, IL: Southern Illinois University Press, 2007.

Golden, James L., ed. *Rhetoric of Western Thought*. Dubuque, IA: Kendall Hunt, 2003.

Gonzalez, Alberto, Marsha Houston, and Victoria Chen. *Our Voices: Essays in Culture, Ethnicity, and Communication*. Oxford: Oxford University Press, 2011.

Gresson, Aaron D, III. "Minority Epistemology and the Rhetoric of Creation." *Philosophy and Rhetoric* 10, no. 4 (1977): 244–262.

——. "Phenomenology and the Rhetoric of Identification: A Neglected Dimension of Coalition Communication." *Communication Quarterly* 26, no. 4 (1978): 14–23.

Hall, Stuart. "Signification, Representation, Ideology: Althusser and the Post-Structuralist Debates." *Critical Studies in Mass Communication* 2, no. 2 (1985): 91–114.

Haraway, Donna. *Simians, Cyborgs and Women: The Reinvention of Nature*. New York: Routledge, 1991.

Harrell Jr., Willie J. "A Call to Political and Social Activism: The Jeremiadic Discourse of Maria Miller Stewart, 1831–1833." *Journal of International Women's Studies* 9, no. 3 (2013): 300–319.

Hecht, Michael, Ronald L. Jackson, II, and Sidney Ribeau. *African American Communication: Exploring Identity and Culture*. Mahwah, NJ: Lawrence Erlbaum Associates, 2003.

Hill Collins, Patricia. *Black Feminist Thought: Knowledge, Consciousness, and the Politics of Empowerment*. New York: Routledge, 1991.

——. *From Black Power to Hip Hop: Racism, Nationalism, and Feminism*. Philadelphia: Temple University Press, 2006.

Hobson, Janell. *Body as Evidence: Mediating Race, Globalizing Gender*. New York: SUNY Press, 2012.

hooks, bell. *Ain't I a Woman: Black Women and Feminism*. Vol. 3. Boston: South End Press, 1981.

Howard, Sheena. *Black Queer Identity Matrix: Towards an Integrated Queer of Color Framework*. New York: Peter Lang Publishing, 2014.

Howard-Pitney, David. "The Jeremiads of Frederick Douglass, Booker T. Washington, and W.E.B. Du Bois and Changing Patterns of Black Messianic Rhetoric, 1841–1920." *Journal of American Ethnic History* 6, no. 1 (1986): 47–61.

Jackson II, Ronald L. and Sonja M. Brown Givens. *Black Pioneers in Communication Research*. Thousand Oaks, CA: Sage, 2006.

Jasinski, James. "Constituting Antebellum African American Identity: Resistance, Violence, and Masculinity in Henry Highland Garnet's (1843) 'Address to the Slaves.'" *Quarterly Journal of Speech* 93 no. 1 (2007): 27–57.

Johnson, E. Patrick and Henderson, Mae G, eds. *Black Queer Studies: A Critical Anthology*. Durham, NC: Duke University Press, 2005.

Karenga, Maulana. "Nommo, Kawaida, and Communicative Practice: Bringing Good into the World." In *Understanding African American Rhetoric: Classical Origins to Contemporary Innovations*, edited by Ronald L. Jackson, II and Elaine B. Richardson, 3–22. New York: Routledge, 2003.

Lanham, Richard A. "Digital Rhetoric: Theory, Practice, and Property." In *Literacy Online: The Promise (and Peril) of Reading and Writing with Computers*, edited by Myron C. Tuman, 221–224. Pittsburgh, PA: University of Pittsburgh Press, 1992.

Lorde, Audre. *Sister Outsider: Essays and Speeches*. Berkeley, CA: Crossing Press, 1984.

Manovich, Lev. *Software Takes Command*. New York: Bloomsbury Academic, 2013.

Mays, Benjamin Elijah. "Desegregate and Integrate to What End?" Founder's Day Speech, Livingstone College, Salisbury, NC, 1964.

McGee, Michael C. "The 'Ideograph': A Link between Rhetoric and Ideology." *Quarterly Journal of Speech* 66, no. 1 (1980): 1–16.

——. "In Search of 'the People': A Rhetorical Alternative." *Quarterly Journal of Speech* 61, no. 3 (1975): 235–249.

McKerrow, Raymie E. "Critical Rhetoric: Theory and Praxis." *Communication Monographs* 56, no. 2 (1989): 91–111.

McPhail, Mark Lawrence. "The Politics of (In)visibility in African American Rhetorical Scholarship: A (Re)quest for an African Worldview." In *Understanding African American Rhetoric: Classical Origins to Contemporary Innovations*, edited by Ronald L. Jackson, II and Elaine B. Richardson, 99–113. New York: Routledge, 2003.

Moody, Richard. "Negro Minstrelsy." *Quarterly Journal of Speech* 30, no. 3 (1944): 321–328.

Moseberry, Lowell Tillry. "An Historical Study of Negro Oratory in the United States to 1915." PhD dissertation, University of Southern California, 1955.

Negroponte, Nicholas. *Being Digital*. New York: Alfred Knopf, 1995.

Nkrumah, Kwame. *Neo-Colonialism, the Last Stage of Capitalism*. New York: International Publishers, 1965.

Pearson, Patricia. "The World of the Atlantic before the 'Atlantic World': Africa, Europe, and the Americas before 1450." In *The Atlantic World, 1450–2000*, edited by Toyin Falola and Kevin David Roberts, 3–26. Bloomington, IN: Indiana University Press, 2008.

Pennington, Dorthy. "A Synoptic Early Social History of the SAA/SCA/NCA Black Caucus: From a Bedroom Community to Center Stage." Washington, DC: Black Caucus Pre-Conference of the National Communication Association Convention, 2013.

Pipes, William Harrison. "Old-Time Negro Preaching: An Interpretative Study." *Quarterly Journal of Speech* 31, no. 1 (1945): 15–21.

Robinson, Cedric. *Black Marxism: The Making of the Black Radical Tradition*. London: Zed Press, 1983.

Rodney, Walter. *How Europe Underdeveloped Africa*. Washington, DC: Howard University Press, 1974.

Scott, Robert Lee, and Wayne Brockriede, eds. *The Rhetoric of Black Power*. New York: Harper & Row, 1969.

Smith, Adam. *An Inquiry into the Nature and Causes of the Wealth of Nations*. Edinburgh: A. and C. Black, 1863 [1776].

——. *The Theory of Moral Sentiments*. London: Penguin, 2010 [1792].

Smith, Arthur L. "Markings of an African Concept of Rhetoric." *Communication Quarterly* 19, no. 2 (1971): 13–18.

——. *Rhetoric of Black Revolution*. Boston: Allyn and Bacon, 1969.

Smith, Barbara. *Home Girls: A Black Feminist Anthology*. New Brunswick, NJ: Rutgers University Press, 1983.

Sowande, Fela. "The Quest of an African Worldview: The Utilization of African Discourse." In *Black Communication: Dimensions of Research and Instruction*, edited by Jack L. Daniel, 67–117. New York: Speech Communication Association, 1974.

Story, Kaila A. "There's No Place Like Home: Mining the Theoretical Terrain of Black Women's Studies, Black Queer Studies and Black Studies." *The Journal of Pan African Studies* 2 (2008): 44–57.

Thonssen, Lester and Albert Craig Baird. *Speech Criticism: The Development of Standards for Rhetorical Appraisal*. New York: Ronald Press Co., 1948.

Toulmin, Stephen. *The Uses of Argument*. Cambridge: Cambridge University Press, 1958.

Truth, Sojourner. "Ain't I a Woman?" Speech, Women's Rights Convention, Akron, OH, May 29, 1851.

Walker, Alice. *In Search of Our Mothers' Gardens: Womanist Prose*. San Diego: Harcourt Brace, 1984.

Walker, David. *Appeal to the Coloured Citizens of the World*. Cambridge, MA: Harvard University Press, 2002.

Wallerstein, Immanuel M. *Centrist Liberalism Triumphant, 1789–1914*. Vol. 4. Berkeley: University of California Press, 2011.

——. *World-Systems Analysis: An Introduction*. Durham, NC: Duke University Press, 2004.

Wander, Philip. "The Ideological Turn in Modern Criticism." *Communication Studies* 34, no. 1 (1983): 1–18.

West, Cornell. "The Paradox of the Afro-American Rebellion." *Social Text* 9/10 (1984): 44–58.

Woodson, Carter Godwin, ed. *Negro Orators and their Orations*. Washington, DC: Associated Publishers, 1925.

8.

A CRITICAL HISTORY OF THE "LIVE" BODY IN PERFORMANCE WITHIN THE NATIONAL COMMUNICATION ASSOCIATION

Tracy Stephenson Shaffer, John M. Allison, Jr., and Ronald J. Pelias

Bodies are the material that make texts happen in the doing of performance.[1]

Since NCA's beginning as the National Association of Academic Teachers of Public Speaking in 1915, performance scholars have been invested in the live body in performance. Over the past two decades, many departments as well as the national organization have removed the term "speech" as a modifier for communication. In doing so, some argue we have diminished the many live contexts in which communication occurs, contexts that depend on interactions between corporeal bodies. While we acknowledge we live in an age where communication is increasingly mediated, and mediation impacts the way we communicate, the majority of our scholarship and pedagogy remains focused on bodies communicating in live contexts. This fact is particularly true for performance.

As we survey the century, two primary trends characterize the live body in performance. Thus, we offer the aesthetic body and the everyday body as categories for critical consideration. At times, these bodies intertwine. The aesthetic body, for example, is as present in contemporary performance scholarship as it was at the origins of the discipline; consequently, it necessarily overlaps with the everyday body. These bodies often compete with and/or complement one another, revealing performance's potential to provide unique insights into human communication. A critical history reveals that these bodies emerged in response to the exigencies of politics, pedagogy, and practice.

In our analysis, we adopt a fairly linear genealogical method, but we also recognize that any history is, of necessity, incomplete.[2] Given the scope of this chapter, we attempt to highlight representative moments in the history that have impacted the live body in interpretation and performance studies.[3] However, we also acknowledge certain approaches to theory, practice and particular scholars, although they are important to the history of the discipline, are necessarily absent due to the constraints of a document of this length.[4] As we trace this history, we hope that these categories will be of use to communication and performance scholars interested in how the live body has been theorized and staged over the past century.

As we begin this discussion, we would do well to remember that all scholars and practitioners of performance recognize three elements necessary to performance: performer, text, and audience.[5] Over the course of our history, then, scholars in the discipline have focused varying amounts of attention on one or more of these elements, leading to emphases on performer training (performer-centered theories), communication (audience-centered theories), and literary study (text-centered theories). While a discussion of the live body in performance would seem to place us squarely in a performer-centered domain, we are actually interested in discovering how any and all of these foci have impacted the body in performance, particularly as our notions of text have expanded over time and the media of performance have evolved.

The Aesthetic Body

From the inception of the national organization, and continuing for well over half a century, performance scholars focused on an aestheticized body. We define the aesthetic body as one made capable of performing certain behaviors through participation in mental, vocal, and physical exercises. For example, a performer learns to gesture with the upstage arm by both imagining the downstage arm blocking the audience's view and by gesturing with the upstage arm repeatedly in rehearsal. Of course, performance scholars debate methods and theories of training, and as a result, what constitutes training and the aesthetic body changes over time. But, from the beginning of the discipline, a passionate group of scholars dedicated their scholarship and pedagogy to live performances of texts enacted by individuals who had received vocal and physical training. Even today, a strong contingent of performance scholars invests its time, training, and talent in studying and creating live aesthetic performance. Many would argue the aesthetic body remains a priority in performance scholarship. Regardless, performance scholarship relied on an aesthetically trained body as a primary site of communication research for at least the first sixty years of the discipline. The following traces a history of the aesthetic body, highlighting significant moments and movements along the way.

In the late nineteenth and early twentieth century, prior to the formation of the national organization, the discipline we now refer to as performance studies was largely the province of private schools and/or teachers, usually of elocution. As performance teachers and scholars sought to make the transition to the academy, they felt the need to distinguish themselves "from the vagaries and vulgarities of elocutionists."[6] Simultaneously, they needed to situate the emerging discipline in relation to other academic disciplines such as English and Theater by demonstrating its unique potential for offering new knowledge and expertise.[7] Maud May Babcock, whose early twentieth-century publications stand as exemplars of this positioning, was prominent in distinguishing interpretation from acting.[8] She did so by promoting *suggestion* as the appropriate performance style, a style that called for vocal dexterity but minimal bodily impersonation. Scholars like Babcock emphasized cognitive methods over theatrical techniques to achieve these goals.

From the start, vigorous debate surrounded the use of the body in performance. Rollo Anson Tallcott, opposing Babcock's perspective, argued that certain literary texts called for more developed characterization. Their scholarly debate on interpretation versus impersonation was featured prominently in early NCA publications.[9] At the time, Babcock triumphed and interpretation, rather than impersonation, became favored in our academic practice. Yet from our historical vantage point, their arguments appear to take place on the same side of the coin. While they disagreed on selections suitable for interpretation and on the degree to which the practice of interpretation should utilize the skills of the actor, they both stated unequivocally that the text takes precedence. While Babcock sought to place the performer (and his or her body) in service to the text, Tallcott allowed the text to influence the type of performance (and bodily investment) created. While he does not explicitly place Babcock and Tallcott in specific camps, Paul Gray associates these differences in philosophy to audience-centered versus text-centered perspectives on performance, and claims that *suggestion* as a performance style arose from the audience-centered philosophy that emphasized interpretation as an act of communication.[10]

The argument about the distinction between interpretation and impersonation, between reading and acting, did not originate with Babcock and Tallcott, however. As Paul Edwards demonstrates, the relatively short-lived "Expression" movement in American education, which served as a transition between elocution and interpretation, had been rehearsing these ideas since the early 1890s. In *The Province of Expression*, S.S. Curry championed suggestion over acting because it appealed not to the eye of the audience member but to the imagination.[11] Beverly Whitaker Long further explains the connection between the ascendance of suggestion and a prominent aesthetic theory of the time.[12] According to aesthetic theory, unlike everyday, practical experiences, art may provide a unique experience characterized by a "dual state" of simultaneous involvement and detachment. As creative artists in their own right, interpreters of literature sought to generate an aesthetic attitude in their audiences through their readings. To do so, they sought to achieve and maintain an appropriate aesthetic distance in their performances, thereby "inviting an audience to participate imaginatively in the fictive world of the text."[13] The appropriate aesthetic distance could be encouraged by the performer through selection of literature, appropriate framing of the performance, use of a manuscript or a lectern, or, perhaps most importantly, through suggestion, a performance style inevitably contrasted with everyday experiences and with acting. From the 1920s through the 1950s, many prominent interpretation textbooks by pedagogues of both the audience-centered and text-centered variety promoted suggestion as the appropriate performance style *because* it appealed to the mind rather than the eye, thereby encouraging audience members to participate imaginatively in aesthetic experiences by completing the action in their minds.

Scholars and pedagogues during this period placed most emphasis on training the voice, while the body, limited by principles of suggestion, was physically constrained.

In the period from 1915 through the 1930s, for example, a majority of the articles in the *Quarterly Journal of Speech* and textbooks published by interpretation scholars emphasized the oral aspects of interpretive practice: oral English, oral expression, vocal interpretation, and public reading.[14] An article by Margaret Prendergast McLean illustrates the emphasis on voice training characteristic of the early part of the period. After devoting several pages to six aspects of the use of the voice, McLean makes a single statement about the use of the body in oral interpretation: "*Bodily action* must be exact and economical to the point of miserliness."[15] While most authors were neither this terse nor this proscriptive with regard to the body, they frequently decried the excesses of performer-centered methods and their unfortunate effects on platform performance behavior.[16]

Numerous textbooks from the beginning of the discipline up through the 1950s also demonstrated similar ratios of space devoted to discussions of voice and body. The fourth edition of Charles Woolbert and Severina Nelson's *The Art of Interpretative Speech*, for example, devoted five chapters to aspects of the voice and vocal training, and only a single chapter to the training and use of the body.[17] Their advice, moreover, is of the most general sort; they discuss muscular tension in everyday life and in theatrical performance and provide exercises for students to learn the art (or skill) of suggestion through the practice of delivering lines "first, as an actor; second, as an impersonator; third, as an interpreter."[18] The implications of such exercises seem to be that the interpreter can learn the appropriate level of physical expressiveness through a process of "toning it down."

Scholars working during the early years of the field found success by separating themselves from elocution with its negative associations and by carving out for themselves a new field of academic study. Thus, in 1942, when Margaret Robb looked back to evaluate the progress of the field since its inception, she described the prehistory of interpretation as one that trains platform readers, and declared that the discipline had successfully driven a stake through the heart of elocution. She claims, proudly in fact, that one might find a course in the oral interpretation of literature where the appreciation of literature is emphasized and no attention is paid to the "preparation of public readers."[19]

Although the leading proponents of the new academic field espoused the centrality of the text in the practice of interpretive reading, they were operating in a historical period in which the majority of practitioners had been trained in elocutionary techniques. Consequently, textbooks and articles published during this period reflected an emphasis either on performer training, a holdover from elocutionary practice, or the practice of communicating literature to an audience, an attempt to justify the location of interpretation in speech departments. In fact, prior to the formation of the *Quarterly Journal of Speech*, in the *Public Speaking Review*, Richard Hollister defined "two main divisions of the speech arts": self-expression, such as conversation, debating, and preaching, and interpretation, the recreation of "the thought of another . . . express[ed] in the words of the other."[20] Hollister argued that interpretation should play a role in departments of public speaking because in addition to voice development, self-mastery, and discipline for the memory, it develops sustained thinking and intellectual sensitivities, quickens the imagination, and enhances good direct speaking. In short, Hollister argued that the act of interpretation makes one a better communicator: the "science" of communication is enhanced through the "art" of interpretation. Thus, even a century ago, performance researchers situated interpretation in a liminal space between art and science, and performance scholars acted as scholar/artists, a title many performance scholars embrace today.

Even though literature has been a major element of interpretation—along with performer training and communication—since Babcock and Tallcott's public argument about interpretation versus impersonation, it became increasingly important at mid-century, achieving its zenith as scholars in interpretation embraced New Criticism and its principles as the primary method of analysis leading to live aesthetic performance. It is important to note, as K.B. Valentine does, that "'New Criticism' stands for a cluster of modern attitudes toward literature rather than a fixed system or school" extending from the 1920s through the 1960s.[21] In an examination of articles and textbooks, Valentine traces the increasing influence of New Critical precepts on scholarship and practice in oral interpretation from 1939 through 1966. The text, though always considered an important element in the triumvirate by theorists of all stripes, from elocutionists up to and including some contemporary theorists, gradually became of prime importance as text-centered theories of performance assumed center stage in both theory and practice.

One of the results of increased emphasis on the text was the gradual weakening of suggestion as the preferred performance style for oral interpretation. Although the style remained prominent in textbook discussions through the 1970s, by the end of the 1950s theorists and pedagogues were beginning to question its prescriptive status.[22] According to Valentine, the influence of the New Critics on interpretation practice began to be felt as early as the late 1930s, when Algernon Tassin encouraged students to think of interpretive reading as a method of literary study rather than as a method for improving their skills as communicators.[23] In the 1940s, advocacy for intrinsic analysis of texts, rather than extrinsic factors such as biographical and historical scholarship, became increasingly prominent. This led to a reversal in the polarity of the relationship: rather than reading texts carefully in order to perform them well, students should perform them in order to fully understand them.

Among the proponents of New Critical precepts, none was more prolific or influential than Don Geiger, whose articles in NCA journals in the 1950s and textbook, *Oral Interpretation and Literary Study* (released later as *The Sound, Sense, and Performance of Literature*), placed literature at the center of the interpretative enterprise.[24] Beverly Whitaker Long notes that like many of his contemporaries, Geiger advocated oral interpretation as a means for understanding and appreciating literary texts, and like many of his contemporaries, he also espoused the belief that the text was the most important of the elements (performer, text, audience) in the performance equation. Geiger distinguished himself from his contemporaries by his insistence that performers "experience and understand the literature *by* performing it." In doing so, he shifted "the interpreter's final accountability ... from the audience to the particularity of the literature."[25] In other words, Geiger popularized the notion that a performer's behaviors should be dictated by a close analysis *and* performance of "the text itself," and not by the abstract demands of a particular performance style. With this change, performers were freed from the constraints of suggestion and began to incorporate characterization and more overt physicalizations appropriate to the literary texts they performed.

The increasing shift to the use of the term "performance," which had been circulating in the discipline at least since the 1950s as a progressively more acceptable synonym for interpretation, signaled the waning of the much-vaunted distinction between acting and interpretation.[26] Significantly, it paralleled an increase in references to theories, theorists, and techniques associated with acting in articles as well as in textbooks, which led in turn to fewer restrictions on the use of the body in performance. Even so, until the mid-to-late 1970s, performance remained, for the most part, a one-item category: that is, when members of the discipline spoke of either interpretation or performance, they were referencing the performance of *literature*.

To this point, our discussion has focused exclusively on performances by individuals. As early as the 1930s, however, group readings of literature became increasingly popular as classroom activities as well as presentations for the public. Mary Margaret Robb attributes the revival of "choric speaking" in the United States to the work of Marjorie Gullan in England, whose methods were brought to the United States through the efforts of her students.[27] In the period beginning in 1931 and continuing throughout the 1940s, disciplinary scholarship on choral reading and verse choirs appeared and increased steadily.[28] As with individual acts of interpretation, descriptions of verse choirs from the period acknowledge the familiar art/science dichotomy. Identifying the practice as an act of "poetry appreciation," Rose Walsh references their artistry and claims that verse choirs "amplify an individual interpretation of a poem, just as an orchestra amplifies the solo rendition of a musical composition."[29] While Dorothy Kaucher defines the purpose of a verse choir similarly, she also claims that choral speaking "offers unrealized possibilities for speech improvement," which include improved vocal control, greater range of expression, development of bodily expression, and enhanced voice and body coordination.[30]

In descriptions of verse choirs, discussions of the body become more overt. Kaucher describes verse choirs as "speaking sounds in rhythm and rhythmically moving."[31] She describes, for example, movement performed by the San Jose College Verse Choir as they interpreted Vachel Lindsay's "Congo": "A group of ten, arms interlocked, start swaying with a decided rhythm left and right . . . the entire group bends backward . . . then all bend far forward, each one's hands clasped tightly in front."[32] Although essays like this introduce and document movement in ways that are not done with individual performances, it is important to note that the movement is neither representational nor impersonation, but presentational and suggestive. In addition, as one takes a broader view of the field, discussions of movement remain minimal in interpretation research. In fact, from 1915 to 1950, words connoting movements of the body (e.g., gesture) appear only a handful of times in titles of journal articles.[33] These emergent discussions of movement anticipate important work in group performance that would begin in the late 1940s and 1950s.

Group performances of literature developed along two parallel paths: Readers Theatre and Chamber Theatre. The forms of group performance that have come to be known collectively as Readers Theatre enjoyed greater popularity, benefiting from professional performances as well as disciplinary publications that resulted in more widespread practice in college classrooms.[34] Chamber Theatre, which began as a classroom exercise in the 1940s at Northwestern University, was documented by its creator, Robert Breen, in an informal format that remained unpublished until 1978;[35] consequently, its principal ideas were disseminated primarily in publications by his colleagues and through the practice of his students.[36] The particularities of the two forms are indicative of the traditions from which they arise.

Readers Theatre, as traditionally conceived, was characterized by the use of stools and stands arranged on a bare stage; the performers wore formal (or other suitable) attire, and utilized scripts read in a presentational manner using off-stage focus (wherein they imaginatively visualized the action beyond the fourth wall and in the realm of the audience rather than on stage); movement was minimal; and lighting, if used, established mood. In such productions, the action took place primarily in the minds of the performers who used their voices and the techniques of suggestion to stimulate the imaginations of the audience. Much of the language used to describe and explain the practice of Readers Theatre is based in the distinctions between acting and interpretation that animated early theoretical arguments in the discipline. The voice was primary and the body, to the extent that it was used, was trained, but highly constrained in performance.

Chamber Theatre, which was designed specifically for staging narrative fiction, was more closely aligned with text-centered theory that was influencing literary study as well as oral interpretation practice. Joanna Maclay notes, "Chamber Theatre took its style ... from a view of literature as experiential and dramatic and a view of interpretation as an *embodiment* of that experience."[37] As such, the form made extensive use of theatrical elements such as sets, lighting, props, costumes, and make-up. It also made extensive use of theatrically trained bodies, as characters enacted scenes with one another using on-stage focus, while a narrator navigated relationships that included the audience (presentational form) and the characters (representational form).

In the 1970s, the forms began to meld as practitioners of Readers Theatre began to adopt more text-centered language and as faculty and students encountered more varied forms of group performance through their attendance at performance festivals. As these brief characterizations of the two forms demonstrate, however, the forms of group performance popular within the discipline reflected the predominant trends with regard to the use of the body in individual performance. Readers Theatre aligned itself with communication-centered classroom practices predominant during the early years of the discipline through its emphasis on the aesthetics of suggestion rather than on physical embodiment. Chamber Theatre, which was more closely associated with the emerging text-centered practices, made fewer distinctions between the kinds of performance practiced by actors in theater departments and those practiced by oral interpreters in speech communication departments.

From the 1980s until today, practitioners have continued to refine, experiment with, and expand Readers and Chamber Theatre using a variety of methods to engage multiple types of texts. For example, Michael and Ruth Laurion Bowman, separately and together, in print and on stage, have advocated a more "writerly" approach to performance composition in which practitioners use the "technologies" through which they communicate (in our case performance) to explore the medium's possibilities, rather than being limited by the technologies, forms, and mindsets that characterized an earlier stage of our evolution.[38] Their work shows that the aesthetic body in live performance creates the "dual perspective" early practitioners aspired toward by igniting the audience's imagination while simultaneously filling the stage with performers' bodies trained using a variety of methods.[39]

The Everyday Body

Two essays published in 1977 can be considered emblematic in understanding the transition from the aesthetic body to the everyday body. The first, Beverly Whitaker Long's "Evaluating Performed Literature," identified the literary text as both the *raison d'être* for performance as well as the foundation for evaluating performances. By defining performance as "*a temporal and spatial actualization of an experience that a literary text notates*," however, she was also implicitly articulating a claim about what constituted the heart of the discipline: the performance of *literature*.[40] This definition represented centripetal forces within the discipline that sought to maintain text-centered scholarship and practice. The second article, Elizabeth Fine and Jean Haskell Speer's "A New Look at Performance," was a counterargument for broadening the discipline. By championing performance rather than literary texts as the disciplinary "center," Fine and Speer were exerting centrifugal force that would gain momentum and eventually lead to the evolution from "interpretation" to "performance studies."[41]

Like scholars from the early years of the discipline who wished to situate themselves in relation to English and Theater, Fine and Speer aspired to place performance scholarship in conversation with scholars across the arts and sciences who studied performance in everyday life. They argued:

> a fuller examination of the phenomenon of performance in human culture can give interpretation study new possibilities for research ... Our task is to join with these other humanists and with the social and behavioral scientists in an exploration of human life. Our contribution will be the result of our experience in creating, participating in, evaluating, and doing performances, experience which is not part of the other disciplines currently interested in the nature of performance.[42]

Thus, Fine and Speer reasoned, our disciplinary experience in the aesthetic body would enable performance scholars to contribute insights on the everyday body. Drawing on the work of scholars in a variety of disciplines who had researched the bodies and behaviors of cultural others, they illustrated connections between the ongoing work of scholars in our discipline and set the stage for sophisticated "performance studies" of cultural and everyday life performance.

This section focuses on the everyday body, which we define as a body engaged in the mundane activities of living. Humans perform certain everyday acts, like engaging in conversations, telling stories, attending funerals, and taking on particular roles through dress and nonverbal behaviors; yet, they may not define themselves as performers. The performance metaphor helps scholar/artists communicate how these meaningful everyday acts create, sustain, and transform culture. In addition, scholars/artists use their own everyday bodies as tools and sites of research. Thus, in the category of the everyday body, performance is an object, method, and metaphor. Whether in the field or at home, performing the other or the self, performance scholars mine their own bodily experiences for insights into human communication and culture. While this perspective's multiple interdisciplinary ties expand performance theory beyond the scope of this chapter, this section focuses on a few significant practices that rely on the live body in performance and that impact the research conducted in the discipline and published in its journals.

If the task of interpretation was bringing life to texts through performance, one of the tasks faced by those interested in everyday bodies was creating performance texts from life. In 1984, Fine's *The Folklore Text* introduced strategies for creating texts from everyday life that included the bodies of the researched, rather than just their language. Fine's approach, informed by folklorists and sociolinguists, developed folklore (the stories of a culture passed down orally) beyond content or theme, and defined it "as a dynamic process encompassing speech, movement, context, and interaction."[43] She advocated for translations of folklore that included notations for the paralinguistic and kinesic behaviors of the cultural performers. Moreover, the collection and creation of these texts relied on the researcher's *experience* of the cultural performance as well as his/her critical and aesthetic judgment of what to include and exclude.[44] Finally, Fine claimed that the translation of the text was "only complete when readers restore the integral presence of the original through performance."[45] In Fine's performance-centered approach to folklore, the aesthetic body and the everyday body intertwine and inform one another. The researcher's everyday body enters the field to observe and collect meaningful behaviors performed by cultural others that the researcher only fully understands when he/she has translated and performed the text. Fine's work validated performance scholars' claims that the body mattered in communication, and that performance was an effective tool for understanding it.[46] Performance ethnography extended the same validation.

The primary paradigmatic research direction emerging from Fine and Speer's visionary essay was performance ethnography. In 1985, Dwight Conquergood's influential "Performing as a Moral Act: Ethical Dimensions of the Ethnography of Performance" appeared in *Literature in Performance*. Conquergood's essay was the first of its kind in the five-year-old *Literature in Performance* still primarily devoted to the analysis and performance of literary texts. Yet, in the lead article of the journal's first issue, Wallace Bacon foreshadowed the turn toward the performer's everyday body by arguing that the process of interpretation relied on the performer's body. While Bacon admitted "some people are embarrassed by so much talk of the body," he declared that "the body is the form in which we live."[47] Inspired by Bacon's concept of the "sense of the other" enabled through performance, anthropologist Clifford's Geertz's "Thinking as a Moral Act," and Bakhtin's dialogical Marxism introduced to him by Mary Strine, Conquergood named dialogical performance as the ethical response to ethnographic research.[48] Simply, Conquergood claimed that ethnography, a participant-observer methodology practiced primarily by anthropologists and sociologists at the time, gained ethos through a performer's body.[49]

Drawing on his background in oral interpretation, Conquergood saw culture as a text one should engage through everyday participation-observation.[50] In fact, he was widely admired for the amount of time he devoted to living in and learning the various cultures he studied.[51] Like Fine, Conquergood's process intertwined the everyday and the aesthetic body. His recommended final step in ethnographic research was to create an aesthetic performance featuring the insights gleaned during participant-observer research. As a practitioner, he "created and presented performances from his fieldwork before a variety of audiences: social service agencies, educators, religious groups, and civic groups."[52] Through his performances, he desired to create genuine conversation between the performer and the culture studied, what he called "dialogical performance." The influence of Conquergood's work is difficult to overestimate. As one of the earliest and most vocal proponents of ethnography within the NCA, now a division in its own right, he inspired a generation of performers who used his concept of dialogic performance to balance the relationship between researcher as performer and culture as text.[53]

Theory and practice inspired by Fine, Speer, Conquergood, and others values embodied knowledge that comes through engaging the cultural other via participant-observation fieldwork and through communicating the resulting knowledge via "thick description" as well as live performance. As these scholars focused our attention on performing the other, those researching and practicing personal narrative and "auto-ethnography" concentrated on performing the self.

In the period from the 1950s through the 1970s, interpretation textbooks began anthologizing nonfiction literature for beginning classes based on the belief that performing texts featuring real life experiences told in the first-person was a worthwhile endeavor.[54] In addition to "literature," performance scholars and students performed essays, diaries, letters, and autobiographical texts. By the 1980s, however, issues of representation and power made many practitioners increasingly nervous about performing the other, particularly in cases where the other was a member of an oppressed group. Moreover, members of oppressed groups found few texts reflecting their own voices and experiences in the anthologized literature they were asked to perform. These circumstances, in part, gave rise to performances of personal narrative. In theorizing personal narrative, Kristin Langellier called the form a "challenger to territory and power, legitimacy and authority" that "promises innovation in theories, models, and methods of analysis as well as in performance and pedagogical practices."[55]

Combining aspects of folklore, rhetoric, and performance art, the personal narrative began to impact performance studies theory and practice in the early 1990s.[56] Performance scholars, such as Craig Gingrich-Philbrook, took to the stage to tell crafted stories based on life experiences.[57] These stories emphasized the relationships between the personal/political and the everyday/aesthetic and responded to a field increasingly interested in critical theories that sought to identify and undermine oppressive societal structures.

As Langellier predicted, the personal narrative also impacted performance practice and pedagogy. While many introductory textbooks continued to focus on the performance of prose and poetry, others included personal narrative.[58] Claiming that personal stories have an aesthetic shape, the authors of these textbooks encourage students to pay attention to the wording and structure of the story. In addition, they also ask students to attend to their bodies as they perform the tales. Stern and Henderson, for example, emphasize the theatrical dimensions of a good narrative, comparing the everyday storyteller to a director or actor,[59] while Ronald Pelias and Tracy Shaffer encourage the performer to consider bodily choices explicitly:

> You may raise your volume or become more exaggerated. You may incorporate dramatic gestures. You might take on the accents and personalities of the other characters or persons in your story . . . How you move on stage may help communicate the setting of your tale as well as the emotional content of your story.[60]

While Stern and Henderson suggest that performers can learn about the theatrics of everyday storytelling by watching storytellers in action, Pelias and Shaffer grant performers freedom to enhance everyday stories by drawing upon their own everyday experiences of self, other, and culture in the creation of aesthetic performances.[61]

As the practice and pedagogy of personal narrative developed, performance scholars continued to theorize the relationships between self, other, and culture. Just as Fine and Speer found value in gathering and performing stories from disparate cultural groups, many who performed personal narratives also saw their work as representing culture through the lens of the self. To capture this connection between self and culture, these performance scholars embraced the term autoethnography.[62]

Autoethnographers draw from autobiography and ethnography. They tell stories of the self situated in culture. Performance autoethnographers who stage their stories, speak from lived experience, place themselves centrally within the tales they tell, and work to create performances that evoke revealing moments in the human condition.[63] In autoethnographic performances, the performing body acts as a cultural site that is both the product of culture and a vantage point for observing and critiquing culture. That is, autoethnography privileges the everyday body as a site of knowing, and the autoethnographic performer demonstrates (through that same body) how one maneuvers through life's contingencies and makes sense of human experience.

Tami Spry's recent book, *Body, Paper, Stage: Writing and Performing Autoethnography*, provides a summary and a practical guide to autoethnographic performance.[64] Spry defines autoethnography as transdiciplinary, used extensively by "the fields of education, medicine, performance studies, sociology, communication studies, and many more [as a] methodology that can articulate the intersections of histories, cultures, and societies through the critical representation of the researcher's experience."[65] Her book provides a systematic journey, moving from experience, to writing, to staging auto-ethnographic accounts. Importantly, Spry cites staging the work, moving it from the everyday experience to the aesthetic performance, as an essential part of the process. She argues, "Rather than a linear path from page to stage, performance is a dialogic space where experience and text affect and are affected by one another."[66] For Spry, the rich history of performance studies provides the methodological tools for the hard work that must accompany the act. Thus, those performing autoethnographic texts may draw from an array of theories and methods from performance practitioners as they rehearse.[67] Spry's work serves as an exemplar of how the everyday body transforms into the aesthetic body in autoethnography, and how the two, working in concert, have the potential to transform both self and culture.[68]

While the everyday body takes center stage when interpretation expands into performance studies, the instances we have provided show that the aesthetic body works in concert with it, both enabling valuable insights as well as communicating those insights. In her 1995 address "Mapping the Cultural Turn In Performance Studies," Mary Susan Strine urged performance scholars to think about the future in terms of a culture–performance matrix. To explain, she quoted social theorist David Chaney: "[A]lthough culture is privileged as a theoretical object, it is a complex layering of meanings that can only be comprehensible as enacted in social practices."[69] Simply, we experience and understand culture through performance. Strine acknowledged that cultural performance, such as oral histories and personal narratives, has commanded our greatest interest in recent years, but she also maintained that our aesthetic practice continues to provide an "effective means of overcoming the abstractive, distancing tendencies in Anglo-American critical practice" through its holistic focus on texts in the act of performance.[70]

Conclusion

Since the beginning of the national organization, performance scholars have skillfully negotiated their investments in the live body in performance with the political demands of the broader discipline. From transitioning to the academy, which constrained the body, to embracing text-centered theories, which ironically freed the body, to creating relationships with other disciplines, which introduced the everyday body into our praxis, performance studies seized these shifts as productive moments to enhance scholarly conversation and to cultivate pedagogy and practice. For performance scholars, the live body in performance has always been a fertile liminal site between art and science, theory and practice, teaching and research, artistry and scholarship, and the aesthetic and the everyday.

Notes

1 Elizabeth Bell, *Theories of Performance* (Thousand Oaks, CA: Sage, 2008): 79.
2 While our genealogical method is not necessarily Foucauldian, we acknowledge that this history is plural, complex, incomplete, sometimes contradictory, and driven by relations of power.
3 We acknowledge that "liveness" is contested and is addressed from a variety of theoretical perspectives. With additional space, we would have added a third category: the virtual body. We recommend a critical history of the virtual body in performance as a future research direction. For more, see the Phelan/Auslander debate: Peggy Phelan, *Unmarked: The Politics of Performance* (New York: Routledge, 1993) and Philip Auslander, *Liveness: Performance in a Mediatized Culture* (New York: Routledge, 1999). Also see Elizabeth Bell and Marcy Rose Chvasta, "Performing Technologies," in Bell's *Theories of Performance*, 233–263.
4 We encourage readers to read other histories of the discipline, including Eugene Bahn and Margaret L. Bahn, *A History of Oral Interpretation* (Minneapolis: Burgess, 1970); Paul Edwards, "Unstoried: Teaching Literature in the Age of Performance Studies," *Theatre Annual* 52 (1999): 1–147; Mary S. Strine, Beverly Whitaker Long, and Mary Frances HopKins, "Research in Interpretation and Performance Studies: Trends, Issues, Priorities," in *Speech Communication: Essays to Commemorate*

the 75th Anniversary of The Speech Communication Association, ed. Gerald M. Phillips and Julia T. Wood (Carbondale, IL: Southern Illinois University Press, 1990): 181–204; Jill Taft-Kaufman, "Oral Interpretation: Twentieth Century Theory and Practice," in *Speech Communication in the 20th Century*, ed. Thomas W. Benson (Carbondale, IL: Southern Illinois University Press, 1985): 157–183; David W. Thompson, ed., *Performance of Literature in Historical Perspectives* (Lanham, MD: University Press of America, 1983).

5 Taft-Kaufman, "Oral Interpretation," 159.

6 W.M. Parrish, "Interpretative Reading," *Quarterly Journal of Speech Education* 13, no. 2 (1927): 161.

7 Paul Gray, "Strange Bedfellows: My Life and Hard Times in a Speech Communication Department," *Southern States Communication Journal* 44, no. 2 (1979): 161–162.

8 Maud May Babcock, "Teaching Interpretation," *Quarterly Journal of Public Speaking* 1, no. 2 (1915): 173–176.

9 Maud May Babcock, "Interpretive Presentation versus Impersonative Presentation," *Quarterly Journal of Public Speaking* 2, no. 1 (1916): 18–25; R.A. Tallcott, "The Place for Personation," *Quarterly Journal of Public Speaking* 2, no. 2 (1916): 116–122; Maud May Babcock, "Impersonation vs. Interpretation," *Quarterly Journal of Public Speaking* 2, no. 4 (1916): 340–343.

10 Gray, "Strange Bedfellows," 160–161.

11 Paul Edwards, "The Rise of 'Expression,'" in Thompson, *Performance of Literature*, 529–548.

12 Beverly Whitaker Long, "A 'Distanced' Art: Interpretation at Mid-Century," in Thompson, *Performance of Literature*, 567–587.

13 Long, "A 'Distanced' Art," 573.

14 J.S. Gaylord, "Preparing Literary Material for Public Utterance," *Quarterly Journal of Public Speaking* 1, no. 1 (1915): 38–43; R.L. Lyman, "Oral English in the High School," *Quarterly Journal of Public Speaking* 1, no. 3 (1915): 241–259; Bertha Forbes Herring, "Vocal Interpretation of Literature in High Schools," *Quarterly Journal of Speech Education* 6, no. 4 (1920): 52–58; Alma M. Bullowa, "The Reading-Telling Method in the Use of the Short Story in Teaching Spoken English," *Quarterly Journal of Speech Education* 8, no. 1 (1922): 1–7; Rollo Anson Tallcott, "Teaching Public Reading," *Quarterly Journal of Speech Education* 9, no. 1 (1923): 53–66.

15 Margaret Prendergast McLean, "Oral Interpretation—A Re-creative Art," in *Studies in the Art of Interpretation*, ed. Gertrude E. Johnson (New York: D. Appleton-Century, 1940): 51.

16 See, for example, Babcock, "Interpretative Presentation," 20.

17 Charles H. Woolbert and Severina E. Nelson, *The Art of Interpretative Speech*, 4th ed. (New York: Appleton-Century-Crofts, 1956).

18 Woolbert and Nelson, *Art of Interpretative Speech*, 228.

19 Margaret Robb, "Looking Backward!," *Quarterly Journal of Speech* 28, no. 3 (1942): 327.

20 Richard D.T. Hollister, "Interpretive Reading and Its Place in a Department of Public Speaking," *Public Speaking Review* 4 (1914): 104.

21 K.B. Valentine, "'New Criticism' and the Emphasis on Literature in Interpretation," in Thompson, *Performance of Literature*, 549.

22 Edwards, "Rise of Expression," 542.

23 Valentine, "'New Criticism,'" 558.

24 Don Geiger, "Oral Interpretation and the 'New Criticism,'" *Quarterly Journal of Speech* 36, no. 4 (1950): 508–513; "A 'Dramatic' Approach to Interpretative Analysis," *Quarterly Journal of Speech* 38, no. 2 (1952): 189–194; "The Oral Interpreter as Creator," *Speech Teacher* 3, no. 4 (1954): 269–277; *Oral Interpretation and Literary Study* (South San Francisco: Pieter Van Vloten, 1958); *The Sound, Sense, and Performance of Literature* (Chicago: Scott, Foresman, 1963).

25 Long, "A 'Distanced' Art," 583.

26 Don Geiger began using the term performance in articles in the 1950s. His initial use of the term was most often in reference to actions performed by a speaker in a poem. He gradually began to use it to reference the actions of the oral interpreter, and eventually included it in the title of his textbook, *The Sound, Sense, and Performance of Literature*.

27 Mary Margaret Robb, *Oral Interpretation of Literature in American Colleges and Universities*, Rev. ed. (New York: Johnson Reprint Corporation, 1968): 191. For a more complete description of one aspect of Gullan's work, see Ronald E. Shields, "Like a Choir of Nightingales: The Oxford Recitations 1923–1930," *Literature in Performance* 3, no. 1 (1982): 15–26.

28 See, for example, Mary Haldeman Armstrong, "Certain Aspects of Choral Speech," *Quarterly Journal of Speech* 24, no. 1 (1938): 117–119; Harvey Scott Hinks, "Choric Speaking," *Southern Speech Bulletin*, 3 (1938): 16–18; Mary Eleanor Lutz, "Choral Reading: Its Application to the Teaching of Speech," *Southern Speech Bulletin* 1 (1935): 26–28; Dorothy J. Lyne, "The Choral Verse Speaking Choir," *Quarterly Journal of Speech* 23, no. 3 (1937): 449–451; Emma Grant Meader, "Choral Speaking and Its Values," *Quarterly Journal of Speech* 22, no. 2 (1936): 235–245.

29 Rose Walsh, "Whither the Verse Choir," *Quarterly Journal of Speech* 21, no. 4 (1935): 463.

30 Dorothy Kaucher, "The Verse Speaking Choir," *Quarterly Journal of Speech* 17, no. 1 (1931): 71–72.

31 Kaucher, "The Verse Speaking Choir," 65.

32 Kaucher, "The Verse Speaking Choir," 66.

33 See, for example, Carrie Rasmussen, "Verse Speaking and Bodily Activity," *Quarterly Journal of Speech* 20, no. 2 (1934): 282–286; Charlotte I. Lee, "Choric Reading and Kinetic Projection," *Quarterly Journal of Speech* 26, no. 4 (1940): 545–550; Sara Lowrey, "Gesture Through Empathy," *Southern Speech Journal* 11, no. 3 (1946): 59–62.

34 The 1951 Broadway Production of *Don Juan in Hell* is frequently cited as significant in the rise of the Readers Theatre movement, as is the seminal article, Leslie Irene Coger, "Interpreters Theatre: Theatre of the Mind," *Quarterly Journal of Speech* 49, no. 2 (1963): 157–164. The principles of Readers Theatre were translated for classroom practice in textbooks such as Leslie Irene Coger and Melvin R. White, *Readers Theatre Handbook* (Glenview, IL: Scott, Foresman, 1967) and Joanna Hawkins Maclay, *Readers Theatre: Toward a Grammar of Practice* (New York: Random House, 1971).

35 Robert Breen, *Chamber Theatre* (Englewood Cliffs, NJ: Prentice-Hall, 1978).

36 Joanna H. Maclay, "Group Performance in Academic Settings," in Thompson, *Performance of Literature*, 396–397.

37 Maclay, "Group Performance," 396.

38 Michael Bowman, "'Novelizing' the Stage: Chamber Theatre after Breen and Bakhtin," *Text and Performance Quarterly* 15, no. 1 (1995): 1–23; Michael S. Bowman, "Performing Literature in an Age of Textuality," *Communication Education* 45, no. 2 (1996): 97–101; Michael S. Bowman and Ruth Laurion Bowman, "Performing the Mystory: A Textshop in Autoperformance," in *Teaching Performance Studies*, ed. Nathan Stucky and Cynthia Wimmer (Carbondale, IL: Southern Illinois University Press, 2002): 161–174; Ruth Laurion Bowman and Michael S. Bowman, "On the Bias: From Performance of Literature to Performance Composition," in *The Sage Handbook of Performance Studies*, ed. Soyini Madison and Judith Hamera (Thousand Oaks, CA: Sage, 2006): 205–226.

39 For example, Ruth Laurion Bowman experimented with the bodily theories of Vsevolod Meyerhold in her 2010 production, *The Double Life of Dr. Dappertutto*, at Louisiana State University.

40 Beverly Whitaker Long, "Evaluating Performed Literature," in *Studies in Interpretation II*, ed. Esther M. Doyle and Virginia Hastings Floyd (Amsterdam: Rodopi N.V., 1977): 268.

41 A number of publications document the years-long struggle over disciplinary identity, including the essays contained in *Renewal & Revision: The Future of Interpretation*, ed. Ted Colson (Denton, TX: NB Omega Publication, 1986). For another argument leading to the name change and placing performance into a broader conversation with communication studies, see Ronald J. Pelias and James VanOosting, "A Paradigm for Performance Studies," *Quarterly Journal of Speech* 73 (1987): 219–231.

42 Elizabeth C. Fine and Jean Haskell Speer, "A New Look at Performance," *Communication Monographs* 44 (1977): 375.

43 Elizabeth C. Fine, *The Folklore Text: From Performance to Print* (Bloomington, IN: Indiana University Press, 1984): 57.

44 Fine, *The Folklore Text*, 161.

45 Fine, *The Folklore Text*, 184.

46 Examples of scholarship/pedagogy that draws from similar scholarly threads include the performance of everyday conversation, featured in a special issue of *Text and Performance Quarterly* 13, no. 2 (1993); the regular teachings of performance artist Anna Devere Smith, illustrated in Kay Ellen Capo and Kristen M. Langellier, "Review/Interview: Anna Devere Smith," *Text and Performance Quarterly* 14, no. 1 (1994): 57–76; Heidi Rose, "A Conversation with Anna Devere Smith," *Text and Performance Quarterly* 31 (2011): 440–448; and the performance work of Danielle Sears Vignes documented in *Text and Performance Quarterly* 28 (2008): 344–365.

47 Wallace A. Bacon, "An Aesthetics of Performance," *Literature in Performance* 1, no. 1 (1980): 2.

48 Dwight Conquergood, "Performing as a Moral Act: Ethical Dimensions of the Ethnography of Performance," *Literature in Performance* 5, no. 2 (1985): 1–13. Conquergood credits all three in his first note. In addition, he also draws upon Beverly Whitaker Long's research on psychic distance and Mary Frances HopKins' discussion of "moral distance" in "From Page to Stage: The Burden of Proof," *Southern Speech Communication Journal* 47, no. 1 (1981): 1–9.

49 John Van Maanen, *Tales of the Field: On Writing Ethnography*, 2nd ed. (Chicago: University of Chicago Press, 2011) provides a useful history of ethnography. Ethnography had begun to expand beyond the confines of anthropology and sociology around the time Conquergood became an advocate for it in performance circles.

50 Excellent examples of participant-observer research inspired by Conquergood are E. Patrick Johnson's "SNAP! Culture: A Different Kind of 'Reading'," *Text and Performance Quarterly* 15, no. 2 (1995): 122–142; and Frederick C. Corey's "Performing Sexualities in an Irish Pub," *Text and Performance Quarterly* 16, no. 2 (1996): 146–160.

51 Conquergood spent February through September of 1985 in Southeast Asia working with Hmong refugees. For examples of his work, see Dwight Conquergood, "Health Theatre in a Hmong Refugee Camp," *TDR* 32, no. 3 (1988): 174–208; "Life in Big Red: Struggles and Accommodations in a Chicago Polyethnic Tenement," in *Structuring Diversity: Ethnographic Perspectives on the New Immigration*, ed. Louise Lamphere (Chicago: University of Chicago Press, 1992).

52 Bell, *Theories of Performance*, 141.

53 Performances (and their subsequent publication) inspired by Conquergood's work include David Olsen's "Flood and Church Secretaries, Buffalo Creek and Northwestern: Struggling with the Seams Between," *Text and Performance Quarterly* 12, no. 4 (1992): 329–348; Shannon Jackson, "Ethnography and the Audition: Performance as Ideological Critique," *Text and Performance Quarterly* 13, no. 1 (1993): 21–43; D. Soyini Madison, "'That Was My Occupation': Oral Narrative, Performance, and Black Feminist Thought," *Text and Performance Quarterly* 13, no. 3 (1993): 213–232; Mariangela Maguire and Laila Farah Mohtar, "Performance and the Celebration of a Subaltern Counterpublic," *Text and Performance Quarterly* 14, no. 3 (1994): 248–252; and Joni L. Jones, "The Self as Other: Creating the Role of Joni The Ethnographer for *Broken Circles*," *Text and Performance Quarterly* 16, no. 2 (1996): 131–145.

54 See, for example, Charlotte I. Lee, *Oral Interpretation* (Boston: Houghton Mifflin, 1952); Wallace A. Bacon and Robert S. Breen, *Literature as Experience* (New York: McGraw-Hill, 1959); Wilma H. Grimes and Althea Smith Mattingly, *Interpretation: Writer Reader Audience* (San Francisco: Wadsworth, 1961); Wallace A. Bacon, *The Art of Interpretation*, 2nd ed. (New York: Holt, Rinehart, and Winston, 1972); Joanna Hawkins Maclay and Thomas O. Sloan, *Interpretation: An Approach to the Study of Literature* (New York: Random House, 1972).

55 Kristin Langellier, "Personal Narratives: Perspectives on Theory and Research," *Text and Performance Quarterly* 9, no. 4 (1989): 272. Langellier and Eric Peterson have most fully theorized the performance of personal narratives. In addition to this article, see also "Voiceless Bodies, Bodiless Voices: The Future of Personal Narrative Performance," in *The Future of Performance Studies: Visions and Revisions*, ed. Sheron J. Dailey (Annandale, VA: National Communication Association, 1998); "Personal Narrative, Performance, Performativity: Two or Three Things I Know for Sure," *Text and Performance Quarterly* 19, no. 2 (1999): 125–144; and Kristin Langellier and Eric Peterson,

Storytelling in Daily Life: Performing Narrative (Philadelphia: Temple University Press, 2004). For additional work, also see the section "Personal Narratives: Problems and Possibilities" in Dailey, *The Future of Performance Studies*, 199–300.

56 Tracy Stephenson Shaffer makes a similar argument in her manuscript "The Place of Performance in Performance Studies" currently under review.

57 Gingrich-Philbrook, who debuted as a personal narrative performance artist in 1991 at the Otis J. Aggert Festival, has presented numerous personal narrative/autobiographical performances in multiple venues over the last twenty-three years.

58 See, for example, Carol Simpson Stern and Bruce Henderson, "The Personal Narrative and the Performance of Ethnography," *Performance: Texts and Contexts* (New York: Longman, 1993): 35–71; and Ronald J. Pelias and Tracy Stephenson Shaffer, "Everyday Storytelling," in *Performance Studies: The Interpretation of Aesthetic Texts* (Dubuque, IA: Kendall Hunt, 2007): 45–58.

59 Stern and Henderson, "The Personal Narrative," 39.

60 Pelias and Shaffer, "Everyday Storytelling," 55.

61 As a result, there was a proliferation of texts and performances under such labels as autobiography, personal narrative, and autoperformance, terms that many in the field still embrace. In a special issue of *Text and Performance Quarterly* 32, no. 3 (2012), guest editors Heather Carver and Bryant Alexander offer the cumbersome term "personal/auto/bio/ethno/graphic performance." Several collections of performance pieces that might fit into this broad category have been published. For example, see Lynn C. Miller, Jacqueline Taylor, and M. Heather Carver, eds., *Voices Made Flesh: Performing Women's Autobiography* (Madison, WI: University of Wisconsin Press, 2003); Frederick C. Corey, ed., *HIV Education: Performing Personal Narratives* (Tempe, AZ: Arizona State University, 1993); Lynn C. Miller and Ronald J. Pelias, eds., *The Green Window: Proceedings of the Giant City Conference on Performative Writing* (Carbondale, IL: Southern Illinois University, 2001).

62 For more extended discussions of autoethnographic performance, see Bryant Keith Alexander, "Performance Ethnography: The Reenacting and Inciting of Culture," in *The Sage Handbook of Qualitative Research*, 3rd ed., ed. Norman K. Denzin and Yvonna S. Lincoln (Thousand Oaks, CA: Sage, 2005): 411–442; Norman K. Denzin, *Performance Ethnography: Critical Pedagogy and the Politics of Culture* (Thousand Oaks, CA: Sage, 2003); Stacy Holman Jones, "Autoethnography: Making the Personal Political," in *The Sage Handbook of Qualitative Research*, 3rd ed., ed. Norman K. Kenzin and Yvonna S. Lincoln (Thousand Oaks, CA: Sage, 2005): 763–792; Stacy Holman Jones, Tony E. Adams, and Carolyn Ellis, eds., *Handbook of Autoethnography* (Walnut Creek, CA: Left Coast Press, 2013); Ronald J. Pelias, "Writing Into Position: Strategies for Composition and Evaluation," in *The Sage Handbook of Qualitative Research*, 4th ed., ed. Norman K. Denzin and Yvonna S. Lincoln (Thousand Oaks, CA: Sage, 2011): 659–668; Tami Spry, "Performative Autoethnography: Critical Embodiments and Possibilities," in *The Sage Handbook of Qualitative Research*, 4th ed., ed. Norman K. Denzin and Yvonna S. Lincoln (Thousand Oaks, CA: Sage, 2011): 497–512.

63 Because autoethnography often recalls and stages momentous life events, some critique its predictability and call for more rigorous attention to its artistry. See Craig Gingrich-Philbrook's "Autoethnography's Family Values: Easy Access to Compulsory Experiences," *Text and Performance Quarterly* 25, no. 4 (2005): 297–314.

64 Tami Spry, *Body, Paper, Stage: Writing and Performing Autoethnography* (Walnut Creek, CA: Left Coast Press, 2011).

65 Spry, *Body, Paper, Stage*, 33.

66 Spry, *Body, Paper, Stage*, 169.

67 For example, Spry asks performers to consider Bacon's concepts of inner form and outer form of literature to bring the inner form of the self, written on the page, to the outer form of the persona, presented on the stage.

68 Another exceptional example of the self in/as culture is a performance, *Nursing Mother*, and essay by Elyse Pineau, "Nursing Mother and Articulating Absence," *Text and Performance Quarterly* 20, no. 1 (2000): 1–19. In the performance, script, and essay, Pineau's body acts as an agent to critique medical interventions into the processes of birth and death.

69 Mary S. Strine, "Mapping the Cultural Turn in Performance Studies," in *The Future of Performance Studies: Visions and Revisions*, ed. Sheron J. Dailey (Annandale, VA: National Communication Association, 1998): 3–9.
70 Strine, "Mapping the Cultural Turn," 4.

References

Alexander, Bryant Keith. "Performance Ethnography: The Reenacting and Inciting of Culture," in *The Sage Handbook of Qualitative Research*, 3rd ed., ed. Norman K. Denzin and Yvonna S. Lincoln, 411–442. Thousand Oaks, CA: Sage, 2005.

Armstrong, Mary Haldeman. "Certain Aspects of Choral Speech." *Quarterly Journal of Speech* 24, no. 1 (1938): 117–119.

Auslander, Philip. *Liveness: Performance in a Mediatized Culture*. New York: Routledge, 1999.

Babcock, Maud May. "Impersonation vs. Interpretation." *Quarterly Journal of Public Speaking* 2, no. 4 (1916): 340–343.

———. "Interpretive Presentation versus Impersonative Presentation." *Quarterly Journal of Public Speaking* 2, no. 1 (1916): 18–25.

———. "Teaching Interpretation." *Quarterly Journal of Public Speaking* 1, no. 2 (1915): 173–176.

Bacon, Wallace A. "An Aesthetics of Performance." *Literature in Performance* 1, no. 1 (1980): 1–9.

———. *The Art of Interpretation*, 2nd ed. New York: Holt, Rinehart, and Winston, 1972.

Bacon, Wallace A. and Robert S. Breen. *Literature as Experience*. New York: McGraw-Hill, 1959.

Bahn, Eugene and Margaret L. Bahn. *A History of Oral Interpretation*. Minneapolis: Burgess, 1970.

Bell, Elizabeth. *Theories of Performance*. Thousand Oaks, CA: Sage, 2008.

Bell, Elizabeth and Marcy Rose Chvasta, "Performing Technologies." In *Theories of Performance*, edited by Elizabeth Bell, 233–263. Thousand Oaks, CA: Sage, 2008.

Bowman, Michael S. "'Novelizing' the Stage: Chamber Theatre after Breen and Bakhtin." *Text and Performance Quarterly* 15, no. 1 (1995): 1–23.

———. "Performing Literature in an Age of Textuality." *Communication Education* 45, no. 2 (1996): 96–101.

Bowman, Michael S. and Ruth Laurion Bowman. "Performing the Mystory: A Textshop in Autoperformance." In *Teaching Performance Studies*, edited by Nathan Stucky and Cynthia Wimmer, 161–174. Carbondale, IL: Southern Illinois University Press, 2002.

Bowman, Ruth Laurion. *The Double Life of Dr. Dappertutto*. Performed at Louisiana State University, 2010.

Bowman, Ruth Laurion and Michael S. Bowman, "On the Bias: From Performance of Literature to Performance Composition." In *The Sage Handbook of Performance Studies*, edited by Soyini Madison and Judith Hamera, 205–226. Thousand Oaks, CA: Sage, 2006.

Breen, Robert. *Chamber Theatre*. Englewood Cliffs, NJ: Prentice-Hall, 1978.

Bullowa, Alma M. "The Reading-Telling Method in the Use of the Short Story in Teaching Spoken English." *Quarterly Journal of Speech Education* 8, no. 1 (1922): 1–7.

Capo, Kay Ellen and Kristin M. Langellier. "Review/Interview: Anna Devere Smith." *Text and Performance Quarterly* 14, no. 1 (1994): 57–76.

Coger, Leslie Irene. "Interpreters Theatre: Theatre of the Mind." *Quarterly Journal of Speech* 49, no. 2 (1963): 157–164.

Coger Leslie Irene and Melvin R. White. *Readers Theatre Handbook*. Glenview, IL: Scott, Foresman, 1967.

Colson, Ted, ed. *Renewal & Revision: The Future of Interpretation*. Denton, TX: NB Omega Publication, 1986.

Conquergood, Dwight. "Health Theatre in a Hmong Refugee Camp." *TDR* 32, no. 3 (1988): 174–208.

———. "Life in Big Red: Struggles and Accommodations in a Chicago Polyethnic Tenement." In *Structuring Diversity: Ethnographic Perspectives on the New Immigration*, edited by Louise Lamphere, 95–144. Chicago: University of Chicago Press, 1992.

——. "Performing as a Moral Act: Ethical Dimensions of the Ethnography of Performance." *Literature in Performance* 5, no. 2 (1985): 1–13.

Corey, Frederick C., ed., *HIV Education: Performing Personal Narratives*. Tempe, AZ: Arizona State University, 1993.

——. "Performing Sexualities in an Irish Pub." *Text and Performance Quarterly* 16, no. 2 (1996): 146–160.

Denzin, Norman K. *Performance Ethnography: Critical Pedagogy and the Politics of Culture*. Thousand Oaks, CA: Sage, 2003.

Edwards, Paul. "The Rise of 'Expression.'" In *Performance of Literature in Historical Perspectives*, edited by David W. Thompson, 529–548. Lanham, MD: University Press of America, 1983.

——. "Unstoried: Teaching Literature in the Age of Performance Studies." *Theatre Annual* 52 (1999): 1–147.

Fine, Elizabeth C. *The Folklore Text: From Performance to Print*. Bloomington, IN: Indiana University Press, 1984.

Fine, Elizabeth C. and Jean Haskell Speer. "A New Look at Performance." *Communication Monographs* 44, no. 4 (1977): 374–389.

Gaylord, J.S. "Preparing Literary Material for Public Utterance." *Quarterly Journal of Public Speaking* 1, no. 1 (1915): 38–43.

Geiger, Don. "A 'Dramatic' Approach to Interpretative Analysis." *Quarterly Journal of Speech* 38, no. 2 (1952): 189–194.

——. "Oral Interpretation and the 'New Criticism.'" *Quarterly Journal of Speech* 36, no. 4 (1950): 508–513.

——. "The Oral Interpreter as Creator." *Speech Teacher* 3, no. 4 (1954): 269–277.

——. *Oral Interpretation and Literary Study*. South San Francisco: Pieter Van Vloten, 1958.

——. *The Sound, Sense, and Performance of Literature*. Chicago: Scott, Foresman, 1963.

Gingrich-Philbrook, Craig. "Autoethnography's Family Values: Easy Access to Compulsory Experiences." *Text and Performance Quarterly* 25, no. 4 (2005): 297–314.

Gray, Paul. "Strange Bedfellows: My Life and Hard Times in a Speech Communication Department." *Southern States Communication Journal* 44, no. 2 (1979): 159–166.

Grimes, Wilma H. and Althea Smith Mattingly. *Interpretation: Writer Reader Audience*. San Francisco: Wadsworth, 1961.

Herring, Bertha Forbes. "Vocal Interpretation of Literature in High Schools." *Quarterly Journal of Speech Education* 6, no. 4 (1920): 52–58.

Hinks, Harvey Scott. "Choric Speaking." *Southern Speech Bulletin* 3, no. 2 (1938): 16–18.

Hollister, Richard D. T. "Interpretive Reading and Its Place in a Department of Public Speaking." *Public Speaking Review* 4 (1914): 104.

HopKins, Mary Frances. "From Page to Stage: The Burden of Proof." *The Southern Speech Communication Journal* 47, no. 1 (1981): 1–9.

Jackson, Shannon. "Ethnography and the Audition: Performance as Ideological Critique." *Text and Performance Quarterly* 13, no. 1 (1993): 21–43.

Johnson, E. Patrick. "SNAP! Culture: A Different Kind of 'Reading'." *Text and Performance Quarterly* 15, no. 2 (1995): 122–142.

Jones, Joni L. "The Self as Other: Creating the Role of Joni The Ethnographer for *Broken Circles*." *Text and Performance Quarterly* 16, no. 2 (1996): 131–145.

Jones, Stacy Holman. "Autoethnography: Making the Personal Political." In *The Sage Handbook of Qualitative Research*, 3rd ed., edited by Norman K. Kenzin and Yvonna S. Lincoln, 763–792. Thousand Oaks, CA: Sage, 2005.

Jones, Stacy Holman, Tony E. Adams, and Carolyn Ellis, eds. *Handbook of Autoethnography*. Walnut Creek, CA: Left Coast Press, 2013.

Kaucher, Dorothy. "The Verse Speaking Choir." *Quarterly Journal of Speech* 17, no. 1 (1931): 64–73.

Langellier, Kristin. "Personal Narrative, Performance, Performativity: Two or Three Things I Know for Sure." *Text and Performance Quarterly* 19, no. 2 (1999): 125–144.

——. "Personal Narratives: Perspectives on Theory and Research." *Text and Performance Quarterly* 9, no. 4 (1989): 243–276.

——. "Voiceless Bodies, Bodiless Voices: The Future of Personal Narrative Performance." In *The Future of Performance Studies: Visions and Revisions*, edited by Sheron J. Dailey, 207–213. Annandale, VA: National Communication Association, 1998.

Langellier, Kristin and Eric Peterson. *Storytelling in Daily Life: Performing Narrative.* Philadelphia: Temple University Press, 2004.

Lee, Charlotte I. "Choric Reading and Kinetic Projection." *Quarterly Journal of Speech* 26, no. 4 (1940): 545–550.

——. *Oral Interpretation.* Boston: Houghton Mifflin, 1952.

Long, Beverly Whitaker. "A 'Distanced' Art: Interpretation at Mid-Century." In *Performance of Literature in Historical Perspectives*, edited by David W. Thompson, 567–587. Lanham, MD: University Press of America, 1983.

——. "Evaluating Performed Literature." In *Studies in Interpretation II*, edited by Esther M. Doyle and Virginia Hastings Floyd, 267–282. Amsterdam: Rodopi N.V., 1977.

Lowrey, Sara. "Gesture through Empathy." *Southern Speech Journal* 11, no. 3 (1946): 59–62.

Lutz, Mary Eleanor. "Choral Reading: Its Application to the Teaching of Speech." *Southern Speech Bulletin* 1 (1935): 26–28.

Lyman, R.L. "Oral English in the High School." *Quarterly Journal of Public Speaking* 1, no. 3 (1915): 241–259.

Lyne, Dorothy J. "The Choral Verse Speaking Choir." *Quarterly Journal of Speech* 23, no. 3 (1937): 449–451.

Maclay, Joanna H. "Group Performance in Academic Settings." In *Performance of Literature in Historical Perspectives*, edited by David W. Thompson, 393–417. Lanham, MD: University Press of America, 1983.

——. *Readers Theatre: Toward a Grammar of Practice.* New York: Random House, 1971.

Maclay, Joanna Hawkins and Thomas O. Sloan. *Interpretation: An Approach to the Study of Literature.* New York: Random House, 1972.

Madison, D. Soyini. "'That Was My Occupation': Oral Narrative, Performance, and Black Feminist Thought." *Text and Performance Quarterly* 13, no. 3 (1993): 213–232.

Maguire, Mariangela and Laila Farah Mohtar. "Performance and the Celebration of a Subaltern Counterpublic." *Text and Performance Quarterly* 14, no. 3 (1994): 238–252.

McLean, Margaret Prendergast. "Oral Interpretation—A Re-creative Art." In *Studies in the Art of Interpretation*, edited by Gertrude E. Johnson, 44–51. New York: D. Appleton-Century, 1940.

Meader, Emma Grant. "Choral Speaking and Its Values." *Quarterly Journal of Speech* 22, no. 2 (1936): 235–245.

Miller, Lynn C. and Ronald J. Pelias, eds. *The Green Window: Proceedings of the Giant City Conference on Performative Writing.* Carbondale, IL: Southern Illinois University, 2001.

Miller, Lynn C., Jacqueline Taylor, and M. Heather Carver, eds. *Voices Made Flesh: Performing Women's Autobiography.* Madison, WI: University of Wisconsin Press, 2003.

Olsen, David. "Flood and Church Secretaries, Buffalo Creek and Northwestern: Struggling with the Seams Between." *Text and Performance Quarterly* 12, no. 4 (1992): 329–348.

Parrish, W.M. "Interpretative Reading." *Quarterly Journal of Speech Education* 13, no. 2 (1927): 161.

Pelias, Ronald J. "Writing Into Position: Strategies for Composition and Evaluation." In *The Sage Handbook of Qualitative Research*, 4th ed., edited by Norman K. Denzin and Yvonna S. Lincoln, 659–668. Thousand Oaks, CA: Sage, 2011.

Pelias, Ronald J. and Tracy Stephenson Shaffer. "Everyday Storytelling." In *Performance Studies: The Interpretation of Aesthetic Texts*, 45–58. Dubuque, IA: Kendall Hunt, 2007.

Pelias, Ronald J. and James VanOosting. "A Paradigm for Performance Studies." *Quarterly Journal of Speech* 73, no. 2 (1987): 219–231.

Phelan, Peggy. *Unmarked: The Politics of Performance.* New York: Routledge, 1993.

Pineau, Elyse. "Nursing Mother and Articulating Absence." *Text and Performance Quarterly* 20, no. 1 (2000): 1–19.

Rasmussen, Carrie. "Verse Speaking and Bodily Activity." *Quarterly Journal of Speech* 20, no. 2 (1934): 282–286.

Robb, Margaret. "Looking Backward!" *Quarterly Journal of Speech* 28, no. 3 (1942): 323–327.

Robb, Mary Margaret. *Oral Interpretation of Literature in American Colleges and Universities*. Rev. ed. New York: Johnson Reprint Corporation, 1968.

Rose, Heidi. "A Conversation with Anna Devere Smith." *Text and Performance Quarterly* 31, no. 4 (2011): 440–448.

Shaffer, Tracy Stephenson. "The Place of Performance in Performance Studies." Manuscript currently under review.

Shields, Ronald E. "Like a Choir of Nightingales: The Oxford Recitations 1923–1930." *Literature in Performance* 3, no. 1 (1982): 15–26.

Spry, Tami. *Body, Paper, Stage: Writing and Performing Autoethnography*. Walnut Creek, CA: Left Coast Press, 2011.

——. "Performative Autoethnography: Critical Embodiments and Possibilities." In *The Sage Handbook of Qualitative Research*, 4th ed., edited by Norman K. Denzin and Yvonna S. Lincoln, 497–512. Thousand Oaks, CA: Sage, 2011.

Stern, Carol Simpson and Bruce Henderson. "The Personal Narrative and the Performance of Ethnography." In *Performance: Texts and Contexts*, 35–71. New York: Longman, 1993.

Strine, Mary S. "Mapping the Cultural Turn in Performance Studies." In *The Future of Performance Studies: Visions and Revisions*, edited by Sheron J. Dailey, 3–9. Annandale, VA: National Communication Association, 1998.

Strine, Mary S., Beverly Whitaker Long, and Mary Frances HopKins. "Research in Interpretation and Performance Studies: Trends, Issues, Priorities." In *Speech Communication: Essays to Commemorate the 75th Anniversary of The Speech Communication Association*, edited by Gerald M. Phillips and Julia T. Wood, 181–204. Carbondale, IL: Southern Illinois University Press, 1990.

Taft-Kaufman, Jill. "Oral Interpretation: Twentieth Century Theory and Practice." In *Speech Communication in the 20th Century*, edited by Thomas W. Benson, 157–183. Carbondale, IL: Southern Illinois University Press, 1985.

Tallcott, R.A. "The Place for Personation." *Quarterly Journal of Public Speaking* 2, no. 2 (1916): 116–122.

——. "Teaching Public Reading." *Quarterly Journal of Speech Education* 9, no. 1 (1923): 53–66.

Thompson, David W. ed. *Performance of Literature in Historical Perspectives*. Lanham, MD: University Press of America, 1983.

Valentine, K.B. "'New Criticism' and the Emphasis on Literature in Interpretation." In *Performance of Literature in Historical Perspectives*, edited by David W. Thompson 549–565. Lanham, MD: University Press of America, 1983.

VanMaanen, John. *Tales of the Field: On Writing Ethnography*, 2nd ed. Chicago: University of Chicago Press, 2011.

Vignes, Danielle Sears. "Hang It Out To Dry: A Performance Script." *Text and Performance Quarterly* 28, no. 3 (2008): 351–365.

——. "'Hang It Out To Dry': Performing Ethnography, Cultural Memory, and Hurricane Katrina in Chalmette, Louisiana." *Text and Performance Quarterly* 28, no. 3 (2008): 344–350.

Walsh, Rose. "Whither the Verse Choir." *Quarterly Journal of Speech* 21, no. 4 (1935): 461–466.

Woolbert, Charles H. and Severina E. Nelson. *The Art of Interpretative Speech*, 4th ed. New York: Appleton-Century-Crofts, 1956.

9.

LISTENING RESEARCH IN THE COMMUNICATION DISCIPLINE

David Beard and Graham Bodie

Claims abound that listening research started in the mid-twentieth century with a handful of scholars employed in the Department of Rhetoric at the University of Minnesota. In a hagiographic gesture that honors the founder of the Association, the public relations materials for the International Listening Association (ILA) claim that (emphasis added):

> Any history of listening would be remiss if it didn't *start* with "The Father of Listening," Dr. Ralph G. Nichols. *All* listening roads *led* to the University of Minnesota for over 25 years prior to the formation of the International Listening Association. Dr. Nichols *pioneered,* popularized and parlayed the missing "L" back into learning the world over.[1]

Pooley and Park would call this "a kind of social science *bildungsroman*,"[2] which imposes a novel-like story, with all the satisfactions that a good story brings, on what would be a richer, if less satisfying, account of history without that artificial narrative structure.

While there are good reasons, within an organizational culture, to salute its founder, this history is partial and incomplete. While not taking anything away from Dr. Nichols as a key figure in listening research, as Keith suggests, "Any honest history will be messy, and not just at the edges."[3] It is our goal to muddle the convergence implied by the ILA's metaphor; to thoroughly understand the history of listening research (at least as it is understood within the Communication Studies discipline), we must recognize that all "roads" sprawl endlessly, usually dead end just short of intersection, and often collide in traffic circles that serve to both smooth and to snarl the work of communication scholars.

It is the work of this chapter to trace some of that roadmap: to recognize that research in listening is as old as the discipline and its oldest professional association, the National Communication Association (NCA), and to recognize that research in listening is a thread in the tapestry of every dimension of work in the Association (from the basic course to media theory; from interpersonal communication to public address). We will map their intersections and trace their developments toward new frontiers, and in so doing, shed a little light on the road ahead in the twenty-first century.

Listening as a Conceptual Problem, Listening as a Historiographical Problem

In writing a chapter for this volume about the history of listening research, we faced both a conceptual problem and a historiographical problem, reflecting larger areas of contention in the Communication Studies discipline. We tackle, albeit briefly, both of these problems separately below.

Concepts

Defining any field or subfield raises problems of definition and questions of emphasis. The definitional problem has been addressed (for example) by the ILA, an affiliate organization of the NCA, which stipulates that listening is "the process of receiving, constructing meaning from, and responding to spoken and/or nonverbal messages."[4] Such a definition is designed to move us from the audiologist's or speech pathologist's attention on *hearing* toward a communication scholar's attention to *listening* (because we can hear an array of sounds which are not *messages*).[5] Indeed, a popular distinction made in textbooks and scholarly writing alike is between hearing and listening with the latter imbued with more conscious awareness and manipulation on the part of an active message recipient.[6] The ILA's definition of listening as a process involving *messages* also moves us away from the musicologist's focus on understanding and appreciating various musical styles, although there are moments when music constitutes at least one dimension or one channel of meaning within the listening process.[7] Conceptually, then, communication scholars have needed to define listening by either excluding particular activities of the ear or, more commonly, by adding certain critical activities that other disciplines ignore.

In some ways, conceptual work in listening research is always pragmatic: each piece of listening research begins with some variation of the claim, "for the ends I intend, I stipulate the following definition of listening . . ."[8] Over time, these definitions are synthesized and analyzed,[9] but the stipulative work of conceptual definition was as ongoing in listening research as it has been in other areas of communication research (for example, in rhetoric, where definitions of the central term proliferate). Interestingly, most definitions, thus far, move us toward understanding listening as a behavior—as intentional a communication behavior as writing, reading, and speech.[10] We share those basic assumptions, though at some points in this chapter we will discuss scholars who further trouble them.

Historiography

Listening has been the subject of intense, focused scrutiny (especially, we shall see, in the post-war period of American communication scholarship). At the same time, it has been a phenomenon visible only indirectly, by its effects on other areas of communication research. We can see this split, for example, in mass communication research. Most mass communication research focuses on the message: on critical interpretation of the message, on the effects of certain types of messages, and on locating the message within larger cultural and economic systems.[11] The role and activities of the listener are only sometimes under direct scrutiny. Most of the time, the role of the listener is a presupposition of the research—a background element, unquestioned and unexamined.[12] Indeed, the listener is often conceptualized as a mere receptor of information, someone acted upon versus an active participant in the meaning-making process.

To attempt to draft a history of listening research that attended only to the scholarship addressing the phenomenon directly would thus be to generate a history already more significant for its absences and lacunae than for its contribution. We have greater ambitions than that. At the same time, we have no intentions to see scholars with no explicit interest in listening as an area of research, as Pooley and Park call it, "retroactively dragooned" as listening scholars.[13] In much the way a conservation biologist must sometimes study the fish and sometimes study the lake, we must move back and forth between (1) analysis of research that directly addresses listening and (2) analysis of research that directly addresses some other dimension of human communication but offers insight into disciplinary presumptions about the nature of listening. By doing so, we will be able to make claims about both the study of listening and the contributions of the study of listening to the larger project of the National Communication Association in its first hundred years.

Toward the goal of writing a history of listening research, this chapter is arranged by intellectual problem set. Some of these problem sets are nearly as old as the NCA—being articulated in the early, most polemical years of the Association's history. Others are recent research trajectories.

(1) First, we will address the early tensions in accounts of listening. Scholarship in the journals prior to World War II (a period usually presumed to be barren of research on listening) focused on the speech teacher as (a) the master listener, (b) diagnostician for speech defects, and (c) expert judge of quality. Audiences were presumed passive recipients of speech; the master speech teachers strove to teach students to listen as they listened.

(2) Second, we will address the turn, at mid-century, to study listening as a behavior. Empirical research in student listening practices was the core of this research (and the core of claims that this period marks the beginning of listening research—claims we here revise). The research here drew attention to best practices for listening, stemming from the larger communications movement in the wartime and post-war period.

(3) Third, we will address listening research that attempts to study listeners. This thread of research asks scholars to account for the actual behaviors of listeners. While scholars in Communication Studies presume that empirical study of listeners and "participatory culture" in media is a recent development, in fact, this research is among the oldest strands in communication scholarship.

(4) Finally, we examine the current intersections between listening and cultural studies research as communication scholars come to participate in larger discussions of the

auditory environment. At the start of the twenty-first century, listening research is just one of the many sites where Communication Studies is making a contribution to interdisciplinary research across the humanities and social sciences.

In the end, we will draw some attention to the evolution of the map of programs for listening research in Communication Studies and the directions that might evolve in the second century of the NCA.

The Mastery of "Speech Teachers" and the Passivity of Audiences

Given the history of the NCA and the prominent focus of early work on "speech" pedagogy,[14] it is no surprise that the earliest conceptualizations of listening are based in this framework. In the early decades of the discipline, however, little explicit attention was paid to listening;[15] indeed "the audience" was itself not a major focus of the earliest work.

The lack of attention was not because the early scholars in the field did not recognize the importance of listening. In 1915, an exhortation to conduct "an observational study of the behavior of audiences" was included in the *Quarterly Journal of Public Speaking* (later renamed the *Quarterly Journal of Speech*) in a report from the research committee.[16] Similarly, preparation for research in public speaking depended upon learning a complex of biological, sociological, and psychological dimensions of the communication process. This list included, among many other factors:

- The processes involved in good English *when it is being heard* (emphasis added).
- To what extent … postures, gestures, and vocal modulation influence one's experience.
- What relations exist between the work of the vital organs (heart, lungs, glands, etc.) and the different kinds of experiences.
- The structure, functions, and development of collective auditors, or audiences, including such topics as:

    (1) The crowd, the mob, the society, and the army.
    (2) The audience.
    (3) Fashion and custom.
    (4) Methods of social intercourse.

        (a) Suggestion (mass and individual), suggestibility.
        (b) Sympathy and contagion.
        (c) Imitation and tradition.[17]

To the contemporary communication scholar, this looks like a scattershot list of the topics that would come to shape research in listening and in audience research more broadly. But in the resulting exchanges between Everett Hunt and Charles Woolbert about the future of research in the discipline (fundamentally, a disagreement about humanistic and social scientific research trajectories), both of these scholars continued to emphasize the *production* of speeches, not the *reception* of speeches in the audience, as the primary site for scholarship.[18] When mentioned in the early journals, audience was generally discussed in terms of how a speaker can make "himself [*sic*] agreeable to an audience."[19] Perhaps unsurprisingly, considerations of *audience* and *listening* that were active in the early years of the discipline primarily included consideration of (1) the speech teacher as the master listener, a diagnostician of speech impediments who taught students to listen as he or she does; and (2) the relatively impoverished model for listening outside the classroom, one which emphasized the audience as acted upon by the speaker and the mass media, instead of acting to create their own meaning.

Early Views of Audience as Passive

The view of the unilateral or unidirectional impact of speakers on audience members is well captured in the literature with the use of terms like "audience reaction."[20] Language such as "the effect of the speech on the hearers"[21] was much more common than language indicative of listeners' active construal of information. The audience as passive receptor was also the implicit model of listening in early work on attitude change, and most of the early work was in the spirit of how speakers can more effectively move audiences. The assumption that listeners are "influenced" by how speakers structure their messages was fully entrenched in the vernacular of those writing articles for the *Quarterly Journal of Speech* (*QJS*),[22] and this same view was also evident in the experimental studies published mostly in *Speech Monographs* that were concerned with speaker effectiveness. To describe the processes by which speakers influenced audiences, a variety of variables were investigated, with intelligibility[23] and articulation[24] mentioned frequently. Research in mass communication focused on similar variables, replicating concerns addressed by traditional speech researchers. For instance, F.H. Lumley investigated "Rates of speech in radio speaking,"[25] while others voiced concerns over how the radio will "change speech"[26]—generally speaking, even in mass communication, emphasis resided in the act of production.

As reviewed by Howard Gilkinson, there were "four distinguishable kinds of criterion-indexes ... employed to record, or measure, the influence of a speaker upon an audience."[27] These included attitude scales, opinion polls, retention tests, and ratings (or judgments about the speech). Interestingly, the third of these (retention tests) was deemed the measure of listening, a trend that lasted well into the 1990s and was influential in efforts to improve student comprehension of lecture material.[28] The focus on how people comprehend messages was also aided by work made necessary by the war effort, in particular reported problems of pilots in "listening accurately and in reporting back accurately what is heard."[29] Whether the population of interest was students or pilots, however, the focus of listening instruction was about "the degree of accuracy with which the theme and main ideas of the speaker are communicated to the listener."[30] Although the listener was recognized, the primary model of the audience (and thus listening) was simple and linear, much like early models of communication more generally.[31]

Speech Teacher as Therapist

Prior to 1930, a primary discussion of listening was as diagnostic, as instructors in voice, speech pathology, and speech clinics needed to attune their ears for purposes of identifying various speech problems to be corrected. Although some were concerned with students "listening" to their own voices in an effort to help with pitch, rate, and so forth,[32] most attention was paid to constituting the speech teacher as an expert interpreter not only of what was said by a student or clinic patient, but of what blocks (psychological and physical) were an impediment to effective speech.[33] Smiley Blanton is the obvious case in support of this focus. Blanton argued that the voice, divided into motor, vibrator, and resonator, is impacted by emotion, and that one could discern the impact that emotion has on each of the components of the voice.[34]

In the public speaking classroom at the University of Minnesota, Bryng Bryngelson continued this line of thinking, arguing that students with difficulties in public speaking had internalized emotional difficulties and social disorders that were complicating their speech. A good speech teacher could listen to diagnose these difficulties and develop treatment. Bryngelson would force the students to speak before a mirror (and so learn to internalize the image that their audiences had of them, rather than their faulty self-image). In addition, he would enlist other students to serve as both audience and makeshift analyst, participating in the diagnosis: Bryngelson writes about "the members of the class all participat[ing] in the discussion, calling attention to the difference as well as remarking about the more normal parts of their persons."[35] This was the work of the public speaking teacher (in the works of Blanton, Bryngelson, and others): to listen attentively, to diagnose, and to treat, in the clinic and in the classroom.

In outlining the public speaking class at Cornell and seeking the ideal speaking situation for classroom exercises, James Winans writes, "We wish to make the conditions as normal as possible, with the audience listening to what the speaker has to say and the speaker rising to communicate his ideas." In this model, audience response or criticism is suppressed until after the class is over when speakers seeking audience feedback could meet with the teacher. Feedback from students was not valuable in the classroom dynamic; students as listeners were no more valuable than the passive audiences discussed above.[36] At best, a handful of scholars were interested in teaching students to listen as the teacher listens—as a therapist. In "Standardization of Grades in Public Speaking," J.R. Pelsma argues that students should attend academic speaking competitions and measure their sense of "the winner" in the competition against those of the judges—learning to listen like the master speech teachers do.[37] In "Some Statistical Investigations in the Field of Speech," Robert West and Helen Larsen argue that a public speaking class can be taught to assess each other with a high degree of reliability to the ways that the teacher assesses the students: in other words, that students can be taught to listen like the teacher listens.[38] Effective listening defines the master Speech Teacher, who teaches students to listen like him or her, and the master Speech Teacher defines the discipline of Communication Studies until the Great Depression.

Listening and the Communications Movement: Training Listeners

No history of communication study and instruction can deny that the world wars were important engines that drove speech research and pedagogy. In this section, we trace a history from wartime communication pedagogy (which was inherently multimodal, written and verbal) through the Communications movement (catalyzed by the influx of students funded by the GI Bill) which picked up that multimodal approach to communication. This is the backdrop against which the earliest formal research in listening is engaged—the work of the "father of listening," Ralph Nichols, and his colleagues at the University of Minnesota. In contextualizing the work of Nichols, we hope to reinterpret somewhat hagiographic histories of listening research, enhancing them with an acute awareness of the developing fullness of the Communication Studies discipline which leads to including listening as a formal area of study in the post-war period.

The War Redefines Communication Pedagogy in Military Training

In the wartime period, it was not unusual to see submissions to *QJS* from teachers and scholars whose institutional identification was not with colleges or universities, but with a military rank and branch of service. For example, Harold Kent's "The Army and its Needs in Speech" outlines, specifically, the skills the military values in oral communication in the midst of World War II (e.g., effective use of microphones).[39] Held and Held reiterate the emphasis on message production, writing that:

> the Army has no pressing need for great orators, nor has it any need whatever for spellbinders and rabble-rousers. But it has a great need for officers who have knowledge, logical conclusions based upon it, and ability to impart it to others.[40]

But the army was also interested in effective listening techniques—Forest Whan tells us that the airplane pilot must be trained in "ear-memory" so that he can retain and process complex, compressed messages from air traffic control towers.[41] And perhaps more significantly, the military was interested in integrated communication. There is no point to the differentiation of speaking, writing, reading, and listening in the military context; disciplinary boundaries that divide curricula in the university have minimal significance in the context of war (or perhaps any "applied context" for that matter). As reported in an unsigned article of 1943 in *QJS*, the "Objectives" of military training in communication are:

> to develop an officer candidate who will (1) be a clear thinker; (2) possess the skill of orderly, concise, and appropriate communication, both oral and written, including the ability to observe and report accurately; (3) possess the ability to listen and to read understandingly.[42]

In a very practical form, this integration of reading, writing, speaking, and listening into a single curriculum prefigures the work engaged by the Communications movement of the post-war period; Jean Malmstrom argued as much, claiming that the curricular innovations developed to better train officers should serve as the backbone of university curricula after the war.[43]

The Communications Movement Redefines Communication Pedagogy within the University

A new wave of systematic exploration of listening seems to happen within the context of the Communications movement in World War II–era United States. The rise in students after the war (enabled by the GI Bill) and the interest in practical communications that these students brought to university life led to the development of "communications courses." These were core courses (liberal education or general education courses) which combined speech and composition, reading and listening, sometimes inflected with the works of Alfred Korzybski and S.I. Hayakawa in General Semantics. According to David Russell:

> the movement was launched in 1947 when the NCTE [National Council of Teachers of English] and SAA [Speech Association of America, later renamed the NCA] sponsored a joint conference on freshman programs (which led the NCTE to found the Conference on College Composition and Communication the next year). The movement amounted to a crash program for initiating into academia a host of GIs from radically different social backgrounds.[44]

Against the backdrop of an integrated curriculum, uniting writing and speaking, reading and listening, a more formal research and pedagogical agenda would develop.

Harlen Adams was one of the first to argue strongly that listening is absent from pedagogy, writing that most teachers would claim that:

> speaking and listening cannot be separated. Probably all teachers would agree on this point, but they then focus their attention upon the teaching of speech and apparently assume that skill in listening will somehow be acquired.[45]

Unfortunately, textbooks prior to World War II were closer to pop psychology than grounded in genuine listening research. By the end of World War II, there would be a hunger in the Speech community for textbooks and pedagogies grounded in theory and research. Robert T. Oliver shares the best of his advice, which again stems from pop psychology: "to be a good listener . . . attention must be so eager and intent as to inspire the best that the speaker of the moment is capable of giving."[46]

It is not unfair to the discipline to note that, prior to the war, energy was focused on the speaker. These pressures are aggravated when faculty are called upon to teach four dimensions of the communication process; if faculty trained in speech barely addressed listening, faculty trained primarily in the teaching of writing might not address it at all in the context of a communications program. After and as a result of the war and the GI Bill, listening could move from the periphery to the center.

Reframing and Refocusing "The Father of Listening"

To understand how the Communications movement reframed pedagogy at the university, and to reframe the origin of listening research as commonly identified in disciplinary histories to this point, we can examine a specific program at the University of Minnesota.

In 1944, the University of Minnesota's Department of Rhetoric in the College of Agriculture converted the first-year composition course into the first-year "communication" course. The university required undergraduate majors to take nine credits (three courses on the quarter system, or one full year) of "Communication I-II-III," a course sequence symptomatic of the Communications movement insofar as it integrated assignments in reading, listening, and speaking as well as writing. Here, the curriculum follows Adams's 1938 claim that "listening is one of the four major aspects of the teaching of English, perhaps the most neglected,"[47] and so the curriculum was redesigned to address all four areas.

To ground their pedagogy in addressing listening, faculty members in the Rhetoric program (like Ralph Nichols and James I. Brown) engaged in social scientific research in processes of listening. Nichols and others, in a series of articles in *QJS* and *Speech Monographs*, outline a model for listening that would define a subfield (including a scholarly association) for some time.[48] Listening should be taught, not presumed in the communication process, Nichols argued, and there were specific skills and habits that were best taught. These were not the folk theories that typified popular (and sometimes scholarly) communication texts but specific skills discerned through systematic study.

To give you a taste of the energy of this period, we can look to Nichols's inaugural address to the first meeting of the International Listening Association (ILA), in which he celebrates the work of his contemporaries at this exciting time:

> Paul Bagwell ... was put in charge of the biggest communication program in the nation, at Michigan State University. Their stated objective was to improve the reading, writing, speaking, and listening of their thousands of under-classmen. He declared that if listening improvement was one of their stated goals, they should spend a fourth of their energy on it ...
>
> James I. Brown at the University of Minnesota ... felt that to prove to people that listening comprehension can be improved, we ought to have a standardized test of effective listening ... and he went ahead and produced his Brown-Carlson Test of Listening Comprehension ...
>
> Grant Fairbanks ... was a chopper and splicer. He would take a tape recording of a previously recorded speech, cut it all up in little pieces, and then paste the residues together. Through this technique he could speed up the presentation time to any degree desired, and determine the consequent effect upon listener comprehension ... [I]t is possible for people to listen to human speech at twice the rate, perhaps three times the rate, that they normally hear it without any significant loss of comprehension of it.[49]

One can feel a general sense of an open horizon here, one that invited many approaches.

The rise of social scientific research methods and the presentation of formal research as the basis for instruction in listening follow from the general blossoming of social science approaches in the post-war period. It is no accident that Ralph Nichols was an agitator for the formation of both the International Listening Association and the National Society for the Study of Communication (NSSC, formed in 1950, renamed the International Communication Association in 1969). The NSSC was the alternative organization to the Speech Association of America (NCA) that privileged empirical and data-driven research. These early figures in listening were also committed to the development of empirical methods.

Nichols's own contribution was to systematize listening as a skill set: to identify behaviors that hurt one's ability to listen and to identify behaviors that made one a better listener. He was also skilled at arguing the value of listening and listening research. So, for example, he noted in various places that focusing on emotional trigger words could interfere with good listening, as does focusing overmuch on evaluating delivery or attempting to take notes on all of the details in a speech (losing sight of the forest for the trees). That last bit should make clear that Nichols was focused on listening among undergraduate students. On the positive side, Nichols recommended that listeners make mental summaries and anticipate next points as they listen—engaging in a kind of meta-cognition that would improve listening practice. Again, this work was grounded in empirical studies of the listening practices of students, though Nichols believed in great generalizability.

At the level of the hortatory, Nichols argued that effective listening was central to efforts to develop our basic human nature:

- The most basic of all human needs is to understand and to be understood.
- It is almost impossible to hate a person whom we fully understand.
- The best way to understand people is to listen to them.[50]

It is clear, within the ILA, that some scholars believe that Nichols (and Brown and others) had a formative and powerful effect on the Communication Studies discipline. Whether Nichols is a force for transforming the discipline or symptomatic of changes already under way (including the larger systematization of social science methods) is an open question; what is clear is that listening was being recognized by a larger body of teacher-scholars. By the 1960s, L. LeRoy Cowperthwaite's 1964 review essay on "Fundamentals and Public Speaking Texts" surveyed a variety of texts that brought listening to the fore for the basic course, manifesting the promise of integrating speaking and listening in the communication curriculum.[51]

By the 1980s, the Communications movement had thoroughly waned,[52] but interest in listening continued to flower. "Communications" courses, teaching a complex inter-play of reading, writing, and speaking, were being eliminated by administrators who succumbed to arguments about expertise: speech teachers should teach speech, writing teachers should teach writing, and expertise in both is not possible. As communications courses began to evaporate, freestanding courses in listening began to appear. Listening developed as an area of inquiry all its own, with studies emerging on listening in health communication, workplace communication, interpersonal communication, intercultural communication, and so on.[53] The subfield became open to ethnographic, qualitative, quantitative, and occasionally even critical and rhetorical methods.[54]

In the last decades of the twentieth century, listening research and pedagogy became at once more thoroughly institutionalized, but fell victim to a catch–22 of communication pedagogy. Listening increasingly becomes viewed as important enough an area of inquiry to establish a course in the undergraduate curriculum. Yet, by establishing a course in listening, it became unnecessary to address listening in other courses. In 2014, it is very nearly impossible to imagine a textbook in the basic course in communication without a chapter on listening. At the same time, the presence of that chapter erases the need to address listening as the textbook addresses other elements of the communication process. As Adams and Cox note, communication textbooks retain a production focus, one that centers on the speaker (and often on the parts of the speaking process that most resemble writing or speech-writing), without a real exploration of the listening process threaded through the text.[55] At the level of research, listening becomes more sharply defined as a subfield—autonomous within the larger field of Communication Studies. Its increasing richness and independence is simultaneous to its segregation from the larger NCA community.[56]

The International Listening Association is the group most caught in that bind. Founded at a "State-of-the-Art of Listening" symposium held on the University of Minnesota campus (where Nichols taught with Brown, Lyman Steil, and others) in 1979, the ILA has grown from a small community holding annual meetings with a newsletter (*Listening Post*) to an organization with an international convention, often held abroad, and three scholarly publications: *International Journal of Listening, The Listening Professional,* and *Listening Education*.[57] The ILA still sponsors or co-sponsors panel and poster sessions at the NCA convention, but these presences are reflections of the joint identification of some ILA members with both the ILA and a larger disciplinary association, rather than a sign that listening research descending from the work of Nichols is thoroughly embedded in NCA disciplinary conversations.[58]

Without a doubt, the received history of the scholars engaged in listening research and pedagogy (identifiable with the International Listening Association) reinforces the tension between autonomy and isolation. By focusing on Nichols's role in the foundation of the ILA (and so at least underplaying his role in the foundation of the ICA), the uniqueness and autonomy of listening research comes to the fore. We want to trouble that narrative. We would argue, instead, that listening research is of a piece with the turn away from speaker-centered rhetorical approaches favored (in the post-war period) by the SAA/SCA community toward the social scientific approaches of the ICA. We lose the idea that Nichols was a single great man, but we may regain a sense that listening research is of a piece with the historical developments of Communication Studies as a field. Additionally, by focusing on the individual genius of Nichols's research program in the study of listening, we may lose sight of the broader disciplinary movements that funded the integrated pedagogies for listening, speaking, writing, and reading that defined the Communications movement. (The post-war period in communication research and pedagogy, the period in which the Communications movement found root, is entirely undertheorized, if not forgotten, by scholars in the history of communication, with rare exception,[59] and so we want to crack open the door here to beginning that kind of re-investigation.)

Recontextualized in the way that we have tried to engage here, we find ways to appreciate both the increasing specialization of methods and the unique scholarly traditions inherent in the community of listening researchers. At the same time, we hope we have demonstrated that the tradition of listening research and pedagogy is embedded in and inseparable from the larger movements in the Communication Studies discipline.

From Studying *Listening* to Studying *Listeners*

The study of listening as Nichols and his contemporaries engaged it was the study of practices and behaviors. While rooted in classroom-based research, this work was generalized to other contexts—the skills for good listening in the classroom were generalized to business, to relationships, to public discourse. But for Nichols, Brown, and others, the study of the actual practices of real listeners in these other contexts was not yet on the horizon. The move from studying listening as a practice in the university setting to studying the diverse actual practices of real listeners in other settings comes slowly to Communication Studies (and some would argue is still not to an adequate level[60]).

We can trace the growing importance of studying the actual practices of people listening across the decades in the twentieth century. While at first just a whisper manifested around the advent of radio, by the end of the century full-scale ethnographic study of real listeners would become one of the defining dimensions of communication study. We will trace those earliest efforts in sources like Cantril and Allport's work in radio listening. But quickly, we will see this impulse to study real people, listening, will spread to researchers interested in business communication, in K–12 education, and more—scholars will bring the study of listening into real listening contexts and so start to make the listener the genuine object of study.

In the 1930s, Cantril and Allport, in *The Psychology of Radio* (reprinted in the 1970s), begin their work with a sketch of "The Mental Setting of Radio," a comprehensive picture of the social-psychological setting in which radio operates, thrown into relief by detailed comparison with the economic and political background of radio broadcasting in other countries.[61] This section of the book considers the effects of the radio upon the listening public and the preferences and habits of the radio audience as inferred from questionnaire data, fan mail, and field studies. For example, the *Survey of Radio Listeners in Louisiana* by Edgar A. Schuler covered nearly every geographical section of the state and outlined listeners' typical daily listening patterns, activities while listening, reasons for not listening, non-available programs desired, types of programs preferred, methods of learning about new programs, reasons for writing to radio stations, station preferences, conditions of radio sets, and extent of shortwave listening. Breakdowns are afforded on many of these items on a basis of sex, age, educational background, race, family income, geography, and location in cities-villages-farms.[62]

With the advent of research on radio listening, then, the Communication Studies discipline is no longer solely about public speaking or speech, but about a broader understanding of communication, including mediated communication. Notably, by studying audiences as much or more than speakers, in the mediated communication environment created by radio, the discipline of Speech Communication comes to widen and grow out of the speaker-centered model for communication research and toward the study of real listeners.

This movement comes to real fruition in the 1970s. In Communication Studies, we see the ascension of the idea that listeners play an "active role in determining both the nature and the outcome of the communicative encounter,"[63] coupled with the recognition that listening will vary across contexts (civic, professional, educational, and relationship). The most popular distinction made to identify listening as a unique phenomenon worthy of study was put forth in texts such as *Listening Behavior* by Larry Barker.[64] In this and other texts one finds the now infamous dichotomy between hearing (a passive form of listening in which "the potential receiver of the message is minimally, if at all, concerned about the listening process") and listening (an active form of listening in which the receiver is involved or has a purpose for information reception). This basic separation is still prominent in textbooks designed for the basic course as well as interpersonal communication. Others added to the notion of active listening abilities not only to be involved but also to adequately judge a speaker's message.[65] This sort of active involvement or engagement as an informed citizen was present in early conceptualizations of the basic course[66] and is still evident in the way many programs still conceptualize this course. Thus the goal of speech education is more than producing adequate elocutionists, or skillful note-takers (in Nichols's case) and information processors (in Brown's case); it is fundamentally about producing engaged citizens, an idea as old as rhetorical studies itself.

Listening research conformed to a trend in the SCA journal space (in particular in *The Speech Teacher*) to publish articles that highlighted the importance of various skills for the workplace and life in general. Within this larger literature can be found several assessment instruments (typically self-report) that attempt to map communicative and listening competence.[67] A focus explicitly on what constitutes listening competence was led by Andrew Wolvin and his colleagues at the University of Maryland, and many of the findings from this research program are obvious within the NCA's list of critical communication skills.[68] In addition, there were, for obvious reasons, complementary efforts targeted toward K–12 education as opposed to the academy[69] with a concern on national standards,[70] or what is now referred to as the Common Core.

Apart from an explicit focus on listening as a distinct set of competencies, others implied the importance of listening as part of a larger communicative construct.[71] Most, though not all, of this research was concerned with how listening (or related competencies) is influenced by certain trait-like predispositions. Some investigations treat listening only tangentially, for example Charles Wigley's study of verbal aggressiveness (VA) in which jurors' listening to testimony is thought to be clouded by traits like VA,[72] while others treat listening directly, for example, William Villaume's work on age-related hearing loss.[73] Again, we are moving more and more deeply into the study of the practices of real listeners in real contexts.

The *International Journal of Listening* has been a center for the study of real listeners— from medical students to nursing professionals, from police to hospitality workers.[74] The annual meeting of the ILA maintains a business communication track that specifically works on researching and training for listening in the corporate context.[75]

In addition to the importance of listening skills for student retention of aurally presented (and largely lecture-based) information, others have made a career out of stressing the importance of training listening skills for various classes of workers like healthcare providers.[76] Finally, there is also an emphasis in communication research that utilizes semi-structured interviewing techniques that listening is a skilled method for data collection.[77] Thus, it appears that our field in part works within a vision of listening as a skilled behavior—one that can be trained and honed and one that is crucial for personal and professional success and well-being.[78] Further research in new contexts of listening will only enhance our understanding of the complexities of the communication process.

Listening and the Mediation of Technology: From Radio to iTunes

The end of the twentieth century and the first decades of the twenty-first have been the time of the rediscovery of the ear by communities beyond Communication Studies. Historians of technology, cultural studies scholars, literary theorists, and others in the humanities have rediscovered sound, noise, music, and voice as complementary areas of critical exploration. Taken together, these studies have constituted a new scholarly area of research, "auditory culture," and significant scholars in Communication Studies are shaping this scholarly dialogue.

Auditory culture is composed of a range of sound phenomena, analyzed from diverse critical and methodological perspectives. Perhaps appropriately, given his dominant position in the interdisciplinary humanities, Michel Foucault is among the scholars who cracked open listening as a phenomenon worthy of critical reflection. He begins by addressing listening in the classical world:

> When you have heard someone say something important, do not start quibbling straightaway but try to collect yourself and spend some moments in silence, the better to imprint what you have heard, and undertake a quick self-examination when leaving the lesson you have listened to, or the conversation you have had, take a quick look at yourself in order to see where you are, whether you have heard and learned something new with regard to the equipment (the *paraskeue*) you already have at hand, and thus see to what extent and how far you have been able to improve yourself.[79]

Listening was, as Foucault described the Pythagoreans, a process engaged with the whole body; listening also requires a "precise physical posture . . . the body must stay absolutely calm."[80] Understanding is to be indicated "by a smile and a slight movement of the head";[81] the body's stillness is essential. In this context, the immobility of the body is "a guarantee of morality."[82] Listening, as a practice, becomes the key to reflection, meditation, and salvation.

The 1986 publication of Jacques Attali's *Noise*[83] and the rise of Cultural Studies scholarship generally in the late 1980s and 1990s opened the door to cultural studies of sound and the socio-cultural processes of listening, broadly conceived. We provide the following three areas of study as examples of the emerging trends in such research.

Music Studies

Theodor Adorno diagnosed the twentieth century as an age of "regressive listening." Mass reproduction and broadcast of music meant that the average person understood less and less about the process of performing music. The experience of music becomes increasingly passive. Botstein tells us that "the cause of the 'impoverishment' of musical culture . . . was that music was no longer practiced in the home."[84] Denied the music literacy to produce songs on instruments of their own, listeners grow ever more passive in their appreciation for music. Adorno aggressively advocated for a rediscovery and revaluation of the processes of attentive listening, an advocacy picked up by others in communication and cultural studies. Contemporary musicologists continue work in this vein.[85]

Critical Technology Studies

Technologies for listening tend to interfere with genuine human interaction. Jonathan Sterne discusses "mediated auscultation" as one of the major phenomena of the twentieth century.[86] Sterne's example of such mediated listening that actually narrows or winnows the range of human interaction is the stethoscope: the stethoscope brings certain sounds into clarity for the doctor, but as it does, it closes out or even suppresses a range of other sounds. The doctor learns to listen *only* through the stethoscope.

Relatedly, technology changes the sociality of listening. Radios, in a crowded room, can push people into solitude. When the sports bar turns on the giant screen television, the room ceases to be a *group* of basketball fans and becomes a *collection of individual fans*, entranced by the screen. As Michael Bull puts it, "users no longer commune with those next to them but with the 'distant' voices'" of the media.[87] The technology yields an experience of "accompanied solitude" in lieu of genuine interaction with the people around us. Bull and Sterne see critical reflection on listening technologies as a key to rethinking the processes of listening.

Soundscape Studies

The environmental movement leads to a rediscovery of "acoustic ecology." Murray Schafer identifies a "soundscape" or an "acoustic environment" that can be documented via "soundwalks," or walks in which the ambient noises of an environment are recorded electronically; the recordings are logged onto a map of the space.[88] The noises include those sounds that exist regardless of the visitor's presence, like ambient bird noises and water or wind, and those caused by the visitor's presence, like the sound of footfalls on the walking surfaces.

Barbara Lorenzkowski (in *Sounds of Ethnicity*) argues persuasively for soundscape as productive of cultural identities. Among German immigrants in North America, "the act of speaking (or singing) the German mother tongue anchored fellow migrants reassuringly in a soundscape of German ethnicity." This process is not simply akin to an immersion program in your local middle school for learning a foreign language. Rather, among some immigrant communities, arguments were made for an "audible homeland—a space liberated from place and translated into sound." Sound, above and beyond physical or political geography, was constitutive of identity for these immigrant families.[89]

Barry Blesser, Linda Ruth Salter, and Alain Corbin have explored the role of nonmusical sound in identity formation. Blesser and Salter, in *Spaces Speak: Are You Listening? Experiencing Aural Architecture*, define "soundmarks"—something like the landmark, but constituted in sound.[90] Soundmarks define an acoustic geography of a space (like the sound of a waterfall or a chiming bell). Corbin analyzes the use of nineteenth-century church and village bells to define a "territorial identity."[91] The Church decreed that cathedrals held five to seven bells while local parishes could hold at most three. Monastery bells could not reach louder or further than the local parish bell, and the cathedral bells should always be rung before local bells within their area. It was bells, not landforms or geographical barriers, which served to define membership in a community: a citizen belonged to the group of people who could hear a specific bell. The soundscape centered on the bell, and local identity developed around the soundscape. Architects have engaged the dialogue on space and sound as well, both as practitioners and as critical scholars.[92]

Taken together, these areas of research into sound are at once richly complex, exploring dimensions of our lived experience that have been unconsidered before. But, to return to our ecological metaphor, these scholars (trained in musicology, technology, and cultural studies) are highly trained limnologists. Their attention to the soundscape, to ambient sounds and the cultural impact of these ambient sounds, is akin to the freshwater scientist who carefully studies the chemical, bacterial, and other makeup of the lake.[93]

We argue that scholars in Communication Studies struggled to locate the study of listening within the larger domain of communication for most of the twentieth century. In the twenty-first, we need to locate the study of listening both in the Communication Studies discipline and within the larger, interdisciplinary exploration of sound. Communication scholars are poised to make these connections. Whether in connecting the speech tradition to media ecology,[94] to performance studies,[95] or to technology studies, scholars rooted in the powerful tradition of Communication Studies have much to offer the contemporary, interdisciplinary turn in sound studies.

For example, Bull's notion of "accompanied solitude" has been extended, in the cultural studies tradition, to account for other sound experiences (e.g., the Walkman).[96] This extension of Bull's concept invites us to explore whether Bull has found a resonant experience in modern life, but it does not push the borders of his theoretical work.[97] Communication scholars Joshua Gunn and co-author Mirko Hall push harder, taking the experience of the iPod and articulating the politics behind it:

> The mirror-work of iPod discourse is an attempt to represent the sonorous envelope, an advertising campaign that appeals to an unconscious desire to return to a prediscursive state of harmonious omnipotence, maintaining the presumed autonomy and independence of the ideal consumer.[98]

To make these claims, Gunn and Hall assess both the experience of the iPod and the discourses around the iPod. Moving a step beyond Bull or Sterne or Schafer, Hall and Gunn do not end with the examination of the auditory environment of the iPod (the "sonorous envelope"), but account, as well, for the media landscape that sends us messages about the iPod. Advertising tells us how to listen to the iPod in ways for which Bull never accounts, but that communication scholars recognize easily. We are attuned to the complexity of the media environment.

There is no time in human history better suited to a research program in the complexities of listening. But these rediscoveries are fragmented; they are puzzle pieces that require integration. The decades of experience in Communication Studies in defining, theorizing, analyzing, and teaching about listening as part of human communication positions us well to shape the future of this interdisciplinary research.

Toward the Twenty-First Century: Reassembly of the Senses

The twenty-first century, then, offers us the possibility of achieving what Marshall McLuhan called the "orchestration" of our senses. McLuhan picks up the concept of the "*sensus communis*" from the classical tradition, the "reassembly" of the senses for an integrated relationship with the world, to explicate a "five sense sensorium."[99] We must be able to bring the eye and the ear and all the senses together to attend to the complexities of our world and the complexities of human communication.

To fulfill this project for a twenty-first century *sensus communis*, we must begin to draw upon the best research in listening in the last century—this is a unique strength of the Communication Studies discipline, honed over decades of research and teaching. In developing an integrated relationship to the world, we must understand listening as integrated, inextricable from other aspects of the communication process (speaking, reading, writing). We must understand listening to the spoken word as integrated, inextricable from the broader auditory environment. And perhaps, we must appreciate that our understanding of listening is an essential part of our understanding of what it means to be human.

Notes

1 International Listening Association, "History," International Listening Association, January 16, 2014, www.listen.org/history.
2 Jefferson D. Pooley and David W. Park, "Communication Research," in *The Handbook of Communication History (ICA Handbook Series)*, ed. Peter Simonson, Janice Peck, and Robert T. Craig (New York: Routledge, 2013): 76.
3 William Keith, *Democracy as Discussion: The American Forum Movement and Civic Education* (Lanham, MD: Rowman & Littlefield/Lexington Books): 345.
4 International Listening Association, "An ILA Definition of Listening," *Listening Post* 53, no. 1 (April 1995): 4–5. Interestingly, this definition was itself a contested issue within the organization for years before its codification and in years since.
5 Margarete Imhof, "The Cognitive Psychology of Listening," in *Listening and Human Communication in the 21st Century*, ed. Andrew D. Wolvin (Boston: Blackwell, 2010): 97–126.
6 Graham D. Bodie and Nathan Crick, "Listening, Hearing, Sensing: Three Modes of Being and the Phenomenology of Charles Sanders Peirce," *Communication Theory* (in press).
7 David Beard, "A Broader Understanding of the Ethics of Listening: Philosophy, Cultural Studies, Media Studies and the Ethical Listening Subject," *International Journal of Listening* 23 (2009): 7–20.

8 Graham D. Bodie, "Listening as Positive Communication," in *The Positive Side of Interpersonal Communication*, ed. T. Socha and M. Pitts (New York: Peter Lang, 2012): 109–125.

9 Ethel C. Glenn, "A Content Analysis of Fifty Definitions of Listening," *Journal of the International Listening Association* 3 (1989): 21–31; Andrew D. Wolvin and Carolyn Gwynn Coakley, "A Listening Taxonomy," in *Perspectives on Listening*, ed. Andrew D. Wolvin and Carolyn Gwynn Coakley (Norwood, NJ: Ablex, 1993): 15–22.

10 Graham D. Bodie, Debra L. Worthington, Magrete Imhof, and Lynn Cooper, "What Would a Unified Field of Listening Look Like? A Proposal Linking Past Perspectives and Future Endeavors," *International Journal of Listening* 22 (2008): 103–122.

11 Annie Lang, "Discipline in Crisis? The Shifting Paradigm of Mass Communication Research," *Communication Theory* 23 (2013): 10–24.

12 Graham D. Bodie, "Treating Listening Ethically," *International Journal of Listening* 24 (2010): 185–188. Graham D. Bodie, "The Understudied Nature of Listening in Interpersonal Communication: Introduction to a Special Issue," *International Journal of Listening* 25 (2011): 1–9.

13 Jefferson D. Pooley and David W. Park, "Communication Research," in *The Handbook of Communication History (ICA Handbook Series)*, ed. Peter Simonson, Janice Peck, and Robert T. Craig (New York: Routledge, 2013): 84.

14 Gerry Philipsen, "The Early Career Rise of 'Speech' in Some Disciplinary Discourse, 1914–1946," *Quarterly Journal of Speech* 93 (2007): 352–354; and William M. Keith, "We Are the Speech Teachers," *Review of Communication* 11, no. 2 (2011): 83–92.

15 For early discussions of the role of listening in communication studies, see Harlen Adams, "Listening," *Quarterly Journal of Speech* 24, no. 2 (1938): 209–211; Harold A. Dressel, "Debating for the Audience," *Quarterly Journal of Speech* 16, no. 2 (1930): 227–231; Winifred H. Littell, "Before and After Taking," *Quarterly Journal of Speech* 23, no. 4 (1937): 616–619; Ralph G. Nichols, "Listening: Questions and Problems," *Quarterly Journal of Speech* 33, no. 1 (1947): 83–86; Robert West, "Speech and Hearing," *Quarterly Journal of Speech* 21, no. 2 (1935): 178–188; Wesley Wiksell, "The Problem of Listening," *Quarterly Journal of Speech* 32, no. 4 (1946): 505–508.

16 The Research Committee, "Research in Public Speaking," *Quarterly Journal of Speech* 1, no. 1 (1915): 24–32.

17 The Research Committee, "Research."

18 Charles H. Woolbert, "The Organization of Departments of Speech Science in Universities," *Quarterly Journal of Public Speaking* 2, no. 1 (1916): 64–77; Everett Lee Hunt, "The Scientific Spirit in Public Speaking," *Quarterly Journal of Public Speaking* 1, no. 2 (1915): 185–193.

19 H.B. Gislason, "The Relation of the Speaker to his Audience," *Quarterly Journal of Public Speaking* 2, no. 1 (1916): 45.

20 William A.D. Millson, "A Review of Research in Audience Reaction," *Quarterly Journal of Speech* 24, no. 3 (1938): 464–483; William A.D. Millson, "A Review of Research in Audience Reaction," *Quarterly Journal of Speech* 24, no. 4 (1938): 655–672.

21 Ernest H. Henrikson, "An Analysis of the Characteristics of Some 'Good' and 'Poor' Speakers," *Speech Monographs* 11, no. 1 (1944): 124.

22 L.B. Tyson, "The Radio Influences Speech," *Quarterly Journal of Speech* 19, no. 2 (1933): 219–224.

23 C. Hess Haagen, "Intelligibility Measurement," *Speech Monographs* 13, no. 2 (1946): 4–7.

24 Gayland L. Draegert, "Intelligibility Related to Articulation," *Speech Monographs* 13, no. 2 (1946): 50–53.

25 F.H. Lumley, "Rates of Speech in Radio Speaking," *Quarterly Journal of Speech* 19, no. 3 (1933): 393–403.

26 Tyson, "The Radio Influences Speech."

27 Howard Gilkinson, "Experimental and Statistical Research in General Speech: II. Speakers, Speeches, and Audiences," *Quarterly Journal of Speech* 30, no. 2 (1944): 180.

28 Larry L. Barker, Robert J. Kibler, and Francis J. Kelly, "Effect of Perceived Mispronunciation on Speech Effectiveness Ratings and Retention," *Quarterly Journal of Speech* 54, no. 1 (1968): 47–58; Larry L. Barker and Robert J. Kibler, "An Experimental Study to Assess the Effects of Three Levels of Mispronunciation on Comprehension for Three Different Populations," *Speech Monographs* 35,

no. 1 (1968): 26–38; Ralph G. Nichols, "Factors in Listening Comprehension," *Speech Monographs* 15, no. 2 (1948): 154–163.

29 Forest L. Whan, "Training in Listening and in Voice and Diction for the Airplane Pilot," *Quarterly Journal of Speech* 30, no. 3 (1944): 263.

30 William H. Ewing, "Finding a Speaking–Listening Index," *Quarterly Journal of Speech* 31, no. 3 (1945): 368–370.

31 David K. Berlo, *The Process of Communication: An Introduction to Theory and Practice* (New York: Holt, Rinehart and Winston, 1960). The model of the audience as passive would remain a force for decades. The Constructivist model advanced by Jesse Delia and his colleagues at the University of Illinois operated with a thin veneer of attention to audience, but eventually collapsed into this oversimplified reflection of the linear model. Constructivism focused on how individual social cognitive ability is associated with abilities to produce listener-adapted communication (which later was renamed person-centered speech; see Graham D. Bodie and S.M. Jones, "Constructivism," in *International Encyclopedia of Interpersonal Communication*, edited by C.R. Berger and M.E. Roloff (New York: Wiley-Blackwell, in press)). Thus, Constructivism, which served as a predominant paradigm for the study of interpersonal communication for nearly two decades, was not unlike the early emphasis on adapting speeches to audiences. As written by Lyon, "For present purposes I shall limit the subject to a brief treatment of the *speaker's consciousness* of his audience. I am thinking of audience consciousness on the part of the speaker as the possession of a proper degree and kind of audience awareness" (C.E. Lyon, "Audience Consciousness," *Quarterly Journal of Speech* 17, no. 3 (1931): 376). Of course, being aware of the presence of an audience and the need to adapt messages to that audience is different from viewing the audience (and the listener) as not only a participant in the communicative transaction (for example, Kristin M. Langellier, "A Phenomenological Approach to Audience," *Literature and Performance* 3, no. 2 (1983): 34–39) but also a "co-narrator" of dialogue (Pamela Cook Miller, "Listen to the Ancients," *Literature and Performance* 5, no. 1 (1984): 29–39; see also Janet B. Bavelas and Jennifer Gerwing, "The Listener as Addressee in Face-to-Face Dialogue," *International Journal of Listening* 25, no. 3 (2011): 178–198).

32 For a review, see Howard Gilkinson, "Experimental and Statistical Research."

33 One reason that listening instruction emphasized effective diagnosis in the early journals of the field may stem from the hybrid relationship with speech pathology at the time. The founding of the American Speech-Language-Hearing Association (ASHA) was marked during the 1925 meeting of the National Association of Teachers of Speech in Iowa City, IA. In December of that year, the Academy of Speech Correction (the first of five names for what is now ASHA) was officially chartered and specialized journals followed soon thereafter. Indeed, this separation aligns well with the fact that by the mid-1920s all but lost in the NCA journal space was an interest in hearing and auditory disorders, something that was integrated with more mainstream scholarship in the beginning (for example, Swift, "Psychological Parallelisms between Speech Disorder and Oral English," *Quarterly Journal of Public Speaking* 3 (1917): 224–228).

34 Smiley Blanton, "The Voice and the Emotions," *Quarterly Journal of Public Speaking* 1, no. 2 (1915): 154–172.

35 Bryng Bryngelson, "The Re-education of Speech Failures," *Quarterly Journal of Speech* 19, no. 2 (1933): 231. Thanks to Joshua Gunn for bringing Bryngelson to our attention.

36 J.A. Winans, "Public Speaking 1 at Cornell University," *Quarterly Journal of Speech* 3, no. 2 (1917): 157.

37 J.R. Pelsma, "Standardization of Grades in Public Speaking," *Quarterly Journal of Public Speaking* 1, no. 3 (1915): 266–271.

38 Robert West and Helen Larsen, "Some Statistical Investigations in the Field of Speech," *Quarterly Journal of Speech Education* 7, no. 4 (1921): 375–382.

39 Harold Kent, "The Army and its Needs in Speech," *Quarterly Journal of Speech* 30, no. 2 (1944): 147–150.

40 McDonald W. Held and Colbert C. Held, "Public Speaking in the Army Training Program," *Quarterly Journal of Speech* 29, no. 2 (1943): 143–146; see also William West, "Speech and the

Signal Corps," *Quarterly Journal of Speech* 30, no. 2 (1944): 151–154, for a take on communication in the signal corps, for example.

41 Whan, "Training in Listening."

42 "Speaking Instruction in College Military Units," *Quarterly Journal of Speech* 29, no. 4 (1943): 399–400.

43 Jean Malmstrom, "The Communications Course," *College Composition and Communication* 7 (1956): 21–24; this argument has been elaborated by David Russell in "Writing across the Curriculum in Historical Perspective: Toward a Social Interpretation," *College English* 52, no. 1 (January, 1990): 52–73.

44 Russell, "Writing across the Curriculum in Historical Perspective," 61.

45 Adams, "Listening," 210.

46 Robert T. Oliver, "Conservation in the Speech Curriculum," *Quarterly Journal of Speech* 18, no. 1 (1932): 108–111.

47 Adams, "Listening," 211.

48 Nichols, "Listening"; Nichols, "Factors in Listening Comprehension"; Wiksell, "The Problem of Listening."

49 Ralph G. Nichols, "The Struggle to be Human," from the International Listening Association website, www.listen.org/Resources/Documents/14.pdf.

50 Nichols, "The Struggle to be Human."

51 L. LeRoy Cowperthwaite, "Fundamentals and Public Speaking Texts," *Quarterly Journal of Speech* 50, no. 4 (1964): 448–452.

52 For discussions of the waning of the Communications movement, see Russell, "Writing across the Curriculum in Historical Perspective." At the University of Minnesota, the freestanding Communications Program (which was designed by faculty in the Department of Communication in opposition to the "Communication 1-2-3" sequence in the Department of Rhetoric) was dismantled in the 1980s, largely as the Department of English made greater claims to the professionalization of the teaching of writing (see David Beard, "More than 100 Years of Rhetoric at the University of Minnesota," *Composition Forum* 18 (Summer 2008). Online at http://compositionforum.com/issue/18/uminnesota-duluth.php).

53 Graham D. Bodie and Margaret Fitch-Hauser, "Quantitative Research in Listening: Explication and Overview," in *Listening and Human Communication in the 21st Century*, ed. Andrew D. Wolvin (Oxford: Blackwell, 2010): 46–93.

54 Michael W. Purdy, "Listening, Culture, and Structures of Consciousness: Ways of Studying Listening," *International Journal of Listening* 14 (2000): 47–68; Michael W. Purdy, "Qualitative Research: Critical for Understanding Listening," in *Listening and Human Communication in the 21st Century*, ed. Andrew D. Wolvin (Oxford: Blackwell, 2010): 33–45.

55 W. Clifton Adams and E. Sam Cox, "The Teaching of Listening as an Integral Part of an Oral Activity: An Examination of Public-Speaking Texts," *International Journal of Listening* 24, no. 2 (2010): 89–105.

56 Interestingly, several members of the ILA were instrumental in the establishment of the Commission on Intrapersonal Communication Processes within the NCA, a group that was officially recognized in 1986. The name of the Commission was changed to the Communication & Social Cognition Division in 2000, and "listening" remains a focal area of research inquiry for its members. Although detailed records are dispersed across various file cabinets (and others likely lost forever), we garnered this information from the bylaws of the CSC Division of the NCA, found here: www.ou.edu/csc/Communication_and_Social_Cognition/Bylaws_files/CSCBylaws.pdf.

57 For more information about the history of the ILA see here: www.listen.org/history.

58 Indeed, in past years the number of NCA convention panel slots allotted to the ILA has varied as a function of those in charge of convention planning. There have been several conversations between leaders of the ILA and leaders of the NCA with respect to the affiliate status of the former to the latter. Of course, these conversations are not part of the "official" history of either organization, but are worth mentioning here as evidence of the tension that exists between these two organizations.

59 For an example of the excavation of the post-war period, see Darrin Hicks, "The New Citizen," *Quarterly Journal of Speech* 93, no. 3 (2007): 358–360.

60 Graham D. Bodie, Kellie St. Cyr, Michelle Pence, Michael Rold, and James M. Honeycutt, "Listening Competence in Initial Interactions I: Distinguishing between What Listening Is and What Listeners Do," *International Journal of Listening* 26, no. 1 (2012): 1–28; Graham D. Bodie, "Issues in the Measurement of Listening," *Communication Research Reports* 30, no. 1 (2013): 76–84.

61 Cantril and Allport's work stretches into mass communication research, but certainly remained significant across subfields of the communication discipline for decades. Hadley Cantril and Gordon W. Allport, *The Psychology of Radio* (New York and London: Harper & Brothers, 1935).

62 Edgar A. Schuler, *Survey of Radio Listeners in Louisiana* (Baton Rouge: General Extension Division, Louisiana State University, 1943).

63 Theodore Clevenger, *Audience Analysis* (Indianapolis, IN: Bobbs-Merrill, 1966).

64 Larry L. Barker, *Listening Behavior* (Englewood Cliffs, NJ: Prentice-Hall, 1971).

65 William Norwood Brigance, *Speech: Its Techniques and Disciplines in a Free Society* (New York: Appleton-Century-Crofts, 1961): 9.

66 B. Paul Wilson, Frederick Sorensen, and Murray Elwood, "A Functional Core for the Basic Communications Course." *Quarterly Journal of Speech* 32, no. 2 (1946): 232–244.

67 John M. Wiemann, "Assessing Communication Literacy," *Communication Education* 27, no. 4 (1978): 310–315; Rebecca Rubin, "Assessing Speaking and Listening Competence at the College Level: The Communication Competency Assessment Instrument," *Communication Education* 31, no. 1 (1982): 19–32.

68 For information on the National Communication Association's "Speaking and Listening Competencies for College Students," see www.natcom.org/uploadedFiles/Teaching_and_Learning/Assessment_Resources/PDF-Speaking_and_Listening_Competencies_for_College_Students.pdf.

69 Donald L. Rubin, John Daly, James C. McCroskey, and Nancy A. Mead, "A Review and Critique of Procedures for Assessing Speaking and Listening Skills among Preschool through Grade Twelve Students," *Communication Education* 31, no. 4 (1982): 285–303.

70 Donald L. Rubin and Sally Hampton, "National Performance Standards for Oral Communication K–12: New Standards and Speaking/Listening/Viewing," *Communication Education* 47 no. 2 (1998): 183–193.

71 Work by Rod Hart and Don Burks on rhetorical sensitivity (Roderick P. Hart and Don M. Burks, "Rhetorical Sensitivity and Social Interaction," *Speech Monographs* 3, no. 2 (1972): 75–91) is just one example of this type of work.

72 Charles J. Wigley, "Verbal Aggressiveness and Communicator Style Characteristics of Summoned Jurors as Predictors of Actual Jury Selection," *Communication Monographs* 66, no. 3 (1999): 266–275.

73 William A. Villaume and Tami Reid, "An Initial Investigation of Aging, Aligning Actions and Presbycusis," *Journal of Applied Communication Research* 18, no. 1 (1990): 8–31.

74 Kittie W. Watson, Cathy J. Lazarus, and Todd Thomas, "First-Year Medical Students' Listener Preferences: A Longitudinal Study," *International Journal of Listening* 13, no. 1 (1999): 1–11; Brenda Comeaux Trahana and Patricia Rockwell, "The Effects of Listening Training on Nursing Home Assistants: Residents' Satisfaction with and Perceptions of Assistants' Listening Behavior," *International Journal of Listening* 13, no. 1 (1999): 62–74; Connie Fletcher, "Listening to Narratives: The Dynamics of Capturing Police Experience," *International Journal of Listening* 13, no. 1 (1999): 46–61; Judi Brownell, "Managerial Listening and Career Development in the Hospitality Industry," *International Journal of Listening* 8, no. 1 (1994): 31–49.

75 Jan Flynn, Tuula-Riitta Valikoski, and Jennie Grau, "Listening in the Business Context: Reviewing the State of Research," *International Journal of Listening* 22, no. 2 (2008): 141–151.

76 Ben W. Morse and Richard N. Piland, "An Assessment of Communication Competencies Needed by Intermediate-Level Health Care Providers: A Study of Nurse-Patient, Nurse-Doctor, Nurse-Nurse Communication Relationships," *Journal of Applied Communication Research* 9, no. 1 (1981): 30–41.

77 Timothy G. Plax, Patricia Kearney, Ted J. Ross, and J. Christopher Jolly, "Assessing the Link Between Environmental Concerns and Consumers' Decisions to Use Clean-Air Vehicles," *Communication*

Education 57, no. 4 (2008): 417–422; Karen Slattery and Ana C. Garner, "Mothers of Soldiers in Wartime: A National News Narrative," *Critical Studies in Media Communication* 24, no. 5 (2007): 429–445.

78 Judi Brownell, "Listening Leaders: The Skills of Listening-Centered Communication," in *Listening and Human Communication in the 21st Century*, ed. Andrew D. Wolvin (Oxford: Blackwell, 2010): 141–157.

79 Michel Foucault, *The Hermeneutics of the Subject: Lectures at the College de France, 1981–1982* (New York: Palgrave Macmillan, 2001): 350.

80 Foucault, *Hermeneutics*, 343.

81 Foucault, *Hermeneutics*, 345.

82 Foucault, *Hermeneutics*, 344.

83 Jacques Attali, *Noise: The Political Economy of Music* (Minneapolis: University of Minnesota Press, 1985).

84 Theodor W. Adorno, "On the Fetish Character in Music and Regressive Listening," in *The Culture Industry* (New York: Routledge, 2001): 143.

85 L. Botstein, "Listening through Reading: Musical Literacy and the Concert Audience," *19th-Century Music* (Special Issue on Music in Its Social Contexts) 16, no. 2 (1992): 129–145; C. Hirchskind, "Hearing Modernity: Egypt, Islam, and the Pious Ear," in *Hearing Cultures: Essays on Sound, Listening and Modernity*, ed. Veit Erlmann (New York: Berg Publishing, 2004): 131–151; D. Wong, "Finding an Asian American Audience: The Problem of Listening," *American Music* (Special Issue on Asian American Music) 19, no. 4 (2001): 365–384.

86 Jonathan Sterne, *The Audible Past: The Cultural Origins of Sound Reproduction* (Durham, NC: Duke University Press, 2006): 99.

87 Michael Bull, "Sound, Proximity, and Distance in Western Experience: The Case of Odysseus's Walkman," in *Hearing Cultures: Essays on Sound, Listening and Modernity*, ed. Veit Erlmann (New York: Berg Publishing, 2004): 134.

88 Murray Schafer, *The Soundscape: Our Sonic Environment and the Tuning of the World* (Rochester, VT: Destiny Books, 1994): 212.

89 Barbara Lorenzkowski, *Sounds of Ethnicity: Listening to German North America* (Winnipeg: University of Manitoba Press, 2010): 10.

90 Barry Blesser and Linda Ruth Salter, *Spaces Speak: Are You Listening? Experiencing Aural Architecture* (Cambridge, MA: MIT Press, 2007): 29.

91 Alain Corbin, "The Auditory Markers of the Village," in *The Auditory Culture Reader*, ed. M. Bull and L. Back (New York: Berg, 2003): 117.

92 Michael Fowler, "Sound, Aurality and Critical Listening: Disruptions at the Boundaries of Architecture," *Architecture and Culture* 1, no. 1–2 (2013): 162–181.

93 In rhetorical studies, itself becoming an increasingly interdisciplinary field, there is continuing attention to the cultural work of listening. Scholars in rhetoric and composition in English departments have turned to listening to drive theory-building; Krista Ratcliffe, in writing about "Rhetorical Listening," calls for listening with intellectual roots in Heidegger and in Fiumara's philosophical work on listening. Similar roots are at the core of calls by Wayne Booth and Lisbeth Lipari for listening in rhetoric; by rethinking rhetoric not from the position of the speaker/author, but from the listener, these scholars open us up to new ways to think through the central problems of communication studies; while these scholars are not in communication studies, their work has resonance. See Krista Ratcliffe, *Rhetorical Listening: Identification, Gender, Whiteness* (Carbondale, IL: Southern Illinois University Press, 2005); see also Wayne C Booth, *The Rhetoric of Rhetoric: The Quest for Effective Communication* (Malden, MA: Blackwell, 2004); Lisbeth Lipari, "Rhetoric's Other: Levinas, Listening and the Ethical Response," *Philosophy and Rhetoric*, 45 (2012): 227–245.

94 Joshua Gunn, "Speech Is Dead; Long Live Speech," *Quarterly Journal of Speech* 94, no. 3 (2008): 343–364; see also Edward Schiappa and Emmanuelle Wessels, "Listening to Audiences: A Brief Rationale and History of Audience Research in Popular Media Studies," *International Journal of Listening* 21 (2007): 14–23.

95 Joshua Gunn, "On Recording Performance; or, Speech, the Cry, and the Anxiety of the Fix," *Liminalities: A Journal of Performance Studies* 7, no. 3 (2011), online at http://liminalities.net/7-3/.
96 Michael Bull, "No Dead Air! The iPod and the Culture of Mobile Listening," *Leisure Studies* 24 (2005): 343–355.
97 Bull, "No Dead Air!"
98 Joshua Gunn and Mirko M. Hall, "Stick it in Your Ear: The Psychodynamics of iPod Enjoyment," *Communication and Critical/Cultural Studies* 5, no. 2 (2008): 135–157.
99 These issues are excavated in Norm Friesen, "Education as a Training of the Senses: McLuhan's Pedagogical Enterprise," Enculturation: http://enculturation.net/education-as-a-training (November 7, 2011).

References

Adams, Harlen. "Listening." *Quarterly Journal of Speech* 24, no. 2 (1938): 209–211.

Adams, W. Clifton and E. Sam Cox. "The Teaching of Listening as an Integral Part of an Oral Activity: An Examination of Public-Speaking Texts." *International Journal of Listening* 24, no. 2 (2010): 89–105.

Adorno, Theodor W. "On the Fetish Character in Music and Regressive Listening." In *The Culture Industry*, 29–60. New York: Routledge, 2001.

Attali, Jacques. *Noise: The Political Economy of Music.* Minneapolis: University of Minnesota Press, 1985.

Barker, Larry L. *Listening Behavior.* Englewood Cliffs, NJ: Prentice-Hall, 1971.

Barker, Larry L. and Robert J. Kibler, "An Experimental Study to Assess the Effects of Three Levels of Mispronunciation on Comprehension for Three Different Populations." *Speech Monographs* 35, no. 1 (1968): 26–38.

Barker, Larry L., Robert J. Kibler, and Francis J. Kelly, "Effect of Perceived Mispronunciation on Speech Effectiveness Ratings and Retention." *Quarterly Journal of Speech* 54, no. 1 (1968): 47–58.

Bavelas, Janet B. and Jennifer Gerwing. "The Listener as Addressee in Face-to-Face Dialogue." *International Journal of Listening* 25, no. 3 (2011): 178–198.

Beard, David. "A Broader Understanding of the Ethics of Listening: Philosophy, Cultural Studies, Media Studies and the Ethical Listening Subject." *International Journal of Listening* 23 (2009): 7–20.

——. "More than 100 Years of Rhetoric at the University of Minnesota." *Composition Forum* 18 (Summer 2008). Online at http://compositionforum.com/issue/18/uminnesota-duluth.php.

Berlo, David K. *The Process of Communication: An Introduction to Theory and Practice.* New York: Holt, Rinehart and Winston, 1960.

Blanton, Smiley. "The Voice and the Emotions." *Quarterly Journal of Public Speaking* 1, no. 2 (1915): 154–172.

Blesser, Barry and Linda Ruth Salter. *Spaces Speak: Are You Listening? Experiencing Aural Architecture.* Cambridge, MA: MIT Press, 2007.

Bodie, Graham D. "Issues in the Measurement of Listening." *Communication Research Reports* 30, no. 1 (2013): 76–84.

——. "Listening as Positive Communication." In *The Positive Side of Interpersonal Communication*, edited by T. Socha and M. Pitts, 109–126. New York: Peter Lang, 2012.

——. "Treating Listening Ethically." *International Journal of Listening* 24, no. 3 (2010): 185–188.

——. "The Understudied Nature of Listening in Interpersonal Communication: Introduction to a Special Issue." *International Journal of Listening* 25, no. 1–2 (2011): 1–9.

Bodie, Graham D. and Nathan Crick. "Listening, Hearing, Sensing: Three Modes of Being and the Phenomenology of Charles Sanders Peirce." *Communication Theory* (in press).

Bodie, Graham D. and Margaret Fitch-Hauser. "Quantitative Research in Listening: Explication and Overview." In *Listening and Human Communication in the 21st Century*, edited by Andrew D. Wolvin, 46–94. Oxford: Blackwell, 2010.

Bodie, Graham D. and S.M. Jones. "Constructivism." In *International Encyclopedia of Interpersonal Communication*, edited by C.R. Berger and M.E. Roloff. New York: Wiley-Blackwell, in press.

Bodie, Graham D., Debra L. Worthington, Magrete Imhof, and Lynn Cooper. "What Would a Unified Field of Listening Look Like? A Proposal Linking Past Perspectives and Future Endeavors." *International Journal of Listening* 22, no. 2 (2008): 103–122.

Bodie, Graham D., Kellie St. Cyr, Michelle Pence, Michael Rold, and James M. Honeycutt, "Listening Competence in Initial Interactions I: Distinguishing between What Listening Is and What Listeners Do." *International Journal of Listening* 26, no. 1 (2012): 1–28.

Booth, Wayne C. *The Rhetoric of Rhetoric: The Quest for Effective Communication*. Malden, MA: Blackwell, 2004.

Botstein, L. "Listening through Reading: Musical Literacy and the Concert Audience." *19th-Century Music* (Special Issue on Music in Its Social Contexts) 16, no. 2 (1992): 129–145.

Brigance, William Norwood. *Speech: Its Techniques and Disciplines in a Free Society*. New York, Appleton-Century-Crofts, 1961.

Brownell, Judi. "Listening Leaders: The Skills of Listening-Centered Communication." In *Listening and Human Communication in the 21st Century*, edited by Andrew D. Wolvin, 141–156. Oxford: Blackwell, 2010.

——. "Managerial Listening and Career Development in the Hospitality Industry." *International Journal of Listening* 8, no. 1 (1994): 31–49.

Bryngelson, Bryng. "The Re-education of Speech Failures." *Quarterly Journal of Speech* 19, no. 2 (1933): 227–232.

Bull, Michael. "No Dead Air! The iPod and the Culture of Mobile Listening." *Leisure Studies* 24, no. 4 (2005): 343–355.

——. "Thinking about Sound, Proximity, and Distance in Western Experience: The Case of Odysseus's Walkman." In *Hearing Cultures: Essays on Sound, Listening and Modernity*, edited by Veit Erlmann, 173–190. New York: Berg Publishing, 2004.

Cantril, Hadley and Gordon W. Allport. *The Psychology of Radio*. New York and London: Harper & Brothers, 1935.

Clevenger, Theodore. *Audience Analysis*. Indianapolis: Bobbs-Merrill, 1966.

Corbin, Alain. "The Auditory Markers of the Village." In *The Auditory Culture Reader*, edited by M. Bull and L. Back. New York: Berg, 2003.

Cowperthwaite, L. LeRoy. "Fundamentals and Public Speaking Texts." *Quarterly Journal of Speech* 50, no. 4 (1964): 448–452.

Draegert, Gayland L. "Intelligibility Related to Articulation." *Speech Monographs* 13, no. 2 (1946): 50–53.

Dressel, Harold A. "Debating for the Audience." *Quarterly Journal of Speech* 16, no. 2 (1930): 227–231.

Ewing, William H. "Finding a Speaking-Listening Index." *Quarterly Journal of Speech* 31, no. 3 (1945): 368–370.

Fletcher, Connie. "Listening to Narratives: The Dynamics of Capturing Police Experience." *International Journal of Listening* 13, no. 1 (1999): 46–61.

Flynn, Jan, Tuula-Riitta Valikoski, and Jennie Grau. "Listening in the Business Context: Reviewing the State of Research." *International Journal of Listening* 22, no. 2 (2008): 141–151.

Foucault, Michel. *The Hermeneutics of the Subject: Lectures at the College de France, 1981–1982*. New York: Palgrave Macmillan, 2001.

Fowler, Michael. "Sound, Aurality and Critical Listening: Disruptions at the Boundaries of Architecture." *Architecture and Culture* 1, no. 1–2 (2013): 162–181.

Friesen, Norm. "Education as a Training of the Senses: McLuhan's Pedagogical Enterprise," Enculturation: http://enculturation.net/education-as-a-training (November 7, 2011).

Gilkinson, Howard. "Experimental and Statistical Research in General Speech: II. Speakers, Speeches, and Audiences." *Quarterly Journal of Speech* 30, no. 2 (1944): 180–186.

Gislason, H.B. "The Relation of the Speaker to his Audience." *Quarterly Journal of Speech* 2, no. 1 (1916): 39–45.

Glenn, Ethel C. "A Content Analysis of Fifty Definitions of Listening." *Journal of the International Listening Association* 3, no. 1 (1989): 21–31.

Gunn, Joshua. "On Recording Performance; or, Speech, the Cry, and the Anxiety of the Fix." *Liminalities: A Journal of Performance Studies* 7, no. 3 (2011), online at http://liminalities.net/7-3/.

——. "Speech Is Dead; Long Live Speech." *Quarterly Journal of Speech* 94, no. 3 (2008): 343–364.

Gunn, Joshua and Mirko M. Hall. "Stick it in Your Ear: The Psychodynamics of iPod Enjoyment." *Communication and Critical/Cultural Studies* 5, no. 2 (2008): 135–157.

Haagen, C. Hess. "Intelligibility Measurement." *Speech Monographs* 13, no. 2 (1946): 4–7.

Hart, Roderick P. and Don M. Burks. "Rhetorical Sensitivity and Social Interaction." *Speech Monographs* 3, no. 2 (1972): 75–91.

Held, McDonald W. and Colbert C. Held. "Public Speaking in the Army Training Program." *Quarterly Journal of Speech* 29, no. 2 (1943): 143–146.

Henrikson, Ernest H. "An Analysis of the Characteristics of Some 'Good' and 'Poor' Speakers." *Speech Monographs* 11, no. 1 (1944): 120–124.

Hicks, Darrin. "The New Citizen." *Quarterly Journal of Speech* 93, no. 3 (2007): 358–360.

Hirchskind, C. "Hearing Modernity: Egypt, Islam, and the Pious Ear." In *Hearing Cultures: Essays on Sound, Listening and Modernity,* edited by Veit Erlmann, 131–151. New York: Berg, 2004.

Hunt, Everett Lee. "The Scientific Spirit in Public Speaking." *Quarterly Journal of Public Speaking* 1, no. 2 (1915): 185–193.

Imhof, Margarete. "The Cognitive Psychology of Listening." In *Listening and Human Communication in the 21st Century,* edited by Andrew D. Wolvin, 97–126. Boston: Blackwell, 2010.

International Listening Association. "An ILA Definition of Listening." *Listening Post* 53, no. 1 (April 1995): 4–5.

——. "History," International Listening Association, January 16, 2014, www.listen.org/history.

Keith, William. *Democracy as Discussion: The American Forum Movement and Civic Education.* Lanham, MD: Rowman & Littlefield/Lexington Books, 2007.

——. "We Are the Speech Teachers." *Review of Communication* 11, no. 2 (2011): 83–92.

Kent, Harold. "The Army and its Needs in Speech." *Quarterly Journal of Speech* 30, no. 2 (1944): 147–150.

Lang, Annie. "Discipline in Crisis? The Shifting Paradigm of Mass Communication Research." *Communication Theory* 23, no. 1 (2013): 10–24.

Langellier, Kristin M. "A Phenomenological Approach to Audience." *Literature and Performance,* 3 no. 2 (1983): 34–39.

Lipari, Lisbeth. "Rhetoric's Other: Levinas, Listening and the Ethical Response." *Philosophy and Rhetoric* 45, no. 3 (2012): 227–245.

Littell, Winifred H. "Before and After Taking." *Quarterly Journal of Speech* 23, no. 4 (1937): 616–619.

Lorenzkowski, Barbara. *Sounds of Ethnicity: Listening to German North America.* Winnipeg: University of Manitoba Press, 2010.

Lumley, F.H. "Rates of Speech in Radio Speaking." *Quarterly Journal of Speech* 19, no. 3 (1933): 393–403.

Lyon, C.E. "Audience Consciousness." *Quarterly Journal of Speech* 17, no. 3 (1931): 375–385.

Malmstrom, Jean. "The Communications Course." *College Composition and Communication* 7, no. 1 (1956): 21–24.

Miller, Pamela Cook. "Listen to the Ancients." *Literature and Performance* 5, no. 1 (1984): 29–39.

Millson, William A.D. "A Review of Research in Audience Reaction." *Quarterly Journal of Speech* 24, no. 3 (1938): 464–483.

——. "A Review of Research in Audience Reaction." *Quarterly Journal of Speech* 24, no. 4 (1938): 655–672.

Morse, Ben W. and Richard N. Piland. "An Assessment of Communication Competencies Needed by Intermediate-Level Health Care Providers: A Study of Nurse-Patient, Nurse-Doctor, Nurse-Nurse Communication Relationships." *Journal of Applied Communication Research* 9, no. 1 (1981): 30–41.

National Communication Association. "Communication and Social Cognition Bylaws." www.ou.edu/csc/Communication_and_Social_Cognition/Bylaws_files/CSCBylaws.pdf.

——. "Speaking and Listening Competencies for College Students." www.natcom.org/uploadedFiles/Teaching_and_Learning/Assessment_Resources/PDF-Speaking_and_Listening_Competencies_for_College_Students.pdf.

Nichols, Ralph G. "Factors in Listening Comprehension." *Speech Monographs* 15, no. 2 (1948): 154–163.

——. "Listening: Questions and Problems." *Quarterly Journal of Speech* 33, no. 1 (1947): 83–86.

——. "The Struggle to be Human," from the International Listening Association website, www. listen.org/Resources/Documents/14.pdf.

Oliver, Robert T. "Conservation in the Speech Curriculum." *Quarterly Journal of Speech* 18, no. 1 (1932): 108–111.

Pelsma, J.R. "Standardization of Grades in Public Speaking." *Quarterly Journal of Public Speaking* 1, no. 3 (1915): 266–271.

Philipsen, Gerry. "The Early Career Rise of 'Speech' in Some Disciplinary Discourse, 1914–1946." *Quarterly Journal of Speech* 93, no. 3 (2007): 352–354.

Plax, Timothy G. Patricia Kearney, Ted J. Ross, and J. Christopher Jolly. "Assessing the Link Between Environmental Concerns and Consumers' Decisions to Use Clean-Air Vehicles." *Communication Education* 57, no. 4 (2008): 417–422.

Pooley, Jefferson D. and David W. Park. "Communication Research." In *The Handbook of Communication History (ICA Handbook Series)*, edited by Peter Simonson, Janice Peck, and Robert T. Craig, 76–92. New York: Routledge, 2013.

Purdy, Michael W. "Listening, Culture, and Structures of Consciousness: Ways of Studying Listening." *International Journal of Listening* 14, no. 1 (2000): 47–68.

——. "Qualitative Research: Critical for Understanding Listening." In *Listening and Human Communication in the 21st Century*, edited by Andrew D. Wolvin, 33–45. Oxford: Blackwell, 2010.

Ratcliffe, Krista. *Rhetorical Listening: Identification, Gender, Whiteness.* Carbondale, IL: Southern Illinois University Press, 2005.

The Research Committee. "Research in Public Speaking." *Quarterly Journal of Speech* 1, no. 1 (1915): 24–32.

Rubin, Donald L. and Sally Hampton. "National Performance Standards for Oral Communication K–12: New Standards and Speaking/Listening/Viewing." *Communication Education* 47, no. 2 (1998): 183–193.

Rubin, Donald L., John Daly, James C. McCroskey, and Nancy A. Mead. "A Review and Critique of Procedures for Assessing Speaking and Listening Skills among Preschool through Grade Twelve Students." *Communication Education* 31, no. 4 (1982): 285–303.

Rubin, Rebecca. "Assessing Speaking and Listening Competence at the College Level: The Communication Competency Assessment Instrument." *Communication Education* 31, no. 1 (1982): 19–32.

Russell, David. "Writing across the Curriculum in Historical Perspective: Toward a Social Interpretation." *College English* 52, no. 1 (1990): 52–73.

Schafer, Murray. *The Soundscape: Our Sonic Environment and the Tuning of the World.* Rochester, VT: Destiny Books, 1994.

Schiappa, Edward and Emmanuelle Wessels. "Listening to Audiences: A Brief Rationale and History of Audience Research in Popular Media Studies." *International Journal of Listening* 21, no. 1 (2007): 14–23.

Schuler, Edgar A. *Survey of Radio Listeners in Louisiana.* Baton Rouge: General Extension Division, Louisiana State University, 1943.

Slattery, Karen and Ana C. Garner. "Mothers of Soldiers in Wartime: A National News Narrative." *Critical Studies in Media Communication* 24, no. 5 (2007): 429–445.

"Speaking Instruction in College Military Units." *Quarterly Journal of Speech* 29, no. 4 (1943): 399–400.

Sterne, Jonathan. *The Audible Past: The Cultural Origins of Sound Reproduction.* Durham, NC: Duke University Press, 2006.

Swift, W.B. "Psychological Parallelisms between Speech Disorder and Oral English." *Quarterly Journal of Public Speaking* 3, no. 3 (1917): 224–228.

Trahana, Brenda Comeaux and Patricia Rockwell. "The Effects of Listening Training on Nursing Home Assistants: Residents' Satisfaction with and Perceptions of Assistants' Listening Behavior." *International Journal of Listening* 13, no. 1 (1999): 62–74.

Tyson, L.B. "The Radio Influences Speech." *Quarterly Journal of Speech* 19, no. 2 (1933): 219–224.

Villaume, William A. and Tami Reid. "An Initial Investigation of Aging, Aligning Actions and Presbycusis." *Journal of Applied Communication Research* 18, no. 1 (1990): 8–31.

Watson, Kittie W., Cathy J. Lazarus, and Todd Thomas. "First-Year Medical Students' Listener Preferences: A Longitudinal Study." *International Journal of Listening* 13, no. 1 (1999): 1–11.

West, Robert. "Speech and Hearing." *Quarterly Journal of Speech* 21, no. 2 (1935): 178–188.

West, Robert and Helen Larsen. "Some Statistical Investigations in the Field of Speech." *Quarterly Journal of Speech Education* 7, no. 4 (1921): 375–382.

West, William. "Speech and the Signal Corps." *Quarterly Journal of Speech* 30, no. 2 (1944): 151–154.

Whan, Forest L. "Training in Listening and in Voice and Diction for the Airplane Pilot." *Quarterly Journal of Speech* 30, no. 3 (1944): 262–265.

Wiemann, John M. "Assessing Communication Literacy." *Communication Education* 27, no. 4 (1978): 310–315.

Wigley, Charles J. "Verbal Aggressiveness and Communicator Style Characteristics of Summoned Jurors as Predictors of Actual Jury Selection." *Communication Monographs* 66, no. 3 (1999): 266–275.

Wiksell, Wesley. "The Problem of Listening." *Quarterly Journal of Speech* 32, no. 4 (1946): 505–508.

Wilson, B. Paul, Frederick Sorensen, and Murray Elwood. "A Functional Core for the Basic Communications Course." *Quarterly Journal of Speech* 32, no. 2 (1946): 232–244.

Winans, J.A. "Public Speaking 1 at Cornell University." *Quarterly Journal of Speech* 3, no. 2 (1917): 153–162.

Wolvin, Andrew D. and Carolyn Gwynn Coakley. "A Listening Taxonomy." In *Perspectives on Listening*, edited by Andrew D. Wolvin and Carolyn Gwynn Coakley, 15–22. Norwood, NJ: Ablex, 1993.

Wong, D. "Finding an Asian American Audience: The Problem of Listening." *American Music* (Special Issue on Asian American Music) 19, no. 4 (2001): 365–384.

Woolbert, Charles H. "The Organization of Departments of Speech Science in Universities." *Quarterly Journal of Public Speaking* 2, no. 1 (1916): 64–77.

10.

CONCEPTUALIZING MEANING IN COMMUNICATION STUDIES

Brian L. Ott and Mary Domenico

Meaning, some have suggested, is the common concern that unifies the diverse and fragmented discipline of communication.[1] As communication scholars, we are all concerned with the matter of meaning, whether it is the meaning of speeches, of small group discussion and dynamics, of interpersonal and intercultural interactions, of organizational roles, rituals, and relations, of everyday cultural practices and performances, or of media events, flows, and assemblages. Our common *concern* with meaning should not be confused with a common *conception* of meaning, however. While communication scholars routinely speak of conveying meaning, sharing meaning, expressing meaning, making meaning, decoding meaning, and uncovering "hidden" meaning, there are nearly as many conceptions of meaning today as there are scholars concerned with it. Indeed, after surveying the literature on meaning in the field, we are tempted simply to agree with Dennis Stampe that:

> The concept of meaning is as dismayingly complex as any concept which suffers the attentions of philosophy. So diverse and apparently miscellaneous are the senses, uses, and meanings of the words *mean* and *meaning* that the very integrity of "the concept of meaning" is subject to doubt.[2]

Despite—or perhaps because of—the "dismaying complexity" of meaning, however, it is crucial that communication scholars continue to wrestle with this singularly important concept. The aim of this chapter is not to reconcile the various ways that meaning has been conceptualized within the discipline and even less so to advocate for some views over others.

Rather, we have something far more modest in mind. Our central objective is to survey the key theories of meaning that have been influential within the field over the past hundred years and to point to a few of the ways they have been taken up by communication scholars. We are not the first to undertake such a task. In a 1974 article for the *Quarterly Journal of Speech*, John Stewart conducted a comparative study of how the field conceptualized meaning from 1953 to 1970.[3] A decade later, Gary Cronkhite comprehensively explored the topic in Carroll C. Arnold and John Waite Bowers's 1984 *Handbook of Rhetorical and Communication Theory*.[4] Cronkhite's whopping 178-page chapter on "Perception and Meaning" was followed more recently by Bryan Crable's five-page synopsis of "Meaning Theories" in Stephen W. Littlejohn and Karen A. Foss's 2009 *Encyclopedia of Communication Theory*.[5] Our own enterprise registers somewhere between Cronkhite's colossal undertaking and Crable's succinct summary.

But before we begin, we would like to briefly reflect on the general approach, scope, and organization of our project. In preparing to write this chapter, we conducted an exhaustive search of the *Communication and Mass Media Complete Index* to identify the scholarship on meaning published in the discipline over the past century. Based on that research, we identified what we take to be the seven key theories of meaning: general semantics, new materialism, the new rhetoric, ordinary language, semiotics, symbolic forms, and symbolic interactionism. Given the broad scope of the topic, however, we limited our research to the field's qualitative, interpretive, and critical work. So, while we present a broad spectrum of views on the meaning of meaning, we make no claims about the centrality of our survey to the discipline's considerable body of social scientific research. We also wish to note that nearly all of the theories of meaning central to communication studies have been imported from other disciplines (e.g., linguistics, sociology, philosophy, and psychology). The study of meaning is a decidedly inter-disciplinary affair.

Given the historic anniversary that this volume marks, it was tempting to organize our discussion chronologically. But such an approach proved both unsuitable and unworkable, as the theories we discuss were not taken up by the discipline in a sequential way. Rather, they were invoked in fits and starts as suited the needs of various sub-specialties within the field at particular historical junctures. Some have influenced the discipline broadly, others have only influenced select segments. Some have steadily exerted their influence over time, while others have risen and fallen in prominence. To prevent the misperception of any sort of developmental progression within the discipline, we have arranged the subsequent survey of theories alphabetically.

Finally, while the seven theories we survey are all distinct, drawing upon different philosophical and intellectual traditions, they nevertheless share some common concerns and governing impulses. Chief among these, we suggest, is a rejection of early trans-mission models of communication, such as the Shannon and Weaver model (1949), the Carroll model (1953), and the Westley-Maclean model (1955).[6] These models tended to reflect a correspondence theory of truth that reduced meaning—inasmuch as they were concerned with it at all—to an uncomplicated representationalism or primitive labeling theory in which words referred to things. Thus, as we proceed, we highlight a few of the ways the theories reviewed challenge and contest the assumptions underlying simple representational and transmission models of communication.

General Semantics

Coming to terms with the aftermath of the moral and material devastation of two world wars, communication scholars in the mid-twentieth century turned to the pressing need to increase the ability of humans to critique communicative phenomena such as propa-ganda, mass media, and consumer media. Support for these efforts was found in the theory of *general semantics* which, rather than strictly a study of language, involves "applying the techniques, habits, and viewpoints of science to problems of everyday living."[7]

The founder of general semantics, Alfred Korzybski (1879–1950), was a Polish-American philosopher and scientist who conceptualized the faculty of *time-binding*—the ability to organize social cooperation at a distance and accumulate knowledge over generations of time—as the most salient human characteristic.[8] For Korzybski, human survival depends on fruitful time-binding in which communication is employed to foster agreement and peaceful coexistence. During the latter half of the twentieth century, Korzybski's student S.I. Hayakawa (1906–1992) continued the effort to make general semantics a discipline that could advance the practice of time-binding by training people to use the scientific principles of observation, hypothesizing, and testing in order to "think more clearly, to speak and write more effectively, and to listen and read with greater understanding."[9] General semantics approaches meaning on several interconnected levels including the relationship of words to external reality, the difference between *extensional* and *intensional* meanings, and the problems inherent in abstractions.

Laying out his theory in *Science and Sanity*, Korzybski claimed that theories of meaning that are based on referents and operational methods are confused and inadequate.[10] Korzybski's famous dictum, "the map is not the territory," spoke to his belief that there is a fundamental difference between the sensory world of experience and the world of symbols and language. The world itself is continually changing and in flux, but words "lock the gaze" on partial phenomena, condense the field of reality, and set up false distinctions between body/mind, emotions/rationality, and objective/subjective.[11] In other words, language is never the territory, but always an abstraction that depends on its context for meaning. For general semanticists, words never *mean*, people do, and to understand what an expression means it is necessary to ask what the person who uses it means. General semantics therefore posits a highly contextual sense of meaning.[12]

The meanings of words—which are in themselves merely complicated noises—are learned from hearing noises as they accompany actual situations in life and learning to associate certain noises with certain situations. This association results in words having both *extensional* and *intensional* meanings. The extensional meaning of an utterance is that to which it points in the physical world. This meaning linguistically maps, or denotes, a territory it can never reach or comprehend. The *intensional* meaning of an utterance is that which is suggested within people's minds, a content that is highly individualized, never consistent from one utterance to the next, and inevitably ambiguous. Critiquing what he terms the *one meaning fallacy*, Hayakawa points out that ambiguity in language use is inherent because words are always shifting and changing meanings. For example, the statement "I *believe* in you" (an expression of confidence) is different than "I *believe* democracy is the best political system" (an acceptance of a set of principles). Likewise, "my computer" denotes a different object when uttered by Donna, Christy, or Jeff. The implication is that the meaning of a word can be known only approximately until it is uttered; all words interact and meanings emerge in the context of other words and the situation in which they arise.

That the *map is not the territory* implies that all words are abstractions, and for general semanticists, it is confusion about the multi-modal character of the various levels of abstraction that confounds communication and makes language dangerous. In *Language in Thought and Action*, Hayakawa introduces his "abstraction ladder" and uses the example of Bessie the Cow to exemplify how, in variously viewing and expressing this creature as "Bessie," "cow," "livestock," "farm asset," "asset," and "wealth," speakers invoke various levels of distance from the actual object under discussion.[13] Abstracting is a necessary human convenience—time-binding and sharing knowledge would be impossible without this process—but when people fail to perceive that they are interacting via abstractions, and often from different levels of abstraction, disagreements and even wars can result. Particularly on the top rungs of the ladder, where high-level abstractions such as *justice, democracy,* and *patriotism* emerge, the actual condition of the world fails to be depicted, arguments result, and lethal antagonisms may develop.

To avoid such confusions in meaning, general semantics seeks to train people to apply scientific ways of thinking so that humans can co-create better discursive maps of the world. Only scientific methodology—observing, hypothesizing, and testing—enables the systematic selection from prevailing ways of abstracting that can ensure the "maximum increase in knowledge through ensuring the maximum of human agreement."[14] In recognizing the map is not the territory, the differences between intentional and extensional meanings, and the pitfalls of abstraction, people are able to strengthen the cultural institutions under which time-binding best flourishes.

In the decades following S.I. Hayakawa's 1939 "General Semantics and Propaganda," communication scholars applied or critiqued general semantics over a range of subjects, including public speaking, speech situations, persuasion, and speech education.[15] From 1953 to 1970, the general semanticists were, according to Stewart, among the "primary sources for referential treatments of meaning,"[16] and general semantics was a standard part of communication curriculum during the 1960s and 1970s.[17] Despite these engagements, interest in general semantics slowed during the latter part of the twentieth century and has been revived only in the last two decades with studies that, for example, explore the influence of general semantics on Kenneth Burke's theories[18] and apply the theory to media ecology and theology.[19]

New Materialism

In the late twentieth century, communications scholars, like other scholars in the humanities and social sciences, developed a renewed interest in "the primacy of matter."[20] This interest, variously dubbed the "material turn" and the "new materialism," has prompted a crucial rethinking of the concept of meaning. The two theorists we have grouped under the banner of *new materialism*, while distinctive, share the belief that meaning is grounded in the materiality of the body. This perspective is, of course, not without precursor. Figures such as Charles Sanders Peirce, Ernst Cassirer, Susanne Langer, I.A. Richards, and Kenneth Burke, among others, have all suggested that meaning involves both sensory experience and human cognition. But what distinguishes new materialists such as Julia Kristeva (1941–) and Mark Johnson (1949–) from the aforementioned scholars is their insistence that body and mind (matter and consciousness) are not separate, ontologically distinct entities. These theorists maintain that physical (material) states and psychical (mental) states are co-extensive, if not entirely reducible to one another.

Julia Kristeva first began to sketch her materialist view of meaning in her 1969 book, *Semiotiké: Recherches pour une sémanalyse* (*Semiotics: Investigations for Semanalysis*). Since only two chapters of *Semiotiké* were translated into English, however, Kristeva's theory of meaning is generally traced to her groundbreaking 1974 text, *La révolution du langage poétique*, a third of which was translated into English and published as *Revolution in Poetic Language* in 1984. In this latter work, Kristeva examines avant-garde literature and the ways "poetic language" undermines a traditional conception of meaning in which words simply denote things or thoughts. Instead of viewing meaning as separate from subjectivity, Kristeva regards it as the outcome of a dynamic *signifying process* in which language discharges the subject's bodily drives and energies. For Kristeva, the signifying process is comprised of two modalities that, while conceptually distinct, are wholly inseparable: the *semiotic* and the *symbolic*.[21]

To avoid confusion, it should be noted that Kristeva's use of the term "the semiotic" (*le sémiotique*) differs from Peirce and others' use of the term "semiotics." Whereas semiotics refers to the science of signs, the semiotic refers to "the heterogeneous, affective, material dimension of language,"[22] which is to say, to the "drive-based dimension of language."[23] The semiotic entails the transverbal qualities of language, "such as rhythmical and melodical inflections."[24] Though the semiotic facet of language does not signify, it motivates (even as it threatens) signification, discharging drives in symbols and making symbols matter.[25] In contrast to the semiotic, the symbolic is associated with syntax and grammar, with the rules that govern language and its use. Following Jacques Lacan, Kristeva regards the symbolic as the domain of logic and law: it is that which provides stability and structure and makes representation possible. Meaning is a product of the dialectical oscillation between the semiotic and the symbolic.

Kristeva's theory of meaning is bound up with her conception of the *chora* (roughly, "space"). Adapting the term from Plato's *Timaeus*, Kristeva understands the *chora*, which she frequently couples with the semiotic, as the "receptacle" that registers (but also provisionally orders) the bodily rhythms, intensities, and pulsations connecting mother and infant before and following birth. Inasmuch as these kinetic energies are discharged in verbal and gestural expression, the *chora* is the locus of the socio-biological drives that underlie the semiotic and, by extension, all signification, though Kristeva prefers the term *signifiance* to signification, as it accounts for the non-signifying facet of language and communication. Just as a baby's "first sounds and gestures express and discharge feelings and energies" of the *chora*,[26] so too do the timbre and tone of one's voice, the rhythm and tempo of poetry, and the melody and movement of music; these are all material manifestations of the semiotic chora. The semiotic, then, is the precondition of the symbolic—the generative "material conditions of meaning construction."[27]

Whereas Kristeva approaches the matter of meaning from a psychoanalytic perspective, Mark Johnson approaches it from a philosophical perspective, though he draws support for his theory from neuroscience, linguistics, and cognitive science. His approach to meaning is most clearly laid out in two works, *The Body in the Mind* and *The Meaning of the Body*, though elements of it have also been developed in his collaborative work with George Lakoff, especially *Philosophy in the Flesh*.[28] The starting point for Johnson's theory is a critique of Anglo-American analytic philosophy and its attendant *objectivist* theory of meaning, which he maintains, "assumes a fixed and determined mind-independent reality, with arbitrary symbols that get meaning by mapping directly onto that objective reality."[29] Like Kristeva, Johnson's theory of meaning rejects a Cartesian mind/body dualism, offering a unified, material, embodied, and non-propositional perspective in its stead.

For Johnson, the material body is the basis of all meaning, for it structures or lends form to all human experience. Combining the pragmatism of John Dewey and William James with the phenomenology of Maurice Merleau-Ponty, Johnson suggests that meaning arises from the felt qualities of events and situations generated by active and moving bodies. According to Johnson, meaning emerges out of (or originates with) pre-conscious sensorimotor experiences that precede and, subsequently, structure perception and other higher cognitive processes such as intellectual feelings and reflective thinking. To explain this process, Johnson invokes the concepts of *image schemata* and *metaphorical projections*. Image schemata are basic patterns or recurring gestalts of embodied (visual, auditory, kinesthetic, or cross-modal) experience typically formed during infancy and early childhood, and metaphorical projections are the abstract concepts and inferences derived from those patterns. Johnson further contends that the basic schemas, which give rise to more abstract understanding and meaning (through metaphorical projections), are themselves tied to the aesthetic dimension of all embodied experience. In short, pervasive aesthetic characteristics of the world appeal to our bodily senses, creating relatively stable patterns of sensorimotor experience that, in turn, contribute to the meanings we make through metaphorical extension to nonphysicalistic realms.

Given that new materialism is a comparatively recent perspective on meaning, it has not been embraced as widely as some other perspectives. But in the past ten years, communication scholars have increasingly begun to draw upon its insights to explain how audiences engage in fully embodied sense making. Taking up Kristeva's notion of the semiotic, for instance, media and rhetorical scholars have explored how literature, plays, films, and war rhetoric move audiences at an affective, bodily level.[30] Similarly, Johnson's work on image schemata and metaphor has variously been taken up by discourse, intercultural, and organizational scholars to study the role of embodied cognition in information processing and meaning-making.[31] Animated both by the "material turn" and a rising interest in the body, new materialism is likely to continue to grow in influence in the coming decades.

The New Rhetoric

For nearly 2,000 years, a classical conception of rhetoric rooted in persuasion dominated rhetorical theory. That conception was problematized in the early to mid-twentieth century, however, as a renewed interest in rhetoric among philosophers, communication scholars, and composition teachers spawned a series of efforts to reconceptualize it. Though diverse, the reconceptualizations of rhetoric that occurred during this period are often grouped, if somewhat uneasily, under the sweeping, nondescript banner of the *new rhetoric*.[32] Chief among the thinkers credited with advancing the new rhetoric were the literary scholars I.A. Richards (1893–1979) and Kenneth Burke (1897–1993), both of whom were introduced to communication scholars in large measure by Marie Hochmuth in the 1950s. In separate essays in the *Quarterly Journal of Speech*, Hochmuth outlined the basic contours of Richards's and Burke's versions of the new rhetoric.[33] Our interest in the new rhetoric is animated by the context-based theory of meaning at its core.

I.A. Richards's conception of meaning emerges directly out of his concern with rhetoric. In his 1936 book *The Philosophy of Rhetoric*, Richards laments the state of rhetoric, suggesting that it has changed little since Aristotle. He objects, in particular, to rhetoric's obsession with persuasion, advocating for a reconceptualization of rhetoric aimed instead at comprehension. Accordingly, Richards defines rhetoric as "a study of misunderstanding and its remedies."[34] In keeping with his desire to promote understanding, he turns to what he regards as the key site of misunderstanding: words. The problem of misunderstanding arises, according to Richards, from two misconceptions about how words work, what he calls the *proper meaning superstition* and the *doctrine of uses*. These principles hold, respectively, that every word has a singular meaning and that its correct usage will eliminate misunderstanding. In contrast, Richards argues that not only do words not possess one correct meaning, but they also have no meaning by themselves. For Richards, meaning resides not in words, but in people and, more specifically, in the contexts in which persons use them.

When Richards insists that meaning is contextual, he intends "context" in two senses. First, meaning is contextual because it depends upon the particular combination of words used in a phrase or sentence. This, the more restricted or literary sense of context, simply refers to the "interinanimation of words"—to the ways in which the meanings of words are mutually dependent. Second, meaning is contextual because words summon or call to mind previous events that shape our experience of the present. This, the more inclusive or technical sense of context, which Richards explored with his co-author C.K. Ogden (1889–1957) in their 1923 book *The Meaning of Meaning*, refers to how humans perceive and experience the world. Every event, according to Ogden and Richards, produces stimuli or sensory experiences that are stored as imprints or "engrams" in our minds for later retrieval. Words activate these engrams—the residual traces of previous events—because words are substitute stimuli or signs of the original stimulus. When a person hears a word such as *apple*, for instance, it evokes thoughts of one's previous experiences with apples, thus triggering the associated engrams—a process called "delegated efficacy." And since no two people have experienced apples in all the same ways, the word *apple* necessarily evokes different engrams and, consequently, different meanings for each person. In light of the inevitable ambiguity of words, meaning can never be determined by analyzing words as if they are "discrete independent tesserae" in a mosaic; to some extent, all understanding is inference and guesswork.[35]

Ogden and Richards sum up their context-based theory of meaning in a model known as the semantic triangle. Like Peirce's triadic theory of the sign, Ogden and Richards' semantic triangle features three primary elements:

(1) a *referent*, which corresponds to Peirce's "object";
(2) a *symbol*, which corresponds to his "sign"; and
(3) a *thought* or reference, which corresponds to his "interpretant."

Though both models seek to explain the relation between an expression and the subject to which that expression refers, they do so in different ways. While Peirce's model depicts an equilateral relationship among all three terms, Ogden and Richards' model indicates (via a dotted line) that "there is no relevant relation other than the indirect one" between the symbol and the referent.[36] This "imputed" relation is much closer to Ferdinand de Saussure's view of signs than to Peirce's. We highlight this distinction to underscore that no directly causal relation exists between a symbol (word) and a referent (object), which is why Richards "sees all language as metaphorical."[37] Words do not refer to objects; rather, they trigger "the missing parts of the context."[38]

Though Kenneth Burke's conception of meaning is far less explicit than Richards's, it can nonetheless be intuited from his theory of rhetoric. While Richards's conception of rhetoric explicitly challenges Aristotle's conception and its focus on persuasion, Burke's view of rhetoric extends Aristotelian rhetoric.[39] In his 1950 book *A Rhetoric of Motives*,

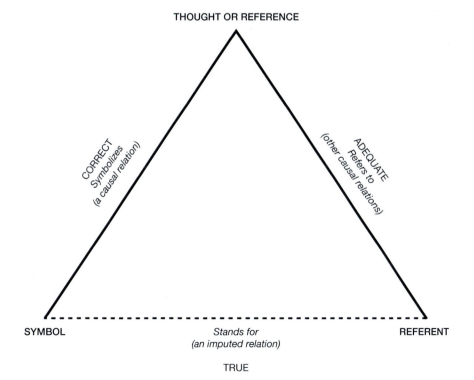

Figure 10.1 Ogden and Richards's semantic triangle.

Burke features *identification*, rather than persuasion, as his key term and defines rhetoric as *"the use of language as a symbolic means of inducing cooperation in beings that by nature respond to symbols."*[40] Identification is critical to Burke's new rhetoric because, like Richards, he regards division (or alienation) and conflict to be endemic to the human condition. But whereas Richards locates the source of conflict in misunderstanding, Burke locates it in social hierarchy and human motives. Thus, Burke's rhetoric is more concerned with *attitudes* than with comprehension. Despite these differences, both Richards's and Burke's new rhetorics were responses to World War I and to the social anxieties that it generated.

Burke's most explicit treatment of meaning and signs appears in a 1962 essay, "What Are the Signs of What? A Theory of 'Entitlement'," published in *Anthropological Linguistics*. In that essay, which Burke had previously delivered as an invited talk at Boston University in 1956, he proposes to "reverse the usual realistic view of the relation between words and things" by arguing that "things are the signs of words."[41] For Burke, the idea that words are unproblematic reflections of the world "clings to a kind of naive verbal realism that refuses to realize the full extent of the role played by symbolicity in his [man's] notions of reality."[42] The position Burke advances is grounded in a constitutive view of rhetoric that sees language as essential to the construction of the social world. While he is quick to acknowledge that there is a material (or nonverbal) world that exists independent of symbolicity, Burke maintains that our experience of that world is so tied up in the way we define, designate, and dramatize it that the "overall 'picture' is but a construct of our symbol system."[43]

Continuing, Burke posits that words distill and "entitle" complex nonverbal situations.[44] By singling out certain attributes (as opposed to others) of a situation, language orients us toward that situation; it shapes our attitudes and, thus, our actions. Language, then, is not simply a transparent representation of the nonverbal world, but a kind of action—symbolic action—in the world. While words entitle situations, nonverbal situations also operate according to the principle of abbreviation, meaning that they exhibit "one fragment or portion that is felt to stand for the essence of the situation."[45] Since our sensory experience of that fragment signifies or is emblematic of the particular motives that inhere in the entitling terms for that situation, situations can be said to be materializations or signs of the spirit peculiar to words. So, while Burke's new rhetoric differs from Richards's in scope, purpose, and terminology, it shares a recognition that meaning is radically contextual in character.

The new rhetoric, generally, and I.A. Richards's, specifically, was seminal to the study of meaning in communication. According to Stewart, Richards was one of the eleven most cited authorities on meaning through 1970,[46] and his belief that meaning is context dependent and, thus, never fixed is widely regarded as axiomatic. Richards's influence continued to be felt, especially in rhetorical studies, throughout the 1970s and 1980s, and, in 1988, *Rhetoric Society Quarterly* hosted a special issue on I.A. Richards and his contributions to rhetorical theory. Burke, perhaps even more so than Richards, has had a profound influence on rhetorical theory and, especially, a constitutive view of language. But Burke's view of meaning is less well known. Indeed, one of the few sustained treatments of it is Stewart's *Language as Articulate Contact*, which dedicates a full chapter to its explication.[47]

Ordinary Language

Ordinary language philosophy—a label that was not used by the philosophers themselves—is primarily associated with the views of Ludwig Wittgenstein (1889–1951), J.L. Austin (1911–1960), and John Searle (1932–). This perspective challenges the view that philosophical inquiry requires a specialized language divorced from ordinary use. For proponents, the distinction between ordinary and non-ordinary language is not that of vernacular use on the one hand and academic or scientific language on the other; rather, the distinction is between language as it is ordinarily used and understood and philosophical, idealized language—such as that employed by logical positivists—thought to be more capable of reflecting reality. Ordinary language philosophy also challenges referential theories of meaning; these referential theories assert that the meaning of a word or phrase consists in its relationship to an object or thing, and that the verifiability of this relationship can be determined to be true or false. Ordinary language philosophers point out that, for many words and phrases, there is no identifiable object that constitutes meaning; the meaning of a word or a phrase emerges only through its use.[48] For ordinary language philosophers, both philosophical methodology and linguistic meaning are found in the ordinary *use* of expressions.

Wittgenstein studied logic and mathematics before becoming a Fellow at Trinity College at Cambridge where he wrote what eventually became one of the most influential philosophical texts of the twentieth century, *Philosophical Investigations*. Published posthumously in 1953, the text explores Wittgenstein's non-referential position toward meaning by analogizing language use with games.[49] For Wittgenstein, to ask, "What is a word?" is analogous to asking, "What is a piece in chess?" Knowing the shape of the king, for example, explains nothing about its use; how the king functions—what it means—is known only through the rules of the game. The shape and sound of a word is like the shape of the king and functions likewise; to know what any word means it is necessary to know its role in the language-game in which it is used.[50] The fundamental error of denotative theories of language is that they appeal to something outside of the system of language-games—to objects in the world—in order to explain the significance of words, an appeal that is analogous to trying to explain how the king functions by referring to something outside of the game of chess. For Wittgenstein, a word's meaning cannot be explained by reference to the thought it expresses, nor the thought by some object in the external world. The word, an indivisible unit of sound-with-sense, is explainable only by contrasting its role with that of other words in the language system of which it is a part.

Wittgenstein's language-games are often communication games.[51] Communication is possible because language (like any game) has recognized, albeit arbitrary, rules.[52] Reference is possible in Wittgenstein's view; the rules of some language-games are founded on conventions through which a language community comes to link sense impressions to conditions in the world. In other words, in the technique of using language, certain elements or objects come to correspond to signs, to words.[53] *Brick*, for example, through practices involving interacting with people and bricks, comes to correspond to a rectangular block of aggregate, but outside of human interactions involving such blocks, *brick* is meaningless. The meanings of words are always highly contextualized, embedded in forms of life that give them meaning. For example, the expression "*Water!*" can be used as an exclamation, an order, a request, or as an answer to a question, depending on how it is used. Language-games are learned by watching others play and by observing utterances and their consequences within the culture and society in which they are used. Without training in the rules of these forms of life, communication between people would be impossible.

British philosopher J.L. Austin and his erstwhile American student John Searle developed ordinary language theory based on what Austin called *speech acts*. In 1955, Austin introduced speech acts by publishing his William James Lectures (which had been delivered at Harvard in 1954) as *How to Do Things with Words*. Like Wittgenstein, Austin challenged traditional notions of meaning and insisted that the meanings of all utterances are not referential, nor truth-conditional and verifiable. Creating a distinction between *constatives*, or utterances that are referential, truth-conditional, and mostly descriptive in function, and *performatives*, or utterances that are not sayings but *doings*, Austin says that only the former have truth value. This constative–performative distinction challenged rhetorical, linguistic, and philosophical traditions that establish equivalence between definitions of literal meaning and truth and considered meaningful only statements that are verifiable according to criteria of truth-falsity.[54] Performatives—"I do" or "I hereby christen this ship *The Queen Elizabeth*," for example—do not describe or report anything that can be considered true or false. Further, these sentences are, or are part of, the doing of an action—marrying or naming.[55] While Austin later abandoned a strict delineation between constatives and performatives, he continued to advocate for the position that not all expressions were truth-verifiable. For Austin, language is not merely representational: a theory of linguistic meaning must take into account social and pragmatic features of language use.

Austin further explicates speech acts by conceptualizing three different linguistic acts that can be performed at the same time by uttering the same words: a *locutionary* act of uttering words with a definite meaning as defined by sense and reference; an *illocutionary* act which by virtue of implicit conventions is accomplished in uttering the words; and a *perlocutionary* act of producing some effect as a result of uttering words.[56] For example, uttering the locutionary act "You're stupid" accomplishes the illocutionary act of insulting someone and the perlocutionary act of causing anger. According to Austin, while the meaning of a constative can be assessed in terms of truth or falsity— the accused person is or is not stupid—the meaning of speech acts is assessed by an alternate criterion, felicity. For a speech act to be felicitous, several conditions must be met: there must exist a conventional procedure having a conventional effect (for example, saying "I do" making one married), and the speech act must be uttered correctly and completely by appropriate persons in appropriate circumstances (in a ceremony by partners capable of being united in a marriage ceremony).

Austin distinguished meaning as sense and reference from meaning resulting from what he termed *force*, or that which gives information as to how an utterance is to be taken or interpreted.[57] For some utterances, it is *force*—accomplished through a number of factors including the situation, mood, tone, grammar, and nonverbal gestures—that informs a hearer that a speaker is joking, insinuating, being sarcastic, or merely reporting. Where wording alone is insufficient to clue a hearer into the meaning intended by a speaker, force—words like "I argue," "I demand," or "I believe"—allows meaning to emerge in a specific context of language use.

John Searle's theory, initially published in 1969 in *Speech Acts: An Essay on the Philosophy of Language* and in 1979 in *Expression and Meaning: Studies in the Theory of Speech Acts*, is an extension of Austin's work. Searle, a professor of philosophy at Berkeley, has continued to develop his language theory, and the remarks included here do not reflect the full evolution of his thinking on consciousness, language, and culture. In communication scholarship, Searle may be best known for his conceptualization of *indirect speech acts*, or speech acts in which "the speaker's utterance meaning and the sentence meaning come apart in various ways" so that the meaning exceeds what is said.[58] Indirect speech act theory, along with Searle's Principle of Expressibility and his Literal Meaning Hypothesis, address meaning in language by contrasting literal meaning with nonliteral meaning.

The Principle of Expressibility states that "whatever can be meant can be said."[59] In other words, whenever the force of an utterance is not clear, it can be made clear. For example, the proposition "Sam smokes habitually" can be explicated by the addition of expressions of force such as "Sam, smoke habitually!" or "Does Sam smoke habitually?"[60] The Principle of Literal Meaning addresses those utterances in which a speaker intends to communicate no more than the literal meaning of a sentence. In these cases, the speaker's meaning and sentence meaning coincide as, for example, when "It's getting hot in here" is uttered to indicate rising temperature in a room.[61] Nonliteral meaning includes utterances such as metaphors—"It's getting hot in here" to describe an escalating argument, for example—as well as uses of language that are intended to be sarcastic or jokes. For Searle, as for Austin and Wittgenstein, meaning does not exist prior to utterances; meaning depends upon and emerges within specific language use.

As the field of communication broadened its scope and methodologies in the latter decades of the twentieth century—away from classical conceptions of rhetoric as public address and a scientific orientation to research—communication scholars turned to ordinary language theories to ground their work. While Edward Shirley argued that a satisfactory theory of meaning could not be derived in terms of speech acts, other researchers found ordinary language principles productive. In the 1970s–1980s, Thomas Farrell and Thomas Frentz turned to J.L. Austin and John Searle while Richard Buttny turned to Wittgenstein, for instance, to shift the focus from what language *symbolizes* to what language *does* in a material arena.[62] During the latter twentieth and early twenty-first centuries, ordinary language theory has been applied to discussions concerning linguistics, the rapprochement of rhetoric and philosophy, realism in news journalism, interpersonal conflict literature, and models of signification and pedagogy, among others.[63]

Semiotics

Ferdinand de Saussure (1857–1913), Charles Sanders Peirce (1829–1913), and Roland
Barthes (1915–1980) are three theorists, influential in the communication field, who
advanced the perspective on meaning known as *semiotics*. Semiotics can be defined as
a "science of meaning" that studies signs and their uses in representation.[64] Two core
assumptions of semiotic theory are that any theory of meaning must be conceptualized
within the context of a theory of language, and any theory of language must be based
on a definition of signs in relation to other signs.[65] Each of the three major semiotic
theorists begins with the sign, but their different conceptualizations yield different
implications for meaning.

The Swiss linguist Ferdinand de Saussure is generally credited with revolutionizing
the study of language by replacing a substantive view of language as a collection of
separate, meaningful units called *words* with a relational, structural model that considers
language in terms of the relationships among words.[66] Saussure's lectures on his semiotic
system—which he termed *semiology*—were delivered at the University of Geneva and
published posthumously in 1915 as *Course in General Linguistics*. Interested in establishing
a general science of signs, Saussure says that "from the very outset we must put both
feet on the ground of language and use language as the norm of all other manifestations
of speech."[67] Accordingly, he isolates language as a field of study independent of both
speakers and of external reality by approaching language as made up of two distinct
parts, a structure and the manifestations of that structure. The structure or system of
rules and conventions that makes speech possible is *la langue*; the actual use of language
by speakers is *la parole*. For Saussure, it is the conceptual structure of *la langue* and not
the social use of *la parole* that determines the meanings of words.

In contrast to how correspondence theories of meaning treat a symbol as the link
between a name and an object, Saussure's linguistic sign is a two-sided psychological
entity consisting of a *signifier* (sound-image) and a *signified* (the concept). The signifier
is the material form of the sign as perceived by the listener's senses, while the signified
is the mental image or idea evoked by the signifier. Importantly, Saussure regarded
the relation between the signifier and the signified to be arbitrary. For example, the
concept "tree" and the sound /tri/ have no necessary connection beyond shared
social convention. Communication is possible because all individuals who are socially
linked by a common language will establish among themselves a kind of average of
meanings: all will reproduce—not exactly, but approximately—the same signs linked to
the same concepts.

Saussure shifts the question of meaning away from how language relates to the
external world and toward the internal relations of signs in a structured system of
"organizational categories and forms through which the mind is able to experience the
world, or to organize a meaning in what is essentially in itself meaningless."[68] For Saussure,
then, given the arbitrary nature of signs, signs do not reference external reality and
meanings do not reside in the signs themselves, but in their relationships. Fixing signs
in relation to one another in the sign-system underlying language use allows the possibility
of meaning. Signs thus *mean* in advance of communication events and exclusively due

to the differences among them in *la langue*. Meaning is possible, but to decipher meaning would require knowledge of exclusively symbolic and abstract language codes.

Charles Sanders Peirce, the founder of modern pragmatism, is considered along with Saussure to be a founder of modern semiotics, calling his theory *semiotics*.[69] Educated at Harvard, Peirce taught logic and philosophy and wrote prodigiously, filling eight dense volumes that began to be published in 1932 as *Collected Papers of Charles Sanders Peirce*. Like Saussure, Peirce rejects a correspondence view of meaning and frames the study of language on the basis of signs. However, Peirce does not approach language from a perspective divorced from language use and he extends the category of signs to include all modes of human communication. Taking a pragmatic stance, Peirce acknowledges that humans cannot directly know external reality, but he asserts that people take for real what their community considers real, including the fact of consciousness. Beginning with consciousness, Peirce approaches his system of signs by asking, "what *must* be the character" of signs used by "an intelligence capable of learning by experience?"[70] He answers this question by theorizing three levels of meaning that correspond to levels of consciousness and result in a triadic theory of the sign.

Peirce notes that signs are not constructed simply to name and classify objects but because people want to understand objects in a sensory-based fashion.[71] This understanding is possible because of the basic components of consciousness which Peirce terms *firstness*, *secondness*, and *thirdness*. Firstness is immediate sensation derived from bodily and sensory processes; firstness is pure experience without recognition, analysis, or reference. Secondness is derived from relating signs to one another; secondness is human lived reality of the fact of things existing in the world. Thirdness is the level of meaning derived from symbolic processes; thirdness is the world of sign relations in abstractions, theories, and concepts. From these levels of consciousness, Peirce theorizes a triadic sign as "an object which stands for another object to some mind."[72]

For Peirce, signification requires a relationship not only between a sign and an object, but also with an interpretant, a human mind that must conceive of the sign as connected with its object. For example, as a hearer encounters the spoken word "flag," there is an immediate, non-conceptual experience of vibrations on the eardrum. Next, there is the experience of having a thought—a sign in the mind as "flag" becomes conscious. Then, the sign's interpretant *re-presents* the thought-object as a sign of the waving, striped object. It is the sign in the mind that meaningfully connects the other two.[73] A sign often has more than one thought-object. "Flag" might mean "my father's coffin cover," "the United States," or "US imperialism." Indeed, any sign or collection of signs resulting from prior experience can become an object in the sign–object–interpretant relationship. Communication is possible because experiences form the basis of sign–object–interpretant relations that are shared by members of a language community.

French philosopher, literary and social critic Roland Barthes built on the language theories of both Saussure and Peirce to develop his own theory of signs which might be termed the *signifying system*. Saussure's and Peirce's conceptualization of a sign is that of a signifier that then leads to a signified; the relationship between the two is one of *equality*. For Barthes, however, the relationship between the signifier and signified is one of *equivalence*, a non-sequential correlation that unites the two in an indivisible unity.[74] What a hearer grasps as *meaning* is the entire sign, the sound-image *and* the associated concept. This insight led Barthes to make one of his most important contributions to semiotic theory—the distinction between *denotative* and *connotative* meanings.

Denotative meaning involves the literal or explicit meanings of words and other phenomena. On a denotative level, the word "lion" (signifier) evokes the mental association of a large feline mammal (signified). But Barthes recognized that meaning goes beyond the literal; the word "lion" also evokes other associations such as "courage" and "pride." This second level of meaning, connotation, operates at the level of ideology and myth. For example, "dog" and "perro" may both denote a hairy mammal that barks, but, depending on the culture, the word might connote "faithful companion," "family member," "pest," or even "food." One consequence of connotative meaning is that all meaning is fundamentally culturally determined.

For Barthes, the semantization of cultural items is inevitable because "*as soon as there is a society, every usage is converted into a sign of itself.*"[75] For any object not to signify would require that it be absolutely divorced from all human experience up to its creation. This insight led Barthes to extend his study of signs beyond language to such areas as myth, clothing, food, advertisements, and photography. All of these for Barthes function as planes of expression (signifiers) associated with planes of content (signifieds).[76]

Though William Hardy first began to explore a semiotic conception of meaning in a 1944 *Quarterly Journal of Speech* article, this perspective did not become popular in communication studies until the late 1960s and early 1970s. The popularity of semiotics largely corresponded with the dominance of structuralism, an (largely European) intellectual tradition concerned with the rules that govern all aspects of social life. As such, semiotics generally reflected an *objectivist* orientation, i.e., "a commitment to the belief that one could describe the world as it exists objectively, without reference to observers."[77] Throughout the 1970s and 1980s, interest in semiotics grew exponentially, especially with regard to the study of media and culture, where it was used to account for the meanings of everything from fashion and film to advertising and architecture. Semiotics, which is still widely used in visual communication and media studies, has spawned thousands of articles in communication. Consequently, it is difficult to overstate the influence of semiotic theory on conceptions of meaning in communication studies throughout the latter half of the twentieth century.

Symbolic Forms

By the late 1960s, communication scholars had developed a keen interest in the complex relation between rhetoric and knowing, one that led them to explore the theory of symbolic forms. Two of the key philosophers responsible for this theory—Ernst Cassirer (1874–1945) and Susanne K. Langer (1895–1985)—believed that reason alone is a "very inadequate term with which to comprehend the forms of man's cultural life in all their richness and variety."[78] Reason as developed in mathematical and scientific thinking is inadequate to study mental phenomena such as the symbolic capacity of human consciousness.[79] Cassirer and Langer revise traditional notions of meaning that focus exclusively on language and discourse by extending symbolic behavior to the realms of sensation and emotion, and to considerations of myth, religion, music, and art.

Cassirer was a philosophy professor at Frankfurt and Hamburg universities before immigrating first to England where he taught at Oxford, and then to the United States where he lectured at Yale and Columbia. In one of his two books written in English, *An Essay on Man* (1944), Cassirer shifts attention from conceiving of objects *substantively* as things independent of conceptualization to considering objects *functionally* through how they are experienced by conceptualization. For Cassirer, experiencing something takes place according to the rules of a *symbolic form*, a framework that encompasses the experiencing agent and that which is experienced and made meaningful. For example, an electron is not an independent, substantial thing, but a functional term in the context of a certain conceptualization; an electron becomes comprehensible only within the framework of a scientific theory like quantum mechanics. Like electrons, all objects are made meaningful only with a symbolic form that determines the "reality" of what one understands.[80] Even a tree is symbolic, something different to an artist or a biologist, depending on the symbolic form through which it is understood. The symbolic form, then, *forms* a world as a meaningful context and what is experienced is not the thing— the electron or the tree—but a phenomenon within this context. Symbolic forms are multiple and vary for different realms of human reasoning such as mythology, language, and science.

Cassirer designates three functions of symbolic meaning that apply to different symbolic forms: *expressive*, *representative*, and *significative*. Expressive meaning, the most basic and primitive type, is the emotional significance of experiences of events in the world. This function of meaning is evident in mythology where a unity of consciousness results in a world where inner and outer realms and the names for objects and the objects themselves are not distinguished. Representative symbolic meaning results in a *natural language* that distinguishes stable and enduring substances that are re-identifiable and communicable. Through natural language, the world of ordinary sense perception is constructed. The third type of meaning, the significative, is exhibited in a scientific view of the world and in the pure concepts that characterize mathematics, logic, and physics. Freed from sense perception, this form of meaning is abstract and universalizing.[81] All three types of meaning are found in human culture: expressive meaning in religion and art, representative meaning in everyday language, and significative meaning in scientific discourse.

Susanne Langer, who taught at Harvard and was the first American woman to receive professional recognition as a philosopher, based her theory of symbolic functions on Cassirer's work. In a 1960 article, "The Origins of Speech and its Communicative Function," published in the *Quarterly Journal of Speech*, Langer challenges the traditional conceptualization of language as having evolved from more primitive forms of animal communication. Building on biological and psychiatric research, Langer claims that human language is the result of a unique human capability—that of generating and using symbols. Like her predecessor, Cassirer, Langer considers symbol use as a natural and biological human characteristic, one that must be adequately conceptualized to distinguish human symbolic behavior from that of other animals.

Langer considers meaning not a quality of objects but a function or pattern viewed with reference to one special term that is related to others.[82] The meaning of any symbol emerges in relationship to other terms and always has both psychological and logical aspects. Psychologically, any item that has meaning must be employed by *someone*. Logically, any item with meaning must be capable of conveying that meaning. Citing Peirce's triadic sense of meaning, Langer posits meaning as involving three things—a function that rests on a pattern, an object that is "meant," and a subject who uses the term. A certain symbol "means" an object to a person; this is the logical meaning. A person also "means" the object by the symbol; this is the psychological meaning. There is no symbolic meaning without these relations.

Langer critiques the traditional philosophical notion that language is the only means of articulating thought and that everything that is not speakable is mere feeling or intuition. Believing this notion, says Langer, leads erroneously to the idea that thought is the only rational intellectual activity.[83] This idea also limits the symbolic function to discourse, a position that Langer finds untenable as a way to explain the range of human thought and understanding. Langer extends the symbolic function beyond discourse to the senses and points out that the forms recognizable through sight or hearing, for example, are genuine symbolic materials that function as media of understanding.[84] In other words, sense organs are not merely receptors or recorders; from a myriad number of sensations, the eye and the ear abstract to make symbolic forms that are meaningful.

To explain the difference between meaning in language and meaning in other symbolic processes, Langer differentiates between *discursive* and *presentational* meanings. Discursive meaning is the type of meaning in language. Every language has a vocabulary and a syntax; its elements are words with relatively fixed meanings that are linked by grammatical structure to make more complex terms whose meanings are special constellations of the united symbols. Language is a temporal series of words and the meaning of language is thus necessarily successively understood. Presentational meaning is the meaning that pertains to art, photography, and music. In these cases, there is no defining dictionary of terms and meaning depends not upon successive understanding or the equivalence of symbols with referents, but upon the simultaneous apprehension of forms through the senses. Like words, visual forms—light, shadow, line, coloration, and proportion, for example—are capable of complex combinations, but the laws governing this articulation differ from the syntax that governs language. Gradations of light and shade cannot be separated from an image, enumerated like words, or correlated in a one-to-one sense with meanings. An image, therefore, has *wordless symbolism*, a meaning that provides a route to understanding that does not involve discourse. Importantly for Langer, her understanding of nondiscursive symbolism established a basis for a symbolic understanding of art, music, and photography by including in human reasoning those mental processes that traditionally have been devalued as emotion and intuition.

The theory of symbolic forms put forward by Cassirer and Langer was central to the ideational views of meaning that were popular in communication studies in the mid- to late twentieth century.[85] In contrast to a referential perspective, which suggests that symbols refer to objects, an ideational view holds that symbols refer to ideas. In locating meaning in the mental idea that a symbol represents, the ideational view, especially as articulated in the theory of symbolic forms, broadened the scope of rhetoric by expanding the range of what constitutes "symbolic" forms beyond that of discourse and language. As Joddy Murray explains, "what philosophers such as Langer and Cassirer do for us is de-emphasize the exclusivity of verbal logic as the only form of legitimate articulation ... [through] a more inclusive definition of symbolization."[86] Although the theory of symbolic forms is cited less frequently today, its insights hold particular promise for the recent "affective turn" in the humanities.

Symbolic Interactionism

One of the most influential conceptions of meaning in the field of communication and, in particular, the qualitative study of interpersonal communication derives from the sociological theory or perspective known as symbolic interactionism. This perspective maintains that human behavior and, therefore, social life are best understood in terms of the subjective meanings that people attribute to the world, as opposed to the world as it objectively exists. This view was attractive to communication scholars, who in the latter half of the twentieth century had increasingly begun to subscribe to the view that reality is socially constructed. Though symbolic interactionism, which has its roots in the philosophy of German idealism, owes a debt to both the German sociologist Max Weber (1864–1920) and the American sociologist Charles Horton Cooley (1864–1929), its development and systematization is typically credited to the pragmatist philosopher and social behaviorist George Herbert Mead (1863–1931).

For Mead, meaning involves more than the simple transmission of messages between persons. Rather, meaning arises from and is endlessly modified through persons' symbolic interactions. In other words, meaning is a social product generated by interactional partners within a shared context. Consequently, it originates in neither objects nor individual psychic processes. To better appreciate this perspective, it is useful to consider Mead's discussion of meaning in his book *Mind, Self, and Society*, which was published posthumously in 1934 based upon the notes of Mead's former students; it was edited by Charles W. Morris, the semiotician responsible for establishing the distinction among semantics, syntactics, and pragmatics.[87] For Mead, the nature of meaning is "implicit in the [triadic] structure of the social act,"[88] which involves:

(1) a gesture made by one person;
(2) a response gesture made by a second person based upon an interpretation of the initiating gesture; and
(3) completion of the act begun by the gesture of the first person based upon an interpretation of the response gesture.

Meaning, then, always involves an interaction between at least two persons engaged in what Mead described as a "conversation of gestures" (unconscious) and "significant gestures" (conscious). While a conversation of gestures is characteristic of all animal communication, a conversation of significant gestures or symbols (such as that involving language) is unique to human communication because responses are not chiefly automatic or reflexive, but call for interpretation. Since one's interpretation will influence one's response, which will then be interpreted by the other human actor and influence her or his response, communication is an ongoing process of modified responses. Emerging as it does from contextual responses, meaning is always collaborative and conditional.

Mead's ideas regarding the nature of meaning and social life would later be refined and extended by Herbert Blumer (1900–1987), a former student of Mead's at the University of Chicago. In his 1969 book, *Symbolic Interactionism: Perspective and Method*, Blumer outlines the three central premises of symbolic interactionism. "The first premise," according to Blumer, "is that human beings act toward things on the basis of the meanings that they have for them."[89] According to Blumer, humans have meanings for everything in their social world, including physical objects, persons, categories, ideals, institutions, activities, events, etc., and these meanings shape our attitudes and actions. Blumer's second premise is that "the meaning of such things is derived from, or arises out of, the social interaction that one has with one's fellows."[90] In locating the source of meaning in interaction, this premise explicitly rejects theories of meaning that regard meaning as either intrinsic to the essence or makeup of a thing or attribute it to a psychical accretion that a person brings to a thing. The third premise holds that "meanings are handled in and modified through, an interpretive process used by the person in dealing with the things he [*sic*] encounters."[91] Interpretation in this schema is not "a mere automatic application of established meanings" but a formative process in which each person revises meaning as a guide for action based upon situated interactions with others.[92] The conception of meaning that underlies the theory of symbolic interactionism reflects an important challenge to those theories that regard meaning as transparent or unimportant. In particular, symbolic interactionism is critical of social science research concerned with human behaviors and the factors—stimuli, motives, attitudes, etc.—thought to produce them. The problem with this approach to the study of human behavior, according to interactionists, is that meaning is either ignored or subsumed to the factors being studied "by regarding it as a neutral link intervening between the initiating factors and the behavior they are alleged to produce."[93] In contrast to this perspective, symbolic interactionism sees meaning as contingent, co-constitutive, and crucial to all human behavior. This view of meaning also contests the belief that meaning is a personal or private affair, e.g., that it is something created in the individual psyche. In fact, for symbolic interactionists, both the concepts of self and mind are social constructions that develop out of "the dynamic, ongoing social process" that is symbolic interaction.

Within a decade of the publication of Blumer's book, symbolic interactionism had begun to gain traction as an approach for studying human communication. Stephen Littlejohn's 1977 *Quarterly Journal of Speech* article outlining the key figures and major schools of thought associated with this perspective was particularly important in its adoption.[94] So, too, was JAI Press's 1978 release of the first volume in a series edited by

Norman Denzin titled *Studies in Symbolic Interaction*. This series, which includes forty volumes to date, consists of "original research and theory within the general sociological perspective known as Symbolic Interactionism."[95] During the 1980s and 1990s, symbolic interactionism was used to study interpersonal and organizational communication, as well as social movements and media. More recently, this perspective has been influential in the study of mobile and online communication.

Conclusion

During the discipline's first few decades, the concept of meaning was only sporadically mentioned in communication scholarship and, even then, it was mentioned only in passing. Meaning was, for nearly forty years, somewhat of a mystery. Indeed, in 1948, Lester Thonssen and A. Craig Baird explicitly reflected on its mysterious nature, observing that "the phonetic and gestural symbols we call language are the external aspects of a highly complex and not too well-known psychological phenomenon, namely the conception and transference of meaning."[96] But that would soon change. By mid-century, as philosophers called into question correspondence theories of truth and communication scholars critiqued transmission models of communication, meaning had become the subject of sustained study and scrutiny.

While no single theory would secure disciplinary consensus in the ensuing decades, all would complicate our ideas about communication, pointing to meaning's subjective character, its relational quality, its contextual nature, its non-linguistic dimensions, its embodied tenor, and its indirect referentiality. Today, there is still no consensus about precisely what meaning is and how it functions. But communication scholars do seem to agree that it is far more complex than the simple "transfer" of ideas through words and symbols. How our understanding of meaning will evolve over the next hundred years is difficult, if not impossible, to predict. But if history is any indicator, then there is good reason to believe the field will not be dominated by a singular view. And perhaps that is as it should be—that a field with such a diverse array of interests, methods, and commitments is built upon an equally diverse conception of its unifying concept: meaning.

Notes

1 David K. Berlo, *The Process of Communication: An Introduction to Theory and Practice* (New York: Holt, Rinehart and Winston, 1960): 169.

2 Dennis Stampe, "Toward a Grammar of Meaning," *The Philosophical Review* 77, no. 2 (1968): 137.

3 John Stewart, "Concepts of Language and Meaning: A Comparative Study," *Quarterly Journal of Speech* 58, no. 2 (1972): 123–135.

4 Gary Cronkhite, "Perception and Meaning," in *Handbook of Rhetorical and Communication Theory*, ed. Carroll C. Arnold and John Waite Bowers (Boston: Allyn and Bacon, 1984): 51–229.

5 Bryan Crable, "Meaning Theories," in *Encyclopedia of Communication Theory*, ed. Stephen W. Littlejohn and Karen A. Foss (Thousand Oaks, CA: Sage Publications, 2009): 618–623.

6 For an overview of these models, see Cronkhite, "Perception."

7 Martin H. Levinson, "Why 'General Semantics'," *ETC: A Review of General Semantics* 70, no. 1 (2013): 22.

8   S.I. Hayakawa, "The Aims and Tasks of General Semantics: Implications of the Time-Binding Theory (Part I)," *ETC: A Review of General Semantics* 58, no. 1 (2001): 65.

9   S.I. Hayakawa and Alan R. Hayakawa, *Language in Thought and Action*, 5th ed. (New York: Harvest Original, 1991): x.

10 Alfred Korzybski, *Science and Sanity: An Introduction to Non-Aristotelian Systems and General Semantics*, 2nd ed. (Fort Worth, TX: Institute of General Semantics, 2010).

11 Korzybski, *Science and Sanity*, 3.

12 Korzybski, *Science and Sanity*, 50.

13 Hayakawa, *Language in Thought and Action*, 168.

14 Hayakawa, "The Aims," 70.

15 See Irving J. Lee, "General Semantics and Public Speaking," *Quarterly Journal of Speech* 26, no. 4 (1940): 594–604; Raymond H. Barnard, "General Semantics and the Controversial Phases of Speech," *Quarterly Journal of Speech* 26, no. 4 (1940): 602–606; Bower Aly, "The Rhetoric of Semantics," *Quarterly Journal of Speech* 30, no. 1 (1944): 23–31; Elton S. Carter, "Making Progress with Speech," *Today's Speech* 4, no. 2 (1956): 3–6.

16 Stewart, "Concepts," 126.

17 Celeste Condit, "Framing Kenneth Burke: Sad Tragedy or Comic Force?" *Quarterly Journal of Speech* 80, no. 1 (1994): 77–82.

18 Jodie Nicotra, "Dancing Attitudes in Wartime: Kenneth Burke and General Semantics," *Rhetoric Society Quarterly* 39, no. 4 (2009): 331–352.

19 Geraldine E. Forsberg, "Media Ecology and Theology," *Journal of Communication & Religion* 32, no. 1 (2009): 135–156.

20 Diana Coole and Samantha Frost, eds., *New Materialism: Ontology, Agency, and Politics* (Durham, NC: Duke University Press, 2010): 1.

21 Julia Kristeva, *Revolution in Poetic Language*, trans. Margaret Walker (New York: Columbia University Press, 1984): 24.

22 S.K. Keltner, *Kristeva* (Malden, MA: Polity Press, 2011): 22.

23 John Lechte and Mary Zournazi, eds., *The Kristeva Critical Reader* (Edinburgh: Edinburgh University Press, 2003): 219.

24 Julia Kristeva, "Europhilia, Europhobia," in *French Theory in America*, ed. Sylvère Lotringer and Sande Cohen (New York: Routledge, 2001): 33–46, at 37.

25 Kelly Oliver, "Introduction: Kristeva's Revolutions," in *The Portable Kristeva*, updated edition, ed. Kelly Oliver (New York: Columbia University Press, 2002): xi–xxix, at xv.

26 Noëlle McAfee, *Julia Kristeva* (New York: Routledge, 2004): 23.

27 Keltner, *Kristeva*, 36.

28 Mark Johnson, *The Body in the Mind: The Bodily Basis of Meaning, Imagination, and Reason* (Chicago: University of Chicago Press, 1987); Mark Johnson, *The Meaning of The Body: Aesthetics of Human Understanding* (Chicago: University of Chicago Press, 2007); George Lakoff and Mark Johnson, *Philosophy in the Flesh: The Embodied Mind and Its Challenge to Western Thought* (New York: Basic Books, 1999).

29 Johnson, *The Body in the Mind*, xxi–xxii.

30 Robin Melrose, "Sites and Parasites of Meaning: Browning's 'My Last Duchess'," *Language and Literature* 15, no. 2 (2006): 123–140; Jennifer Givhan, "Crossing the Language Barrier: Coalescing the Mind/Body Split and Embracing Kristeva's Semiotic in Margaret Edson's *Wit*," *Women and Language* 32, no. 1 (2009): 77–81; Brian L. Ott and Diane Marie Keeling, "Cinema and Choric Connection: *Lost in Translation* as Sensual Experience," *Quarterly Journal of Speech* 97, no. 4 (2011): 363–386; Marita Gronnvoll and Kristen McCauliff, "Bodies that Shatter: A Rhetoric of Exteriors, the Abject, and Female Suicide Bombers in the 'War on Terrorism'," *Rhetoric Society Quarterly* 43, no. 4 (2013): 335–354.

31 Kevin M. Clark and Donald J. Cunningham, "Metaphors We Teach By: An Embodied Cognitive Analysis of *No Child Left Behind*," *Semiotica* 161 (2006): 265–289; Enrico Monti, "Translating the Metaphors We Live By: Intercultural Negotiations in Conceptual Metaphors," *European Journal of*

English Studies 13, no. 2 (2009): 207–221; Celia V. Harquail and Adelaide Wilcox King, "Constructing Organizational Identity: The Role of Embodied Cognition," *Organization Studies* 31, no. 12 (2010): 1619–1648.

32 The "new rhetoric" is sometimes reductively associated with Chaim Perelman and Lucie Olbrechts-Tyteca, who wrote a well-known treatise on argument by the same name. See C. H. Perelman and L. Olbrechts-Tyteca, *The New Rhetoric: A Treatise on Argumentation*, trans. John Wilkinson and Purcell Weaver (Notre Dame, IN: University of Notre Dame Press, 1969). But in the 1950s and 1960s, the new rhetoric was employed by communication scholars to describe a wide array of developments in philosophy and psychology aimed at broadening rhetoric beyond its classical conception.

33 Marie Hochmuth, "Kenneth Burke and the 'New Rhetoric'," *Quarterly Journal of Speech* 38, no. 2 (1952): 133–144. Marie Hochmuth, "I. A. Richards and the 'New Rhetoric'," *Quarterly Journal of Speech* 44, no. 1 (1958): 1–16.

34 I.A. Richards, *The Philosophy of Rhetoric* (New York: Oxford University Press, 1936): 3.

35 Richards, *The Philosophy*, 55.

36 C.K. Ogden and I.A. Richards, *The Meaning of Meaning: A Study of the Influence of Language upon Thought and of the Science of Symbolism*, 4th ed. rev. (London: Kegan Paul, Trench, Trubner & Co, Ltd., 1936.): 11.

37 John F. Wilson, "Six Rhetorics for Perennial Study," *Today's Speech* 19, no. 1 (1971): 50.

38 Richards, *The Philosophy*, 34.

39 Kenneth Burke, *A Rhetoric of Motives* (Berkeley, CA: University of California Press, 1969): xiv.

40 Burke, *A Rhetoric*, 43.

41 Kenneth Burke, "What Are the Signs of What? A Theory of 'Entitlement'," *Anthropological Linguistics* 4, no. 6 (1962): 7, 5.

42 Kenneth Burke, *Language as Symbolic Action: Essays on Life, Literature, and Method* (Berkeley, CA: University of California Press, 1966): 5.

43 Burke, *Language*, 5.

44 Burke, "What," 6, 15.

45 Burke, "What," 6.

46 Stewart "Concepts," 124, fn. 10.

47 John Stewart, *Language as Articulate Contact: Toward a Post-Semiotic Philosophy of Communication* (SUNY Press, 1995).

48 Danny Steinberg and Leon Jakobovits, eds., *Semantics: An Interdisciplinary Reader in Philosophy, Linguistics, and Psychology* (London: Cambridge University Press, 1971): 8.

49 Ludwig Wittgenstein, *Philosophical Investigations*, 3rd ed., trans. G.E.M. Anscombe (Englewood Cliffs, NJ: Prentice-Hall, 1958): §43.

50 Wittgenstein, *Philosophical Investigations*, §15.

51 William Keith, "Wittgenstein and Communication: From Language to Forms of Life," in *Philosophical Profiles in the Theory of Communication*, ed. Jason Hannan (New York: Peter Lang, 2012): 463–497, 477.

52 Roy Harris, *Language, Saussure and Wittgenstein: How to Play Games With Words* (London: Routledge, 1988): 97.

53 Wittgenstein, *Philosophical Investigations*, §25.

54 Mava Jo Powell, "Conceptions of Literal Meaning in Speech Act Theory," *Philosophy and Rhetoric* 18, no. 3 (1985): 136.

55 J.L. Austin, *How to Do Things with Words* (Oxford: Oxford University Press, 2009): 5.

56 Edward Shirley, "The Impossibility of a Speech Act Theory of Meaning," *Philosophy and Rhetoric* 8, no. 2 (1975): 114.

57 Austin, *How to Do Things with Words*, 121.

58 John Searle, *Expression and Meaning: Studies in the Theory of Speech Acts* (Cambridge: Press Syndicate of the University of Cambridge, 1979): 30.

59 John Searle, *Speech Acts: An Essay in the Philosophy of Language* (Cambridge: Press Syndicate of the University of Cambridge, 1969): 19.

60 Searle, *Speech Acts*, 22.

61 Powell, "Conceptions," 150.

62 Thomas B. Farrell and Thomas S. Frentz, "Communication and Meaning: A Language-Action Synthesis," *Philosophy and Rhetoric* 12, no. 4 (1979): 215–255; Richard Buttny, "The Ascription of Meaning: A Wittgensteinian Perspective," *Quarterly Journal of Speech* 72 (1986): 261–273.

63 Talbot J. Taylor, "A Wittgensteinian Perspective in Linguistics," *Language & Communication* 1, no. 2/3 (1981): 263–271; Paul R. Falzer, "Wittgenstein's Path to Rapprochement," *Philosophy and Rhetoric* 25, no. 1 (1992): 45–58; Giles Gauthier, "The Reality of Journalism, An Exploration Has to Leave the Philosophy of John Searle," *Communication* 23, no. 2 (2004): 150–181; Christian K. Nelson, "If it Sounds Too Good to be True, it is: A Wittgensteinian Approach to the Conflict Literature," *Language & Communication* 21, no. 1 (2001): 1–22; Johanna Hartelius, "Models of Signification and Pedagogy in J. L. Austin, John Searle, and Jacques Derrida," *Review of Communication* 13, no. 1 (2013): 23–47.

64 Marcel Danesi, *The Quest for Meaning: A Guide to Semiotic Theory and Practice* (Toronto: University of Toronto Press, 2012): 11.

65 John Sheriff, *The Fate of Meaning* (Princeton, NJ: Princeton University Press, 1989): xiii–xiv.

66 Terence Hawkes, *Structuralism and Semiotics* (New York: Routledge, 2003): 8.

67 Ferdinand de Saussure, *Course in General Linguistics*, trans. Wade Baskin (New York: Columbia University Press, 1959): 9.

68 Fredric Jameson, *The Prison-House of Language: A Critical Account of Structuralism and Russian Formalism* (Princeton, NJ: Princeton University Press, 1972): 109.

69 Danesi, *Quest*, 10.

70 Sheriff, *Fate*, 55.

71 Danesi, *Quest*, 10.

72 James Hoopes, ed., *Peirce on Signs: Writings on Semiotic by Charles Sanders Peirce* (Chapel Hill, NC: University of North Carolina Press, 1991): 141.

73 Sheriff, *Fate*, 57.

74 Hawkes, *Structuralism*, 106.

75 Roland Barthes, *Elements of Semiology*, trans. Annette Lavers (New York: Hill and Wang, 1968): 41.

76 Barthes, *Elements*, 38.

77 Klaus Krippendorf, *On Communicating Otherness, Meaning, and Information*, ed. Fernando Bermejo (New York: Routledge, 2009): 173.

78 Ernst Cassirer, *An Essay on Man* (New Haven, CT: Yale University Press, 1944): 26.

79 Susanne K. Langer, *Philosophy in a New Key: A Study in the Symbolism of Reason, Rite, and Art* (New York: The New American Library, 1954): 14.

80 Sebastian Luft, "Cassirer's Philosophy of Symbolic Forms: Between Reason and Relativism; a Critical Appraisal," *Marquette University e-Publications@Marquette*, 5.

81 Michael Friedman, "Ernst Cassirer," *The Stanford Encyclopedia of Philosophy*, Spring 2012 Edition, last modified January 21, 2011, accessed January 28, 2014, http://plato.stanford.edu/archives/spr2011/entries/cassirer/.

82 Langer, *Philosophy*, 55.

83 Langer, *Philosophy*, 87.

84 Langer, *Philosophy*, 92.

85 Stewart, "Concepts," 126.

86 Joddy Murray, *Non-discursive Rhetoric: Image and Affect in Multimodal Composition* (New York: SUNY Press, 2009): 75.

87 Charles W. Morris, *Signs, Language and Behavior* (New York: Prentice-Hall, 1946).

88 George Herbert Mead, *Mind, Self, and Society: From the Standpoint of a Social Behaviorist*, ed. Charles W. Morris (Chicago: University of Chicago Press, 1934): 81.

89 Herbert Blumer, *Symbolic Interactionism: Perspective and Method* (Berkeley, CA: University of California Press, 1969): 2.

90 Blumer, *Symbolic Interactionism*, 2.
91 Blumer, *Symbolic Interactionism*, 2.
92 Blumer, *Symbolic Interactionism*, 5.
93 Blumer, *Symbolic Interactionism*, 3.
94 Stephen W. Littlejohn, "Symbolic Interactionism as an Approach to the Study of Human Communication," *Quarterly Journal of Speech* 63, no. 1 (1977): 84–91.
95 Norman K. Denzin, ed., *Studies in Symbolic Interaction, Volume 1* (Greenwich, CT: JAI Press, 1978): vii.
96 Lester Thonssen and A. Craig Baird, *Speech Criticism: The Development of Standards for Rhetorical Appraisal* (New York: The Ronald Press Company, 1948): 6.

References

Aly, Bower. "The Rhetoric of Semantics." *Quarterly Journal of Speech* 30, no. 1 (1944): 23–31.

Austin, J.L. *How to Do Things with Words*. Oxford: Oxford University Press, 2009.

Barnard, Raymond H. "General Semantics and the Controversial Phases of Speech." *Quarterly Journal of Speech* 26, no. 4 (1940): 602–606.

Barthes, Roland. *Elements of Semiology*. Translated by Annette Lavers. New York: Hill and Wang, 1968.

Berlo, David K. *The Process of Communication: An Introduction to Theory and Practice*. New York: Holt, Rinehart and Winston, 1960.

Blumer, Herbert. *Symbolic Interactionism: Perspective and Method*. Berkeley, CA: University of California Press, 1969.

Burke, Kenneth. *Language as Symbolic Action: Essays on Life, Literature, and Method*. Berkeley, CA: University of California Press, 1966.

——. "(Nonsymbolic) Motion/(Symbolic) Action." *Critical Inquiry* 4, no. 4 (1978): 809–838.

——. *A Rhetoric of Motives*. Berkeley, CA: University of California Press, 1969.

——. "What Are the Signs of What? A Theory of 'Entitlement'." *Anthropological Linguistics* 4, no. 6 (1962): 1–23.

Buttny, Richard. "The Ascription of Meaning: A Wittgensteinian Perspective." *Quarterly Journal of Speech* 72 (1986): 261–273.

Carter, Elton S. "Making Progress with Speech." *Today's Speech* 4, no. 2 (1956): 3–6.

Cassirer, Ernst. *An Essay on Man*. New Haven: Yale University Press, 1944.

Clark, Kevin M. and Donald J. Cunningham. "Metaphors We Teach By: An Embodied Cognitive Analysis of *No Child Left Behind*." *Semiotica* 161 (2006): 265–289.

Coole, Diana and Samantha Frost, eds. *New Materialism: Ontology, Agency, and Politics*. Durham, NC: Duke University Press, 2010.

Condit, Celeste. "Framing Kenneth Burke: Sad Tragedy or Comic Force?" *Quarterly Journal of Speech* 80, no. 1 (1994): 77–82.

Crable, Bryan. "Meaning Theories." In *Encyclopedia of Communication Theory*, edited by Stephen W. Littlejohn and Karen A. Foss, 618–623. Thousand Oaks, CA: Sage Publications, 2009.

Cronkhite, Gary. "Perception and Meaning." In *Handbook of Rhetorical and Communication Theory*, edited by Carroll C. Arnold and John Waite Bowers, 51–229. Boston: Allyn and Bacon, 1984.

Danesi, Marcel. *The Quest for Meaning: A Guide to Semiotic Theory and Practice*. Toronto: University of Toronto Press, 2012.

Denzin, Norman K., ed. *Studies in Symbolic Interaction, Volume 1*. Greenwich, CT: JAI Press, 1978.

Falzer, Paul R. "Wittgenstein's Path to Rapprochement." *Philosophy and Rhetoric* 25, no. 1 (1992): 45–58.

Farrell, Thomas B. and Thomas S. Frentz. "Communication and Meaning: A Language-Action Synthesis." *Philosophy and Rhetoric* 12, no. 4 (1979): 215–255.

Forsberg, Geraldine E. "Media Ecology and Theology." *Journal of Communication and Religion* 32, no. 1 (2009): 135–156.

Friedman, Michael. "Ernst Cassirer." *The Stanford Encyclopedia of Philosophy*. Last modified January 21, 2011. http://plato.stanford.edu/archives/spr2011/entries/cassirer/.

Gauthier, Giles. "The Reality of Journalism: An Exploration Has to Leave the Philosophy of John Searle." *Communication* 23, no. 2 (2004): 150–181.

Givhan, Jennifer. "Crossing the Language Barrier: Coalescing the Mind/Body Split and Embracing Kristeva's Semiotic in Margaret Edson's *Wit*." *Women and Language* 32, no. 1 (2009): 77–81.

Gronnvoll, Marita and Kristen McCauliff. "Bodies that Shatter: A Rhetoric of Exteriors, the Abject, and Female Suicide Bombers in the "War on Terrorism'." *Rhetoric Society Quarterly* 43, no. 4 (2013): 335–354.

Hardy, William G. "The Philosophy of Modern Semantics." *Quarterly Journal of Speech* 30, no. 2 (1944): 191–199.

Harquail, Celia V. and Adelaide Wilcox King. "Constructing Organizational Identity: The Role of Embodied Cognition." *Organization Studies* 31, no. 12 (2010): 1619–1648.

Harris, Roy. *Language, Saussure and Wittgenstein: How to Play Games With Words*. London: Routledge, 1988.

Hartelius, Johanna. "Models of Signification and Pedagogy in J. L. Austin, John Searle, and Jacques Derrida." *Review of Communication* 13, no. 1 (2013): 23–47.

Hawkes, Terence. *Structuralism and Semiotics*. New York: Routledge, 2003.

Hayakawa, S.I. "The Aims and Tasks of General Semantics: Implications of the Time-Binding Theory (Part I)." *ETC: A Review of General Semantics* 58, no. 1 (2001): 64–73.

——. "General Semantics and Propaganda." *The Public Opinion Quarterly* 3, no. 2 (1939): 197–208.

——. *Language in Thought and Action*. New York: Harcourt, Brace & World, 1949.

Hayakawa, S.I. and Alan R. Hayakawa, *Language in Thought and Action*. 5th ed. New York: Harvest Original, 1991.

Hochmuth, Marie. "I. A. Richards and the 'New Rhetoric'." *Quarterly Journal of Speech* 44, no. 1 (1958): 1–16.

——. "Kenneth Burke and the 'New Rhetoric'." *Quarterly Journal of Speech* 38, no. 2 (1952): 133–144.

Hoopes, James, ed. *Peirce on Signs: Writings on Semiotic by Charles Sanders Peirce*. Chapel Hill, NC: University of North Carolina Press, 1991.

Jameson, Fredric. *The Prison-House of Language: A Critical Account of Structuralism and Russian Formalism*. Princeton, NJ: Princeton University Press, 1972.

Johnson, Mark. *The Body in the Mind: The Bodily Basis of Meaning, Imagination, and Reason*. Chicago: University of Chicago Press, 1987.

——. *The Meaning of The Body: Aesthetics of Human Understanding*. Chicago: University of Chicago Press, 2007.

Keith, William. "Wittgenstein and Communication: From Language to Forms of Life." In *Philosophical Profiles in the Theory of Communication*, edited by Jason Hannan, 463–497. New York: Peter Lang, 2012.

Keltner, S.K. *Kristeva*. Malden, MA: Polity Press, 2011.

Korzybski, Alfred. *Science and Sanity: An Introduction to Non-Aristotelian Systems and General Semantics*. 2nd ed. Fort Worth, TX: Institute of General Semantics, 2010.

Krippendorf, Klaus. *On Communicating Otherness, Meaning, and Information*. Edited by Fernando Bermejo. New York: Routledge, 2009.

Kristeva, Julia. "Europhilia, Europhobia." In *French Theory in America*, edited by Sylvère Lotringer and Sande Cohen, 33–46. New York: Routledge, 2001.

——. *Revolution in Poetic Language*. Translated by Margaret Walker. New York: Columbia University Press, 1984.

Lakoff, George and Mark Johnson. *Philosophy in the Flesh: The Embodied Mind and Its Challenge to Western Thought*. New York: Basic Books, 1999.

Langer, Susanne K. "The Origins of Speech and Its Communicative Function." *Quarterly Journal of Speech* 46, no. 2 (1960): 121–135.

——. *Philosophy in a New Key: A Study in the Symbolism of Reason, Rite, and Art*. New York: The New American Library, 1954.

Lechte, John, and Mary Zournazi, eds. *The Kristeva Critical Reader*. Edinburgh: Edinburgh University Press, 2003.

Lee, Irving J. "General Semantics and Public Speaking." *Quarterly Journal of Speech* 26, no. 4 (1940): 594–604.

Levinson, Martin H. "Why 'General Semantics'." *ETC: A Review of General Semantics* 70, no. 1 (2013): 22–24.

Littlejohn, Stephen W. "Symbolic Interactionism as an Approach to the Study of Human Communication." *Quarterly Journal of Speech* 63, no. 1 (1977): 84–91.

Luft, Sebastian. "Cassirer's Philosophy of Symbolic Forms: Between Reason and Relativism; a Critical Appraisal." *Marquette University e-Publications@Marquette*.

McAfee, Noëlle. *Julia Kristeva*. New York: Routledge, 2004.

Mead, George Herbert. *Mind, Self, and Society: From the Standpoint of a Social Behaviorist*. Edited by Charles W. Morris. Chicago: University of Chicago Press, 1934.

Melrose, Robin. "Sites and Parasites of Meaning: Browning's 'My Last Duchess'." *Language and Literature* 15, no. 2 (2006): 123–140.

Monti, Enrico. "Translating the Metaphors We Live By: Intercultural Negotiations in Conceptual Metaphors." *European Journal of English Studies* 13, no. 2 (2009): 207–221.

Morris, Charles W. *Signs, Language and Behavior*. New York: Prentice-Hall, 1946.

Murray, Joddy. *Non-discursive Rhetoric: Image and Affect in Multimodal Composition*. New York: SUNY Press, 2009.

Nelson, Christian K. "If it Sounds Too Good to be True, it is: A Wittgensteinian Approach to the Conflict Literature." *Language & Communication* 21, no. 1 (2001): 1–22.

Nicotra, Jodie. "Dancing Attitudes in Wartime: Kenneth Burke and General Semantics." *Rhetoric Society Quarterly* 39, no. 4 (2009): 331–352.

Ogden, C.K. and I.A. Richards. *The Meaning of Meaning: A Study of the Influence of Language upon Thought and of the Science of Symbolism*. 4th ed. rev. London: Kegan Paul, Trench, Trubner, 1936.

Oliver, Kelly. "Introduction: Kristeva's Revolutions." In *The Portable Kristeva*, edited by Kelly Oliver, xi–xxix. New York: Columbia University Press, 2002.

Ott, Brian L. and Diane Marie Keeling. "Cinema and Choric Connection: *Lost in Translation* as Sensual Experience." *Quarterly Journal of Speech* 97, no. 4 (2011): 363–386.

Perelman, C.H. and L. Olbrechts-Tyteca. *The New Rhetoric: A Treatise on Argumentation*. Translated by John Wilkinson and Purcell Weaver. Notre Dame, IN: University of Notre Dame Press, 1969.

Powell, Mava Jo. "Conceptions of Literal Meaning in Speech Act Theory." *Philosophy and Rhetoric* 18, no. 3 (1985): 133–157.

Richards, I.A. *The Philosophy of Rhetoric*. New York: Oxford University Press, 1936.

Saussure, Ferdinand de. *Course in General Linguistics*. Translated by Wade Baskin. New York: Columbia University Press, 1959.

Searle, John. *Expression and Meaning: Studies in the Theory of Speech Acts*. Cambridge: Press Syndicate of the University of Cambridge, 1979.

——. *Speech Acts: An Essay in the Philosophy of Language*. Cambridge: Press Syndicate of the University of Cambridge, 1969.

Sheriff, John. *The Fate of Meaning*. Princeton, NJ: Princeton University Press, 1989.

Shirley, Edward. "The Impossibility of a Speech Act Theory of Meaning." *Philosophy and Rhetoric* 8, no. 2 (1975): 114–122.

Stampe, Dennis. "Toward a Grammar of Meaning." *The Philosophical Review* 77, no. 2 (1968): 137–174.

Steinberg, Danny, and Leon Jakobovits, eds. *Semantics: An Interdisciplinary Reader in Philosophy, Linguistics, and Psychology*. London: Cambridge University Press, 1971.

Stewart, John. "Concepts of Language and Meaning: A Comparative Study." *Quarterly Journal of Speech* 58, no. 2 (1972): 123–135.

——. *Language as Articulate Contact: Toward a Post-Semiotic Philosophy of Communication*. Albany: SUNY Press, 1995.

Taylor, Talbot J. "A Wittgensteinian Perspective in Linguistics." *Language & Communication* 1, no. 2/3 (1981): 263–271.

Thonssen, Lester and A. Craig Baird. *Speech Criticism: The Development of Standards for Rhetorical Appraisal.* New York: The Ronald Press Company, 1948.

Wilson, John F. "Six Rhetorics for Perennial Study." *Today's Speech* 19, no. 1 (1971): 49–54.

Wittgenstein, Ludwig. *Philosophical Investigations.* 3rd ed. Translated by G.E.M. Anscombe. Englewood Cliffs, NJ: Prentice-Hall, 1958.

11.

COMMUNICATIVE MEETING

From Pangloss to Tenacious Hope

Ronald C. Arnett

Existentially, authentic communication issues do not emerge within a vacuum or in the abstract, but rather arise from attentive meeting of questions and demands that shape a given historical moment, prompting necessity of response. Communication issues exist before and after their most visible points of entry into the public domain; their identity becomes transparent when a historical moment saturated with conversation about them emerges. A public historical welcome of communicative meeting ensued in the 1960s, just as free speech was entwined with the events of World War II and small group communication leadership studies organically emerged during the Korean War. The 1960s ushered forth the public identity of communicative meeting; this communication reality was not, of course, created in the 1960s, but it was disciplined into daily consciousness in that era.

    This chapter elucidates a story about the continuing evolution of diverse conceptions of communicative meeting, foregrounding the creative heart of the discipline of Communication Studies and the vital ethical belief that relationships and others matter. I employ "communicative meeting" as an umbrella term encompassing diverse and disparate understandings of relational communication, and as a bridge concept in order to link a vast array of relational communication approaches. The key assumptions that undergird communicative meeting are relational contact via understanding of and responsibility for another and the basic existential fact that relationships matter. Communicative meeting is a prescriptive ethical stance resistive to provincial self-preoccupation within an individualistic culture. Communicative meeting is central to human sociality and antithetical to relational colonization, possession, and control. I conceive this term in response to Richard Johannesen's stress on freedom and responsibility.[1] Communicative meeting assumes relational freedom anchored in responsibility for an Other and the relationship. Additionally, the prescriptive nature of communicative meeting is consistent with the ethics of responsibility called forth by Emmanuel Levinas and illustrative of the scholarly corpus of Michael Hyde.[2] Communicative meeting works as an everyday counter to impersonal systems and policies void of relational responsibility. Communicative meeting is a "unity of contraries," consisting of unremarkable everyday communicative action and an extraordinary communicative ethic of social resistance.[3] This term, as I conceive it, has roots in local American and Western soil, emanating from resistance and serving as a rejoinder to concrete impersonal social realities.

The Performance of Everyday Defiance

During the 1960s, communicative meeting offered an oasis in the face of oppressive social realities of war in Vietnam and Jim Crow laws. Turning the world upside down, leaving Vietnam, and empowering the Civil Rights movements for African Americans and for women required, of course, multiple forms of communicative influence and power. This chapter suggests, however, that one component of the ethical engine that fueled this transformation lived within a communicative assumption and practice of everyday defiance: the Other and relationships matter. The notion of communicative meeting is far from neutral; it is a relational rejection of processes, systems, and structures that forget the fundamental importance of attentiveness to the Other and accompanying relational responsibility. The praxis of communicative meeting manifested itself in scorn against complacent "blind loyalty,"[4] which initiated social rebellion in response to parallel social conditions of impersonal attentiveness/injustice and increasing prosperity.[5] Imposed and impersonal demands defined an era in which questioning was made *plus facile* in a historical moment ever-distant from the pervasive poverty of the Great Depression (1929–1939) that haunted a nation into the throes of World War II (1939–1945).

The 1960s heritage of communicative meeting commenced with a desire for social change that vacillated between a Panglossian optimism and tenacious hope. Optimism is the natural attitude of a consumer society, assuming the postulation that the world will turn in accordance with one's own expectations and demands. Optimism is a central ingredient in the over-reach of therapeutic language into political life, thoughtfully articulated by Dana Cloud in *Control and Consolation in American Culture and Politics: Rhetoric of Therapy*[6] and social critics such as Richard Sennett and Christopher Lasch.[7]

Tenacious hope, on the other hand, lives in the actions of those who do not cease laboring and struggling for change—no matter the obstacles or difficulties. Tenacious hope as tied to communicative meeting is manifest in one of my favorite quotations from Ernest Boyer, president of the Carnegie Foundation for the Advancement of Teaching. When asked about the "crucial ingredient for student success," he offered the following response: "A parent, friend, teacher, or someone significant offering a sense of hope that the young person is worthwhile and can and will succeed."[8] Tenacious hope tied to communicative meeting engages in a labor of care for the Other, explicated in *The Communicative Relationship Between Dialogue and Care* by Marie Baker-Ohler and Annette Holba.[9]

I contend that essential coordinates for Communication Studies are attentiveness to embryonic cultural and social questions and creative scholarly responses. The field of communication has historically augmented its relational identity through attentiveness to emergent questions and issues that shape a given historical moment, which is then followed by creative responses.[10] Disciplinary diversity naturally follows multiplicity, which yields differences in conceptual, methodological, and theoretical communication responses to historical questions and concerns. The diversity of scholarly responses in the study and practice of communication has historically been accompanied by a democratic bent within the communication field. The responsive nature of Communication Studies and its alignment with local soil privileged democracy as a practical counter against hegemonic demands insisting on uniform response and ideological purity.[11]

Communication Studies has originative ties to classical discourses of policy argument and political defense.[12] This rhetorical tradition eschews pristine truth, uniting content/evidence with the reality of audience opinion. Sociality of the human condition via the interplay of ideas and audience moved Hannah Arendt to privilege opinion over pristine truth as the heart of a vibrant public domain resistive to a universal, a singular view of truth.[13] This standpoint rejects hegemony, whether in the guise of totalitarianism, colonialism, or corporatization of everyday life.[14] The value-laden nature of this position is illustrated by Thomas Nilsen's emphasis on an "ethic of choice" and the communication ethics and dialogue scholarship of Johannesen.[15] Communicative choice links communication and journalism, valuing the function of the "fourth estate" as the guardian of decision-making choice.[16] Additionally, the connection between free speech and informed choice is a heritage of the communication field, personified by Franklin Haiman's scholarly contributions, such as "The Rhetoric of the Streets: Some Legal and Ethical Considerations."[17]

The notion of difference and the choice of a situated/limited communicative agent are reflected in a post-modern championing of difference, which rejects universal certainty.[18] This perspective advocated the pragmatic return of rhetoric and rejected hegemonic control of ideas and interpretive limits.[19] Andrew King, in a significant edited volume on post-modernity, *Postmodern Political Communication: The Fringe Challenges the Center*, offers a short history of "post-modern." He details renewed attention to community, to fringe groups, to awareness of a loss of center, and to the emergence of a new rhetoric, a "third sophistic," that embraces a "decentered rhetoric" and shuns "any particular institutional commitments."[20] This orientation jettisons universal and monolithic assertions, uniting choice with embedded understanding and the temporality of truth claims.

Modernity, on the other hand, seeks to "freeze social reality," as stated by Mats Alvesson and Stanley Deetz, permitting change within a given limited perspective, tradition, or paradigm.[21] Modernity embraces a "secular trinity of efficiency, individual autonomy, and progress."[22] The amalgamating factor of this secular trinity is a contempt for messiness. Efficiency is paradigmatically bound to a given outcome. Progress in everyday discourse assumes that new is better, a position contrary to Immanuel Kant's conception of the term.[23] Finally, individual autonomy, understood as a relational abstraction, walks above the messiness of relational life and communicative meeting. Modernity's possessive limits even affect democratic discourse when "democracy and diversity" are used to "impos[e] homogeneity"; such an effort coopts difference and choice and embraces marketing and branding. The danger of imposed democracy via marketing is articulated in Bilijana Scott's "Multiculturalism for the Masses: Social

Advertising and Public Diplomacy Post-9/11."[24] Genuine democracy finds nourishment and reason for its importance in the realm of messiness.

My contention is that the field of communication is at its best when it remains a champion of the frayed and the unkempt, a home for public communicative deliberation that attends to others and relationships with public evidence. From the notion of self-talk (internal dialogue of choice) of Charles Brown and Paul Keller to the invitational rhetoric of Sonja Foss and Cindy Griffin, relationships and choice matter.[25] The construct of communicative meeting forges an identity with depth and breadth, beginning as a relational alternative to impersonal and imposing authority structures. The public origin of communicative meeting was nourished by a 1960s milieu constituted by the interplay of wealth, youth, and social contention,[26] and its influence continues. Such work still energizes this field of study. Scholars such as Josina Makau, Lawrence Frey, Charles Morris, Lester Olson, Cloud, and Brenda Allen unmask and de-privilege mindless adherence to authority that fails to engage in relational responsibility.[27] The following steps of this chapter explicate communicative meeting as a value-laden presumption: relationships matter, calling forth responsibility. First, I proffer communicative meeting as story, a hermeneutic frame that guides this investigative understanding of the ever-changing conception of communicative meeting. Then through a pragmatically tempered cosmopolitan perspective I explore the interplay of local conviction and an enlarged mentality willing to learn from difference. Next, through reviewing difference in action I examine significant summary essays related to what I term *communicative meeting*, which announce differing images of communicative meeting. The concluding section, on the gift of rival versions, underscores the creative importance of competing and, at times, incommensurable understandings of communicative meeting. The significance of communicative meeting finds public evidence in communication scholarship that displays choice, relationship, and responsibility in communicative engagement from a diversity of theoretical perspectives.

Communicative Meeting as Story

Before I begin my story of response to impersonal structures of authority, I offer another version, thoughtfully generated by William Rawlins, which connects the expansion of relational communication with responsiveness to the historical moment. In "Stalking Interpersonal Communication Effectiveness: Social, Individual, or Situational Integration?" Rawlins reviews the insights of Raymond Howes and Robert Oliver and their investigation of "conversation."[28] Rawlins stressed the general semantics work of Alfred Korzybski that united practical utility and spoken interaction between persons, emphasizing a 1940s accent on "communication effectiveness" through appropriate employment of "interactional means." Rawlins noted contrasting views on the goals and methods of relational communication in three different historical periods:

(1) social integration (1940s–1960s);
(2) individual integration (1950s–1980s); and
(3) situational integration (1970s–1980s).[29]

Rawlins cited Elwood Murray's work on "efficacious communicators" as a reflection of the importance of the social dimension of communicative life, which aligned with Mary Parker Follett's fusing of communication with "decision-making."[30] Rawlins sketched this strand of scholarship as "communal" with a "social" focus, which gave way to a personal view of interpersonal communication, moving from social conformism to "individual integration." Dean Barnlund, Johannesen, Kenneth Williams, John Stewart, W. Barnett Pearce, John Poulakos, and Charles Wise led this scholarship, stressing a "humanizing" and "individualized self," which was followed by an emphasis on "situational integration."[31] Personal navigation of an increasingly complex set of standards set by social groups and individuals propelled the objective of situational integration.[32] Rawlins provides us with an initial story about interpersonal health that shifted from the social to a humanized self to an emphasis on communicative competence attentive to social integration led by James McCroskey.[33]

In a moment of narrative and virtue contention, an era termed post-modern by many, the rhetorical interruption of the 1960s afforded communicative meeting a sense of Kantian "publicity"[34] through multiple relational movements, such as humanistic psychology, William Glasser's *Schools without Failure*,[35] and the liberation theology of Gustavo Gutiérrez.[36] The discipline of communication was equally responsive, represented by Keller and Brown's *Monologue to Dialogue: An Exploration of Interpersonal Communication* and "An Interpersonal Ethic for Communication."[37] Brown and Keller pointed to the historical necessity of communication as relational connections between and among persons.

The 1960s initiated a disparate and contradictory set of directions in communicative meeting that continues. In the 2011 *Handbook of Interpersonal Communication*, Mark Knapp and John Daly conclude their introductory chapter by citing a 1994 essay by Art Bochner: "A singularly 'correct' perspective, he argues, does not exist, because natural events and processes lend themselves to a multiplicity of descriptions depending on the individual's point of view."[38] I suggest that when and if solidified agreement surfaces, the inventiveness of this area of study will rest dormant until paradigmatic differences once again jar possibilities for renewed life within the creative heart of the story of communicative meeting.

Arendt stated that "behavior" must be vetted within a story in order to be understood as "action" capable of conveying public meaning.[39] Communicative meeting, understood as a story, begins with attentiveness to the demands for an alternative to impersonal structures that gave rise to a kaleidoscope of communicative responses. This perspective assumes that there is no single conception of relational communication, no one story, no one unassailable covering law,[40] no single formulation of communicative meeting that trumps immemorially.

Karen Tracy, in her use of "reasonable hostility," and Pearce and Littlejohn, in their work on moral conflict, explicate the dangers of singularity of perspective.[41] This story's claim of breadth and diversity in relational discourse follows the empirical common sense of the Scottish Enlightenment.[42] The stress on difference is not contrived, but is descriptive of a historical moment resistive to demands for isomorphic agreement.

A Pragmatically Tempered Cosmopolitan Perspective

A story-centered conception of communicative meeting can be understood through the interpretive lens of philosophical hermeneutics, which Stewart illuminated in his work on Hans-Georg Gadamer and dialogue.[43] The obligation in this interpretive perspective is threefold:

(1) begin with public confession of a particular interpretative bias;[44]
(2) elucidate the text or story under study; and
(3) render a public account of possibilities and implications.

Such interpretative scholarship is responsive to questions that shape the particularity of a historical moment. The interpretative scholarship of Gadamer and Paul Ricoeur[45] privileges questions that give identity to a unique historical moment and the unique bias or prejudice, or the standpoint, one takes to a given communicative activity.[46] Gadamer contended that without bias of perspective, novel communicative insights would cease.[47]

Nancy Harding, Jackie Ford, and Marianna Fotaki explicate the importance of contrasting perspectives with reference to Judith Butler's analysis of *Antigone*.[48] Butler exposed interpretative positions as dependent upon "contingent social norms."[49] Interpretive voices announce from a position. The content of our assumptions guides and shapes how we meet the world—what matters is not just the events before us, but the interplay between our postulations and existential events.

The Gadamer/Habermas debate centered on contrasting readings of tradition;[50] however, both scholars concurred that "interest" and "bias" are central to the human condition and integral to the interpretive process. Their argument concentrates on two contrasting conceptions of tradition. Habermas rejects the bias of tradition, while Gadamer understands tradition as a source of creative prejudice that spawns new insight. Habermas is currently the key representative of the Frankfurt School, which began in 1923 at the Institute of Social Research at Frankfurt University with the objective of developing a critical theory in the form of a cultural Marxism. When the Nazis came to power in 1933, much of the creative energy of the school shifted to the United States. Habermas, on the other hand, was not old enough to fight during World War II, but he, like many, was deeply affected by the war. He witnessed Nazi fixation with local soil; the Nazis turned tradition into an oppressive weapon. Habermas's scholarship then rejected tradition as he embraced a discourse ethic that relied upon a collective reasoning unresponsive to the bias of a single perspective. Habermas recognizes the fact that discourse embodies interests; using Gadamer's terms, Habermas suggests that bias and prejudice account for what matters to a communicator.

Gadamer, in contrast, understands traditions as vital in generating new insight. He does not seek to eliminate bias, but rather to infuse prejudice within the very process of interpretive understanding.[51] For Gadamer, bias and prejudice of traditions fuel contrary insights. Gadamer, unlike Habermas, does not work from a universal position. He links tradition(s) to bias, while recognizing the necessity of rhetoric in sorting out contrasting assumptions/prejudices. John Arthos stresses the communal, social, and creative use of tradition that Gadamer adopted. Arthos states that Gadamer emphasized an "ethical dimension of *sensus communis*[, which] takes center stage [in Gadamer's project]."[52] A Gadamerian interpretive perspective examines the interaction between bias of a given tradition and a specific historical moment, while a Habermasian viewpoint explores the "interests" that drive our interpretive positions.[53] In both cases, bias or interests guide conversation. Habermas unmasks interests. Gadamer embraces the reality of bias as a pragmatic commonplace, using rhetoric to sort through contrasting traditions. Arthos, in a number of essays and book projects, explicates the intimate link between Gadamer's hermeneutics and rhetoric.[54] Both bias and interests matter in interpretation and in this framing of a story about communicative meeting. This perspective is central to Pat J. Gehrke's *The Ethics and Politics of Speech*;[55] he traces the historical development of the discipline of communication, suggesting a theme of creative responsiveness to changing historical moments. Shifting historical conditions can be understood as a fluctuation of interests on what "matters."[56]

This interpretive story's reliance on Gadamer in the exposition of communicative meeting is apropos in light of Stewart's interest in Gadamer's work.[57] Stewart popularized multiple senses of what I call communicative meeting. His perspective rests alongside the work of Leslie Baxter, Virginia Richmond, Charles Berger, Julia Wood, Ronald Jackson, McCroskey, Morris, Bochner, Michael Roloff, and Lynn Turner—to name but a few. This diverse ensemble suggests minimalist agreement and incommensurability. Thomas Kuhn and Paul Feyerabend brought incommensurability into the vernacular,[58] announcing the reality of multiple paradigms or focused presuppositions that often remain at irreconcilable odds. Contrasting points of assumptive origin make agreement and understanding potentially impossible. Their insights are tied to a world of difference, which has a long and eventful history.

For instance, in the fourth century B.C.E., Diogenes the Cynic disdained the power of conventional standards. He championed the reality of multiple perspectives and famously claimed citizenship with the world, not his local home, Sinope, along the southern coast of the Black Sea. Additionally, Kant is known as an eighteenth-century proponent of cosmopolitanism, with its connection to a global community. Pauline Kleingeld, in *Kant and Cosmopolitanism: The Philosophical Ideal of World Citizenship*, offers a further textured account of Kant's position; she claims that Kant did not reject all local attachments and was contextually attentive.[59] More recently Kwame Anthony Appiah brought cosmopolitanism to the public table once again with an emphasis on learning and obligation to the Other.[60] The common key to cosmopolitanism is the recognition of multiple perspectives and a willingness to learn about them, accompanied by skepticism about local attachments.

Kleingeld's assertion that Kant refused to ignore the local resonates with the voice of Stephen Toulmin, who warned against certainty and the disregard of local roots.[61] I make a similar case about the importance of the local in an essay in *Communication Ethics: Cosmopolitanism and Provinciality*.[62] Pearce offers a pragmatic understanding of cosmopolitanism. He both accepted the inevitability of bias from the local and stated that "cosmopolitan communicators [turn] to the possibility of coordinating among them [differing local and translocal perspectives]."[63] Pearce's perspective points to the reality of difference, the recognition of incommensurability, and a pragmatic hope that one can learn from difference as one negotiates and coordinates communication amidst such realities. Pearce gestures toward what I now term a *pragmatically tempered cosmopolitan attentiveness and response.* Such a perspective is attentive to Diogenes in the fourth century, Kant in the eighteenth century, and Appiah in the twenty-first century. Each sought a counter to blind loyalty, to unreflective provinciality. They recognized the inevitability of bias as part of the human condition.

A *pragmatically tempered cosmopolitanism* unites diversity of perspectives with the vitality and energy of single-minded conviction. Milton Rokeach described such passion, defining certainty as the uniting of conviction with openness.[64] This position rests at the heart of dialogue—one works from a ground of interests (a provinciality) with openness to learn from diverse positions (a cosmopolitanism).[65] A pragmatically tempered cosmopolitan perspective suggests a creative wariness that dwells between the local and an "enlarged mentality," acknowledging that as one learns from contrary perspectives, one simultaneously can affirm one's own.[66] In the construction of a story about communicative meeting composed of a non-provincial depiction of differing particulars, affirmation of contrasting perspectives assumes ongoing disagreement and conflict, which counters insular, self-righteous assurance.

A pragmatically tempered cosmopolitan perspective provides a practical *bienvenue* for further paradigmatic explication, offering a heuristic welcome for further inquiry. Such a perspective embraces a tenacious hope that demands courage to continue to meet and learn from difference. I differentiate two sanguine metaphors: "optimism" and "hope."[67] Optimism is a product of a consumerist/narcissist culture that demands conformity to *my* idiosyncratic wishes. On the other hand, a tenacious hope recognizes the demanding reality that emerges between communicative agent and existence. A pragmatically tempered cosmopolitan story of communicative meeting acknowledges the importance of devotion to a given perspective and is accompanied by a tenacious hope that assumes responsibility for acknowledging the reality of multiple perspectives and learning from them. This reading of communicative meeting conceptualizes a drama without end. A pragmatically tempered cosmopolitan position understands Heraclitus's "unity in opposites" and Martin Buber's "unity of contraries" as suggesting that under-standability within the human condition rests with the difference of either and or, not either/or.[68]

Communicative Meeting: Reviewing Difference in Action

This section examines the extraordinary diversity of scholarly inquiry tied to what I term communicative meeting. I have foregone the convention of dividing this review into distinct categories of quantitative, qualitative, and interpretive studies. I am interested in the conversation generated between and among perspectives, which yields an impressionistic picture of the diversity of orientations and insights within this sizeable area of study. My objective is to reveal the insightful signification that has emerged and continues to emerge from the messiness of a responsive field of study. As stated above, my contention is that the field of communication is at its best when it remains a champion of the frayed and the unkempt.

This story of communicative meeting begins by recognizing that content matters and requires careful and thoughtful attention. Our field has generated a plethora of substantive differences in assumptions about methods of studying and meanings of communicative meeting. For instance, in 1975, Gerald Miller and Mark Steinberg's *Between People: A New Analysis of Interpersonal Communication* provided insight into the embryonic beginnings of relational communication, demarcating the relational term "interpersonal communication" from "non-interpersonal communication" with the common link being "prediction."[69] These differing views of communication pivot on distinctive predictive sources:

(1) non-interpersonal uses "cultural" and "sociological" data; and
(2) interpersonal relies upon "psychological" information.[70]

This early work suggests the importance of prediction and reliance upon a psychological inclination.

Miller and Steinberg remind us of the seminal importance of psychology in the early stages of relational discourse, providing a focus on prediction and issuing a call for increasingly sophisticated scientific methodology. Donald Cushman and Thomas Florence, in "The Development of Interpersonal Communication Theory," reprised the scientific rigor refrain as they stressed the importance of relational "coordination" of human activity.[71] Scientific clarity sought predictability with quantitative experimental investigation that countered both rhetorical and humanistic perspectives.

In a 1977 review, Berger summarized swings in the field of communication, highlighting the shift from studies of small groups and persuasion of the 1940s to the early 1960s with a move toward "interpersonal-like" settings connected to the humanistic psychology movement, which then matured into rule-based research attentive to the particular and the contextual.[72] Miller, in 1978, advocated a turn to "law-governed" and, when necessary, "rule-governed" perspectives.[73] The importance of theory increased as social science research pursued causes for communicative behavior.

Two decades later, Berger outlined the results of continuing theoretical sophistication in the area of communicative meeting. In "Interpersonal Communication: Theoretical Perspective, Future Prospects," he provided a short historical introduction of the perspectives in this area of study, beginning with the encounter group and ending with mediated social interaction.[74] Berger then outlined six categories of theories. First, "Interpersonal Adaptation Theories" examine interpersonal adjustments and self-disclosure in close relationships with an increasing emphasis on "functional complexes of behaviors," not isolated behaviors[75]

Second, "Message Production Theories" began with constructivism of the 1980s, which "devised hierarchical coding schemes . . . to assess [how] messages take into account the goals of those for whom they are intended" and continued with a focus on "cognitive-rule based inquiry" and models.[76] Berger recommended examination of choice, multiple rules, imagination, and rumination about past and future social interactions.

Third, Claude Shannon and Warren Weaver worked mathematically to frame Information Theory, followed by extensive work by Berger and Calabrese in the 1970s on Uncertainty Reduction Theory. In 1986, Michael Sunnafrank introduced Predicted Outcome Value and, in 1992, Austin Babrow followed with Problematic Integration Theory, both complicating the role of uncertainty as a consistent goal or aim.[77] Babrow introduced complexity of the communicative environment and creative use of ambiguity. Humans seek to increase their uncertainty in some communicative settings, either by choice or by interruptions that emerge from the environment.

Fourth, Berger cited Erving Goffman's assertion that in order to save face, deceit is a communicative option.[78] In 1996, David Buller and Judee Burgoon developed "Interpersonal Deception Theory," which included multiple pre-interactional dimensions.[79] The theory generated controversy with the assertion that deceivers engage in predictions about the possibilities of success before engaging in deception.[80]

The fifth perspective centers on "dialectical perspectives" initiated in 1996 by Baxter and Barbara Montgomery.[81] They explored interrelated propositions that offer clarity to personal relationships through dialectical tensions of autonomy–connection, predictability–novelty, and openness–closedness.[82] Communicative partners sort out what matters through the interplay of dialectical energy, which fuels insight and energy. Berger also cited Rawlins's understanding of friendship, which follows this dialectical framework by examining the dialectical tensions in relationships.

Berger's final classification, "Mediated Social Interaction," examines the differences and similarities between face-to-face and computer mediated interaction. Berger ends by suggesting that conceptual precision entails differentiating "interpersonal communication" and "interpersonal relationships" in order to examine the public dimension of the service sector. He advocated investigating our increased reliance on computer mediated communication and how it "insinuates" into routines and patterns within "nonmediated social interaction" and problematizes everyday communicative processes, emphasizing issues of practical import for the public domain. In 2005, Berger continued to emphasize the obligation to develop increasingly sophisticated theories that lend insight into problematized communication processes, discerning the "why" of particular communicative actions and assisting generalizability of findings.[83]

Theories offer a contrasting public lens to the study of communicative meeting, a point emphasized by Bochner and Dorothy Lenk Krueger in "Interpersonal Communication Theory and Research: An Overview of Inscrutable Epistemologies and Muddled Concepts."[84] Their insights reveal an already-present theoretical richness with a highlighting of conceptual and theoretical complexity in relational communication. They cited the importance of Kuhn's assertions about paradigmatic diversity[85] and stated that in 1975, the Research Board of the Speech Communication Association[86] sponsored a special session on "Alternative Theoretical Bases for the Study of Human Communication."[87] The implications of the national organization's endorsement of the investigation of multiple theoretical perspectives accompanied by the insights of Bochner and Krueger are noteworthy. They bear witness to the creative heart of a field of study— do not close the door to inquiry, but rather volunteer to keep the door open for others to follow differently.

Bochner and Krueger acknowledged the conceptual scope of the theoretical debate that ranged from "covering law model of science," "rules perspectives," "systems theory," and "interpretative schemas" to "constructivism" and "hermeneutic phenomenology."[88] Their essay offered publicity for the reality of an aggregate conception of communicative meeting and rejected "monolithic" past tendencies, contending with the notions of ordinary language philosophers and calling for a shift to the study of "culture, contexts, and convention." Bochner and Krueger emphasized that new research paradigms do not focus on how behavior is to be observed, but on how it is described.[89] They stressed the importance of systems theory, noting the originative work of Ludwig von Bertalanffy and the creative insights of Gregory Bateson, which shifted communication research from "substance" to "form" of systems. They noted an increasing "skepticism about the progress of social science" and its claim of "accumulative achievement,"[90] eschewing polemic and evangelical exclusion of alternative perspectives. Bochner and Krueger recognized communication messages as "bimodal," requiring study of "metacommunication" reflected in the work of Paul Watzlawick[91] and attentive to "context" and "meaning," which necessitated examination of ethnomethodology and the contextual methods of Harold Garfinkel[92] and Clifford Geertz.[93] The explication of the importance of meaning by Goffman with an emphasis on "frames" and "reframing" in communicative practice suggested bias associated with methodological choices.[94]

Joe Ayres followed the expanded view of theory with a detailed discussion of "Four Approaches to Interpersonal Communication: Review, Observation, and Prognosis."[95] I include this review because it adds rhetoric and the notion of dialogue to the conversation. Ayres grouped diverse perspectives on relational communication into four categories: dialogue, cohesion, message process, and rhetoric.[96] In the following discussion of his essay, I bring additional scholars and articles into the conversation, remaining within the horizon of Ayres's categories. His macro-categories of dialogue, cohesion, message process, and rhetoric continue to offer an insightful commencement of conversation about the diversity of what I term "communicative meeting." The "dialogic" conception of communicative meeting began with Poulakos's stress on the revelatory space of the "between" as the creative point of connection between communicators.[97] Johannesen and Stewart then followed with substantial contributions on dialogue.[98] Arnett, Pat Arneson, and Holba examined the enduring importance of *Bridges Not Walls: A Book about Interpersonal Communication* to relational communication and dialogue in particular.[99]

Ayres then cited the argument between Arnett and Rob Anderson on the differences between a humanistic and a phenomenological understanding of dialogue,[100] announcing diversity within the dialogic perspective. Ayres asserted that there is an unstated and implicit assumption about dialogue—it is actually an ethic that argues for "how people should communicate," with later scholarship verifying Ayres's assertion.[101]

Two major reviews of the *dialogic* approach announcing the diversity of the perspective come from Ken Cissna and Anderson, and Arnett, Celeste Grayson, and Christina McDowell.[102] The reviews acknowledged the work of Carl Rogers, Buber, Gadamer, and Mikhail Bakhtin, with the latter essay emphasizing the insights of Levinas, known for his assertion of "ethics as first philosophy."[103] The work of Lisbeth Lipari also forges the connection between dialogue and ethics with a focus on listening to the Other.[104] The work of Wood, tied to symbolic interactionism and feministic commitments to care, provided an ethic of attentiveness and response to and for the Other,[105] contending with impersonal authority.

Ayres considered the construct of *cohesion* a central dwelling place for the discipline's understanding of relational communication. The literature on this view of communicative meeting focused on forces that generate dyadic bonds. The notion of cohesion, for Ayres, broadly united "covering law" and "rules" approaches[106] to uncover trajectories of relationships and variables that influence interpersonal bonding or association. Ayres stated that the "coherence construction" work of Jesse Delia and of Pearce and Vernon Cronen[107] was theoretically rich, which J. Kevin Barge and Pearce, in 2004, affirm in their review of more than one hundred research projects directly tied to Coordinated Management of Meaning.[108]

Although Ayres did not link Coordinated Management of Meaning to ethics, Gerry Philipsen did make this connection, noting the theory's stress on "personal liberation" from oppressive communicative systems,[109] a perspective underscored in an essay published in memory of Pearce.[110] Additionally, ethics of communicative meeting emerges in Pearce's and Branham's reminder to attend to the inarticulate in their highlighting of the importance of the ineffable, which renders insight without reliance upon undue certainty.[111]

Ayres discussed *message process* as having "linguistic and anthropological heritages."[112] The connecting link between these approaches is pattern, with linguistic interests reflected in everyday conversation and anthropological exploration of meaning residing at a "metacommunicative" level of communicative exchange.[113] Ayres considered this perspective a linguistic approach that offers descriptive data. This outlook also united phenomenology and semiotics in the theoretical development of communicology, supported by the research and leadership of Richard Lanigan.[114] In *Communicology: The New Science of Embodied Discourse*, Isaac Catt and Deborah Eicher-Catt announce the continuing development of communicology.[115] The anthropological understanding of relational engagement also had deep roots within the Palo Alto group, where the research links message patterns with insight into the psychological processes of communicators.[116]

The final approach discussed by Ayres was *rhetoric*. He contended that rhetoric is the only approach to interpersonal communication with "roots in the speech communication discipline."[117] Ayres alleged that early efforts linking rhetoric to interpersonal communication had little success, but the theoretical construct of rhetorical sensitivity, developed by Roderick Hart and Don Burks, generated a number of related essays.[118] The work of Foss and Cindy Griffin in 1995 brought forth "invitational rhetoric," which counters impersonal power structures. Invitational rhetoric reminds us of a relational obligation to the Other and the importance of transforming systems of oppression.[119] Additionally, Makau has been an advocate of debate with a human face, providing alternatives to impersonal structures that fail to listen and learn from the other.[120] Recent work on professional civility by Janie Harden Fritz articulates civility as a modality of communicative meeting marked by respect and attentiveness among conversational partners in organizational settings.[121]

Ayres warned that ongoing debates between Miller and Gerald Phillips were healthy to a point, but could generate an "irreparable division in the area."[122] It seems that Ayres wanted to preserve the creative heart of the field of communication and argued for paradigmatic difference and respect. Paradigmatic argument (one paradigm countering another) does not lead to resolution, but often to dissolution of conversation. Pragmatic paradigmatic respectfulness champions multiple modes of inquiry. Ayres's insights offer a thoughtful picture of the diversity of communicative meeting scholarship that continues to influence differing segments of the field of communication.

The final word goes to Roloff and Lefki Anastasiou in "Interpersonal Communication Research: An Overview," a thoughtful statement on future directions. First, the authors called for an increased emphasis on ongoing connections with the "everyday" and "ordinary individuals." Second, Roloff and Anastasiou suggested that "contextual boundaries" between close, intimate, family, and workplace relationships have blurred. Third, researchers must address the pervasive presence of technology and its impact on relationships. Fourth, the "insularity" of such research must cease, moving toward real-world applicability. Their final comment laments the reality of multiple definitions and calls for increased clarity.[123] I concur with Roloff and Anastasiou that recommendations regarding the ordinary, the blurring of boundaries, the presence of technology, and the danger of insularity are pragmatic common-sense suggestions for ongoing inquiry in this historical moment. I both agree and disagree with their call for increased definitional clarity. My "yes" understands the legitimacy and importance of such an objective from their vantage point. My equally passionate "no" rests within a basic conviction that disagreement pushes the boundaries of understanding about communicative meeting, which centers my final comments below.

The Gift of Rival Versions

The diversity of the story of communicative meeting is an exemplar of the genius of this field. Difference, not commonality, gives rise to paradigmatically contrary insights necessary for heuristic and generative creativity responsive to changing historical and existential demands. I encourage Roloff and Berger with the same enthusiasm that I offer for the work of Lipari and Foss. New directions for communicative meeting need to be embraced with a pragmatic openness. We live in the aftermath of Kuhn, Werner Heisenberg, Martin Luther King, Jr., and Dorothy Day. Paradigmatic rigidity in theory construction is yet another form of impersonal authority that must be challenged.

I contend that the rhetorical heritage of this field is its saving grace—rhetorically, the pursuit of truth is in conversation. Such is the creative legacy upon which we continue to stumble and within which we continue to thrive. Paradigmatic differences in the study and practice of communicative meeting necessitate persons of conviction. Such is the reason that I have called for a return to the study of monologue. Ignoring the monologic passion of another returns us to a strange spot: becoming an impersonal authority unwilling to learn from the contrary and the different.[124] My tenacious hope embraces a pragmatically tempered cosmopolitan position that engages scholarship out of conviction while taking the time to study and learn from positions otherwise than our own.

This story of tenacious hope about communicative meeting is otherwise than a convention of frail optimism reminiscent of Voltaire's Doctor Pangloss in *Candide*.[125] In Voltaire's narrative, Candide has a scholar/tutor, Pangloss, who displays the danger of optimism. The story rotates between the misfortunes of Candide and Pangloss, who consistently utters that good things will come from misfortune, repeatedly announcing the absurdity of optimism. Voltaire wrote the story as a counter to the philosophical optimism of Alexander Pope and Gottfried Wilhelm Leibniz.[126] The mid-eighteenth-century novel ends with Pangloss arguing and unable to find happiness and with Candide discovering a respite void of philosophical optimism in the labor of cultivating a garden. Voltaire's conception of Pangloss originated in a single assumption, an optimistic assertion that this is the best of all possible worlds;[127] this position, which Voltaire critiques, was central to Pope's *Essay on Man* which explicated his position on philosophical optimism.[128]

The diversity in communicative meeting scholarship permits no such optimism. There is no assumption that all will work out on its own. We have scholars passionately committed to positions contending with one another. Such active scholarship does not assume that an optimistic goodwill rights all wrongs; the task of scholarship in the public domain is to seek to influence the environment. This position was central to Arendt's view of the public domain.[129] Multiplicity requires active participation; such engagement embodies the spirit of tenacious hope of communicative meeting—meet existence on its own terms and respond with passion and commitment, with a simultaneous attentiveness to others and relationships.

Communicative meeting aligned with tenacious hope is a form of social resistance to party-approved scripts, those of a corporatized world and a narcissistic inclination; we must struggle with passion for perspectives and, as scholars, engage self-doubt and questioning about our own convictions. The story of communicative meeting dwells within a field of communication that continues to embrace democracy and free speech, not because they generate the right answers, but due to an existential fact: people and researchers stumble toward both the good and the mistaken. Pragmatically, we must let diversity of conversation about communicative meeting continue within a field rhetorically suspicious of paradigmatic certainty. A pragmatically tempered cosmopolitan position rejects optimism that all will work out and enters the fray with tenacious hope. Communicative meeting announces that the Other matters, that relationships matter, making communicative meeting worth the burden of investigation and scholarship in a world of paradigmatic contention. A pragmatically tempered cosmopolitan is not timid about conviction, just wary of final answers.

I end with both thanks and apologies to my good colleagues who have written in this area and most certainly would have offered another version about communicative meeting. I genuinely believe it is from rival versions of communicative meeting that tenacious hope springs. The complex heritage of communicative meeting has breadth, depth, and, often, confounding dissimilarities. I have tenacious hope that we will have the courage to continue to meet one another in dispute—not just to persuade the Other about incorrectness, but to learn from one another.

This particular story about communicative meeting celebrates the unity of contraries, honoring passion for a unique position that demands conviction and simultaneously honoring the gift of rival versions. The contention between and among approaches to communicative meeting makes "thoughtlessness," which is at the heart of Arendt's "banality of evil,"[130] pragmatically less likely. This story of rival traditions empowers scholarship within the field of communication with a uniting conviction that fuels tenacious hope—communicative meeting matters.

Notes

1 Richard L. Johannesen, "Diversity, Freedom, and Responsibility in Tension," in *Communication Ethics in an Age of Diversity*, ed. Josina M. Makau and Ronald C. Arnett (Urbana, IL: University of Illinois Press, 1997).

2 Emmanuel Levinas, *Totality and Infinity: An Essay on Exteriority* (Leiden, Netherlands: M. Nijhoff Publishers, 1979); Michael J. Hyde, "The Call of Conscience: Heidegger and the Question of Rhetoric," *Philosophy & Rhetoric* 27, no. 4 (1994): 374–396; Michael J. Hyde, *The Call of Conscience: Heidegger and Levinas: Rhetoric and the Euthanasia Debate* (Columbia, SC: University of South Carolina Press, 2001).

3 Martin Buber, *Israel and the World: Essays in a Time of Crisis* (Berlin: Schocken Books, 1948; 1979).

4 Albert Camus, *Resistance, Rebellion and Death: Essays* (New York: Alfred A. Knopf, Inc., 1960; 1995).

5 See preface of Howard Brick, *Age of Contradiction: American Thought and Culture in the 1960s* (Ithaca, NY: Cornell University Press, 1998).

6 Dana Cloud, *Control and Consolation in American Culture and Politics: Rhetoric of Therapy* (London: Sage Publications, 1998).

7 Richard Sennett, *The Fall of Public Man* (Alfred A. Knopf, Inc., 1976; London: Cambridge University Press, 1977); Christopher Lasch, *The True and Only Heaven: Progress and Its Critics* (New York: W.W. Norton & Company, Inc., 1991).

8 Ronald C. Arnett, *Dialogic Education: Conversation about Ideas and Between Persons* (Carbondale, IL: Southern Illinois University Press, 1992): 102.

9 Marie Baker-Ohler and Annette M. Holba, *The Communicative Relationship Between Dialogue and Care* (Amherst, NY: Cambria Press, 2009).

10 Pat J. Gehrke, *The Ethics and Politics of Speech: Communication and Rhetoric in the Twentieth Century* (Carbondale, IL: Southern Illinois University Press, 2009); Julia T. Wood, *Relational Communication: Continuity and Change in Personal Relationships* (Belmont, CA: Wadsworth, 1995).

11 Ronald C. Arnett, Janie M. Harden Fritz, and Leeanne M. Bell, *Communication Ethics Literacy: Dialogue and Difference* (Thousand Oaks, CA: Sage, 2009): 46–48; Karl R. Wallace, "An Ethical Basis of Communication," *Speech Teacher* 4, no. 1 (1955): 1–9.

12 For instance, see Christopher Lyle Johnstone, *Listening to the Logos: Speech and the Coming of Wisdom in Ancient Greece* (Columbia, SC: University of South Carolina Press, 2009); John Poulakos, *Sophistical Rhetoric in Classical Greece* (Columbia, SC: University of South Carolina Press, 1995).

13 Hannah Arendt, "Collective Responsibility," in *Responsibility and Judgment*, ed. Jerome Kohn (New York: Schocken Books, 2003).

14 Richard L. Johannesen, "Communication Ethics: Centrality, Trends, and Controversies," in *Communication Yearbook* 25, ed. William B. Gudykunst (Mahwah, NJ: Lawrence Erlbaum Associates, Inc., 2001).

15 Thomas R. Nilsen, *Ethics of Speech Communication* (Indianapolis: Bobbs-Merrill, 1974); Richard L. Johannesen, "The Emerging Concept of Communication as Dialogue," *Quarterly Journal of Speech* 57, no. 4 (1971): 373–384.

16 David Berry, *Journalism, Ethics, and Society* (Surrey: Ashgate Publishing Limited, 2008): 67.

17 Franklyn S. Haiman, "The Rhetoric of the Streets: Some Legal and Ethical Considerations," *Quarterly Journal of Speech* 53, no. 2 (1967): 99–114. Additionally, the National Communication Association awards the Franklyn S. Haiman Award for Distinguished Scholarship in Freedom of Expression in his honor.

18 Post-modernity, as defined by Jean-François Lyotard, is characterized by "incredulity toward metanarratives." Jean-François Lyotard, *The Postmodern Condition: A Report on Knowledge* (France: Ed. de Minuit, 1974; Minneapolis: University of Minnesota Press, 1984): xxiv.

19 Richard H. Brown, "Rhetoric, Textuality, and the Postmodern Turn in Sociological Theory," in *The Postmodern Turn: New Perspectives on Social Theory*, ed. Steven Seidman (New York: Cambridge University Press, 1994).

20 Andrew King, ed., *Postmodern Political Communication: The Fringe Challenges the Center* (Westport, CT: Greenwood Publishing Group, 1992): 15.

21 Mats Alvesson and Stanley Deetz, *Doing Critical Management Research* (Thousand Oaks, CA: Sage, 2000): 9.

22 Ronald C. Arnett, *Communication Ethics in Dark Times: Hannah Arendt's Rhetoric of Warning and Hope* (Carbondale, IL: Southern Illinois University Press, 2013).

23 Immanuel Kant, *Observations on the Feelings of the Beautiful and Sublime*, trans. J.T. Goldthwait (1764; Berkeley, CA: University of California Press, 1960).

24 Bilijana Scott, "Multiculturalism for the Masses: Social Advertising and Public Diplomacy Post-9/11," *Intercultural Communication and Diplomacy, Washington International Social Science Journal* 50, no. 156 (2004): 166.

25 Charles T. Brown and Paul W. Keller, *Monologue to Dialogue: An Exploration of Interpersonal Communication* (Upper Saddle River, NJ: Prentice-Hall, 1979); Sonja K. Foss and Cindy L. Griffin, "Beyond Persuasion: A Proposal for an Invitational Rhetoric," *Communication Monographs* 62, no. 1 (1995): 2–18.

26 Brick, *Age of Contradiction*.

27 For example, see Josina M. Makau and David Lawrence, "Administrative Judicial Rhetoric: The Supreme Court's New Thesis of Political Morality," *Argumentation & Advocacy* 30, no. 4 (1994): 191–205; Lawrence R. Frey and Kevin M. Carragee, *Communication Activism: Media and Performance Activism* (New York: Hampton Press, 2007); Charles E. Morris, ed., *Queering Public Address: Sexualities in American Historical Discourse* (Columbia, SC: University of South Carolina, 2007); Lester C. Olson, "Public Memory of Christopher Isherwood's Novel, *A Single Man*: Communication Ethics, Social Differences, and Alterity in Media Portrayals of Homosexuality," in *Philosophy of Communication Ethics: Alterity and the Other*, ed. Ronald C. Arnett and Pat Arneson (Madison, NJ: Fairleigh Dickinson University Press, forthcoming); Cloud, *Control and Consolation*; Brenda J. Allen, "'Diversity' and Organizational Communication," *Journal of Applied Communication Research* 23, no. 2 (1995): 143–155.

28 William K. Rawlins, "Stalking Interpersonal Communication Effectiveness: Social, Individual, or Situational Integration?" in *Speech Communication in the Twentieth Century*, ed. Thomas W. Benson (Carbondale, IL: Southern Illinois University Press, 1985): 109–129.

29 Rawlins, "Stalking," 110.

30 Rawlins, "Stalking," 112.

31 Rawlins, "Stalking," 111–112.

32 Rawlins, "Stalking," 126.

33 James C. McCroskey, "Communication Competence and Performance: A Research and Pedagogical Perspective," *Communication Education* 31, no. 1 (1982): 1–8.

34 Arnett, *Communication Ethics in Dark Times*, 111; Hannah Arendt, *The Human Condition*, 2nd ed. (Chicago: University of Chicago Press, 1958).

35 William Glasser, *Schools Without Failure* (New York: HarperCollins Publishers, Inc., 1975).

36 Gustavo Gutiérrez, *A Theology of Liberation: History, Politics, and Salvation* (Lima: CEP, 1971; Maryknoll, NY: Orbis Books, 1988).

37 Paul W. Keller and Charles T. Brown, "An Interpersonal Ethic for Communication," *Journal of Communication* 18, no. 1 (1968): 73–81; Brown and Keller, *Monologue to Dialogue.*

38 Mark L. Knapp and John A. Daly, "Background and Current Trends in the Study of Interpersonal Communication," in *The Sage Handbook of Interpersonal Communication*, 4th ed., ed. Mark L. Knapp and John A. Daly (Thousand Oaks, CA: Sage, 2011): 19.

39 Arnett, *Communication Ethics in Dark Times*; for example, see 65–75; Arendt, *Human Condition*, 175–176.

40 See Charles R. Berger, "Interpersonal Communication Theory and Research: An Overview," in *Communication Yearbook* 1, ed. Brent D. Ruben (New Brunswick, NJ: Transaction Books, 1977): 217–228.

41 Karen Tracy, "'Reasonable Hostility': Situation-Appropriate Face-Attack," *Journal of Politeness Research: Language, Behavior, Culture* 4, no. 2 (2008): 169–191; W. Barnett Pearce and Stephen Littlejohn, *Moral Conflict: When Social Worlds Collide* (New York: Sage, 1997).

42 Gerard Hauser, "Machiavelli's Question Mark and the Problem of Ethical Communication," in *Philosophy of Communication Ethics: Alterity and the Other*, ed. Ronald C. Arnett and Pat Arneson (Madison, NJ: Fairleigh Dickinson University Press, forthcoming).

43 John Stewart, "Interpretive Listening: An Alternative to Empathy," *Communication Education* 32, no. 4 (1983): 381–382.

44 Ronald C. Arnett, *Dialogic Confession: Bonhoeffer's Rhetoric of Responsibility* (Carbondale, IL: Southern Illinois University Press, 2003).

45 For example, see Hans-Georg Gadamer, *Truth and Method* (London: Sheed & Ward, Ltd., Continuum Publishing, 1975; London: Continuum, New York: Bloomsbury, 2013); Paul Ricoeur, *Time and Narrative*, trans. Kathleen McLaughlin and David Pellauer (France: Editions du Seuil, 1983; Chicago: University of Chicago Press, 1985). Additionally, communication scholars such as Pat Arneson, Ronald C. Arnett, Lisbeth Lipari, Annette Holba, Ramsey Eric Ramsey, and Michael Hyde display this interpretive perspective.

46 Sandra G. Harding, *The Feminist Standpoint Theory Reader: Intellectual and Political Controversies* (New York: Routledge, 2004).

47 Gadamer, *Truth and Method.*

48 Nancy Harding, Jackie Ford, and Marianna Fotaki, "Is the 'F'-Word Still Dirty? A Past, Present and Future of/for Feminist and Gender Studies," *Organization* 20, no. 1 (2013): 51–65; Judith Butler, *Antigone's Claim: Kinship Between Life and Death* (New York: Columbia University Press, 2000).

49 Harding et al., "Is the 'F'-Word Still Dirty?" 59; Butler, *Antigone's Claim*, 30.

50 Jürgen Habermas, "A Review of Gadamer's *Truth and Method*," in *Understanding and Social Inquiry*, ed. Fred R. Dallmayr and Thomas A. McCarthy (Notre Dame, IN: University of Notre Dame Press, 1977): 335–363.

51 Ronald C. Arnett, "Hans-Georg Gadamer: Philosophical Hermeneutics and the Interplay of Understanding and Meaning," in *Philosophical Profiles in the Theory of Communication*, ed. Jason Hannan (New York: Peter Lang, 2012).

52 John Arthos, *Gadamer's Poetics: A Critique of Modern Aesthetics* (London: Bloomsbury Academic, 2013): 103.

53 Jürgen Habermas, *Knowledge and Human Interests* (Frankfurt: Surkamp Verlag, 1968; Toronto: Beacon Press, 1971).

54 For example, see Arthos, *Gadamer's Poetics*; John Arthos, *The Inner Word of Gadamer's Hermeneutics* (Notre Dame, IN: University of Notre Dame Press, 2009).

55 Gehrke, *Ethics and Politics of Speech.*

56 François Cooren thoughtfully explicates the importance of "matter," weightiness, and attentiveness for people, places, contexts, and surroundings. See François Cooren, *Action and Agency in Dialogue* (Amsterdam: John Benjamins Publishing Co., 2010).

57   John Stewart, "Foundations of Dialogic Communication," *Quarterly Journal of Speech* 64, no. 2 (1978): 183–201; John Stewart, "Dialogue as Tensional, Ethical Practice," *Southern Communication Journal* 65, no. 2/3 (2000): 224–242; Gadamer, *Truth and Method*; Hans-Georg Gadamer, *Reason in the Age of Science*, trans. Frederick G. Lawrence (Cambridge, MA: MIT Press, 1982).

58   See Thomas S. Kuhn, *The Structure of Scientific Revolutions* (Chicago: University of Chicago Press, 1962; 2012); Paul Feyerabend, *Realism, Rationalism, & Scientific Method: Philosophical Papers*, Vol. 1 (New York: Cambridge University Press, 1981; 1995).

59   Pauline Kleingeld, *Kant and Cosmopolitanism: The Philosophical Ideal of World Citizenship* (Cambridge: Cambridge University Press, 2012).

60   Appiah writes, "There are two strands that intertwine in the notion of cosmopolitanism. One is the idea that we have obligation to others, obligations that stretch beyond those to whom we are related by the ties of kith and kind, or even the more formal ties of a shared citizenship. The other is that we take seriously the value not just of human life but of particular human lives, which means taking an interest in the branches and beliefs that lend them significance." Kwame Anthony Appiah, *Cosmopolitanism: Ethics in a World of Strangers (Issues of Our Time)* (New York: W.W. Norton & Company, 2006): xv.

61   Stephen Toulmin, *Cosmopolis: The Hidden Agenda of Modernity* (New York: Free Press, 1990).

62   Ronald C. Arnett, "Provinciality and the Face of the Other: Levinas on Communication Ethics, Terrorism—Otherwise than Originative Agency," in *Communication Ethics: Cosmopolitanism and Provinciality*, ed. Kathleen Glenister Roberts and Ronald C. Arnett (New York: Peter Lang, 2008): 69–88.

63   W. Barnett Pearce, *Communication and the Human Condition* (Carbondale, IL: Southern Illinois University Press, 1989): 186.

64   Milton Rokeach, *Understanding Human Values* (New York: The Free Press, 1979): 42.

65   Arnett, *Dialogic Confession*; Ronald C. Arnett, *Communication and Community: Implications of Martin Buber's Dialogue* (Carbondale, IL: Southern Illinois Press, 1986).

66   Immanuel Kant, *Critique of Judgment*, trans. J.H. Bernard (1790; New York: Hafner Press, 1951): 136–137.

67   Lasch, *True and Only Heaven*; for example, see 80, 373, 530.

68   Vivian Jerauld McGill and William Tuthill Parry, "The Unity of Opposites: A Dialectical Principle," *Science and Society* 12, no. 4 (1948): 418–444; Buber, *Israel and the World*.

69   Gerald R. Miller and Mark Steinberg, *Between People: A New Analysis of Interpersonal Communication* (Minneapolis: University of Minnesota Press, 1975): 7–9.

70   Miller and Steinberg, *Between People*, 22.

71   Donald P. Cushman and B. Thomas Florence, "The Development of Interpersonal Communication Theory," *Today's Speech* 22, no. 4 (1974): 13.

72   Berger, "Interpersonal Communication Theory and Research," 217.

73   Gerald R. Miller, "The Current Status of Theory and Research in Interpersonal Communication," *Human Communication Research* 4, no. 2 (1978): 164–178.

74   Charles R. Berger, "Interpersonal Communication: Theoretical Perspective, Future Prospects," *Journal of Communication* 55, no. 3 (2005): 419.

75   Berger, "Interpersonal Communication."

76   Berger, "Interpersonal Communication," 420–422.

77   Michael Sunnafrank, "Predicted Outcome Value During Initial Interactions: A Reformulation of Uncertainty Reduction Theory," *Human Communication Research* 13, no. 1 (1986): 3–33; Austin S. Babrow, "Communication and Problematic Integration: Understanding and Diverging Probability and Value, Ambiguity, Ambivalence, and Impossibility," *Communication Theory* 2, no. 2 (1992): 95–130.

78   Berger, "Interpersonal Communication," 425.

79   David Buller and Judee Burgoon, "Interpersonal Deception Theory," *Communication Theory* 6, no. 3 (1996): 203–242.

80   Berger, "Interpersonal Communication," 427.

81 Leslie A. Baxter and Barbara M. Montgomery, *Relating: Dialogues and Dialectics* (New York: Guillford Press, 1996).

82 Berger, "Interpersonal Communication," 428.

83 Berger, "Interpersonal Communication," 430–436.

84 Arthur Bochner and Dorothy Lenk Krueger, "Interpersonal Communication Theory and Research: An Overview of Inscrutable Epistemologies and Muddled Concepts," in *Communication Yearbook* 3, ed. Dan Nimmo (New York: Transaction Books, 1979): 197.

85 Kuhn, *Structure of Scientific Revolutions*.

86 The National Communication Association was known as the Speech Communication Association from 1970 until 1997.

87 Bochner and Krueger, "Interpersonal Communication," 198. Essays from that program were published in *Communication Quarterly* and *Western Journal of Speech Communication*. *Quarterly Journal of Speech* and *Human Communication Research* produced special editions devoted to the topic.

88 Bochner and Krueger, "Interpersonal Communication," 198–199.

89 Bochner and Krueger, "Interpersonal Communication," 198–199.

90 Bochner and Krueger, "Interpersonal Communication," 200–201.

91 Bochner and Krueger, "Interpersonal Communication," 204.

92 Harold Garfinkel, *Studies in Ethnomethodology* (New Jersey: Englewood Cliffs, 1967).

93 Clifford Geertz, *The Interpretation of Cultures: Selected Essays* (London: Fontana, 1973).

94 Erving Goffman, *Frame Analysis: An Essay on the Organization of Experience* (Cambridge, MA: Harvard University Press, 1974).

95 Joe Ayres, "Four Approaches to Interpersonal Communication: Review, Observation, and Prognosis," *Western Journal of Speech Communication* 48, no. 4 (1984): 408–440.

96 Ayres, "Four Approaches," 409.

97 John Poulakos, "The Components of Dialogue," *Western Journal of Communication* 38, no. 3 (1974): 199–212.

98 John Stewart, *Bridges Not Walls: A Book about Interpersonal Communication*, 11th ed. (New York: McGraw-Hill Education, 2011); Johannesen, "The Emerging Concept of Communication as Dialogue."

99 Ronald C. Arnett, Pat Arneson, and Annette Holba, "Bridges Not Walls: The Communicative Enactment of Dialogic Storytelling," *Review of Communication* 8, no. 3 (2008): 217–234.

100 Ronald C. Arnett, "Toward a Phenomenological Dialogue," *Western Journal of Speech Communication* 45, no. 3 (1981): 201–212; Rob Anderson, "Phenomenological Dialogue, Humanistic Psychology, and Pseudo-Walls: A Response and Extension," *Western Journal of Communication* 46, no. 4 (1982): 344–357.

101 Ayres, "Four Approaches," 411; Richard L. Johannesen, *Ethics in Human Communication* (Columbus, OH: Charles E. Merrill, 1975); Arnett et al., *Communication Ethics Literacy*.

102 Kenneth N. Cissna and Rob Anderson, "Communication and the Ground of Dialogue," in *The Reach of Dialogue: Confirmation, Voice, and Community*, ed. Rob Anderson, Kenneth N. Cissna, and Ronald C. Arnett (New York: Hampton Press, 1994): 9–30; Ronald C. Arnett, Celeste Grayson, and Christina McDowell, "Dialogue as an 'Enlarged Communicative Mentality,'" *Communication Research Trends* 27, no. 2 (2008): 3–25.

103 Levinas, *Totality and Infinity*.

104 Lisbeth Lipari, "Listening Otherwise: The Voice of Ethics," *The International Journal of Listening* 23, no. 1 (2009): 44–59.

105 Julia T. Wood, *Who Cares? Women, Care, and Culture* (Carbondale, IL: Southern Illinois University Press, 1994).

106 Ayres, "Four Approaches," 411.

107 See Jesse G. Delia, "Constructivism and the Study of Human Communication," *Quarterly Journal of Speech* 63, no. 1 (1977): 66–83; W. Barnett Pearce and Vernon E. Cronen, *Communication, Action, and Meaning* (New York: Praeger, 1980).

108 J. Kevin Barge and W. Barnett Pearce, "A Reconnaissance of CMM Research," *Human Systems* 15, no. 1 (2004): 13–32.

109 Barge and Pearce, "A Reconnaissance," 17.

110 Arnett, "Philosophy of Communication."

111 W. Barnett Pearce and Robert J. Branham, "The Ineffable: An Examination of the Limits of Expressiblity and the Means of Communication," in *Communication Yearbook* 2, ed. Brent D. Ruben (New York: Routledge, 1978): 345–360.

112 Ayres, "Four Approaches," 417.

113 Gregory Bateson, *Steps to an Ecology of Mind: Collected Essays in Anthropology, Psychiatry, Evolution, and Epistemology* (Chicago: University of Chicago Press, 2000).

114 Richard L. Lanigan, *The Human Science of Communicology: A Phenomenology of Discourse in Foucault and Merleau-Ponty* (Pittsburgh, PA: Duquesne University Press, 1992).

115 Isaac E. Catt and Deborah Eicher-Catt, eds., *Communicology: The New Science of Embodied Discourse* (Cranbury, NJ: Associated University Press, 2010).

116 The Palo Alto Group is a network of communication researchers who, over a span of decades in the mid-twentieth century, published hundreds of articles and multiple books on "New Communication" and the "Interactional View." Carol Wilder, "The Palo Alto Group: Difficulties and Directions of the Interactional View for Human Communication Research," *Human Communication Research* 5, no. 2 (1979): 171.

117 Ayres, "Four Approaches," 419.

118 Roderick P. Hart and Don M. Burks, "Rhetorical Sensitivity and Social Interaction," *Communications Monographs* 39, no. 2 (1972): 75–91.

119 Foss and Griffin, "Beyond Persuasion."

120 Josina Makau, "Adapting the Judicial Model of Reasoning to the Basic Argument and Debate Course," *Communication Education* 34, no. 3 (1985): 227; Josina Makau, "The Supreme Court and Reasonableness," *Quarterly Journal of Speech* 70, no. 4 (1984): 379.

121 Janie M. Harden Fritz, *Professional Civility: Communicative Virtue at Work* (New York: Peter Lang, 2013).

122 Ayres, "Four Approaches," 420–421.

123 Michael Roloff and Lefki Anastasiou, "Interpersonal Communication Research: An Overview," in *Communication Yearbook* 24, ed. William B. Gudykunst (Thousand Oaks, CA: Sage, 2012): 64–65.

124 Ronald C. Arnett, "The Fulcrum Point of Dialogue: Monologue, Worldview, and Acknowledgement," *The American Journal of Semiotics* 28, no. 1/2 (2012): 105–127.

125 Voltaire, *Candide*, trans. H. Morley (1759; New York: Barnes and Noble Classics, 2003).

126 Alexander Pope (1688–1744), "the first true professional poet in English" (x), aided in producing the literary marketplace in the nineteenth and twentieth centuries. His works include translations of the *Iliad* and the *Odyssey*. Pat Rodgers, "Introduction," in *Essays on Criticism and Pastorals: The Major Works of Alexander Pope* (Oxford: Oxford University Press, 1993). Gottfried Wilhelm Leibniz (1646–1716) was a metaphysician who aimed at advancing research by making science and language "more definite." He was offered a professorship at the University of Altdorf but declined because the university was too small to support his interests. His works include *Discourse on Metaphysics* and *New Essays on Human Understanding*. See John Theodore Merz, *Leibniz* (Edinburgh: William Blackwood and Sons, 1884): 18.

127 Gottfried Wilhelm Leibniz, *Theodicy: Essay on the Goodness of God, the Freedom of Man, and the Origin of Evil* (1710; New York: Cosimo, 2009).

128 Alexander Pope, *Essay on Man*, edited by Mark Pattison (1733/1734; Oxford: Clarendon Press Series, 1879).

129 Arendt, *Human Condition*.

130 Hannah Arendt, *Eichmann in Jerusalem: A Report on the Banality of Evil* (New York: The Viking Press, 1963; New York: Penguin, 2006).

References

Allen, Brenda. "'Diversity' and Organizational Communication." *Journal of Applied Communication Research* 23, no. 2 (1995): 143–155.

Alvesson, Mats and Stanley Deetz. *Doing Critical Management Research*. Thousand Oaks, CA: Sage, 2000.

Anderson, Rob. "Phenomenological Dialogue, Humanistic Psychology, and Pseudo-Walls: A Response and Extension." *Western Journal of Communication* 46, no. 4 (1982): 344–357.

Appiah, Kwame Anthony. *Cosmopolitanism: Ethics in a World of Strangers (Issues of Our Time)*. New York: W. W. Norton & Company, 2006.

Arendt, Hannah. "Collective Responsibility." In *Responsibility and Judgment*, edited by Jerome Kohn, 147–158. New York: Schocken Books, 2003.

——. *Eichmann in Jerusalem: A Report on the Banality of Evil*. New York: Penguin, 2006. First published 1963 by The Viking Press.

——. *The Human Condition*. 2nd ed. Chicago: University of Chicago Press, 1958.

Arnett, Ronald C. *Communication and Community: Implications of Martin Buber's Dialogue*. Carbondale, IL: Southern Illinois Press, 1986.

——. *Communication Ethics in Dark Times: Hannah Arendt's Rhetoric of Warning and Hope*. Carbondale, IL: Southern Illinois University Press, 2013.

——. *Dialogic Confession: Bonhoeffer's Rhetoric of Responsibility*. Carbondale, IL: Southern Illinois University Press, 2003.

——. *Dialogic Education: Conversation about Ideas and Between Persons*. Carbondale, IL: Southern Illinois University Press, 1992.

——. "Hans-Georg Gadamer: Philosophical Hermeneutics and the Interplay of Understanding and Meaning." In *Philosophical Profiles in the Theory of Communication*, edited by Jason Hannan, 235–259. New York: Peter Lang, 2012.

——. "Philosophy of Communication as the Carrier of Meaning: Adieu to W. Barnett Pearce." *Qualitative Research Reports in Communication* 14, no. 1 (2013): 1–9.

——. "Provinciality and the Face of the Other: Levinas on Communication Ethics, Terrorism— Otherwise than Originative Agency." In *Communication Ethics: Cosmopolitanism and Provinciality*, edited by Kathleen Glenister Roberts and Ronald C. Arnett, 69–88. New York: Peter Lang, 2008.

——. "The Fulcrum Point of Dialogue: Monologue, Worldview, and Acknowledgement." *The American Journal of Semiotics* 28, no. 1/2 (2012): 105–127.

——. "Toward a Phenomenological Dialogue." *Western Journal of Speech Communication* 45, no. 3 (1981): 201–212.

Arnett, Ronald C., Pat Arneson, and Annette Holba. "Bridges Not Walls: The Communicative Enactment of Dialogic Storytelling." *Review of Communication* 8, no. 3 (2008): 217–234.

Arnett, Ronald C., Janie M. Harden Fritz, and Leeanne M. Bell. *Communication Ethics Literacy: Dialogue and Difference*. Thousand Oaks, CA: Sage, 2009.

Arnett, Ronald C., Celeste Grayson, and Christina McDowell, "Dialogue as an 'Enlarged Communicative Mentality.'" *Communication Research Trends* 27, no. 2 (2008): 3–25.

Arthos, John. *Gadamer's Poetics: A Critique of Modern Aesthetics*. London: Bloomsbury Academic, 2013.

——. *The Inner Word of Gadamer's Hermeneutics*. Notre Dame, IN: University of Notre Dame Press, 2009.

Ayres, Joe. "Four Approaches to Interpersonal Communication: Review, Observation, and Prognosis." *Western Journal of Speech Communication* 48, no. 4 (1984): 408–440.

Babrow, Austin S. "Communication and Problematic Integration: Understanding and Diverging Probability and Value, Ambiguity, Ambivalence, and Impossibility." *Communication Theory* 2, no. 2 (1992): 95–130.

Baker-Ohler, Marie and Annette M. Holba. *The Communicative Relationship between Dialogue and Care*. Amherst, NY: Cambria Press, 2009.

Barge, J. Kevin and W. Barnett Pearce. "A Reconnaissance of CMM Research." *Human Systems* 15, no. 1 (2004): 13–32.

Bateson, Gregory. *Steps to an Ecology of Mind: Collected Essays in Anthropology, Psychiatry, Evolution, and Epistemology.* Chicago: University of Chicago Press, 2000.

Baxter, Leslie A. and Barbara M. Montgomery. *Relating: Dialogues and Dialectics.* New York: Guilford Press, 1996.

Berger, Charles R. "Interpersonal Communication: Theoretical Perspective, Future Prospects." *Journal of Communication* 55, no. 3 (2005): 415–447.

———. "Interpersonal Communication Theory and Research: An Overview." In *Communication Yearbook 1*, edited by Brent D. Ruben, 217–228. New Brunswick, NJ: Transaction Books, 1977.

Berry, David. *Journalism, Ethics, and Society.* Surrey: Ashgate Publishing Limited, 2008.

Bochner, Arthur and Dorothy Lenk Krueger. "Interpersonal Communication Theory and Research: An Overview of Inscrutable Epistemologies and Muddled Concepts." In *Communication Yearbook 3*, edited by Dan Nimmo, 197–211. New Brunswick, NJ: Transaction Books, 1979.

Brick, Howard. *Age of Contradiction: American Thought and Culture in the 1960s.* Ithaca, NY: Cornell University Press, 1998.

Brown, Charles Thomas and Paul W. Keller. *Monologue to Dialogue: An Exploration of Interpersonal Communication.* Upper Saddle River, NJ: Prentice-Hall, 1973.

Brown, Richard H. "Rhetoric, Textuality, and the Postmodern Turn in Sociological Theory." In *The Postmodern Turn: New Perspectives on Social Theory*, edited by Steven Seidman, 229–241. New York: Cambridge University Press, 1994.

Buber, Martin. *Israel and the World: Essays in a Time of Crisis.* Berlin: Schocken Books, 1979. First published 1948.

Buller, David and Judee Burgoon, "Interpersonal Deception Theory." *Communication Theory* 6, no. 3 (1996): 203–242.

Butler, Judith. *Antigone's Claim: Kinship between Life and Death.* New York: Columbia University Press, 2000.

Camus, Albert. *Resistance, Rebellion and Death: Essays.* New York: Alfred A. Knopf, Inc., 1995. First published 1960.

Catt, Isaac E. and Deborah Eicher-Catt, eds. *Communicology: The New Science of Embodied Discourse.* Cranbury, NJ: Associated University Press, 2010.

Cissna, Kenneth and Rob Anderson. "Communication and the Ground of Dialogue." In *The Reach of Dialogue: Confirmation, Voice, and Community*, edited by Rob Anderson, Kenneth Cissna, and Ronald C. Arnett, 9–30. Cresskill, NJ: Hampton Press, 1994.

Cloud, Dana. *Control and Consolation in American Culture and Politics: Rhetoric of Therapy.* London: Sage Publications, 1998.

Cooren, François. *Action and Agency in Dialogue.* Amsterdam: John Benjamins Publishing Co., 2010.

Cushman, Donald P. and B. Thomas Florence. "The Development of Interpersonal Communication Theory." *Today's Speech* 22, no. 4 (1974): 11–15.

Delia, Jesse G. "Constructivism and the Study of Human Communication." *Quarterly Journal of Speech* 63, no. 1 (1977): 66–83.

Feyerabend, Paul. *Realism, Rationalism, & Scientific Method: Philosophical Papers.* Vol. 1. New York: Cambridge University Press, 1995. First published 1981.

Foss, Sonja K. and Cindy L. Griffin. "Beyond Persuasion: A Proposal for an Invitational Rhetoric." *Communication Monographs* 62, no. 1 (1995): 2–18.

Frey, Lawrence and Kevin M. Carragee. *Communication Activism: Media and Performance Activism.* New York: Hampton Press, 2007.

Fritz, Janie M. Harden. *Professional Civility: Communicative Virtue at Work.* New York: Peter Lang, 2013.

Gadamer, Hans-Georg. *Reason in the Age of Science.* Translated by Frederick G. Lawrence. Cambridge, MA: MIT Press, 1982.

———. *Truth and Method.* New York: Bloomsbury, 2013. First published 1975 by Sheed & Ward Ltd., Continuum Publishing Group.

Garfinkel, Harold. *Studies in Ethnomethodology.* Maiden, MA: Blackwell Publishers Inc.; Policy Press. First published 1967 by Prentice-Hall.

Geertz, Clifford. *The Interpretation of Cultures: Selected Essays.* London: Fontana, 1973.

Gehrke, Pat. J. *The Ethics and Politics of Speech: Communication and Rhetoric in the Twentieth Century.* Carbondale, IL: Southern Illinois University Press, 2009.

Glasser, William. *Schools without Failure.* New York: HarperCollins Publishers, Inc., 1975.

Goffman, Erving. *Frame Analysis: An Essay on the Organization of Experience.* Cambridge, MA: Harvard University Press, 1974.

Gutiérrez, Gustavo. *A Theology of Liberation: History, Politics, and Salvation.* Maryknoll, NY: Orbis Books, 1988. Originally published as *Teologia de la liberación, Perspecitival* (Lima: CEP, 1971).

Habermas, Jürgen. *Knowledge and Human Interests.* Toronto: Beacon Press, 1972. Originally published as *Erkenntnis und Interesse* (Frankfurt: Suhrkamp Verlag, 1968).

——. "A Review of Gadamer's *Truth and Method.*" In *Understanding and Social Inquiry*, edited by Fred R. Dallmayr and Thomas A. McCarthy, 335–363. Notre Dame, IN: University of Notre Dame Press, 1977.

Haiman, Franklyn S. "The Rhetoric of the Streets: Some Legal and Ethical Considerations." *Quarterly Journal of Speech* 53, no. 2 (1967): 99–114.

Harding, Nancy, Jackie Ford, and Marianna Fotaki. "Is the 'F'-Word Still Dirty? A Past, Present and Future of/for Feminist and Gender Studies." *Organization* 20, no. 1 (2013): 51–65.

Harding, Sandra G. *The Feminist Standpoint Theory Reader: Intellectual and Political Controversies.* New York: Routledge, 2004.

Hart, Roderick P. and Don M. Burks. "Rhetorical Sensitivity and Social Interaction." *Communications Monographs* 39, no. 2 (1972): 75–91.

Hauser, Gerard. "Machiavelli's Question Mark and the Problem of Ethical Communication." In *Philosophy of Communication Ethics: Alterity and the Other*, edited by Ronald C. Arnett and Pat Arneson. Madison, NJ: Fairleigh Dickinson University Press, forthcoming.

Hyde, Michael J. *The Call of Conscience: Heidegger and Levinas: Rhetoric and the Euthanasia Debate.* Columbia, SC: University of South Carolina Press, 2001.

——. "The Call of Conscience: Heidegger and the Question of Rhetoric." *Philosophy & Rhetoric* 27, no. 4 (1994): 374–396.

Johannesen, Richard L. "Communication Ethics: Centrality, Trends, and Controversies." In *Communication Yearbook* 25, edited by William B. Gudykunst, 201–236. Mahwah, NJ: Lawrence Erlbaum Associates, Inc., 2001.

——. "Diversity, Freedom, and Responsibility in Tension." In *Communication Ethics in an Age of Diversity*, edited by Josina M. Makau and Ronald C. Arnett, 155–186. Urbana, IL: University of Illinois Press, 1997.

——. "The Emerging Concept of Communication as Dialogue." *Quarterly Journal of Speech* 57, no. 4 (1971): 373–382.

——. *Ethics in Human Communication.* Columbus, OH: Charles E. Merrill, 1975.

Johnstone, Christopher Lyle. *Listening to the Logos: Speech and the Coming of Wisdom in Ancient Greece.* Columbia, SC: University of South Carolina Press, 2009.

Kant, Immanuel. *Critique of Judgment.* Translated by J.H. Bernard. New York: Hafner Press, 1951. First published 1790.

——. *Observations on the Feelings of the Beautiful and Sublime.* Translated by J.T. Goldthwait. Berkeley, CA: University of California Press, 1960. First published 1764.

Keller, Paul W. and Charles T. Brown. "An Interpersonal Ethic for Communication." *Journal of Communication* 18, no. 1 (1968): 73–81.

King, Andrew, ed. *Postmodern Political Communication: The Fringe Challenges the Center.* Westport, CT: Greenwood Publishing Group, 1992.

Kleingeld, Pauline. *Kant and Cosmopolitanism: The Philosophical Ideal of World Citizenship.* Cambridge: Cambridge University Press, 2012.

Knapp, Mark L. and John A. Daly. "Background and Current Trends in the Study of Interpersonal Communication." In *The Sage Handbook of Interpersonal Communication*, edited by Mark L. Knapp and John A. Daly, 3–24. 4th ed. Thousand Oaks, CA: Sage, 2011.

Kuhn, Thomas S. *The Structure of Scientific Revolutions*. Chicago: University of Chicago Press, 2012. First published 1962.

Lanigan, Richard L. *The Human Science of Communicology: A Phenomenology of Discourse in Foucault and Merleau-Ponty*. Pittsburgh: Duquesne University Press, 1992.

Lasch, Christopher. *The True and Only Heaven: Progress and Its Critics*. New York: W. W. Norton & Company, Inc., 1991.

Leibniz, Gottfried Wilhelm. *Theodicy: Essay on the Goodness of God, the Freedom of Man, and the Origin of Evil*, edited by Austin M. Farrer. New York: Cosimo, 2010. First published 1710.

Levinas, Emmanuel. *Totality and Infinity: An Essay on Exteriority*. Leiden, Netherlands: M. Nijhoff Publishers, 1979.

Lipari, Lisbeth. "Listening Otherwise: The Voice of Ethics." *The International Journal of Listening* 23, no. 1 (2009): 44–59.

Lyotard, Jean-François. *The Postmodern Condition: A Report on Knowledge*. Translated by Geoff Bennington and Brian Massumi. Minneapolis: University of Minnesota Press, 1984. Originally published as *La Condition postmoderne: rapport sur le savoir* (France: Ed. de Minuit, 1979).

MacIntyre, Alasdair C. *Three Rival Versions of Moral Enquiry: Encyclopaedia, Genealogy, and Tradition*. Notre Dame, IN: University of Notre Dame Press, 1990.

Makau, Josina. "Adapting the Judicial Model of Reasoning to the Basic Argument and Debate Course." *Communication Education* 34, no. 3 (1985): 227–234.

——. "The Supreme Court and Reasonableness." *Quarterly Journal of Speech* 70, no. 4 (1984): 379–396.

Makau, Josina M. and David Lawrence. "Administrative Judicial Rhetoric: The Supreme Court's New Thesis of Political Morality." *Argumentation & Advocacy* 30, no. 4 (1994): 191–205.

McCroskey, James C. "Communication Competence and Performance: A Research and Pedagogical Perspective." *Communication Education* 31, no. 1 (1982): 1–8.

McGill, Vivian Jerauld and William Tuthill Parry. "The Unity of Opposites: A Dialectical Principle." *Science and Society* 12, no. 4 (1948): 418–444.

Merz, John Theodore. *Leibniz*. Edinburgh: William Blackwood and Sons, 1884.

Miller, Gerald R. "The Current Status of Theory and Research in Interpersonal Communication." *Human Communication Research* 4, no. 2 (1978): 164–178.

Miller, Gerald R. and Mark Steinberg. *Between People: A New Analysis of Interpersonal Communication*. Minneapolis: University of Minnesota Press, 1975.

Morris, Charles, ed. *Queering Public Address: Sexualities in American Historical Discourse*. Columbia, SC: University of South Carolina, 2007.

Nilsen, Thomas R. *Ethics of Speech Communication*. Indianapolis: Bobbs-Merrill, 1974.

Olson, Lester C. "Public Memory of Christopher Isherwood's Novel, *A Single Man*: Communication Ethics, Social Differences, and Alterity in Media Portrayals of Homosexuality." In *Philosophy of Communication Ethics: Alterity and the Other*, edited by Ronald C. Arnett and Pat Arneson. Madison, NJ: Fairleigh Dickinson University Press, forthcoming.

Pearce, W. Barnett. *Communication and the Human Condition*. Carbondale, IL: Southern Illinois University Press, 1989.

Pearce, W. Barnett and Robert J. Branham. "The Ineffable: An Examination of the Limits of Expressibility and the Means of Communication." In *Communication Yearbook* 2, edited by Brent D. Ruben, 345–360. New York: Routledge, 1978.

Pearce, W. Barnett and Vernon E. Cronen. *Communication, Action, and Meaning*. New York: Praeger, 1980.

Pearce, W. Barnett and Stephen Littlejohn. *Moral Conflict: When Social Worlds Collide*. New York: Sage, 1997.

Pope, Alexander. *Essay on Man*. 6th ed., edited by Mark Pattison. London: Macmillan and Co., 1879. First published in 1733/1734.

Poulakos, John. "The Components of Dialogue." *Western Journal of Communication* 38, no. 3 (1974): 199–212.

——. *Sophistical Rhetoric in Classical Greece*. Columbia, SC: University of South Carolina Press, 1995.

Rawlins, William K. "Stalking Interpersonal Communication Effectiveness: Social, Individual, or Situational Integration?" In *Speech Communication in the Twentieth Century*, edited by Thomas W. Benson, 109–129. Carbondale, IL: Southern Illinois University Press, 1985.

Ricoeur, Paul. *Time and Narrative*. Translated by Kathleen McLaughlin and David Pellauer. Chicago: University of Chicago Press, 1985. Originally published as *Temps et récit* (France: Editions du Seuil, 1983).

Rodgers, Pat. Introduction to *Essays on Criticism and Pastorals: The Major Works of Alexander Pope*. Oxford: Oxford University Press, 1993.

Rokeach, Milton. *Understanding Human Values*. New York: The Free Press, 1979.

Roloff, Michael and Lefki Anastasiou. "Interpersonal Communication Research: An Overview." In *Communication Yearbook* 24, edited by William B. Gudykunst, 51–71. Thousand Oaks, CA: Sage, 2009.

Scott, Bilijana. "Multiculturalism for the Masses: Social Advertising and Public Diplomacy Post-9/11." *Intercultural Communication and Diplomacy, Washington International Social Science Journal* 50, no. 156 (2004): 157–173.

Sennett, Richard. *The Fall of Public Man*. London: Cambridge University Press, 1977. First published 1976 by Alfred A. Knopf, Inc.

Stewart, John. *Bridges Not Walls: A Book about Interpersonal Communication*. 11th ed. New York: McGraw-Hill Education, 2011.

——. "Dialogue as Tensional, Ethical Practice." *Southern Communication Journal* 65, no. 2/3 (2000): 224–242.

——. "Foundations of Dialogic Communication." *Quarterly Journal of Speech* 64, no. 2 (1978): 183–201.

——. "Interpretive Listening: An Alternative to Empathy." *Communication Education* 32, no. 4 (1983): 379–391.

Sunnafrank, Michael. "Predicted Outcome Value during Initial Interactions: A Reformulation of Uncertainty Reduction Theory." *Human Communication Research* 13, no. 1 (1986): 3–33.

Toulmin, Stephen. *Cosmopolis: The Hidden Agenda of Modernity*. New York: Free Press, 1990.

Tracy, Karen. "'Reasonable Hostility': Situation-Appropriate Face-Attack." *Journal of Politeness Research: Language, Behavior, Culture* 4, no. 2 (2008): 169–191.

Voltaire. *Candide*. Translated H. Morley. New York: Barnes and Noble Classics, 2003. First published 1759.

Wallace, Karl L. "An Ethical Basis of Communication." *Speech Teacher* 4, no. 1 (1955): 1–9.

Wilder, Carol. "The Palo Alto Group: Difficulties and Directions of the Interactional View for Human Communication Research." *Human Communication Research* 5, no. 2 (1979): 171–186.

Wood, Julia T. *Relational Communication: Continuity and Change in Personal Relationships*. Belmont, CA: Wadsworth, 1995.

——. *Who Cares? Women, Care, and Culture*. Carbondale, IL: Southern Illinois University Press, 1994.

AFTERWORD

What Next?

William F. Eadie

However artificial it might be, the NCA centennial serves as something of a set point: as a collection of scholars, we pause to look back at our history, to assess our present, and to speculate about our future. The chapters in this volume, taken collectively, do not tell us where we are now, but they do give us some understanding of our progress as an intellectual enterprise (and we can debate what to call that enterprise, though I see many inching toward my preferred label, "discipline"). Taken together, they may suggest what sort of progression would be important to undertake when we put away the party hats and settle back into the business of making scholarship.

I wish to take as my guiding thought a history centering around "communication" rather than "speech," and use it to reflect on these chapters in three ways:

(1) what sort of histories they represent;
(2) what they might be trying to tell us about state of communication today; and
(3) what they suggest for "communication" as a concept moving forward.

I realize that my method here is a bit at odds with the drift of the volume; I do not mean to ignore or slight the important work done in speech history[1] but to create a meaningful sense of contrast that will help illuminate the contributions of this volume and my thoughts about the future.

Kinds of Disciplinary History

Elsewhere, I have noted that there seem to be three kinds of disciplinary history: biographical history, which focuses on the contribution of individuals to a field of study; intellectual history, which focuses on concepts, theories, and meta-theories that a discipline has developed as its unique scholarly contribution; and political history, which focuses on the decisions that members of a scholarly discipline have made, the scholarly societies that have encouraged or impeded such decision-making, and the consequences of those decisions for the directions in which scholarship in a discipline has developed.[2]

Biographical history is the easiest to write. Pick someone, research their contributions, and write about them. Then, wait for others to react. Sometimes, these biographical histories have the effect of calling someone's perhaps unfairly neglected scholarship to the attention of contemporary researchers. Sometimes, biographical history serves to honor someone thought to be worth honoring. Sometimes, biographical history calls to mind a culture that has been created through the hard work of disciplinary leaders of one sort or another. Occasionally, biographical history serves to focus a discipline on a particular important individual.

The potentially most important history of this sort to date was Everett Rogers's *History of Communication Study: A Biographical Approach*. Rogers's book worked its way through a series of acknowledged "great thinkers" (Darwin, Freud, and Marx), traced the influence of these individuals on a series of "big thinkers" (e.g., Lasswell, Lazarsfeld, Lewin, Hovland, Wiener, and Shannon) from other disciplines whose ideas came to focus at least in part on communication phenomena, and concluded with naming Wilbur Schramm as the "father" of the communication discipline.[3] Interestingly, despite Rogers's reputation as one of the discipline's finest scholars, his ideas were only partially accepted, and his book went out of print in fairly short order. I'll have more to say about biographical history once I've explained the other two types of histories.

Intellectual history is potentially the most important for a scholarly discipline, as it draws together the strands of scholarship that make up the core of what the discipline endeavors to study. It is interrelated to some degree with biographical history, as it took individual scholars to create the theories that the discipline considers to be at its core, but it is ideas and concepts on which the discipline coalesces that matter, not so much the people who created those ideas.

There are not very many comprehensive examples of intellectual history in communication, and those that exist are sometimes quirky and sometimes exasperated in tone. The quirky, but certainly brilliant, example of intellectual history may be found in John Durham Peters's book, *Speaking into the Air: A History of the Idea of Communication*. Peters received for this project one of the first National Endowment for the Humanities fellowships won by a communication scholar, and its wide-ranging use of humanistic sources illustrated a keen and thoughtful mind at work. Peters made a basic distinction between dialogue and dissemination in describing varying historical conceptualizations of communication, and he focused his attention heavily on how communication is temporal and how it requires some sort of spiritual, as well as "erotic," dimension in order to be successful. While his argument was intriguing, Peters's examples of phenomena such as telepathy and using "mediums" to communicate with the dead represented historical concepts that didn't particularly influence contemporary communication scholars.[4]

Two other works, both published in journals, proved to be seminal, though perhaps discouraging. The first, Robert Craig's "Communication Theory as a Field," was published in the journal *Communication Theory*. Craig's essay explored the nature of theory in communication and generated seven "traditions" of communication study: rhetorical, semiotic, phenomenological, cybernetic, socio-psychological, socio-cultural, and critical. Craig distinguished each by how the tradition conceptualized "communication," the vocabulary it used to study communicative phenomena, and to some degree the ontological and epistemological underpinnings of each tradition. Ultimately pessimistic,

Craig's essay concluded that these different traditions represented such disparate ways of conceiving and studying these phenomena (even disagreeing fundamentally on what to study) that "communication" was unlikely ever to coalesce into a discipline, from an intellectual point of view.[5]

Providing metatheoretical support for Craig's position but without the pessimism was a 2004 *Journal of Communication* essay by James Anderson and Geoffrey Baym titled "Philosophies and Philosophic Issues in Communication, 1995–2004." Anderson and Baym classified representative articles from communication journals to determine how they fell on four dimensions: ontology, epistemology, axiology, and praxeology. They characterized ontological positions in communication scholarship as being relatively foundational (that is, building systematically on established concepts and relationships) or reflexive (that is, building theories through reflecting on data, ranging from individual cases to large groups). Epistemological positions fall on a continuum from empirical to analytical, while praxeology argues about the relative utility of the theories produced. Axiology, on the other hand, is characterized by the article's authors as a means by which collections of scholars find common ground and distinguish themselves from other collections of scholars. Anderson and Baym might attribute Craig's pessimism to axiological differences.[6]

There are not many seminal examples of political history, which focuses on the decision-making processes where groups of scholars engage each other over controversies that the groups consider to be important (and sometimes are). As these groups often assemble in fora sponsored by scholarly societies, political histories often focus on the activities of these scholarly societies.

My own work has emphasized the actions of three scholarly societies (the NCA, ICA, and AEJMC) in bringing speech and journalism scholars to the "communication" table.[7] I have written that communication really has three histories: a speech history, a journalism history, and a communication history.[8] The speech history harkens to the development of rhetorical theory and the pragmatic use of speech and debate to educate future leaders in the United States in considering the great issues of the day from a critical and analytical viewpoint. It coalesces around the founding story of the organization now known as the NCA. That story is often told in heroic terms[9] as a group of individuals walked out of a hostile environment at a meeting of the National Council of Teachers of English (NCTE) and, with some difficulty and a few false starts, formed a speech discipline.

Consideration of a perspective on that period by Lewis Menand puts the founding story in a somewhat different light. Menand wrote that higher education went through a period of foment, particularly in public institutions, around the turn of the twentieth century.[10] Interdisciplinarity gave way to disciplinarity, which was defined as the organization of "departments" within universities. Departments and disciplines were considered to be synonymous: if you were a discipline you were represented in the university by a department. Menand estimated that the process of disciplinary formation through the establishment of departments was mostly concluded by 1920.

In large universities, some departments of journalism had already formed, sometimes free-standing, sometimes within larger units, such as agriculture. But speech teachers had often functioned as co-curricular coaches for debate teams and speaking contests, and many didn't have a comfortable departmental home. English served as a home for some, because it shared some common tradition in rhetoric (though, there were often substantial and fundamental disagreements about the nature of rhetoric and its roles in both speaking and literature).

As disciplines gained an adequate number of departments, disciplinary societies began to form. English already had the Modern Language Association, but it also formed the NCTE in 1912 as a group that focused on teaching and included high school teachers. There was an active speech section within the NCTE, but from the beginning there were questions about whether speech should have its own discipline. We know that the members of the speech section were unable to decide this question but agreed to poll the membership on it. The poll was inconclusive, as was a vote by the membership following the publication of the poll's results.

A group then met to discuss forming a separate scholarly society in any case. This group consisted entirely of professors, most of them from established programs in the Midwest, and several of them from institutions that offered doctor of philosophy degrees. It is entirely possible that the members of this group saw the handwriting on the wall: they had to form departments at their universities or be subsumed by other disciplines. And, they had to form the right departments: they couldn't be clustered with people who taught elocution, a formalistic and regimented system of public performance that speech teachers disdained for its focus on style over content. High school teachers did not face these problems; in fact, they were often comfortable to be part of English. But, the NCTE was not thrilled to lose the speech professors; the long-serving Executive Director was still fuming about it in his memoir.[11]

So, if speech was formed through a political process, journalism was formed by the actions of strong personalities, such as Joseph Pulitzer, whose donation to Columbia University legitimized the profession, and Willard "Daddy" Bleyer, a University of Wisconsin-Madison professor who founded the first doctoral program in journalism and was a force in establishing the principles of journalism education that have lasted to this day. Journalism also served as a refuge for working journalists who wished to quit the daily grind and teach the craft of journalism instead. Often these individuals had outsized personalities, and so journalism's disciplinary history became primarily biographical, focusing on the contributions of those who led the profession and the institutions serving that profession.

The communication story, on the other hand, came into focus, almost accidentally, through the study of other topics. Robin Goret and I have identified five such scholarly endeavors from which communication scholarship arose:

(1) communication as shaper of public opinion;
(2) communication as language use;
(3) communication as information transmission;
(4) communication as developer of relationships; and
(5) communication as definer, interpreter, and critic of culture.

Each of these scholarly endeavors had roots in twentieth-century scholarship emanating from one or more "big thinkers," including many for whom it might be difficult to classify in terms of their disciplinary commitments.[12] Those who come to mind include Walter Lippmann, John Dewey, George Herbert Mead, Kenneth Burke, Harold Lasswell, Norbert Wiener, Alfred Korzybski and his student S.I. Hayakawa, Carl Hovland, and a collection of Jewish émigrés to the United States who had trouble finding conventional professorial positions because of their religion and ended up studying topics that were considered outside of the mainstream, such as communication. These scholars included Paul Lazarsfeld, Kurt Lewin, and Theodor Adorno.

Speech and journalism scholars were generally on the sidelines of these strands of communication scholarship, but both groups recognized bit by bit, and accelerating following World War II, that communication would emerge as an important topic and one that they should study. A group of speech scholars, concerned initially that they might be pushed aside by the larger and better-organized rhetorical scholars in what was then known as the Speech Association of America, set up a parallel organization called the National Society for the Study of Communication (NSSC). The NSSC's goal was to foster the interdisciplinary study of communication and to produce results that would be useful to practitioners. Unfortunately, the NSSC did not have a great deal of luck attracting scholars outside of speech, save journalism professors who were interested in mass communication research. For mass communication scholars in journalism programs, their scholarly society, the Association for Education in Journalism (AEJ), was at least initially unfriendly toward them, confining their scholarly exchanges to "rump" meetings held either before or after the AEJ's regular sessions.

It was in the 1960s where speech and journalism scholars became more prominent in the communication story. One marker might have been 1963, when the speech association hired a full-time Executive Secretary and staff and set up an office in New York City, where the Modern Language Association was also located. Another, perhaps more significant marker came in 1964, when AEJ members revised its constitution to include the mass communication scholars as part of the organization, eliminating the rump sessions. Interestingly, the AEJ delegates rejected a proposal that year to rename the organization the Association for Education in Communications; apparently allowing the mass communication scholars access to the regular sessions was the step that the journalists who were focused on professional and curricular concerns were ready to tolerate.

Following those two events, there was a rush of change for both speech and journalism. Speech held its New Orleans conference on communication and came out of it with a vastly revised definition of the discipline and an uncomfortable new name: "speech-communication" (which didn't stick and which quickly became the almost-as-uncomfortable compound noun "speech communication"). The NSSC dissolved in a stream of disagreement over how communication should be studied and re-emerged as the International Communication Association, whose members formed "divisions" committed to four major strands of scholarship: information systems; interpersonal communication; mass communication; and organizational communication. ICA members quickly realized that they also had to value culture if they expected to attract international members—and so began the intercultural communication division. The ICA hired its first Executive Secretary in 1974 and established the journal *Human Communication Research* shortly thereafter. Mass communication scholars made great strides in understanding media effects on individuals and public opinion with the establishment of agenda-setting and cultivation theories. Rhetoricians were energized by Robert L. Scott's focus on epistemic and Lloyd Bitzer's concept of the rhetorical situation; they began to make common ground with their rhetoric colleagues in English. Finally, the AEJ became the last of the three major associations to professionalize, in 1981; the following year, the membership voted to add "mass communication" to the association's name. During this time, speech and journalism departments remade their curricula to feature communication scholarship. They also added "communication" to their department names in some form or another. Doing so set the stage for an onslaught of new majors in the 1980s; neither students nor faculty always knew what "communication" was, but they knew that it was definitely in fashion. My contention is that as departments became named "communication" their faculties were also in the process of establishing communication as a scholarly discipline.

Interestingly, the chapters in this volume clearly come from the speech tradition. This is as it should be; for all of its emphasis on being the "big tent" scholarly organization, the NCA came from the speech tradition and remains firmly rooted in it, despite its attempts to reach out to journalism and communication scholars from other traditions. The majority of the chapters focus on intellectual history, and that, too, is as it should be for a volume that celebrates one hundred years of evolution from speech to com-munication (without actually giving up speech, the protestations of Professors Gunn and Dance to the contrary). There is also a smattering of political history, which is encouraging. No chapter, however, focuses entirely on biographical history, which also demonstrates a commitment to a certain maturity in the telling of disciplinary history as the NCA reaches one hundred.

The State of Communication

The chapters in this volume divide fairly evenly into intellectual histories and political histories. I will provide an overview of these chapters by category with an eye to identifying key characteristics of each type. Taken collectively, we can guess at some elements within the state of communication, but clearly this volume was not intended to define such a state.

Intellectual Histories

I classified the following chapters as intellectual histories:

- "Discovering Communication: Five Turns toward Discipline and Association," by J. Michael Sproule
- "Conceptualizing Meaning in Communication Studies," by Brian L. Ott and Mary Domenico

- "Listening Research in the Communication Discipline," by David Beard and Graham Bodie
- "Communicative Meeting: From Pangloss to Tenacious Hope," by Ronald C. Arnett
- "The Scholarly Communication of Communication Scholars: Centennial Trends in a Surging Conversation," by Timothy D. Stephen
- "Epistemological Movements in the Field of Communication: An Analysis of Empirical and Rhetorical/Critical Scholarship," by James A. Anderson and Michael K. Middleton

Of these the Sproule chapter provides a dazzling analysis of five intellectual developments across around 150 years that could be claimed to have led speech scholars toward communication as a disciplinary marker. An experienced disciplinary historian, Professor Sproule draws on pedagogical developments that both drew on and contributed to intellectual developments to find some key moments that he could identify as turning points in communication's intellectual history. These turning points are:

(1) the encouragement of vernacular English as a significant form of speech;
(2) the division of speech and writing on the concept of expression (which became a key intellectual argument for separation of speech professors from the NCTE);
(3) emphasis on speaker–audience interaction in defining oral expression;
(4) a shift in emphasis from scholarship on the speaker to scholarship on the audience, which formed the basis for the beginning of integration of the "speech," "journalism," and "communication" stories I referenced earlier; and
(5) the rise of culture as a significant area of communication study.

Two of the chapters focus on surveying the development of key concepts in communication study: meaning and listening. On the topic of meaning, Professors Ott and Domenico synthesized the writing that could be found in the Communication and Mass Media Complete database into seven key theories: general semantics, new materialism, new rhetoric, ordinary language, semiotics, symbolic forms, and symbolic interactionism. The authors carefully delineate the bases of each approach, as well as the ontological and epistemological differences underlying the various theories. The authors conclude that there is no agreement in the discipline on the nature of meaning and yet the concept continues to be studied productively from a variety of viewpoints.

Professors Beard and Bodie's chapter on listening almost veers into biographical history, with the acknowledgment of Professor Ralph Nichols as the founder and "patron saint" of listening scholarship. And yet, the authors quickly reject this approach and attack listening as both a conceptual problem and a historiographical problem. Like Professor Sproule, these authors find intellectual development embedded in pedagogical practice, and they are able to draw insights from the implicit assumptions of those practices. The authors conclude with a few comments about how the evolution of the study of listening might continue beyond 2014, based on how the study of listening has become less separate and more integrated with other communication processes.

Professor Stephen and Professors Anderson and Middleton have somewhat similar projects, though they approach them in somewhat different manners. Both are attempting to chart the ebb and flow of scholarship in the communication discipline over time. Stephen, working from a database he was instrumental in creating, used a dictionary of predetermined descriptors to show how scholarship in communication exploded beginning in the 1970s. Anderson and Middleton, following the epistemological scheme laid out in the Anderson and Baym article, which I described earlier in this chapter, narrowed their comparisons to articles following a rhetorical/critical method and articles following an empirical method.

Findings of the two studies showed some similarities to each other. Research began as an adjunct to teaching but has since moved outside of the pedagogical realm. Empirical studies often pile small sets of findings on top of each other, but while a large number of theories have been propagated, few have emerged as attracting a great deal of research attention. And, almost no grand theories have emerged that have attracted great support (though, some of those theories have passionate adherents). Similarly, critical/rhetorical studies, while professing allegiance to theory, have done little to build theory in any sort of reliable manner. The coin of the realm in rhetorical study is analysis and critique, and these qualities do not always lead to building, as opposed to using, theory.

I was also intrigued by Anderson and Middleton's finding that the *Quarterly Journal of Speech*, the publication originally begun by the founders of the speech association, is the journal that best tracks current trends in rhetorical study by what it publishes issue to issue.

The final chapter in this section is Professor Arnett's recasting of relational communication into what he calls "communicative meeting." Drawing on hermeneutic principles, Arnett provides a historically-based perspective on relational communication that draws together the work of a number of humanistic writers in support of his own theorizing about the nature of dialogue and narrative. I wouldn't call it intellectual history per se; rather, the chapter summarizes a number of historical approaches in service of an original theory.

Political History

Recall that political disciplinary history focuses on the decisions made by scholars, often in the context of their scholarly associations, in the development of disciplinary scholarship and practices. Not surprisingly, the chapters in this section focus on disciplinary controversies, most of which still bring feelings to the surface.

The first controversy revolves around the creation of "speech" as the historical name for the scholarship of the area of study founded by public speaking teachers. As I mentioned earlier, the "speech" tradition is alive and well in this volume in many ways, but it is at its most overt in two of the chapters.

The first is "Paying Lip Service to 'Speech' in Disciplinary Naming, 1914–1954," by Gerry Philipsen. Professor Philipsen has produced a model of careful historical scholarship that addresses in considerable detail how the term "speech" became the term of art in discussing the scholarly enterprise in which the members of the speech association were engaged. Philipsen has also traced how academic departments adopted "speech" as their title, as well as the alternatives (such as "speech and drama") that were used. Recall Menand's argument that disciplines are defined by their departments, and you see how important this careful work is to understanding the dominance of speech for so many years, only to see its relatively quick undoing in the rush to adopt "communication" as the new disciplinary moniker.

Mourning the loss of speech as the dominant disciplinary term are Professors Joshua Gunn and Frank E.X. Dance. In their chapter, "The Silencing of Speech in the Late Twentieth Century," Professors Gunn and Dance argue that the elimination of "speech" as a disciplinary term and the substitution of "communication" was primarily a means of "disciplining" humanistic scholars by those who had adopted a social scientific perspective. If the founders of the NSSC (and Professor Dance was president of this organization when it remade itself as the International Communication Association) were motivated by a concern that they would be pushed out of the speech association by the humanistic scholars, the authors seem to be arguing that the tables had turned by the 1970s and the humanists were fighting for their lives against being pushed aside by the social scientists. The culminating evidence for this argument is the publication of Michael Burgoon's infamous essay, "Divorcing Dame Speech," where Burgoon argued that scholarship in speech would hold back the recognition of scholarship in communication.[13] Gunn and Dance conclude their chapter by noting that the speech tradition lives on, even if speech is no longer in the name of the association founded by speech professors.

Related to the Gunn and Dance chapter is another on the nature of performance and how the study of performance has changed over time. In "A Critical History of the 'Live' Body in Performance within the National Communication Association," Tracy Stephenson Shaffer, John M. Allison, Jr., and Ronald J. Pelias chronicle the movement away from acting or "oral reading" and toward "interpretation" amongst public speaking teachers and how the de-emphasis on classroom performance described by Gunn and Dance led to a reconsideration of how to bring performance into a more "scholarly" realm. Working with textbooks in the field (where, indeed, many scholars in the 1970s and earlier published their overarching theoretical work), the authors discussed how the focus on the body shifted from classroom performances of literary texts to how people naturally performed in their everyday lives. Performance texts shifted toward personal narrative, ethnography, and autoethnography, and the journal associated with this area of study shifted from being called *Literature in Performance* to being titled *Text and Performance Quarterly*. Overall, these authors detail a successful change in focus as the discipline shifted its emphasis, though certainly this shift was not without its turmoil and need for the new perspectives to gain traction and respect among the discipline's scholars.

The final two chapters, "Liberalism and its Discontents: Black Rhetoric and the Cultural Transformation of Rhetorical Studies in the Twentieth Century," by Reynaldo Anderson, Marnel Niles Goins, and Sheena Howard, and "Sexing Communication: Hearing, Feeling, Remembering Sex/Gender and Sexuality in the NCA," by Charles E. Morris III and Catherine Helen Palczewski, both focus on the development of scholarship from historically under-represented groups within speech and communication study. The chapter by Professors Anderson, Goins, and Howard correctly identifies a great interest in civil and human rights and the formation within the speech association of the Committee on Social Responsibility (which quickly became the Black Caucus) served to aid speech scholars to accept communication as a focus of disciplinary scholarship. Much of the chapter, however, really is intellectual in nature, tracing the development of perspectives on communication and rhetoric arising from the intellectual thought of Africans and the African diaspora.

Professors Morris and Palczewski focus on events that served to "discipline" scholars who were women or who represented sexual minorities. Much of the history recounted here is relatively recent, and the telling of it is still fresh with the feelings engendered by the procedures used in the "disciplining" process. This chapter's story is every bit as engaging as that told by Professor Philipsen, but the two histories as scholarship could not be further apart. Nevertheless, both should be read.

Taken together, these chapters represent a diverse collection of how a historical approach can be used to explain a discipline. And yet, the parts remain parts, and there is little connection among them. What they do have in common, at least to a degree, is a willingness to consider overarching issues, rather than parochial concerns. And, that willingness is a good sign.

What's Next?

As a discipline, communication is still relatively unorganized, and much of its scholarship is still in the formative stages. There is little agreement about what communication scholarship is *for*, other than, perhaps, the personal satisfaction of the individual scholars. "Communication" is also a "big tent" term that has proven to be vague enough to house a wide variety of scholarly enterprises, perhaps more than any one discipline can accommodate adequately.

It is folly to attempt to forecast the future based on an uncertain past, and, as the chapters in this volume show, there is disagreement about what "the past" is really like. But, perhaps a way forward that makes a certain amount of sense is to focus on what Celeste Condit has recently termed a series of "scholarly conversations."[14]

If we want to assess the state of our discipline, perhaps we should look at the content and the quality of the scholarly conversations we are having. Doing so might allow us to see that some "conversations" are not dialogues at all but instead represent monologues for which there is little or no response required. Professor Condit suggests that the discipline's journals might productively use "level of contribution to a scholarly conversation" as a primary criterion for judging whether a submission ought to be published. If I can elaborate on that suggestion, I'd add these questions that might clarify the use of the term:

(1) What is the scholarly conversation about? Is the topic a large or small one in the grand scheme of the discipline? If large, is it too large to matter? If small, does it lack significance?

(2) How does the scholarly conversation advance knowledge in communication? If the conversation has practical implications, what are the potential outcomes for improving communication practice?

(3) What is the societal benefit of the conversation? To what extent is the societal benefit of this conversation important? Is the conversation actually about communication, or is it more focused on a societal problem? If it's not about communication, why are we having it in the first place?

(4) What are the important disciplinary conversations that should be going on about communication? Are those conversations occurring? If not, how should they be started? What contribution does the current conversation make to these larger conversations?

(5) How do we know when the conversation is over, when it's time to move on?

Disciplines consist of big and small ongoing conversations. If too many of the conversations are small ones, the discipline's scholars tend to lose sight of disciplinary boundaries—the "big picture." If too many of the conversations are large ones, there might not be enough specific scholarship going on to fill in the details.

With communication, the conversations have been diffuse, perhaps too much so. Maybe we need to pause and talk about what's really important to study, as well as what would be required to achieve these overarching goals. Given the current state of the discipline, I'm not optimistic that these kinds of conversations are possible. Perhaps the current Centennial celebration can give us pause enough to allow these sorts of conversations to get started. If not, what's next may well be more of the same.

Notes

1 For example, Herman Cohen, *The History of Speech Communication: The Emergence of a Discipline, 1914–1945* (Annandale, VA: Speech Communication Association, 1994); Pat J. Gehrke, *The Ethics and Politics of Speech Communication and Rhetoric in the Twentieth Century* (Carbondale, IL: Southern Illinois University Press, 2009); Patti P. Gillespie, ed., *Our Stories: Twentieth-Century Women Presidents of NCA* (Washington, DC: National Communication Association, 2010); William M. Keith, *Democracy as Discussion: Civic Education and the American Forum Movement* (Lanham, MD: Lexington Books, 2007); Jim A. Kuypers and Andrew King, eds., *Twentieth-Century Roots of Rhetorical Studies* (Westport, CT: Praeger, 2001).

2 William F. Eadie, "Stories We Tell: Fragmentation and Convergence in Communication Disciplinary History," *Review of Communication* 11, no. 3 (2011): 161–176.

3 Everett M. Rogers, *A History of Communication Study: A Biographical Approach* (New York: The Free Press, 1994).

4 John Durham Peters, *Speaking Into the Air: A History of the Idea of Communication* (Chicago: University of Chicago Press, 1999).

5 Robert T. Craig, "Communication Theory as a Field," *Communication Theory* 9, no. 2 (1999): 119–161.

6 James A. Anderson and Geoffrey Baym, "Philosophies and Philosophic Issues in Communication, 1995–2004," *Journal of Communication* 54, no. 4 (2004): 589–615.

7 William F. Eadie, "Communication Societies in the U.S. and the Transition from Field to Discipline." Paper presented to the "New Histories of Communication Study," a preconference offered by the International Communication Association's Communication History Interest Group, in concert

with the history sections of the European Communication Research and Education Association and the International Association for Media and Communication Research, London Metropolitan University. June 17, 2013.

8 Eadie, "Stories."

9 See Andrew Thomas Weaver, "Seventeen Who Made History—The Founders of the Association," *Quarterly Journal of Speech* 45, no. 2 (1959): 195–199.

10 Lewis Menand, "The Demise of Disciplinary Authority," in *What's Happened to the Humanities?*, ed. A. Kernan (Princeton, NJ: Princeton University Press, 1997): 201–219.

11 J.N. Hook, *A Long Way Together: A Personal View of NCTE's First Sixty-Seven Years* (Urbana, IL: National Council of Teachers of English, 1979).

12 William F. Eadie and Robin Goret, "Theories and Models of Communication: Foundation and Heritage," in *Theories and Models of Communication*, ed. Paul Cobley and Peter J. Schulz (Berlin and Boston: Walter de Gruyter GmbH, 2013): 17–36.

13 Michael Burgoon, "Instruction about Communication: On Divorcing Dame Speech," *Communication Education* 38, no. 4 (1989): 303–308.

14 Celeste Michelle Condit, "How Ought Critical Communication Scholars Judge, Here, Now?" *Western Journal of Communication* 77, no. 5 (2013): 550–558.

References

Anderson, James A. and Geoffrey Baym. "Philosophies and Philosophic Issues In Communication, 1995–2004." *Journal of Communication* 54, no. 4 (2004): 589–615.

Burgoon, Michael. "Instruction about Communication: On Divorcing Dame Speech." *Communication Education* 38, no. 4 (1989): 303–308.

Cohen, Herman. *The History of Speech Communication: The Emergence of a Discipline, 1914–1945.* Annandale, VA: Speech Communication Association, 1994.

Condit, Celeste Michelle. "How Ought Critical Communication Scholars Judge, Here, Now?" *Western Journal of Communication* 77, no. 5 (2013): 550–558.

Craig, Robert T. "Communication Theory as a Field." *Communication Theory* 9, no. 2 (1999): 119–161.

Eadie, William F. "Communication Societies in the U.S. and the Transition from Field to Discipline." Paper presented to the "New Histories of Communication Study," a preconference offered by the International Communication Association's Communication History Interest Group, in concert with the history sections of the European Communication Research and Education Association and the International Association for Media and Communication Research, London Metropolitan University. June 17, 2013.

———. "Stories We Tell: Fragmentation and Convergence in Communication Disciplinary History." *Review of Communication* 11, no. 3 (2011): 161–176.

Eadie, William F. and Robin Goret. "Theories and Models of Communication: Foundation and Heritage." In *Theories and Models of Communication*, edited by Paul Cobley and Peter J. Schulz, 17–36. Berlin and Boston: Walter de Gruyter GmbH, 2013.

Gehrke, Pat J. *The Ethics and Politics of Speech Communication and Rhetoric in the Twentieth Century.* Carbondale, IL: Southern Illinois University Press, 2009.

Gillespie, Patti P., ed. *Our Stories: Twentieth-Century Women Presidents of NCA.* Washington, DC: National Communication Association, 2010.

Hook, J.N. *A Long Way Together: A Personal View of NCTE's First Sixty-Seven Years.* Urbana, IL: National Council of Teachers of English, 1979.

Keith, William M. *Democracy as Discussion: Civic Education and the American Forum Movement.* Lanham, MD: Lexington Books, 2007.

Kuypers, Jim A. and Andrew King. *Twentieth-Century Roots of Rhetorical Studies.* Westport, CT: Praeger, 2001.

Menand, Lewis. "The Demise of Disciplinary Authority." In *What's Happened to the Humanities?*, edited by A. Kernan, 201–219. Princeton, NJ: Princeton University Press, 1997.

Peters, John Durham. *Speaking Into the Air: A History of the Idea of Communication.* Chicago: University of Chicago Press, 1999.

Rogers, Everett M. *A History of Communication Study: A Biographical Approach.* New York: The Free Press, 1994.

Weaver, Andrew Thomas. "Seventeen Who Made History—The Founders of the Association." *Quarterly Journal of Speech* 45, no. 2 (1959): 195–199.

INDEX